TRADEMARKS AND UNFAIR COMPETITION
LAW AND POLICY

TRADEMARKS AND UNFAIR COMPETITION
LAW AND POLICY

Third Edition

Case and Statutory Supplement
2012-2013

Graeme B. Dinwoodie

Professor of Intellectual Property and Information Technology Law
University of Oxford

Mark D. Janis

Robert A. Lucas Chair of Law
Indiana University Maurer School of Law

Wolters Kluwer
Law & Business

Published by Wolters Kluwer Law & Business in New York.

Wolters Kluwer Law & Business serves customers worldwide with CCH, Aspen Publishers, and Kluwer Law International products. (www.wolterskluwerlb.com)

To contact Customer Service, e-mail customer.service@wolterskluwer.com, call 1-800-234-1660, fax 1-800-901-9075, or mail correspondence to:

Wolters Kluwer Law & Business
Attn: Order Department
PO Box 990
Frederick, MD 21705

Printed in the United States of America.

1 2 3 4 5 6 7 8 9 0

ISBN 978-1-4548-1105-3

About Wolters Kluwer Law & Business

Wolters Kluwer Law & Business is a leading global provider of intelligent information and digital solutions for legal and business professionals in key specialty areas, and respected educational resources for professors and law students. Wolters Kluwer Law & Business connects legal and business professionals as well as those in the education market with timely, specialized authoritative content and information-enabled solutions to support success through productivity, accuracy and mobility.

Serving customers worldwide, Wolters Kluwer Law & Business products include those under the Aspen Publishers, CCH, Kluwer Law International, Loislaw, Best Case, ftwilliam.com and MediRegs family of products.

CCH products have been a trusted resource since 1913, and are highly regarded resources for legal, securities, antitrust and trade regulation, government contracting, banking, pension, payroll, employment and labor, and healthcare reimbursement and compliance professionals.

Aspen Publishers products provide essential information to attorneys, business professionals and law students. Written by preeminent authorities, the product line offers analytical and practical information in a range of specialty practice areas from securities law and intellectual property to mergers and acquisitions and pension/benefits. Aspen's trusted legal education resources provide professors and students with high-quality, up-to-date and effective resources for successful instruction and study in all areas of the law.

Kluwer Law International products provide the global business community with reliable international legal information in English. Legal practitioners, corporate counsel and business executives around the world rely on Kluwer Law journals, looseleafs, books, and electronic products for comprehensive information in many areas of international legal practice.

Loislaw is a comprehensive online legal research product providing legal content to law firm practitioners of various specializations. Loislaw provides attorneys with the ability to quickly and efficiently find the necessary legal information they need, when and where they need it, by facilitating access to primary law as well as state-specific law, records, forms and treatises.

Best Case Solutions is the leading bankruptcy software product to the bankruptcy industry. It provides software and workflow tools to flawlessly streamline petition preparation and the electronic filing process, while timely incorporating ever-changing court requirements.

ftwilliam.com offers employee benefits professionals the highest quality plan documents (retirement, welfare and non-qualified) and government forms (5500/PBGC, 1099 and IRS) software at highly competitive prices.

MediRegs products provide integrated health care compliance content and software solutions for professionals in healthcare, higher education and life sciences, including professionals in accounting, law and consulting.

Wolters Kluwer Law & Business, a division of Wolters Kluwer, is headquartered in New York. Wolters Kluwer is a market-leading global information services company focused on professionals.

CONTENTS

Preface xi

PART I – FOUNDATIONS AND PURPOSES OF TRADEMARK AND UNFAIR COMPETITION LAW

Chapter 1 – Introduction to Trademark and Unfair Competition Law 3

PART II – CREATION OF TRADEMARK RIGHTS

Chapter 2 – Distinctiveness 7

      AMAZING SPACES, INC. v. METRO MINI STORAGE 11
      UNIVERSAL FURNITURE INT'L, INC.
          v. COLLEZIONE EUROPA USA, INC. 22

Chapter 3 – Functionality... 27

      FRANCO & SONS, INC v. FRANEK... 27
      IN RE BECTON, DICKINSON AND COMPANY 32
      SPECIALIZED SEATING, INC. v. GREENWICH INDUS., L.P. 42
      ERBE ELEKTROMEDIZIN GMBH
          v. CANADY TECHNOLOGY LLC.. 48
      CHRISTIAN LOUBOUTIN S.A. v. YVES SAINT LAURENT
          AMERICA, INC... 53

Chapter 4 – Use 65

Chapter 5 – Registration... 69
      PROBLEM 5-7A: CELEBRITY NAMES 71

PART III – SCOPE AND ENFORCEMENT OF TRADEMARK RIGHTS

Chapter 6 – Geographic Limits on Trademark Rights 75

Chapter 7 – Confusion-Based Trademark Liability Theories................................... 79
    PROBLEM 7-12A: BROTHER BILLY AND THE
        BAPTISTS' BATHROOMS... 93

Chapter 8 – Non-Confusion-Based Trademark Liability Theories 95

    VISA INT'L SERVICE ASSOC. v. JSL CORP......................................98
        NOTES AND QUESTIONS 102
    DSPT INT'L, INC. v. NAHUM.. 103
    NEWPORT NEWS HOLDINGS CORP.
        v. VIRTUAL CITY VISION, INC. 108
    MICROSOFT CORP. v. SHAH.. 114

Chapter 9– Permissible Uses of Another's Trademark..123

    FORTUNE DYNAMIC, INC. v. VICTORIA'S SECRET STORES
    BRAND MGM'T, INC. 123
        NOTES AND QUESTIONS 129
    TOYOTA MOTOR SALES, U.S.A., INC. v. TABARI.............. 130
    THE UNIV. OF ALABAMA BOARD OF TRUSTEES
        v. NEW LIFE ART, INC.. 141
        NOTES AND QUESTIONS. 148
    ROSETTA STONE LTD. v. GOOGLE, INC.. 149

Chapter 10 – False Advertising... 155
    PROBLEM 10-3A: LANHAM ACT FALSE ADVERTISING
        v. OTHER FEDERAL LABELING REGULATIONS 155
    TRAFFICSCHOOL.COM, INC. v. EDRIVER, INC 160
        NOTES AND QUESTIONS 165

Chapter 11 – Trade Identity Rights in One's Persona:
    Endorsement, Attribution, and Publicity 167

Chapter 12 – Remedies.. 169

    VOICE OF THE ARAB WORLD
        v. MDTV MEDICAL NEWS NOW, INC............................. 169
    NIGHTINGALE HOME HEALTHCARE, INC.
        v. ANODYNE THERAPY, LLC. 174

PART IV – EXPLOITATION OF TRADEMARKS

Chapter 13 – Trademark Transactions 185

STATUTORY MATERIALS

I. U.S. – FEDERAL LAW

A. Trademark Act of 1946 ("Lanham Act") 193
B. Counterfeiting 249
C. Rules of Practice in Trademark Cases (Excerpts) 265
D. Trademark Manual of Examining Procedure (TMEP) –8th ed. (Excerpts) 273

II. U.S – STATE LAW (RIGHTS OF PUBLICITY)

A. California 283
B. Indiana 291
C. New York 299
D. Tennessee 303

III. INTERNATIONAL MATERIALS

A. Agreement on Trade-Related Aspects of Intellectual Property Rights ("TRIPS")
    (Excerpts) 311
B. Paris Convention for the Protection of Industrial Property (Excerpts) 321
C. Uniform Domain Name Dispute Resolution Policy 331
D. Protocol Relating to the Madrid Agreement Concerning the International
    Registration of Marks 339
E. North American Free Trade Agreement (Excerpts) 347
F. EC Trademark Directive (Excerpts) 353

PREFACE

This Supplement contains the current version of the Lanham Act and related federal statutes, along with relevant regulatory materials, selected state right-of-publicity statutes, and some international materials, along with excerpts from, and notes about, cases and other materials that have been published in the time since the casebook was published.

The purpose of the Supplement is to keep the casebook materials up to date in an era when the volume of trademark law makes for a continually moving target. In compiling the Supplement, we have intentionally been more inclusive in some respects than in the main casebook. We have included as full excerpts only leading cases or cases that highlight an important developing aspect of trademark and unfair competition law. However, we have also included notes about other cases (including many district court cases from the last two years) that, when taken with the existing casebook, are more extensive than are necessary to understand or teach the subject matter of the Trademarks course. We have done so because we believe it helpful, as part of the updating process, to provide current examples of issues raised explicitly by notes and questions in the main casebook. We hope this enhances the pedagogical value of our casebook, and provides a currency that stimulates students and instructors alike. As a result, when *we* teach from the casebook, we do not add to our existing reading assignments every last page of the Supplement. Instead, we are more selective. We almost always assign the cases that are excerpted in full (where indicated, in lieu of cases excerpted in the casebook). But we use the notes and questions more selectively, as more up-to-date examples that provide the basis for vibrant class discussion.

As always, we welcome your comments on the wisdom of this editorial choice, as well as on any other aspect of the casebook or the Supplement.

G.B.D.
M.D.J.

FOUNDATIONS AND PURPOSES OF TRADEMARK AND UNFAIR COMPETITION LAW

I

INTRODUCTION TO TRADEMARK AND UNFAIR COMPETITION LAW

At p. 27, add as Note 4:

4.   *New top-level domains.* As suggested in note 6 of the Dinwoodie article, ICANN is open to the creation of new generic top-level domains. That strategy has, however, met with substantial resistance from trademark owners. *See* Casebook, p. 685. One aspect of this expansion of gTLDs is that ICANN will consider applications for domains based on brands (e.g., .CANON). On June 13, 2012 (which ICANN designated "Reveal Day"), ICANN published the first list of applications for gTLDs, the first step in a public review process in which trademark owners may object to the applications. See <http://www.wipo.int/amc/en/domains/lro> (providing details on the process). How do you think will this change the relationship between marks and domain names?

CREATION OF TRADEMARK RIGHTS

II

DISTINCTIVENESS

At p. 56, add as Notes 3 and 4:

3.   *Adding TLDs to generic terms.* In *Advertise.com, Inc. v. AOL Advertising, Inc.*, 616 F.3d 974 (9th Cir. 2010), the plaintiff claimed rights in a stylized version of the phrase ADVERTISING.COM for a range of online advertising services. The defendant argued that the standard text mark ADVERTISING.COM was generic and that the plaintiff's rights in the stylized mark did not accord it rights in the standard text term. The plaintiffs argued that in *Oppedahl & Larson*, the Federal Circuit had found that the mark PATENTS.COM was descriptive rather than generic, and, therefore, that ADVERTISING.COM was also not generic. The Ninth Circuit rejected that argument, explaining that "the issue before the court in that case was whether the TTAB had correctly concluded that the mark was not protectable because it was merely descriptive; the court had no occasion to consider whether the mark was generic." The court noted that the TMEP, § 1209.02(a), provides that descriptiveness, rather than genericness, should be the initial basis for the agency's refusal to register a mark. Do you agree with the Ninth Circuit's reading of *Oppedahl & Larson?* We will return to the question of generic terms and domain names later in the Chapter. *See* Casebook, page 84, Note 9.

4.   *Trademark rights in gTLDs.* ICANN has in recent years indicated a willingness to issue many new generic top-level-domains. If a new .music gTLD were created, should the operator of that TLD be granted a registration for .MUSIC for domain name related services? *See* US Trademark Registration, No. 3313153 (.TRAVEL for services involving the registration of sponsored domain names to serve the travel and tourism community on a global computer network); *cf. In re theDot Comm's Network LLC*, 101 U.S.P.Q.2d (BNA) 1062 (TTAB 2011) (denying registration of .MUSIC for a variety of online music-related services, taking account of the fact that other groups not affiliated with the applicant had previously sought to petition ICANN to add .music to the authorized list of TLDs).

At p. 63, add as Note 1A:

1A.   *Descriptiveness of what?* A mark will be treated as descriptive if it is descriptive of any of the features of a product in respect of which rights are claimed. Likewise, the Federal Circuit has stressed that a mark will be regarded as descriptive, and denied registration, if it is descriptive of any of the services for which registration is sought. *See In re The Chamber of Commerce of the United States*, 675 F.3d 1297, 1301 (Fed. Cir. 2012) (affirming descriptiveness rejection because NATIONAL CHAMBER described at least one service within the application); *cf. Valu Engineering, Inc. v. Rexnord Corp.*, 278 F.3d 1268 (Fed. Cir. 2002) ("functionality may be established by a single competitively significant application in the recited identification of goods, even if there is no anticompetitive effect in any other areas of use" . . .).

At p. 66, Note 10, add the following at end of Note:

See also In re Country Music Ass'n, Inc., 100 U.S.P.Q.2d (BNA) 1824 (TTAB 2011) (discussing relevance of placement of mark owner's advertisement in paid advertising listings on search engine results page).

At p. 67, add as Note 13A:

13A.   *Secondary meaning and fractured ownership.* In *Fleischer Studios, Inc. v. A.V.E.L.A., Inc.*, 654 F.3d 958 (9th Cir. 2011), the Court of Appeals for the Ninth Circuit adopted the theory that "fractured ownership of a trademark may make it legally impossible for a trademark holder to prove secondary meaning," although the argument was not made out on the facts of that case. *Id.* at 967. Review the definition of "trademark" in Section 45 of the Lanham Act. To what extent should confusion regarding the identity of the trademark owner be relevant to the assessment of distinctiveness? *Cf. Knights Armament Co. v. Optical Sys. Technology, Inc.*, 654 F.3d 1179, 1189 (11th Cir. 2011).

At p. 68, Note 18, add the following at end of Note:

Suppose that, after filing suit, Zatarain's became concerned that Oak Grove would ultimately succeed in showing that Zatarain's marks lacked distinctiveness. If Zatarain's unilaterally covenanted not to sue Oak Grove for Oak Grove's currently-used marks, and Zatarain's voluntarily dismissed its infringement claims, could Oak Grove still press forward with its distinctiveness challenge? That is, does Section 37 provide an independent basis for jurisdiction? Does it matter whether Oak Grove asserted its distinctiveness challenge as a counterclaim as opposed to an affirmative defense to infringement? *See Nike, Inc. v. Already, LLC*, 663 F.3d 89 (2d Cir. 2011).

At p. 83, Note 7, after *Welding Servs.* cite, add:

See generally Mary LaFrance, *Initial Impressions: Trademark Protection for Abbreviations of Generic or Descriptive Terms*, 45 AKRON L. REV. 201 (2012).

At p. 84, Note 9, add the following:

In *Advertise.com, Inc. v. AOL Advertising, Inc.*, 616 F.3d 974 (9th Cir. 2010), the Ninth Circuit held that ADVERTISING.COM was generic for online advertising services. The putative trademark owner had argued that "refusing to protect such marks will result in 'parasite' marks such as 'addvertising.com' diverting business from marks like ADVERTISING.COM." The Ninth Circuit was unimpressed, noting that "this is the peril of attempting to build a brand around a generic term." Moreover, the court feared that affording rights in ADVERTISING.COM would potentially allow the mark owner to control all combinations of the generic term with any TLD (e.g., ".com"; ".biz"; ".org"). Do you think this is a legitimate fear? On what would your answer depend?

At p. 86, Note 11, add the following:

In December 2011, the French legislature adopted a provision precluding pharmaceutical producers from enjoining the unauthorized use of their marks by legitimate producers of generic pharmaceutical products after expiry of the pharmaceutical patent. This provision is not unlike one that was considered (but eventually dropped) in debates leading to the passage of the Lanham Act, effectively deeming certain marks to be generic as a matter of law. *See* Graeme B. Dinwoodie, *The Story of* Kellogg v. National Biscuit Company: *Breakfast with Brandeis*, *in* INTELLECTUAL PROPERTY STORIES 220, 241-42 (Dreyfuss & Ginsburg eds., 2005).

At p. 88, add the following at the end of Problem 2-2(1):

See Elliott v. Google Inc., D. Ariz., No. 12-1072, *complaint filed* 5/21/12 (arguing that the term "Google" is generic for online searching).

At p. 88, add the following at the end of Problem 2-2(2):

Trademark owners frequently make efforts to educate the public to make proper uses of their marks, such as the advertisement below run by Xerox. To what extent should courts take these efforts into account in assessing whether a mark has become a generic term?

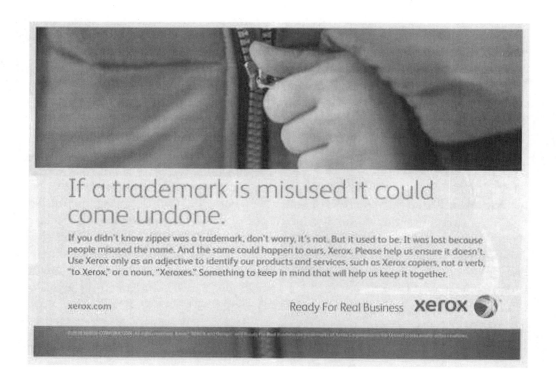

At p. 97, add the following case before Problem 2-5:

AMAZING SPACES, INC. v. METRO MINI STORAGE
608 F.3d 225 (5th Cir. 2010)

KING, Circuit Judge:

Amazing Spaces, Inc., and Metro Mini Storage are rival self-storage businesses in Houston, Texas. Amazing Spaces brought this action against Metro . . . alleging infringement of a star design that it claims as a service mark. The district court concluded that the design was not a legally protectable mark and dismissed Amazing Spaces's claims on summary judgment. We agree that the design was not legally protectable, and we affirm the judgment dismissing Amazing Spaces's service mark infringement claims. However, we also conclude that the district court erred in dismissing Amazing Spaces's claims relating to infringement of its trade dress, and we reverse and remand for further proceedings.

I. BACKGROUND

Amazing Spaces and Metro compete directly with each other in providing self-storage services in Houston, Texas. . . . Amazing Spaces claims, in connection with providing storage services, exclusive use rights in a design consisting of a raised, five-pointed star set within a circle (the "Star Symbol"). . . . Metro uses a similar star design on its buildings. . .

Amazing Spaces was founded in 1998 by Scott and Kathy Tautenhahn, and it currently operates three storage facilities in the greater Houston area. The facilities opened in 1998, 2001, and 2006, respectively. Landmark [Construction] was hired to build each of these facilities and, at Amazing Spaces's request, installed the Star Symbol under the peaks of the facilities' gabled roofs. Amazing Spaces has used the Star Symbol in its facilities' architecture and in its advertising, and it claims to have done so since at least April 1998. One trade magazine has recognized Amazing Spaces for its storage services, and the magazine displayed the Star Symbol in connection with the accompanying article. Amazing Spaces has also used the Star Symbol to designate the locations of its facilities on maps, and it claims to have directed customers—through telephone advertisements—to "look for the star."

The Star Symbol is registered as a service mark with the United States Patent and Trademark Office. [*See* Appendix A reproduced at bottom of opinion]. Prior to applying for registration, Amazing Spaces engaged a company to perform a database search to determine whether other storage companies had registered a similar star mark; the search revealed no such registrations. . . .

Landmark has also constructed self-storage facilities for Metro; these facilities feature a similar five-pointed-star-in-a-circle design (but not raised) on their gables. Despite Amazing Spaces's demand that Metro cease its use of a star, Metro continued to use its design and remodeled existing facilities to include the design. According to Amazing Spaces, this has caused confusion among its customers, who mistook Metro's facilities for new Amazing Spaces facilities. According to Kathy Tautenhahn, existing or prospective customers have inquired about whether new Amazing Spaces facilities had opened where Metro facilities were located. The record also includes a declaration from a customer to similar effect.

. . .

Metro moved for summary judgment on the ground that the Star Symbol was not a valid service mark. It argued primarily that the Star Symbol was not inherently distinctive and that Amazing Spaces could not establish that it had acquired secondary meaning. It supported this contention by presenting evidence that the same or a similar five-pointed star was used in commerce "in at least 63 different industries and businesses on buildings, property, and as part of logos" and on the buildings of "at least 28 other self-storage locations." The court concluded that "[t]he ubiquitous nature of the five-pointed star set within a circle precludes a finding that it is inherently distinctive or that it can serve as an indicator of origin for a particular business," and that "the record d[id] not raise a fact issue material to determining whether the star mark has acquired distinctiveness through a secondary meaning."

. . .

III. Discussion

In reviewing the parties' dispute over whether summary judgment was proper in this case, we first consider the issue addressed by the district court's opinion below—whether the Star Symbol is legally protectable as a service mark. We then evaluate whether summary judgment was appropriately granted on Amazing Spaces's trade dress claims as well.

A. The Star Symbol

. . . .

2. Inherent Distinctiveness

["A] mark is inherently distinctive if 'its intrinsic nature serves to identify a particular source.'" Wal-Mart Stores, Inc. v. Samara Bros., Inc., 529 U.S. 205, 210 (2000) (alteration omitted) (quoting Two Pesos, Inc. v. Taco Cabana, 505 U.S. 763, 768 (1992). Inherent distinctiveness is attributable to a mark when the mark "almost automatically tells a customer that it refers to a brand and . . . immediately signal[s] a brand or a product source." Id. at 212 (alterations and internal quotation marks omitted) (quoting Qualitex Co. v. Jacobson Prods. Co., 514 U.S. 159, 162-63)). The parties disagree over not only the answer to whether the Star Symbol is inherently distinctive but also over the proper method for conducting the inquiry. Metro urges that the familiar *Abercrombie* test cannot be used to categorize the Star Symbol and instead asks that we apply the *Seabrook Foods* test to determine that the Star Symbol is not inherently distinctive. Amazing Spaces, by contrast, presses the application of the *Abercrombie* test, under which it claims the Star Symbol is inherently distinctive, and it argues alternatively that the Star Symbol is inherently distinctive under the *Seabrook Foods* test.

a. *Abercrombie*

[W]e agree with Metro that the Star Symbol resists categorization under the *Abercrombie* test, and we consequently do not rely on a rote application of its categories in determining whether the Star Symbol is inherently distinctive . . .

As the district court discovered, the challenge of placing the Star Symbol into *Abercrombie's* constellation of categories is a futile endeavor. . . .

The district court briefly probed the utility of applying the *Abercrombie* test and concluded that the Star Symbol did not fit as a generic, descriptive, or suggestive mark. The district court first rejected the notion that the Star Symbol was generic because "[a] five-pointed star within a circle does not refer to a product or service provided by a self-storage company" and "[t]he evidence of widespread use of a five-point star or a five-point star set within a circle by many diverse businesses and government offices supports the conclusion that the star mark is not related to or a generic symbol for self-storage goods or services." It next determined that the Star Symbol was not descriptive because "[i]t does not identify a characteristic or quality of self-storage service, such as its function or quality." Nor was the Star Symbol suggestive, according to the district court, because "[t]here is no basis to conclude that a five-pointed star set within a circle suggests an attribute of self-storage services." We discern no flaws in the district court's analysis with respect to these three categories. However, the logical extension of the district court's analysis is the conclusion that the Star Symbol is arbitrary or fanciful, which under the *Abercrombie* test would render it inherently distinctive and thus entitled to protection. Yet the district court refused to so conclude, stating that "the star mark cannot be classified as arbitrary or fanciful unless it is inherently distinctive so as to serve as a source identifier for Amazing Spaces." It then turned to the *Seabrook Foods* test in conducting its inquiry into the Star Symbol's inherent distinctiveness.

We agree that the Star Symbol—indeed, any mark—lacks inherent distinctiveness if its intrinsic nature does not serve to identify its source. [cit]. Furthermore, as we have already indicated, we approve the district court's decision to apply a test other than *Abercrombie* in this case. However, we disagree somewhat with the district court's reasoning that a mark cannot be categorized as arbitrary or fanciful unless it is inherently distinctive. Under the *Abercrombie* test, it is the categorization of a mark that dictates its inherent distinctiveness, not the other way around. A rote application of the *Abercrombie* test yields the conclusion that the Star Symbol is an arbitrary or fanciful mark because it "'bear[s] no relationship to the products or services to which [it is] applied.'" [Pebble Beach Co. v. Tour 18 I Ltd., 155 F.3d 526, 540 (5th Cir. 1998)] (quoting *Zatarains*, 698 F.2d at 791).[13] Were we to apply the *Abercrombie* test mechanically to the Star Symbol, without an eye to the question the test seeks to answer, we would be left with the conclusion that the Star Symbol is inherently distinctive. The district court, aware of that result, proceeded to apply the *Seabrook Foods* test.

Both the Supreme Court and scholars have questioned the applicability of the *Abercrombie* test to marks other than words. See Wal-Mart Stores, 529 U.S. at 210-13 (noting that the *Abercrombie* test was developed and applied "[i]n the context of word marks" and declining to apply it to a mark consisting of product design); Qualitex, 514 U.S. at 162-63 (referring to the *Abercrombie* test but not applying it to a mark consisting of a shade of color); Restatement § 13 cmt. d, at 107 ("[U]nless the symbol or design is striking, unusual, or otherwise likely to differentiate the products of a particular producer, the designation is not inherently distinctive."); [cit]; 2 [McCarthy on Trademarks and Unfair Competition] § 11:2, at 11-7 ("Use of the spectrum of descriptive, suggestive, arbitrary and fanciful is largely confined to word marks. It is usually not suitable for nonword designations such as shapes and images making up trade dress."). We do not go so far as to hold that the *Abercrombie* test is eclipsed every time a mark other than a word is at issue. Instead, we hold that the *Abercrombie* test fails to illuminate the fundamental inquiry in this case: whether the Star Symbol's "'intrinsic nature serves to identify'" Amazing Spaces and its storage services. For the answer to that question, we now turn to the *Seabrook Foods* test employed by the district court.

  b. *Seabrook Foods*

In contrast to the *Abercrombie* test, the *Seabrook Foods* test, articulated by the U.S. Court of Customs and Patent Appeals in 1977, applies expressly to marks consisting of symbols and designs:

> In determining whether a design is arbitrary or distinctive this court has looked to [1] whether it was a "common" basic shape or design, [2] whether it

---

[13] One commentator has noted that marks consisting of symbols and designs are typically arbitrary with respect to their associated goods and services where the marks are "nonrepresentational":
Nonverbal and nonrepresentational designs and figures are perfectly acceptable as trademarks. Indeed, they have the advantage of being totally arbitrary, and so cannot be descriptive of the goods or services. The only problem which may be encountered is the question of whether such designs or figures are regarded by the public as identifying indicia or merely as decorations. Especially is this true of such simple figures as rectangles, diamonds, circles, triangles, or lines.
Louis Altman & Malla Pollack, 3 Callman on Unfair Competition, Trademarks and Monopolies § 18:24 (4th ed.2010) (footnotes omitted). Under this reasoning, nonverbal marks-even though "arbitrary"-must still be shown to serve as identifying indicia. Professor McCarthy appears to share the view that such marks are arbitrary when they are nonrepresentational. See 1 McCarthy on Trademarks § 7:36, at 7-91 ("A picture that is merely a representation of the goods themselves is regarded as merely descriptive of the goods.").

was unique or unusual in a particular field, [3] whether it was a mere refinement of a commonly-adopted and well-known form of ornamentation for a particular class of goods viewed by the public as a dress or ornamentation for the goods, or [4] whether it was capable of creating a commercial impression distinct from the accompanying words.

Seabrook Foods, 568 F.2d at 1344 (footnotes omitted).[14] The first three of the *Seabrook Foods* "'questions are merely different ways to ask whether the design, shape or combination of elements is so unique, unusual or unexpected in this market that one can assume without proof that it will automatically be perceived by customers as an indicator of origin-a trademark.'" I.P. Lund Trading ApS v. Kohler Co., 163 F.3d 27, 40 (1st Cir. 1998) (quoting 1 McCarthy on Trademarks § 8:13, at 8-58.5). As is true of the *Abercrombie* test, the *Seabrook Foods* test seeks an answer to the question whether a mark's "'intrinsic nature serves to identify a particular source.'" [cit].

We agree with the assessment of the I.P. Lund Trading court and Professor McCarthy that the *Seabrook Foods* factors are variations on a theme rather than discrete inquiries. In Star Industries v. Bacardi & Co., the Second Circuit noted that "'[c]ommon basic shapes' or letters are, as a matter of law, not inherently distinctive . . ., [but] stylized shapes or letters may qualify, provided the design is not commonplace but rather unique or unusual in the relevant market." 412 F.3d 373, 382 (2d Cir. 2005) (*citing Seabrook Foods,* 568 F.2d at 1344); [cit]. This statement, turning on whether the symbol or design is "common," comprises, essentially, the first two *Seabrook Foods* factors. However, the third *Seabrook Foods* factor similarly asks whether a symbol or design is "common" in the sense that it is likely to be perceived by the public as ornamentation rather than a mark. See Wiley v. Am. Greetings Corp., 762 F.2d 139, 142 (1st Cir. 1985) (equating a red heart shape on a teddy bear to "an ordinary geometric shape" because it "carrie[d] no distinctive message of origin to the consumer, . . . given the heart shape's widespread use as decoration for any number of products put out by many different companies"). A "common" symbol or design— lacking inherent distinctiveness—is the antithesis of a symbol or design that "'is so unique, unusual or unexpected in this market that one can assume without proof that it will automatically be perceived by customers as an indicator of origin—a trademark.'" I.P. Lund Trading, 163 F.3d at 40 (quoting 1 McCarthy on Trademarks § 8:13, at 8-58.5); accord Restatement § 13 cmt. d, at 107 ("Commonplace symbols and designs are not inherently distinctive since their appearance on numerous products makes it unlikely that consumers will view them as distinctive of the goods or services of a particular seller.").

The district court determined that the Star Symbol was "not a plain five-pointed star" but was instead "shaded and set within a circle," rendering it "sufficient[ly] styliz[ed]" to be "more than a common geometric shape. It then proceeded to conclude that the Star

---

[14] [T]he district court omitted discussion of the fourth factor, which by its terms applies only when a party seeks trademark protection for a background design typically accompanied by words. Similarly, we will not consider the fourth *Seabrook Foods* factor.

Symbol "[wa]s not inherently distinctive and d[id] not act as an indicator of origin for any self-storage business, including Amazing Spaces." It supported this assertion with a discussion of "[t]he ubiquitous nature of the five-pointed star set within a circle" in Texas, specifically its "use[ ] as a decoration or ornamentation on innumerable buildings, signs, roads, and products." The court concluded that this ubiquity-including use of the same or a similar star design in 63 industries businesses and 28 other self-storage locations-"preclude[d] a finding that [the Star Symbol wa]s inherently distinctive or that it c[ould] serve as an indicator of origin for a particular business."

Undoubtedly, the Star Symbol is stylized relative to an unshaded five-pointed star design not set within a circle. However, we disagree that the issue of stylization revolves around comparing a design's actual appearance to its corresponding platonic form. Instead, as discussed above, asking whether a shape is stylized is merely another way of asking whether the design is "commonplace" or "unique or unusual in the relevant market," Star Indus., 412 F.3d at 382, or whether it is "a mere refinement of a commonly-adopted and well-known form of ornamentation for a particular class of goods viewed by the public as a dress or ornamentation," Seabrook Foods, 568 F.2d at 1344.[3] The stylization inquiry is properly conceived of as asking whether a particular symbol or design is stylized such that prospective purchasers of goods or services are likely to differentiate it from other, similar symbols or designs. See Wiley, 762 F.2d at 142 (holding that a red heart on a teddy bear "carrie[d] no distinctive message of origin to the consumer . . . given the heart shape's widespread use as decoration for any number of products put out by many different companies"); Brooks Shoe Mfg. Co. v. Suave Shoe Corp., 716 F.2d 854, 858 (11th Cir. 1983) (holding that a design consisting of a "V," "7," or arrow on athletic shoes was common ornamentation such that it was not inherently distinctive); Restatement § 13 cmt. d, at 107 ("The manner in which a symbol or design is used is also relevant to the likelihood that it will be perceived as an indication of source. In some instances a design is likely to be viewed as mere ornamentation rather than as a symbol of identification."); 1 McCarthy on Trademarks § 3.3, at 3-11 ("Usually, if when viewed in context, it is not

---

[3] The parties dispute the scope of the "relevant market"-specifically, whether the district court correctly considered use of a similar or identical star design beyond the self-storage service industry. Amazing Spaces contends that we should limit our analysis to the self-storage services industry, while Metro argues that we may take into account uses of star designs in a larger context. The second Seabrook Foods factor refers to uniqueness or unusualness "in a particular field," and the Second Circuit has stated that a stylized design may be protectable when it "is not commonplace but rather unique or unusual in the relevant market," Star Indus., 412 F.3d at 382. Similarly, the third factor refers to whether a mark is commonly used as ornamentation for a "particular class of goods." Seabrook Foods, 568 F.2d at 1344. In contrast, the First Circuit, in considering whether a red heart on the chest of a teddy bear was inherently distinctive, appeared to consider the broader use of red hearts in determining whether the use at issue was unique or unusual. See Wiley, 762 F.2d at 142 . . . . Because a mark must distinguish one person's services from another, we agree that our inquiry is whether the Star Symbol identifies and distinguishes Amazing Spaces's self-storage services from others' self-storage services. This does not mean, however, that we must blind ourselves to uses beyond the self-storage services industry: the fact that the same or a similar star is used in countless other ways certainly bears on whether it is "likely that prospective purchasers will perceive [a given star design] as an indication of source" within a particular industry because a "[c]ommonplace symbol [']s . . . appearance on numerous products makes it unlikely that consumers will view [it] as distinctive of the goods or services of a particular seller." Restatement § 13 cmt. d, at 107.

immediately obvious that a certain designation is being used as an indication of origin, then it probably is not. In that case, it is not a trademark."). The record evidence is replete with similar or identical five-pointed stars, both raised and set in circles, and used in similar manners, such that-notwithstanding the residual evidence of the presumption of validity-no reasonable jury could find that the Star Symbol is even a mere refinement of this commonly adopted and well-known form of ornamentation.[20] The Star Symbol is thus not "'so unique, unusual or unexpected in this market that one can assume without proof that it will automatically be perceived by customers as an indicator of origin-a trademark,'" I.P. Lund Trading, 163 F.3d at 40 (quoting 1 McCarthy on Trademarks § 8:13, at 8-58.5), and it "does not almost automatically tell a customer that it refers to a brand . . . [or] immediately signal a brand or a product source." Because the Star Symbol does not, by "'its intrinsic nature [,] serve[] to identify a particular source,'" it is not inherently distinctive, and it can be protected only upon a showing of secondary meaning.

3. Secondary Meaning

The parties disagree over whether the Star Symbol has acquired distinctiveness through secondary meaning. "Secondary meaning occurs when, in the minds of the public, the primary significance of a mark is to identify the source of the product rather than the product itself." [Bd. of Supervisors for La. State Univ. Agric. & Mech. Coll. v. Smack Apparel Co. (Smack Apparel), 550 F.3d 465, 476 (5th Cir. 2008)] (alteration and internal quotation marks omitted) (quoting Wal-Mart Stores, 529 U.S. at 211) . . .

In the context of trade dress, we have articulated seven factors to consider in determining whether secondary meaning has been shown:

> "(1) length and manner of use of the mark or trade dress, (2) volume of sales, (3) amount and manner of advertising, (4) nature of use of the mark or trade dress in newspapers and magazines, (5) consumer-survey evidence, (6) direct consumer testimony, and (7) the defendant's intent in copying the trade dress."

Smack Apparel, 550 F.3d at 476 (quoting Pebble Beach, 155 F.3d at 541). "In considering this evidence, the focus is on how it demonstrates that the meaning of the mark or trade

---

[20] This is what differentiates the Star Symbol from the examples of registered marks containing stars that Amazing Spaces cites to support the protectability of five-pointed stars. The Dallas Cowboys star is stylized through the inclusion of a white border. The star in the Wal-Mart registration is a plain, five-pointed star, but the registered mark consists of more than just the star—the mark is the words "Wal" and "Mart" on either side of the star. The LanChile Airlines star is set against a circle that is 50% filled in, and it is adjacent to the words "LanChile Airlines." Finally, the USA Truck mark is a complex design consisting of a white star within a blue circle, set against a white rectangle with blue borders and a red stripe running across the middle. Each of these marks contains elements distinguishing it from the commonplace stars in the record. See Union Nat'l Bank of Tex., Laredo, Tex., 909 F.2d at 848 n. 25 (noting that the appropriate inquiry is whether the mark as a whole is protectable, not whether its component parts are individually protectable (citing Estate of P.D. Beckwith v. Comm'r of Patents, 252 U.S. 538).

dress has been altered in the minds of consumers." Pebble Beach, 155 F.3d at 541 (citing Zatarains, 698 F.2d at 795); accord Zatarains, 698 F.2d at 795 ("'[T]he question is not the extent of promotional efforts, but their effectiveness in altering the meaning of the term to the consuming public.'" (alteration omitted) (quoting Aloe Creme Labs., Inc. v. Milsan, Inc., 423 F.2d 845, 850 (5th Cir. 1970))). We have consistently expressed a preference for "an objective survey of the public's perception of" the mark at issue. [cit].

The district court considered the following evidence that Amazing Spaces claimed raise a fact issue regarding secondary meaning: (1) the Star Symbol was used for ten years; (2) Amazing Spaces had spent nearly $725,000 in advertising and promoting the Star Symbol; (3) Amazing Spaces had realized over $11.5 million in revenue since it first began using the Star Symbol; (4) Kathy Tautenhahn's statement in her declaration that the Star Symbol identifies Amazing Spaces's self-storage services; and (5) declarations of a customer and an alarm technician about confusion when seeing rival self-storage facilities (Metro and Community) that displayed symbols similar to the Star Symbol. The district court concluded that no fact issue was raised. It based this conclusion partly on the absence of survey evidence, but primarily on its determination that the remaining evidence was not probative regarding secondary meaning: the advertisements did not prominently display the Star Symbol but instead prominently featured the Peaks and Sky Symbol, and the declarations described confusion only in reference to the overall architecture of the facilities.

We agree with the district court that no fact issue has been raised regarding the existence of secondary meaning. [A]mazing Spaces's use of the Star Symbol has been primarily decorative and ornamental. Moreover, the record discloses that the Star Symbol was almost invariably used not as a stand-alone mark but was rather, as Amazing Spaces states in its brief, "an integral part of several marks that Amazing Spaces uses-indeed it is the one common element across its non-word marks." While this argument might support secondary meaning as to those other marks, it does not support secondary meaning as to the Star Symbol. Cf. Taco Cabana Int'l, Inc. v. Two Pesos, Inc., 932 F.2d 1113, 1120 (5th Cir. 1991) ("[C]ompetitors may use individual elements in Taco Cabana's trade dress, but the law protects the distinctive totality."), aff'd, 505 U.S. 763. This logic extends to the advertising present in the record. While the Star Symbol (or a variation thereof) constitutes a minor piece of the Peaks and Sky Symbol, marks Amazing Spaces's locations on a map, or replaces the bullet in a bulleted list, it is virtually absent as a stand-alone mark from Amazing Spaces's advertising in the record. This predominant advertising use belies the force Amazing Spaces would attribute to its telephonic advertising directing customers to "look for the star." Nor does Amazing Spaces's volume of sales-to the extent that it applies to a service mark rather than a trademark, trade dress, or product design-reveal secondary meaning: the advertising attempted to attract customers using marks other than the Star Symbol.

We also agree with the district court's assessment that the two declarations evidencing consumer confusion do not bear on the secondary meaning of the Star Symbol. Shane

Flores averred that he was confused by the appearance of a Metro facility's "use of a star logo in conjunction with the similarity in the architectural features and designs" and believed it to be an Amazing Spaces facility. Glen Gilmore averred similarly with respect to a [use by a third party that had since ceased]. While these instances of confusion may bear on Amazing Spaces's trade dress claims, they do not have relevance as to the secondary meaning of the Star Symbol itself. Amazing Spaces also claims that intentional copying has been shown because Metro constructed a facility that incorporated a star design after this lawsuit had been filed. But this chronology does not bear on whether Metro's use of a common design was intentional copying of Amazing Spaces's design. Amazing Spaces also contends that the district court placed undue emphasis on the lack of a survey. We have already noted this court's preference for survey evidence as proof of secondary meaning, and we also note that the other factors do not weigh in Amazing Spaces's favor. As Professor McCarthy has stated, "in a borderline case where it is not at all obvious that [a] designation has been used as a mark, survey evidence may be necessary to prove trademark perception." 1 McCarthy on Trademarks § 3.3, at 3-8.

In conclusion, we agree with the district court's assessment that Amazing Spaces has failed to raise a fact issue regarding the existence of secondary meaning with respect to the Star Symbol. In light of the overwhelming evidence that the Star Symbol is not distinctive, we hold that it does not serve "to identify and distinguish the services of" Amazing Spaces.

. . . .

B. Trade Dress Claims

Having concluded that the district court correctly held that the Star Symbol is not protectable as a mark, we next address whether the district court correctly dismissed Amazing Spaces's causes of action relating to its trade dress and facility design. Amazing Spaces asserts that [these] causes of action were improperly dismissed because they do not "rest entirely on whether the Star Logo is entitled to trademark protection" . . .

In addition to its claim that Metro had infringed its Star Symbol service mark, Amazing Spaces also brought claims for trade dress infringement under § 43(a) of the Lanham Act and Texas common law. See Blue Bell Bio-Med. v. Cin-Bad, Inc., 864 F.2d 1253, 1256 (5th Cir. 1989) ("The Lanham Act creates a cause of action for trade dress infringement. This action is analogous to the common law tort of unfair competition." (citing cases)). "Trade dress refers to the total image and overall appearance of a product and may include features such as the size, shape, color, color combinations, textures, graphics, and even sales techniques that characterize a particular product." . . . .

Amazing Spaces is correct that, to protect the overall appearance of its facilities as trade dress, it need not establish that the Star Symbol is legally protectable. Amazing Spaces's claimed trade dress, unlike the Star Symbol, consists of the entirety of the facilities' design, including placement of the Star Symbol under the roof peaks. See Taco Cabana Int'l, 932

F.2d at 1120 ("[T]he existence of [non-distinctive] elements does not eliminate the possibility of inherent distinctiveness in the trade dress as a whole."). The district court limited discovery to the issue of the trademarkability of the Star Symbol, and Amazing Spaces was therefore unable to present its trade dress and unfair competition claims. We therefore reverse the dismissal of those claims and remand for further proceedings.

APPENDIX

Int. Cl.: 39

Prior U.S. Cls.: 100 and 105

United States Patent and Trademark Office

Reg. No. 2,859,845
Registered July 6, 2004

SERVICE MARK
PRINCIPAL REGISTER

AMAZING SPACES (TEXAS CORPORATION)
9040 LOUETTA ROAD, SUITE B
SPRING, TX 77379

FOR: STORAGE SERVICES, IN CLASS 39 (U.S. CLS. 100 AND 105).

FIRST USE 4-0-1998; IN COMMERCE 4-0-1998.

SER. NO. 76-540,854, FILED 8-15-2003.

DOMINIC J. FERRAIUOLO, EXAMINING ATTORNEY

At p. 119, Note 10, add the following:

Is *Seabrook* still good law? *See In re Chippendales*, 622 F.3d 1346, 1357-58 (Fed. Cir. 2010). In *Chippendales*, the Federal Circuit applied *Seabrook*, describing it as a "four-part test", and suggesting that "if a mark satisfies any of the first three tests, it is not inherently distinctive." *See id.* at 1351. Is that how the court applies the test in *Amazing Spaces*?

At p. 129, Note 2, add the following:

See Keurig v. Strum Foods, 769 F.Supp.2d 699 (D. Del. 2011) (dismissing trade dress claim for failure to show a consistent overall look on packaging of single serve coffee cartridges).

At p. 131, Note 8, add the following:

The decision in *Chippendales* has been affirmed by the Federal Circuit. *See In re Chippendales*, 622 F.3d 1346 (Fed. Cir. 2010). How would you classify the mark in that case (depicted below) for "adult entertainment services, namely exotic dancing for women"? What test would you apply? Can any costume for a service be inherently distinctive?

At p. 134, Note 2, add the following:

In March 2012, the Canadian Intellectual Property Office reversed long-standing policy and began accepting registrations of sound marks. The decision was prompted by litigation involving the "Roaring Lion" sound mark used by Metro-Goldwyn-Mayer in its movies.

At p. 145, Note 6, add the following:

In *Fleischer Studios, Inc. v. A.V.E.L.A., Inc.*, 636 F.3d 1115 (9th Cir. 2011), a dispute about rights (copyright and trademark) in the Betty Boop character, the parties argued to the court about whether cartoon characters could be trademarks. The Ninth Circuit did not address that issue, instead holding initially that because the defendant was "not using Betty Boop as a trademark, but instead as a functional product", no trademark claim could lie. However, the court withdrew that opinion sua sponte.

At p. 151, Note 3, add the following:

If a defendant scraped data from a website, and hosted the data on the defendant's own website (without attribution), would *Dastar* preclude an action by the owner of the first website? Would it matter whether the data was copyrightable? *See Cvent, Inc. v Eventbrite*, 739 F.Supp.2d 927 (E.D. Va. 2010). What did the Court mean by "repackaging them as its own"? *See Dutch Jackson IATG, LLC v. Basketball Marketing Co.*, 2012 WL 124579 (E.D. Mo. Jan. 17, 2012).

At p. 152, Note 7, add the following at end of Note:

If Peter designed a range of popular furniture with a distinctive design, and Donnie copied the drawings thereof from Peter's catalog, would *Dastar* preclude a Lanham Act claim if Donnie presented the unauthorized copies of the drawings to potential purchasers as showing his furniture? Would your answer change if Donnie simply showed potential purchasers a page ripped from Peter's catalog showing the design (having removed any references to Peter on that page)? *See Victor Stanley, Inc. v. Creative Pipe, Inc.* 2011 Copr. L. Dec. ¶ 30,157 (D. Md. 2011). Does your answer depend on the consequences of Donnie's conduct under copyright law? Does your answer depend on whether Donnie secures and fills purchase orders? Do any of your answers turn on the meaning of the word "origin"?

At p. 155, add the following case after *Bretford*:

UNIVERSAL FURNITURE INT'L, INC. v. COLLEZIONE EUROPA USA, INC.
618 F.3d 417 (4th Cir. 2010)

PER CURIAM:

Appellant Collezione Europa USA, Incorporated ("Collezione"), and its adversary in this proceeding, appellee Universal Furniture International, Incorporated ("Universal"), are competing furniture companies. In 2004, Universal sued Collezione, alleging infringement under the Copyright Act with respect to two of Universal's furniture collections as well as violations of the Lanham Act.

. . .

In 1994, Universal's predecessor . . .entered into a design-service agreement with the Norman Hekler design firm. . . . Steven Russell was the Hekler designer who created the two Universal collections that are the subject of this dispute: the Grand Inheritance Collection (the "GIC") and the English Manor Collection (the "EMC"). Russell designed the GIC in 2001 and the EMC in 2002, and both collections were manufactured for Universal by a Chinese corporation called Lacquercraft. The GIC line became available to the public in April 2001 and the EMC line became available in April 2003. . . .

In 2004, Rhodes Furniture-a major purchaser of the EMC and GIC lines-approached Collezione seeking a cheaper alternative to Universal's furniture. As a result, Collezione agreed to design furniture that would mimic the EMC and GIC lines. . . .

In 2004, Collezione introduced one collection (the "20000") to imitate the GIC line and another collection (the "20200") to imitate the EMC line. Collezione displayed the 20200 collection at the High Point, North Carolina furniture market in October 2004. Upon learning that Collezione was displaying furniture that was nearly identical to the EMC line, Universal's Senior Vice President Stephen Giles visited the High Point market. Giles was shocked by the similarity between Collezione's 20200 collection and the EMC line, and also concluded that Collezione was displaying furniture actually manufactured by Universal. Indeed, Giles believed that Collezione had simply removed Universal stickers from some pieces. In some instances, he noticed stickers (which he had designed) bearing the name of Universal's manufacturer, Lacquercraft. Giles took photographs of what he observed and provided the evidence to Universal's Vice President Victor Hsu

[The court affirmed the finding of copyright infringement and proceeded to the Lanham Act claims.] Collezione . . . challenges the district court's determination that it violated the Lanham Act by marketing actual pieces from Universal's EMC line as its own furniture at the High Point furniture market in October 2004. The Lanham Act prohibits a "false designation of origin" that is "likely to cause confusion, or to cause mistake, or to deceive as to the affiliation, connection, or association . . . or as to the origin" of "goods, services, or commercial activities." 15 U.S.C. § 1125(a)(1)(A). The type of false designation of origin at issue here is a "reverse passing off," which occurs when a "producer misrepresents someone else's goods or services as his own." Dastar Corp. v. Twentieth Century Fox Film Corp., 539 U.S. 23, 28 n. 1 (2003). A reverse passing off claim requires the plaintiff to prove four elements: "(1) that the work at issue originated with the plaintiff; (2) that origin of the work was falsely designated by the defendant; (3) that the false designation of origin was likely to cause consumer confusion; and (4) that the plaintiff was harmed by the defendant's false designation of origin." Syngenta Seeds, Inc. v. Delta Cotton Coop., Inc., 457 F.3d 1269, 1277 (Fed. Cir. 2006).

On the first element, Universal is the "origin" of the EMC even though it does not manufacture the furniture. Although "the most natural understanding of the 'origin' of 'goods'-the source of wares-is the producer of the tangible product," origin may also encompass "the trademark owner who commissioned or assumed responsibility for ('stood behind') production of the physical product." Dastar, 539 U.S. at 31-32. Universal is the company that markets and "stands behind" its furniture collections. Universal labels the furniture with its name, distributes the furniture, and owns the copyrights in the designs.

With respect to the second element—that the origin of the work was falsely designated—the district court found this element satisfied by Collezione's display of actual pieces from Universal's EMC line at the 2004 High Point furniture market. . .The court examined and assessed photographs of the showroom furniture and heard testimony from Universal Vice-President Stephen Giles, who took the photographs after learning that Collezione was selling furniture strikingly similar to the EMC line. Giles confirmed that Collezione's display samples bore lot control stickers that he had designed for Universal. The court compared photographs of Universal's EMC pieces to the photographs taken by Giles and concluded that Collezione was marketing Universal's furniture at the showroom. The photographs in evidence amply support the court's finding. Because Collezione displayed actual pieces from Universal's EMC line and marketed them as belonging to its 20200 collection, Collezione falsely designated the origin of such furniture.

The third element of the reverse passing off claim, consumer confusion, requires a showing that a "substantial number . . . of consumers are likely to be misled." Scotts Co. v. United Indus. Corp., 315 F.3d 264, 280 (4th Cir. 2002). "While there is no bright line test to determine the existence of a likelihood of consumer confusion, recovery under the Lanham Act requires, at a minimum, that confusion, mistake, or deception be likely, not merely possible." Custom Mfg. & Eng'g, Inc. v. Midway Servs., Inc., 508 F.3d 641, 651 (11th Cir. 2007) (internal citation and quotation marks omitted). As the Sixth Circuit has observed, when a "defendant has taken the plaintiff's product and has represented it to be his own work," it is "difficult to imagine how a designation of origin of a product could be more false, or could be more likely to cause confusion or mistake as to the actual origin of the product." Johnson v. Jones, 149 F.3d 494, 503 (6th Cir. 1998). Collezione's display of Universal's furniture at a lower price was likely to mislead a substantial number of consumers. As the district court recognized, "[i]t would be difficult to fathom a situation where a customer would not be confused by seeing two different companies marketing the same furniture under different names." Indeed, consumer confusion is what prompted Giles to visit the showroom for inspection; he learned of Collezione's display from a confused dealer.

Finally, turning to the fourth element, we must reject Collezione's contention that, because it did not actually sell the EMC furniture and recalled its sales photos of the furniture,

Universal suffered no harm from the false designation. Even if the EMC furniture never left the High Point showroom, the district court properly found that Universal suffered harm simply from the display of its furniture by Collezione. A significant harm of reverse passing off is that the "originator of the misidentified product is involuntarily deprived of the advertising value of its name and of the goodwill that otherwise would stem from public knowledge of the true source of the satisfactory product." Smith v. Montoro, 648 F.2d 602, 607 (9th Cir. 1981). As the Supreme Court explained in Dastar, the Lanham Act "assure[s] a producer that it (and not an imitating competitor) will reap the financial, reputation-related rewards associated with a desirable product." 539 U.S. at 34 (internal citation and quotation marks omitted). We thus agree with the district court that Collezione's display of the EMC furniture deprived Universal of "the opportunity to earn sales and profits." By displaying Universal's furniture as its own for a lower price, Collezione appears to have retained customers that would have otherwise purchased from Universal, even if it did not actually sell the EMC pieces in question. Universal introduced evidence that Collezione sold pieces in its 20200 collection to customers who placed their orders during the period in which Collezione displayed corresponding pieces of Universal's EMC line. We therefore affirm the court's ruling that Collezione violated the Lanham Act.

Affirmed.

3

FUNCTIONALITY

At p. 202, add the following cases after *Eppendorf*:

FRANCO & SONS, INC v. FRANEK
615 F.3d 855 (7th Cir. 2010)

EASTERBROOK, Chief Judge:

The same year Huey Lewis and the News informed America that it's "Hip To Be Square", Clemens Franek sought to trademark the circular beach towel. His company, CLM Design, Inc., pitched the towel as a fashion statement—"the most radical beach fashion item since the bikini," declared one advertisement. "Bound to be round! Don't be square!" proclaimed another. CLM also targeted lazy sunbathers: "The round shape eliminates the need to constantly get up and move your towel as the sun moves across the sky. Instead merely reposition yourself."

The product enjoyed some initial success. Buoyed by an investment and promotional help from the actor Woody Harrelson (then a bartender on the TV show Cheers), CLM had sold more than 30,000 round beach towels in 32 states by the end of 1987. To secure its status as the premier circular-towel maker, the company in 1986 applied for a trademark on the towel's round design. The Patent and Trademark Office registered the "configuration of a round beach towel" as trademark No. 1,502,261 in 1988. But this was not enough to save CLM: Six years later it dissolved. The mark was assigned to Franek, who continues to sell circular towels.

In 2006 Franek discovered that Jay Franco & Sons, a distributor of bath, bedding, and beach accessories, was selling round beach towels. After settlement negotiations failed. . . Franco sued . . . Franek to invalidate his mark. . . . The district judge . . . granted summary judgment in Jay Franco's favor, and . . . Franek appeals from that judgment. . .

One way to void a trademark is to challenge its distinctiveness. . . But this type of invalidation is unavailable to Jay Franco. Franek (and before him CLM) has continuously used the round-towel mark since its 1988 registration. That makes the mark "incontestable," 15 U.S.C. § 1065, a status that eliminates the need for a mark's owner in an infringement suit to show that his mark is distinctive. See 15 U.S.C. § 1115(b); Park 'N Fly, Inc. v. Dollar Park and Fly, Inc., 469 U.S. 189 (1985).

Unfortunately for Franek, incontestable marks are not invincible. The Lanham Act lists a number of affirmative defenses an alleged infringer can parry with; one is a showing that the mark is "functional." See § 1115(b)(8); Specialized Seating, Inc. v. Greenwich Industries, L.P., 616 F.3d 722, 724 (7th Cir. 2010) (discussing functionality and other ways to defeat incontestable marks). As our companion opinion in *Specialized Seating* explains, patent law alone protects useful designs from mimicry; the functionality doctrine polices the division of responsibilities between patent and trademark law by invalidating marks on useful designs. This was the route Jay Franco pursued. The district judge agreed, finding Franek's mark "functional" under the definition the Supreme Court gave that concept in TrafFix Devices, Inc. v. Marketing Displays, Inc., 532 U.S. 23, 32-35 (2001). The judge got it right.

TrafFix says that a design is functional when it is "essential to the use or purpose of the device or when it affects the cost or quality of the device," 532 U.S. at 33, a definition cribbed from Inwood Laboratories, Inc. v. Ives Laboratories, Inc., 456 U.S. 844, 850 n. 10 (1982). So if a design enables a product to operate, or improves on a substitute design in some way (such as by making the product cheaper, faster, lighter, or stronger), then the design cannot be trademarked; it is functional because consumers would pay to have it rather than be indifferent toward or pay to avoid it. A qualification is that any pleasure a customer derives from the design's identification of the product's source-the joy of buying a marked good over an identical generic version because the consumer prefers the status conferred by the mark-doesn't count. That broad a theory of functionality would penalize companies for developing brands with cachet to distinguish themselves from competitors, which is the very purpose of trademark law. In short, a design that produces a benefit other than source identification is functional.

Figuring out which designs meet this criterion can be tricky. Utility patents serve as excellent cheat sheets because any design claimed in a patent is supposed to be useful. [cit]. For this reason, *TrafFix* held that expired utility patents provide "strong evidence that the features therein claimed are functional." The parties in this case wrangle over the relevance of a handful of utility patents that claim circular towels. We need discuss only one (No. 4,794,029), which describes a round beach towel laced with drawstrings that can be pulled to turn the towel into a satchel. This patent's first two claims are:

1. A towel-bag construction comprising: a non-rectangular towel;

a casing formed at the perimeter of said towel;

a cord threaded through said casing; and

a section of relatively non-stretchable fabric of a shape geometrically similar to that of said towel attached with its edges equidistant from the edges of said towel.

2. A towel-bag construction as set forth in claim 1 wherein said towel is circular in shape, whereby a user while sunbathing may reposition his or her body towards the changing angle of the sun while the towel remains stationary.

Claim 2 sounds like Franek's advertisements, which we quoted above. The patent's specification also reiterates, in both the summary and the detailed description, that a circular towel is central to the invention because of its benefit to lazy sunbathers.

Franek argues that claim 2 does not trigger the *TrafFix* presumption of functionality because his towel does not infringe the '029 patent. He notes that claim 2 incorporates claim 1 (in patent parlance, claim 1 is "independent" and claim 2 "dependent," see 35 U.S.C. § 112) with the added condition that the towel be circular. An item can infringe a dependent claim only if it also violates the independent claim incorporated by the dependent claim. [cit]. Franek reasons that because his towel lacks a perimeter casing, drawstring, and non-stretchable section of fabric, it does not infringe claim 1, and thus cannot infringe claim 2. Even if his towel could infringe claim 2, Franek maintains that the claim is invalid because the towel-to-bag patent was sought in 1987, two years after Franek started selling a round beach towel, and thus too late to claim its invention. See 35 U.S.C. § 102(b); [cit].

Proving patent infringement can be sufficient to show that a trademarked design is useful, as it means that the infringing design is quite similar to a useful invention. See Raytheon Co. v. Roper Corp., 724 F.2d 951, 959 (Fed. Cir. 1983). But such proof is unnecessary. Functionality is determined by a feature's usefulness, not its patentability or its infringement of a patent. *TrafFix*'s ruling that an expired patent (which by definition can no longer be infringed) may evince a design's functionality demonstrates that proof of infringement is unnecessary. If an invention is too useless to be patentable, or too dissimilar to a design to shed light on its functions, then the lack of proof of patent infringement is meaningful. Otherwise it is irrelevant. A design may not infringe a patented invention because the invention is obvious or taught by prior art, see 35 U.S.C. §§ 102(a), 103(a), but those and other disqualifiers do not mean that the design is not useful. Just so here: Franek's towel may lack some of the components in claim 1 necessary to infringe claim 2, but claim 2's coverage of a circular beach towel for sunbathing is enough to signal that a round-towel design is useful for sunbathers. Each claim in a patent is evaluated individually, [cit], each must be substantially different, [cit], and each is presumed valid, 35 U.S.C. § 282. We must therefore presume that the unique component in claim 2—the round shape of the towel—is useful.

Nor does it matter that the '029 patent application was filed two years after Franek began selling round towels. As we've explained, a patent's invalidity for a reason other than uselessness says nothing about the claimed design's functionality. And a design patented yesterday can be as good evidence of a mark's functionality as a design patented 50 years ago. Indeed, more recent patents are often better evidence because technological change can render designs that were functional years ago no longer so. See Eco Manufacturing LLC v. Honeywell International Inc., 357 F.3d 649, 653 (7th Cir. 2003). The Court in TrafFix may have dealt only with expired utility patents, but the logic it employed is not limited to them.

To put things another way, a trademark holder cannot block innovation by appropriating designs that under-gird further improvements. Patent holders can do this, but a patent's life is short; trademarks can last forever, so granting trademark holders this power could permanently stifle product development. If we found Franek's trademark nonfunctional, then inventors seeking to build an improved round beach towel would be out of luck. They'd have to license Franek's mark or quell their inventiveness. That result does not jibe with the purposes of patent or trademark law.

This "strong evidence" of the round towel's functionality is bolstered by Franek's own advertisements, which highlight two functional aspects of the round beach towel's design. One, also discussed in the '029 patent, is that roundness enables heliotropic sunbathers-tanners who swivel their bodies in unison with the sun's apparent motion in order to maintain an even tan-to remain on their towels as they rotate rather than exert the energy to stand up and reposition their towels every so often, as conventional rectangular towels require.

Franek responds that whatever its shape (golden-ratio rectangle, square, nonagon) any towel can satisfy a heliotropic tanner if it has enough surface area-the issue is size, not shape. That's true, and it is enough to keep the roundness of his towel from being functional under the first prong of TrafFix's definition ("essential to the use or purpose of the device") but not the second. For heliotropic sunbathers, a circle surpasses other shapes because it provides the most rotational space without waste. Any non-circle polygon will either limit full rotations (spinning on a normal beach towel leads to sandy hair and feet) or not use all the surface area (a 6' tall person swiveling on a 6' by 6' square towel won't touch the corners). Compared to other shapes that permit full rotations, the round towel requires less material, which makes it easier to fold and carry. That's evidence that the towel's circularity "affects the . . . quality of the device." (The reduction in needed material also suggests that round towels are cheaper to produce than other-shaped towels, though Franek contends that cutting and hemming expenses make them costlier. We express no view on the matter.)

But let us suppose with Franek—who opposed summary judgment and who is thus entitled to all reasonable inferences—that round towels are not measurably better for spinning with the sun. After all, other shapes (squircles, regular icosagons) are similar enough to circles that any qualitative difference may be lost on tanners. Plus, the ability to rotate 180 degrees may be an undesired luxury. Few lie out from dawn 'til dusk (if only to avoid skin cancer) and the daily change in the sun's declination means it will rise due east and set due west just twice a year, during the vernal and autumnal equinoxes. A towel shaped like a curved hourglass that allows only 150 or 120 degrees of rotation (or even fewer) may be all a heliotropic tanner wants. No matter. Franek's mark still is functional.

Franek's advertisements declare that the round towel is a fashion statement. Fashion is a form of function. A design's aesthetic appeal can be as functional as its tangible characteristics. See Qualitex Co. v. Jacobson Products Co., 514 U.S. 159 (1995); Wal-Mart, 529 U.S. at 214; TrafFix, 532 U.S. at 33; W.T. Rogers Co. v. Keene, 778 F.2d 334 (7th Cir. 1985); [cit]; Abercrombie & Fitch Stores, Inc. v. American Eagle Outfitters, Inc., 280 F.3d 619 (6th Cir. 2002). And many cases say that fashionable designs can be freely copied unless protected by patent law. See, e.g., Bonito Boats, Inc. v. Thunder Craft Boats, Inc., 489 U.S. 141 (1989); Sears, Roebuck & Co. v. Stiffel Co., 376 U.S. 225 (1964); Compco Corp. v. Day-Brite Lighting, Inc., 376 U.S. 234 (1964); Kellogg Co. v. National Biscuit Co., 305 U.S. 111 (1938); Singer Manufacturing Co. v. June Manufacturing Co., 163 U.S. 169 (1896).

The chief difficulty is distinguishing between designs that are fashionable enough to be functional and those that are merely pleasing. Only the latter group can be protected, because trademark law would be a cruel joke if it limited companies to tepid or repugnant brands that discourage customers from buying the marked wares. We discussed this problem at length in *Keene*. [cit.] The Supreme Court broached the subject in *Qualitex* when it discussed the functionality of the green-gold color of a dry cleaning pad. Unwilling to say that the pad required a green-gold hue or was improved by it, the Court still thought that the color would be functional if its exclusive use by a single designer "would put competitors at a significant non-reputation-related disadvantage." This is a problem for Franek's round-towel mark.

Franek wants a trademark on the circle. Granting a producer the exclusive use of a basic element of design (shape, material, color, and so forth) impoverishes other designers' palettes. See, e.g., Brunswick Corp., v. British Seagull Ltd., 35 F.3d 1527 (Fed. Cir. 1994) (black color of boat engines is functional because it is compatible with boats of many different colors). Qualitex's determination that "color alone, at least sometimes, can meet the basic legal requirements for use as a trademark" means that there is no per se rule against this practice. See also Thomas & Betts Corp. v. Panduit Corp., 138 F.3d 277, 299 (7th Cir. 1998). The composition of the relevant market matters. But the more rudimentary and general the element-all six-sided shapes rather than an irregular, perforated hexagon; all labels made from tin rather than a specific tin label; all shades of the color purple rather than a single shade-the more likely it is that restricting its use will significantly impair competition. See, e.g., Keene, 778 F.2d at 343; [cit.]. Franek's towel is of this ilk. He has trademarked the "configuration of a round beach towel." Every other beach towel manufacturer is barred from using the entire shape as well as any other design similar enough that consumers are likely to confuse it with Franek's circle (most regular polygons, for example).

Contrast Franek's mark with the irregular hexagon at issue in *Keene* or the green-gold hue in *Qualitex*. Those marks restrict few design options for competitors. Indeed, they are so distinctive that competitors' only reason to copy them would be to trade on the goodwill of the original designer. Cf. Service Ideas, Inc. v. Traex Corp., 846 F.2d 1118, 1123-24 (7th Cir. 1988) (purposeful copying of a beverage server's arbitrary design indicated a lack of aesthetic functionality). That's not so here. A circle is the kind of basic design that a producer like Jay Franco adopts because alternatives are scarce and some consumers want the shape regardless of who manufactures it. There are only so many geometric shapes; few are both attractive and simple enough to fabricate cheaply. Cf. Qualitex, 514 U.S. at 168 (functionality doctrine invalidates marks that would create color scarcity in a particular market). And some consumers crave round towels-beachgoers who prefer curved edges to sharp corners, those who don't want to be "square," and those who relish the circle's simplicity. A producer barred from selling such towels loses a profitable portion of the market. The record does not divulge much on these matters, but any holes in the evidence are filled by the TrafFix presumption that Franek's mark is functional, a presumption he has failed to rebut.

Franek chose to pursue a trademark, not a design patent, to protect the stylish circularity of his beach towel. Cf. Kohler Co. v. Moen Inc., 12 F.3d 632, 647 (7th Cir. 1993) (Cudahy, J., dissenting) (calling Franek's mark a "horrible example[ ]" of a registered trademark that should have been a design patent). He must live with that choice. We cannot permit him to keep the indefinite competitive advantage in producing beach towels this trademark creates.

If Franek is worried that consumers will confuse Jay Franco's round beach towels with his, he can imprint a distinctive verbal or pictorial mark on his towels. [cit.]. That will enable him to reap the benefits of his brand while still permitting healthy competition in the beach towel market.

Affirmed.

IN RE BECTON, DICKINSON AND COMPANY
675 F.3d 1368 (Fed. Cir. 2012)

CLEVENGER, Circuit Judge:

Becton, Dickinson and Company ("BD") appeals from the final decision of the Trademark Trial and Appeal Board ("Board") affirming the examining attorney's refusal to register BD's design of a closure cap for blood collection tubes as a trademark on the ground that the design is functional. [W]e affirm the Board's conclusion that the mark as a whole is functional.

BD applied to register with the United States Patent and Trademark Office ("PTO") the following mark on the Principal Register for "closures for medical collection tubes":

U.S. Trademark Application Serial No. 77/254,637 (filed August 14, 2007). The application asserts acquired distinctiveness based on five years of substantially exclusive and continuous use in commerce. The required description of the mark, as amended, reads as follows:

> The mark consists of the configuration of a closure cap that has [1] an overall streamlined exterior wherein the top of the cap is slimmer than at the bottom and the cap features [2] vertically elongated ribs set out in combination sets of numerous slim ribs bordered by fatter ribs around most of the cap circumference, where [3] a smooth area separates sets of ribs. [4] The slim ribs taper at their top to form triangular shapes which intersect and blend together at a point where [5] a smooth surface area rings the top of the cap above the ribs, thus [6] extending the cap's vertical profile. At the bottom, [7] a flanged lip rings the cap and protrudes from the sides in two circumferential segments with the bottom-most segment having [8] a slightly curved contour. The matter in dotted lines is not claimed as a feature of the mark, but shows the tube on which the closure is positioned.

The numbers in brackets in the description above are not part of the trademark application, but were used by BD in conjunction with the following illustration to illustrate key features of the mark:

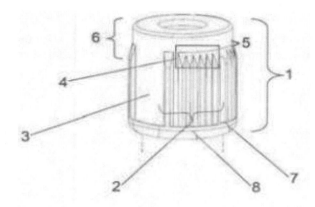

[The examining attorney refused registration under Section 2(e)(5) on the basis inter alia that the cap design is functional. In response to an initial office action, BD submitted several of its utility and design patents, including U.S. Patent No. 4,741,446 (filed Dec. 29, 1986) ("the '446 patent"), samples of advertising materials, and copies of website printouts showing medical closure caps manufactured by other entities.] BD also submitted numerous advertising samples for its VACUTAINER® collection tubes with HEMOGARD™ closure—the brand name of the closure cap for which BD seeks registration. . . .

[On appeal, the] Board found that the proposed mark is a configuration of the outer shell portion of BD's HEMOGARD™ collection tube closure caps. BD argued that its amended mark description and a numbered illustration in its reply brief set out the features of the cap design, but the Board explained that the features described in the amended description do not embody the mark in its entirety. The Board saw additional elements not recited in the mark description, including the circular opening on the top of the cap. Thus, the Board concluded that the proposed mark included all elements shown in the drawing except the tube, which was shown in dotted lines.

The Board considered the four factors from *In re Morton–Norwich Prods., Inc.*, 671 F.2d 1332 (CCPA 1982), in finding that the cap design, considered in its entirety, is functional. . . .

[I]n conducting the analysis, the Board gave less weight to less prominent features, such as the exact spacing or shape of the ribs, because it found them to be incidental to the overall adoption of those features and hardly discernible when viewing the mark. In this regard, the Board relied on *Textron, Inc. v. International Trade Commission*, 753 F.2d 1019, 1025 (Fed.Cir.1985), for the proposition that presence of non-functional features in a mark would not affect the functionality decision where the evidence shows the overall design to be functional. The Board concluded that the overall design is dictated by utilitarian concerns and that the " 'overall composite design' engendered by [BD's] proposed mark is functional." . . .

II

The functionality of a proposed mark is a question of fact. *In re Bose Corp.*, 476 F.3d 1331, 1334 (Fed.Cir.2007); *Valu Eng'g, Inc. v. Rexnord Corp.*, 278 F.3d 1268, 1273 (Fed.Cir.2002) . . . .

Legal conclusions of the Board are reviewed de novo, but the factual findings of the Board are upheld unless they are unsupported by substantial evidence. [cit]. Evidence is substantial if a "reasonable person might find that the evidentiary record supports the agency's conclusion." [cit.] The possibility that two inconsistent conclusions may be drawn from the evidence does not preclude a Board finding from being supported by substantial evidence. . . .

III

BD presents two challenges to the Board's conclusion that the mark as a whole is functional. Its lead argument posits legal error by the Board in its determination that certain features of the mark, which are admittedly non-functional, will not serve to remove the mark as a whole from the realm of functionality. BD asserts that the elongated shape of the closure cap, the spacing of the ribs and their particular shapes, as well as the design relationship of those features to the whole of the closure cap are the design embraced by the mark. As such, BD asserts that the scope of its mark is "extremely modest and limited." BD does not contest that the ribs themselves are functional, as is the opening in the top of the closure cap. These prominent and important functional features, which are common to the closure caps made by BD's competitors, led the Board to conclude that admitted non-functional features could not save the mark from being deemed overall functional. BD contends that the Board committed reversible error by discounting the significance of the non-functional elements.

BD's secondary argument is that the Board's analysis of the *Morton–Norwich* factors is unsupported by substantial evidence. BD appreciates the more deferential standard of review we apply to its second argument.

A

BD's first argument fails to recognize that one object of the *Morton–Norwich* inquiry is to weigh the elements of a mark against one another to develop an understanding of whether the mark as a whole is essentially functional and thus non-registrable. Whenever a proposed mark includes both functional and non-functional features, as in this case, the critical question is the degree of utility present in the overall design of the mark. This court recognized as much in *Morton–Norwich*, where Judge Rich harked back to the design in *In re*

Deister Concentrator Co., 48 CCPA 952, 289 F.2d 496, 506 (1961), in which the design was judged "in essence utilitarian." In *In re R.M. Smith, Inc.*, 734 F.2d 1482, 1484 (Fed.Cir.1984), this court reiterated the importance of the "degree of utility" proposition, and explained how the distinction between de facto and de jure functionality gives shape to a court's inquiry into a mark's "degree of utility."

De facto functionality simply means that a design has a function, like the closure cap in this case. Such functionality is irrelevant to the question of whether a mark as a whole is functional so as to be ineligible for trademark protection. De jure functionality "means that the product is in its particular shape because it works better in this shape." Further, as the Board recognized in this case, *Textron* instructs that where a mark is composed of functional and non-functional features, whether "an overall design is functional should be based on the superiority of the design as a whole, rather than on whether each design feature is 'useful' or 'serves a utilitarian purpose.'" *Textron* cited as an example the Coca-Cola® bottle, noting that the bottle's significant overall non-functional shape would not lose trademark protection simply because "the shape of an insignificant element of the design, such as the lip of the bottle, is arguably functional." Likewise, a mark possessed of significant functional features should not qualify for trademark protection where insignificant elements of the design are non-functional.

The foregoing authority makes clear that the Board committed no legal error by weighing the functional and non-functional features of BD's mark against each other. Our functionality precedent indeed mandates that the Board conduct such an assessment as part of its determination of whether a mark in its entirety is overall de jure functional. As the court explained in *Morton–Norwich*, "we must strike a balance between the 'right to copy' and the right to protect one's method of trade identification." To decide as a matter of fact "whether the 'consuming public' has an interest in making use of [one's design], superior to [one's] interest in being [its] sole vendor," we are guided by the *Morton–Norwich* factors.

B.

. . . .

BD challenges the Board's ultimate factual determination that the mark as a whole is functional by homing in on the Board's *Morton–Norwich* analysis, arguing that the Board's analysis lacks substantial evidence support. As to the first *Morton–Norwich* factor, the Board did not err in finding that this factor weighs in favor of finding functionality. In *TrafFix Devices, Inc. v. Marketing Displays, Inc.*, 532 U.S. 23 (2001), the Supreme Court stated that "the disclosure of a feature in the claims of a utility patent constitutes strong evidence of functionality." As discussed by the Board, claim 4 of the '446 patent shows the utilitarian nature of at least two prominent features of BD's mark: (1) the two concentric circles at the top of the closure cap, which allow a needle to be inserted, and (2) the ribs, which serve as a gripping surface.

BD does not contest the Board's finding that the '446 patent teaches the functional benefits of two important features of its proposed mark. Rather it argues that those features, while disclosed in the '446 patent, were not themselves claimed in that patent. BD's argument lacks merit. *TrafFix* does not require that a patent claim the exact configuration for which trademark protection is sought in order to undermine an applicant's assertion that an applied-for mark is not de jure functional. Indeed, *TrafFix* teaches that statements in a patent's specification illuminating the purpose served by a design may constitute equally strong evidence of functionality. *See TrafFix*, 532 U.S. at 32–33, 34–35. The Board correctly read the '446 patent to indicate that at least two of the important elements of the proposed mark were functional.

BD argues that its design patents are persuasive evidence of the non-functionality of the closure caps' overall design. However, while evidence of a design patent may be some evidence of non-functionality under *Morton–Norwich*, "the fact that a device is or was the subject of a design patent does not, without more, bestow upon said device the aura of distinctiveness or recognition as a trademark." *R.M. Smith*, 734 F.2d at 1485 (citation omitted). Furthermore, the design patents BD claims as evidence of non-functionality do not reflect the specific design for which trademark protection is sought. Our law recognizes that the existence of a design patent for the very design for which trademark protection is sought "presumptively ... indicates that the design is *not de jure* functional." *Morton–Norwich*, 671 F.2d at 1342 n. 3. Absent identity between the design patent and the proposed mark, the presumption loses force, and the "similar" design patents lack sufficient evidentiary value to overcome the strong conclusion in this case that BD's utility patents underscore the functionality of significant elements of the proposed mark.

As to the second *Morton–Norwich* factor, substantial evidence supports the Board's assessment of BD's advertising. BD's advertising touts the utilitarian advantages of the prominent features of the mark, such as the top's circular opening (which maximizes the possible useful area of the opening), the side's ribs, and the bottom's flanged lip. The advertisements emphasize that the "ridges on the outer surface permit for a more secure grip," and praise the "enhanced handling features" that are "inherent in the design." The advertisements explain that the top's "plastic shield" is an "important design innovation that keeps the blood safely contained within the closure" and "encourages safer opening—discourages use of the thumb roll technique, which can result in spattering of the specimen," and that the "hooded feature of closure reduces the possibility of catching glove between stopper and tube on reclosing." Against this substantial evidence of functionality, BD offers two explanations, each of which we reject. First, BD argues that the designs shown in the advertisements are not exactly the same as the proposed mark's design. For purposes of an overall functionality assessment, this distinction is without a difference. While the spire-like tops of the ribs may not be shown in the advertisements, the arrangement of the ribs along the side of the top and the shape of the opening are sufficiently like the features of the claimed mark to show an identity of functionality between the articles shown in the advertising and the proposed mark's prominent features. Second, BD would characterize the advertisements as "look for" advertising—the kind that pulls out of an overall article a few features to catch the viewer's attention. Thus BD argues that its advertisements were not really intended to tout functional aspects of its design, but merely to cause the viewer to look at one part of a design in particular. This argument fails. Nothing in the text of the advertisements underscores this "look for" concept. Instead the advertisements taken as a whole are more than substantial evidence that the proposed mark as a whole is functional. Indeed, the enlarged photographs of parts of the device actually highlight the functional aspects of the mark.

As to the third factor, if functionality is found based on other considerations, there is "no need to consider the availability of alternative designs, because the feature cannot be given trade dress protection merely because there are alternative designs available." *Valu Eng'g*, 278 F.3d at 1276. Thus, since the patent and advertising evidence established functionality, the Board did not need to analyze whether alternative designs exist. Nonetheless, the Board did conduct this analysis and found that one of the proposed designs was irrelevant and the other two could not be characterized as alternative designs because they shared the same utilitarian features of BD's design. BD has not shown that this finding is unsupported by substantial evidence.

Finally, as to the fourth factor, there was little record evidence before the Board to establish whether the cap design results from a comparatively simple or inexpensive method of manufacture. The sole evidence in the record on this factor consists of the declarations of Jaeger and Newby, two BD witnesses, who both averred that the design features did not lower the cost of manufacture. Given this scarce evidence, the Board did not err in refusing to weigh this factor in its analysis.

In *New England Butt Co. v. International Trade Commission*, 756 F.2d 874 (Fed.Cir.1985), we explained that the public policy underlying the rule that de jure functional designs cannot be protected as trademarks is "not the *right* to slavishly copy articles which are not protected by patent or copyright, but the *need* to copy those articles, which is more properly termed the right to compete *effectively*." *Id.* at 877 (citing *Morton–Norwich*, 671 F.2d at 1339). The record in this case shows that BD's competitors in the closure cap industry also feature ribs for sure gripping and similar functional openings on their products. The Board thus concluded that the record failed to establish that there are meaningful alternative designs for collection tube closure caps. Substantial evidence supports this conclusion, which underscores the competitive need to copy the functional features of BD's proposed mark.

Because the Board committed no legal error in its assessment of the functionality of BD's proposed mark, and because substantial evidence supports the Board's findings of fact under the *Morton–Norwich* factors, we affirm the final decision of the Board.

LINN, Circuit Judge, dissenting.

Because the [Board] incorrectly applied the legal standards in assessing the functionality of the trademark of [BD] and because substantial evidence does not support the Board's conclusion of functionality, I respectfully dissent.

It is undisputed that certain individual features of BD's closure cap design are functional, but the evidence falls short in supporting a conclusion that the mark, as a whole and as shown in the drawing, is in essence utilitarian, and thus *de jure* functional. While various individual features of a mark may be *de facto* functional if they are directed to the performance of certain identified functions, *In re Morton–Norwich Prods., Inc.,* 671 F.2d 1332, 1337 (CCPA 1982), *de jure* functionality is directed to the *appearance* of the design (*not* the thing itself) and is concerned with whether the design is "made in the form it must be made if it is to accomplish its purpose"—in other words, whether the appearance is dictated by function. *Morton–Norwich,* 671 F.2d at 1338–39 (internal citation omitted); *see TrafFix Devices, Inc. v. Mktg. Displays, Inc.,* 532 U.S. 23, 33 (2001) ("[A] feature is ... functional when it is essential to the use or purpose of the device or when it affects the cost or quality of the device.") [(citing *Qualitex and Inwood*).]

I agree with the majority that the degree of design utility must be considered in determining *de jure* functionality. I part company with the majority, however, when it approves the Board's "weigh[ing] the elements of a mark against one another to develop an understanding of whether the mark as a whole is essentially functional and thus non-registrable." The presence of functional features may be relevant, but not in the sense of comparing dissociated functional features against non-functional features. The proper inquiry is to examine the degree to which the mark as a whole is dictated by utilitarian concerns (functional or economic superiority) or is arbitrary ("without complete deference to utility"). *See Morton–Norwich,* 671 F.2d at 1338–39, 1342–43.

Weighing individual elements of a mark against each other is analytically contrary to the consideration of the mark as a whole. As this court has previously held, "[s]imply dissecting appellant's alleged trademark into its design features and attributing to each a proven or commonly known utility is not, without more, conclusive that the design, considered as a whole, is de jure functional and not registrable." *In re Teledyne Indus., Inc.,* 696 F.2d 968, 971 (Fed.Cir.1982).

This court's decision in *Morton–Norwich* is instructive. . . .The examining attorney [in that case] rejected the mark on the basis that the design "is no more than a non-distinctive purely functional container for the goods plus a purely functional spray trigger controlled closure . . . essentially utilitarian and non-arbitrary." *Id.* at 1335. The Board similarly concluded that the mark "is dictated primarily by functional (utilitarian) considerations, and is therefore unregistrable." *Id.* (original emphasis omitted).

Our predecessor court reversed finding that the applicant sought to register "no single design feature or component but the overall composite design comprising both bottle and spray top." *Id.* at 1342. Thus, the degree of design utility was analyzed for the whole mark, not the dissociated functional elements. Although the bottle and spray top each served a function, there was a complete absence of evidence to show that the shape of the bottle and spray top were required to look as they did to serve those functions. Indeed, the evidence before the Board established that the bottle and spray top could take a number of diverse forms, equally as suitable from a functional standpoint. The court concluded that there would be no injury to competition if Morton–Norwich were entitled to protection of this particular design; competitors could obtain the functions of the container without copying the trade dress. *Id.* at 1342–43. In sum, the evidence failed to prove that the overall design was "the best or one of a few superior designs available." *Id.* at 1341.

The facts in the present case are very much like those in *Morton–Norwich*. . . As in *Morton–Norwich*, there is no evidence that the overall design of the BD closure cap is required to look the way it does or that the design is "the best or one of a few superior designs available." The Board and the majority place principal focus on the function served by certain features of the mark, including, *inter alia,* the top's opening (to allow for the insertion of a needle), the ribs on the side of the cap (to allow for increased grip), and the bottom's flanged lip (to allow for a safer opening). These considerations relate to the *de facto* functionality of individual product features and not the *de jure* functionality of the overall design—whether the design as a whole must look this way to serve some identified function. In focusing on the functional attributes of individual components, the Board and the majority overlook the arbitrary nature of BD's overall design.

Even under the improper analysis accepted by the majority, if the individual attributes with recognized functions are examined, there is no support for the proposition that the form of those components was dictated by their function. There is no evidence that: (1) the hole in the top *must* be that particular shape and size for a needle to pass through the opening; (2) the side of the cap *must* possess horizontally spaced ribs in the precise shape, size, and spacing depicted in BD's design to provide for increased grip; or (3) the bottom lip *must* be flanged and tapered in the precise manner depicted to avoid being unsafe.

While the proposed mark must be examined as a whole, evidentiary concerns allow the [PTO] to establish a prima facie case of functionality by analyzing *de facto* functional features of a design. *Teledyne,* 696 F.2d at 971; [cit]. The burden then shifts to the applicant to rebut the prima facie case of functionality. *Teledyne,* 696 F.2d at 971 ("Determination that the design as a whole is not de jure functional may well be possible only in light of evidence more readily available to, or uniquely in the possession of, the applicant."). However, the ultimate determination of *de jure* functionality still requires a consideration of the design as a whole. *Id.*; *Textron*, 753 F.2d at 1026 (following *Teledyne*, 696 F.2d at 971).

Here, the examiner focused on functional features to establish a prima facie basis for the rejection and BD, in turn, submitted evidence on functionality to rebut that rejection. While the Board and the majority correctly cite the *Morton–Norwich* factors to determine the functionality of the overall design based on the evidence presented, both the Board and the majority fail to consider the design as a whole in analyzing these factors.

First, while the Board and the majority put great weight in the existence of a utility patent, the '446 Patent, that patent fails to illuminate the functionality inquiry. The Supreme Court recognized that "[a] utility patent is strong evidence that the features therein claimed are functional." *TrafFix*, 532 U.S. at 29. However, the '446 Patent claims none of the features of BD's design mark. Specifically, the claims of the '446 Patent do not cover the appearance or pattern of the ridges, the flanged lip, or the top opening of BD's design. *See* '446 Patent col.8 ll.23–29 ("(f) a flexible cap body for mounting on said stopper body; (g) said cap body having an open end and a substantially closed end; ... (i) said closed end having a needle receiving bore in the top surface thereof....").

Second, the majority correctly notes that the advertisements tout the features of BD's design that serve a functional purpose, which weighs against a finding of non-functionality. However, the advertisements do support the finding of non-functionality based on the third *Morton–Norwich* factor: the presence of alternative designs. While the majority finds no relevance in the fact that the designs featured in BD's advertisements were not exactly the same as the current mark, this fact indicates the existence of alternative designs that are nonetheless functionally identical.

Addressing the third *Morton–Norwich* factor, the Board and the majority discounted the most probative evidence submitted in this case—the design patents and evidence of alternative designs. Because "the effect upon competition is really the crux of the matter, it is, of course, significant that there are other alternatives available." *Morton–Norwich*, 671 F.2d at 1341 (internal quotation omitted).

The three design patents noted by the majority are not identical to the specific design for which trademark protection is sought. However, the fact that three distinct design patents were granted on similar, but not identical, designs performing the same overall function as the current design at issue suggests that the current design is not "made in the form it must be made if it is to accomplish its purpose." *Morton–Norwich*, 671 F.2d at 1339 (internal citation omitted). If a design patent can show that one design in a group of functionally identical alternative designs is non-functional, the entire class of arbitrary alternative designs is likely nonfunctional.

. . . .

Further, the Board and the majority wholly disregarded the evidence submitted by BD of alternative designs utilized by BD's competitors. The majority is correct that there is no need to consider alternative designs when functionality has been established; however, "that does not mean that the availability of alternative designs cannot be a legitimate source of evidence to determine whether a feature is functional in the first place." *Valu Eng'g,* 278 F.3d at 1276. In this case, the Board disregarded two alternative designs—designs actually used by BD's competitors—because it found that they shared the same utilitarian features and were therefore not "alternative designs." The disqualification of an alternative design because it shares the same utilitarian features is unsupported by law. *See Morton-Norwich,* 671 F.2d at 1342 ("[C]ompetitors may even copy and enjoy all of [the design's] *functions* without copying the external appearance of appellant's spray top." (emphasis added)). In fact, this evidence strongly suggests that BD's design is not functional because BD faces competition from products with similar functionality, yet differing designs. As in *Morton-Norwich,* BD's "[c]ompetitors have apparently had no need to simulate" BD's product design "in order to enjoy all of the *functional* aspects" of a closure cap. *Id.* at 1342 (emphasis in original). Any concern that BD will unfairly assert its mark against these competitors rings hollow when BD, in seeking protection of this mark, has already distinguished those designs of its competitors.

Finally, the Board may not ignore the fourth *Morton-Norwich* factor—whether the design results from a less expensive method of manufacture—when evidence was presented on it. There were undisputed statements from BD indicating that the design did not result from reduced costs of manufacture. This uncontroverted evidence should have been taken into consideration in the Board's weighing of the factors. While the majority characterizes this as "little record evidence," it is evidence that must be considered nonetheless.

Because the Board committed legal error in failing to analyze the functionality of BD's mark as a whole and lacked substantial evidence for its findings, I would reverse the Board's decision on functionality. On the functionality determination, I therefore respectfully dissent. . . .

SPECIALIZED SEATING, INC. v. GREENWICH INDUS., L.P.
616 F.3d 722 (7th Cir. 2010)

EASTERBROOK, Chief Judge:

For more than 80 years, Clarin has been making x-frame folding chairs. In 1999 it applied for registration of one particular x-frame design as a trademark. The Patent and Trademark Office issued Registration No. 2,803,875 in January 2004. This is the registered mark:

The principal register describes it thus: "a configuration of a folding chair containing an X-frame profile, a flat channel flanked on each side by rolled edges around the perimeter of the chair, two cross bars with a flat channel and rolled edges at the back bottom of the chair, one cross bar with a flat channel and rolled edges on the front bottom, protruding feet, and a back support, the outer sides of which slant inward."

[S]pecialized competes in Clarin's principal market: the sale of folding chairs to auditoriums, sports stadiums, convention centers, and other places that need to deploy lots of seats, which owners want to be as light and compact as possible for storage when not in use. Specialized sells a folding chair that to an untrained eye looks like Clarin's trademark chair. There are differences in construction and detail; the chair is not a slavish knockoff, but the basic design tracks the registered mark. That similarity had led to this litigation in which Specialized sought a declaratory judgment that its design does not violate Clarin's rights under the Lanham Act, 15 U.S.C. §§ 1051-1129, and Clarin counterclaimed for an injunction.

. . . .

The district court held a bench trial and ruled in Specialized's favor on both of these issues. The judge found that the x-frame construction is functional because it was designed to be an optimal tradeoff between a chair's weight (and thus its cost, since lighter chairs use less steel) and its strength; an x-frame chair also folds itself naturally when knocked over (an important consideration for large auditoriums, where it is vital that chairs not impede exit if a fire or panic breaks out); the flat channel at the seat's edge, where the attachment to the frame slides so that the chair can fold, was designed for strength and attaching hooks to link a chair with its nearest neighbor; the front and back cross bars contribute strength (and allow thinner tubing to be used in the rest of the frame); and the inward-sloping frame of the back support allows the chair to support greater vertical loads than Clarin's older "a-back" design, which the "b-back" design, depicted in the trademark registration, succeeded. The a-back design is on the left and the b-back on the right:

Clarin chairs with a-back designs failed when the audience at rock concerts, seeking a better view, sat on top of the chairs' backs and put their feet on the seats. The tubing buckled at the bend in the frame. The b-back design is less likely to buckle when someone sits on it, and it also produces a somewhat wider back, which concert promoters see as a benefit. (Patrons sometimes try to get closer to the stage by stepping through rows of chairs. The gap between b-back chairs is smaller, so they are more effective at keeping crowds in place.)

. . .

Findings of fact made after a bench trial must stand unless clearly erroneous. [cit.] Although "functionality" is the "ultimate issue" in a case such as this, an "ultimate" issue (such as whether the defendant was negligent or engaged in racial discrimination) remains one of "fact" under this standard, because it is generated by applying legal principles to factual conclusions. [cit.] "Functionality" certainly isn't an issue of law; it represents a fact-specific conclusion about whether aspects of a design are "essential to the use or purpose of the article or if it affects the cost or quality of the article." Inwood Laboratories, Inc. v. Ives Laboratories, Inc., 456 U.S. 844, 850 n. 10; [cit]. Many decisions apply Rule 52's standard to a finding that a mark is functional. [cit].

Clarin tries to evade this standard of review by contending that the district judge's findings were influenced by legal errors. We don't see any. The district judge started from the proposition, which the Supreme Court articulated in TrafFix, that claims in an expired utility patent presumptively are functional. Since utility patents are supposed to be restricted to inventions that have utility, and thus are functional, that's a sensible starting point-and since inventions covered by utility patents pass into the public domain when the patent expires, it is inappropriate to use trademark law to afford extended protection to a patented invention. See also Jay Franco, 615 F.3d at 857-59. 5-8. Clarin itself obtained four utility patents for aspects of the x-frame folding chair. These patents disclose every aspect of the asserted trademark design except for the b-back. And the district judge did not commit a clear error by concluding that the b-back design is a functional improvement over the a-back design. This means that the trademark design is functional as a unit, and that every important aspect of it is independently functional. It looks the way it does in order to be a better chair, not in order to be a better way of identifying who made it (the function of a trademark).

We do not doubt that there are many other available functional designs. Sometimes the function of the functionality doctrine is to prevent firms from appropriating basic forms (such as the circle) that go into many designs. Our contemporaneous opinion in Jay Franco discusses that aspect of the functionality doctrine. This does not imply that preserving basic elements for the public domain is the doctrine's only role.

Another goal, as TrafFix stressed, is to separate the spheres of patent and trademark law, and to ensure that the term of a patent is not extended beyond the period authorized by the legislature. A design such as Clarin's x-frame chair is functional not because it is the only way to do things, but because it represents one of many solutions to a problem. Clarin tells us that other designs are stronger, or thinner, or less likely to collapse when someone sits on the backrest, or lighter and so easier to carry and set up. Granted. But as Clarin's '248 patent states, the x-frame design achieves a favorable strength-to-weight ratio. Plastic chairs are lighter but weaker. Y-frame chairs are stronger but use more metal (and so are heavier and more expensive); some alternative designs must be made with box-shaped metal pieces to achieve strength, and this adds to weight and the cost of fabrication. The list of alternative designs is very long, and it is easy to see why hundreds of different-looking folding chairs are on the market.

What this says to us is that all of the designs are functional, in the sense that they represent different compromises along the axes of weight, strength, kind of material, ease of setup, ability to connect ("gang") the chairs together for maximum seating density, and so on. A novel or distinctive selection of attributes on these many dimensions can be protected for a time by a utility patent or a design patent, but it cannot be protected forever as one producer's trade dress. When the patent expires, other firms are free to copy the design to the last detail in order to increase competition and drive down the price that consumers pay. See, e.g., Bonito Boats, Inc. v. Thunder Craft Boats, Inc., 489 U.S. 141 (1989); Sears, Roebuck & Co. v. Stiffel Co., 376 U.S. 225 (1964). . .

Clarin reminds us that a product whose overall appearance is distinctive can be protected under the trademark laws, even though most of the product's constituent elements serve some function. See, e.g., . . .W.T. Rogers Co. v. Keene, 778 F.2d 334, 339-40 (7th Cir. 1985). That's true enough, but what made the appearance "distinctive" in these and similar decisions was a non-functional aspect of the design. For example, Keene dealt with a letter tray that had irregular hexagons as end caps; each hexagon had an interior cutout. End caps serve the function of making letter trays stable and separating the lower tray from the upper tray, and cutouts make them lighter while reducing the cost of materials, but neither the irregular shape of the hexagon nor the shape of the cutout served any function. They made the tray distinctive and enabled consumers to determine which firm made it. If Clarin had placed a cutout in the backrest, or given it a distinctive pattern, it could claim those attributes as trade dress. But what Registration No. 2,803,875 claims is the x-frame profile with three cross bars and a slanted back support. All of the claimed features are functional; none was added to produce a distinctive appearance that would help consumers identify the product's source.

[Affirmed].

At p. 209-210, Note 2, add the following:

See Georgia-Pacific Consumer Prods. v. Kimberly-Clark Corp., 647 F.3d 723, 727-28 (7th Cir. 2011) ("In *TrafFix*, the Supreme Court found that a design is functional "if it is essential to the use or purpose of the article or if it affects the cost or quality of the article." Courts look to several factors to determine whether a design is functional: '(1) the existence of a utility patent, expired or unexpired, that involves or describes the functionality of an item's design element; (2) the utilitarian properties of the item's unpatented design elements; (3) advertising of the item that touts the utilitarian advantages of the item's design elements; (4) the dearth of, or difficulty in creating, alternative designs for the item's purpose; (5) the effect of the design feature on an item's quality or cost.'"); *see also Secalt SA v. Wuxi Shenxi Const. Mach. Co.*, 668 F.3d 677 (9th Cir. 2012) (applying factors from pre-*TrafFix* case law in the Ninth Circuit). In what ways has *TraFix* altered the factors to which courts look in determining functionality?

At p. 211, Note 4, add the following:

The Sixth Circuit has affirmed the decision of the district court in *Maker's Mark*. *See* 102 U.S.P.Q.2d (BNA) 1693 (6th Cir. 2012).

In several recent cases, litigants have advanced the argument that what they have described as the functionality" of the *defendant's* should sustain a finding of non-infringement. Indeed, in cases *not* involving features of product design, two courts were in cases *not* involving features of product design, initially receptive to the argument. Thus, in *Fleischer Studios, Inc. v. A.V.E.L.A., Inc.*, 636 F.3d 1115 (9th Cir. 2011), a cartoon character merchandising case, the Ninth Circuit held inter alia that because the defendant was "not using Betty Boop as a trademark, but instead as a functional product", no trademark claim could lie. Likewise, in *Rosetta Stone Ltd. v. Google, Inc.*, 730 F.Supp.2d 531 (E.D. Va. 2010), a case involving liability for keyword advertising, a district court held that "because Google uses Rosetta Stone's trademark to identify relevant information to users searching on those trademarks, the use is a functional and noninfringing one." Neither conclusion of "functionality of defendant's use" caused the invalidation of the plaintiff's mark. Rather, it provided a defense to the third party user in the particular case. However, the Ninth Circuit withdrew its initial opinion in *Fleischer* and superseded it with an opinion that did not address that argument. And the *Rosetta Stone* decision was reversed by the Court of Appeal for the Fourth Circuit. It is arguably unhelpful (and confusing) to describe these new cases as "functionality cases."

At pp. 211-12, add the following at end of Note 7:

In *Georgia-Pacific Consumer Prods. v. Kimberly-Clark Corp.*, 647 F.3d 723 (7th Cir. 2011), the plaintiff claimed trade dress rights in the quilted design of its toilet paper. The design had been the subject of several utility patents. The Seventh Circuit gave effect to the inference of functionality based on *TrafFix*, reasoning as follows:

> The parties agree that the essential feature of the trademarks is the Quilted Diamond Design, which is embossed on the toilet paper, giving it a quilt-like appearance. Therefore, the question is whether the Quilted Diamond Design is also the "central advance" claimed in any of the utility patents. Unfortunately for [the plaintiff], all five utility patents disclose a diamond lattice design filled with signature bosses and claim the benefits of this design as the "central advance." Each of the patents discusses the benefits of the Quilted Diamond Design. [Defendant] argues that this language is strong evidence of functionality. We agree.
>
> [Plaintiff] argues, however, that the Quilted Diamond Design is merely "incidental" under *TrafFix*. Accordingly, we will "[go] beyond" the patent claims to the specifications. *See TrafFix*, 532 U.S. at 34. The abstracts for the '639 and '156 patents state that "[t]he perceived *softness of embossed tissue can be increased greatly while avoiding nesting* when a particular pattern is embossed into the tissue." (Emphasis added.) The '776 abstract describes that patent as "[a]n embossed tissue having *improved bulk and puffiness* while being non-nesting by having a lattice pattern and at least two signature bosses." (Emphasis added.) And the '057 patent states that "[t]his invention relates to the discovery that *perceived softness of embossed tissue can be increased greatly while avoiding prior art nesting problems if a particular pattern is embossed into the tissue.*" (Emphasis added.) So [plaintiff's] argument fares no better here; these abstracts all refer to the Quilted Diamond Design's utilitarian benefits of softness, bulk, and non-nesting.
>
> Moreover, the patents claim the Quilted Diamond Design as the "most preferred embodiment." (The preferred embodiment of the '057 patent is a lattice pattern of diamond cells filled with signature debossments; the most preferred embodiment for the '639 patent is a lattice comprised of "diamond shaped" cells filled with a "signature boss.") And while the preferred embodiment alone is not definitive of functionality, the language [plaintiff] uses in the preferred embodiment (a lattice pattern filled with hearts and flowers) matches the language in the claims (a lattice structure and diamond-shaped cells). As with the language in the specifications, the consistency in language between the preferred embodiment and the claims is evidence of functionality.
>
> Thus, reading the language of the patents, we find that the "central

advance" claimed in the utility patents is embossing a quilt-like diamond lattice filled with signature designs that improves (perceived) softness and bulk, and reduces nesting and ridging. This is the same "essential feature" claimed in the trademarks. Thus, the language of the patents—the claims, abstracts, and preferred embodiment—is "strong evidence" that the Quilted Diamond Design is functional, and Georgia-Pacific has failed to offer evidence that the design is merely incidental.

Is this analysis consistent with how the *TrafFix* Court intended lower courts to use patents? Does it incorporate undue (or too little) patent technicality into trademark law?

At p. 213, Note 11, add the following:

See also Secalt SA v. Wuxi Shenxi Const. Mach. Co., 668 F.3d 677 (9th Cir. 2012) (emphasizing that the existence of a design patent on the feature for which trade dress protection is sought will not of itself overcome a presumption of functionality).

At p. 214, add as Note 15:

15.   *Derivative functionality.* In *Georgia-Pacific Consumer Prods. v. Kimberly-Clark Corp.*, 647 F.3d 723 (7th Cir. 2011), the plaintiff argued that even if the design of its toilet paper was functional as used on toilet paper, it was not functional as used on packaging. The Court of Appeals for the Seventh Circuit rejected that argument, affirming that if a product design is found to be functional, the accurate depiction of that product design is also functional. *Cf.* Casebook, page 86 (discussing *de iure genericism* of the terms used to identify products covered by expired patents).

At p. 217, add the following two cases between *Abercrombie & Fitch* and *Au-Tomotive Gold*:

ERBE ELEKTROMEDIZIN GMBH v. CANADY TECHNOLOGY LLC
629 F.3d 1278 (Fed. Cir. 2010)

PROST, Circuit Judge:

Appellants ERBE Elektromedizin GmbH and ERBE USA, Inc. (collectively, "ERBE") appeal from a final decision of the United States District Court for the Western District of Pennsylvania . . . which [inter alia] granted summary judgment . . . on ERBE's . . . trade dress claims in Canady's favor based on the lack of a legally protectable mark. . .

Background

This is a patent infringement case involving three competitor companies that create argon gas-enhanced electrosurgical products for electrosurgery. Argon gas-enhanced electrosurgery is typically performed with an electrosurgical generator to which various surgical accessories, including endoscopic probes, are attached. . . . Three different patents are implicated. . . ERBE is owner by assignment of [one of these patents].

ERBE unsuccessfully tried to register the color blue as applied to these "flexible endoscopic probes for use in argon plasma coagulation (APC)" on the U.S. Patent and Trademark Office's Principal Register. . . .

In 2005, Dr. Canady contracted with KLS Martin GmbH & Co. ("KLS Martin") to manufacture blue 2.3 mm diameter probes ("Canady probes") with black range marking rings along the tip end. . . .

[ERBE sued Dr. Canady and others alleging patent infringement as well as infringement of its purported trade dress, consisting of the blue tube with black markings at the end. The district court granted Canady's motion for summary judgment of non-infringement as to the asserted claims of the relevant patent and also granted Canady's motion for summary judgment with respect to ERBE's trade dress claims because ERBE failed to establish a genuine issue of material fact that the blue color and black markings were nonfunctional and had acquired secondary meaning.]

II

We next address ERBE's challenge to the district court's grant of summary judgment as to its . . . trade dress claims based on the court's determination that the color blue is functional and has not acquired the requisite secondary meaning. When reviewing Lanham Act claims, we look to the law of the regional circuit where the district court sits, here the Third Circuit. See Tone Bros., Inc. v. Sysco Corp., 28 F.3d 1192, 1200 (Fed. Cir. 1994). . . .

The Third Circuit analyzes federal trademark infringement and federal unfair competition under identical standards. A & H Sportswear, Inc. v. Victoria's Secret Stores, Inc., 237 F.3d 198, 210 (3d Cir. 2000). . . .

To survive summary judgment here, ERBE would have to establish a genuine issue of material fact that both the color blue is non-functional and has acquired secondary meaning. [cit.] It fails to do either.

We first look to functionality. A mark is functional if it "'is essential to the use or purpose of the article or if it affects the cost or quality of the article, that is,' if exclusive use of the feature would put competitors at a significant non-reputation-related disadvantage." L.D.

Kichler Co., 192 F.3d at 1352 (quoting Qualitex, 514 U.S. at 165). Some factors courts use to determine functionality include whether the design yields a utilitarian advantage, alternative designs are available in order to avoid hindering competition, and the design achieves economies in manufacture or use. See, e.g., In re Owens-Corning Fiberglas Corp., 774 F.2d 1116, 1121 (Fed. Cir. 1985).

Color may not be granted trademark protection if the color performs a utilitarian function in connection with the goods it identifies or there are specific competitive advantages for use. Brunswick Corp. v. British Seagull Ltd., 35 F.3d 1527, 1530-33 (Fed. Cir. 1994), cert. denied, 514 U.S. 1050 (1995) (color black for outboard engines was functional and could not be protected where black offered the advantage of being compatible with a wider variety of boat colors); Keene Corp. v. Paraflex Indus., Inc., 653 F.2d 822, 824 (3d Cir. 1981). However, "[m]ere taste or preference cannot render a color—unless it is 'the best, or at least one, of a few superior designs'—de jure functional." L.D. Kichler Co., 192 F.3d at 1353; see Brunswick Corp., 35 F.3d at 1531 (explaining that de jure functional features, which rest on utility and the foundation of effective competition, are not entitled to trademark protection). The Third Circuit has explained that the policy behind the functionality doctrine invokes the inquiry of whether prohibiting the mark's imitation by others will deprive those others of something that will substantially hinder them in competition. Keene, 653 F.3d at 827. As a result, the existence of other, equally usable colors is relevant to determine whether a particular color is functional. Qualitex, 514 U.S. at 166.

ERBE asserts that there is a genuine issue of material fact whether the color blue is functional because the evidence demonstrates that blue is not uniquely superior for APC probes, has no competitive advantage because it is not essential to the use or purpose of the APC probes, does not have an aesthetic function, and that many other colors are equally visible against human tissue and are available for selection. For support, ERBE offers the declaration of Managing Director Christian Erbe. In this declaration, Mr. Erbe explained that "[b]lue is one of the many colors available for APC probes. Any color, other than beige or red, would be clearly visible during endoscopic procedures."

We reject ERBE's argument that the district court misapplied Keene. In Keene, the Third Circuit explained that the "functionality doctrine stems from the public interest in enhancing competition" and avoiding improper hindrance of competition in the marketplace. 653 F.2d at 827. ERBE fails to present a genuine issue of material fact that the color blue does not make the probe more visible through an endoscopic camera or that such a color mark would not lead to anti-competitive effects. Cf. In re Owens-Corning Fiberglas Corp., 774 F.2d at 1122 (holding that the color pink for fiber glass insulation was not functional because it did "not deprive competitors of any reasonable right or competitive need"). The evidence in the record is that the color blue is prevalent in the medical field, the blue color enhances identification of the endoscopic tip, and several companies use blue endoscope probes. See, e.g., Biosearch Medical Products Inc. advertisement (explaining that "[b]lue color enhances positive Endoscopic identification of the tip.") There is no evidentiary support that other colors are as visible through an endoscopic camera as the color blue other than a conclusory, self-serving statement by Mr. Erbe. Because the record evidence demonstrates that appropriation by ERBE alone would place others at a competitive disadvantage, we conclude that the district court properly found that there is no genuine issue of material fact that the color blue is functional.

Moreover, even if the color blue is non-functional, we would still affirm the district court's grant of summary judgment because ERBE fails to present a genuine issue of material fact that there is secondary meaning for the mark. . . .

NEWMAN, Circuit Judge, concurring in part, dissenting in part:

I respectfully dissent from the grant of summary judgment whereby the court holds, summarily, that there can be neither patent . . . nor trade dress infringement of ERBE's proprietary rights. I write separately with respect particularly to the . . . trade dress issues, for the court has departed from established law and precedent. Canady does not dispute that it copied the blue color and the particular shade of blue of the ERBE probe; that is, that it copied the trade dress. The public interest in avoidance of deception or confusion looms particularly large in the medical/surgical field, where the surgeon's experience of quality and performance, on recognition of the surgical device by its unique color, is a matter of public concern.

Common law property rights are of practical significance, and their sustenance is as much a judicial responsibility as are statutory rights. This court's cursory authorization to a competitor to copy the distinctive color of this surgical probe, despite the evidence of likelhood of confusion as to the source and identity of the probe, is surely not subject to summary disposition in favor of the copier. ERBE suggests that there is deception and free-riding, for it was not disputed that the blue probes with black markings, manufactured by KLS Martin GmbH & Co. and imported by Canady for use with the ERBE equipment, are intended to mirror the blue color and black markings of the ERBE probes. Canady represented to the FDA that its imported probes are "the same as" the ERBE probes, and obtained expedited FDA approval based on that representation. Indeed, Canady's probes are compatible only with ERBE's electrosurgical equipment.

The district court held, on summary judgment, that the blue color is "functional." However, ERBE established at least a genuine issue as to this question. . . .

The district court improperly granted summary judgment on the . . . trade dress issues. Precedent does not support this judgment. Canady's argument that blue, this shade of blue, is the only color that can be distinguished from body fluids was directly contradicted by the expert declaration of Christian Erbe, Chairman of ERBE, USA, who declared that "Blue is one of many colors available for APC Probes. Any color, other than beige or red, would be clearly visible during endoscopic procedures." At the summary judgment stage, the factual issue of whether blue, or this shade of blue, is the only color of the spectrum that contrasts with bodily fluids was fairly placed into dispute. For this factual question to be decided in favor of Canady at the summary judgment stage, Canady must establish that it is entitled to judgment in its favor, even on ERBE's factual position. [cit].

My colleagues criticize Mr. Erbe's declaration as "conclusory." However, his statement about the visibility of other colors is straightforward and in accord with common sense, and its correctness is unchallenged by Canady. The evidence offered by Canady in support of functionality is that one company advertises that its coagulation probe's "blue color enhances positive endoscopic identification of the tip." . . . A reasonable jury could decide . . . that the color blue for argon plasma coagulation tubes is not functional, and is capable of serving as a trademark.

The court also errs in its summary judgment that ERBE cannot establish secondary meaning. . . .

As to copying, which the majority acknowledges in its list of factors relevant to secondary meaning but does not discuss, ERBE raises significant issues of possible passing off and consumer deception. The laws of trademark and trade dress are designed to protect the consumer as well as the purveyor. It does not serve the consuming public to eliminate legal protection of indicia of source and quality. See Qualitex, 514 U.S. at 164 ("The law thereby 'encourage[s] the production of quality products,' and simultaneously discourages those who hope to sell inferior products by capitalizing on a consumer's inability quickly to evaluate the quality of an item offered for sale." (internal citation omitted)).

ERBE states that its blue color serves to protect the consumer/user, for it is a conspicuous identification of its particular probe for argon plasma coagulation. ERBE states that of the many colors that could be used, Canady selected the ERBE shade of blue for the sole purpose of profiting from the reputation established for ERBE's product. The panel majority discounts this unrebutted evidence, and observes only the absence of other possible types of evidence relating to secondary meaning. However, the Third Circuit, like other circuits, does not set rigid rules for all forms of trademark and trade dress. See E.T. Browne Drug Co. v. Conocare Prods. Inc., 538 F.3d 185, 200 n. 15 (3d Cir. 2008) ("We do not suggest that a party attempting to establish secondary meaning always must show that marketing materials succeeded in creating buyer association or that the term contributed to sales growth.").

My colleagues state that there is "evidence . . . that the color blue is prevalent in the medical field . . . and several companies use blue endoscope probes," apparently drawing this conclusion from the advertisement considered by the PTO and [co-]plaintiff ConMed's authorized blue probe. Whether secondary meaning was established is a question of fact, not subject to adverse inferences on summary judgment. The factual issue of likelihood of confusion, upon the undisputed intentional copying of this shade of blue, must be considered. ERBE has created at least a genuine issue of material fact as to whether its trade dress, as well as its trademark, is protectable. My colleagues err in finding these facts adversely, on summary judgment.

The judicial obligation is more complex than simply to facilitate "competition," as the panel majority asserts. The avoidance of deception of the consumer is a purpose of trade dress law. At the summary judgment stage, ERBE provided sufficient evidence to negate the movant's arguments with respect to the functionality and distinctiveness of its trade dress. Summary judgment that ERBE has no protectable right in its blue endoscopic argon probe was improperly granted. From my colleagues' contrary holding, I must, respectfully, dissent.

CHRISTIAN LOUBOUTIN S.A. v. YVES SAINT LAURENT AMERICA, INC.
778 F.Supp.2d 445 (S.D.N.Y. 2011), *appeal pending*

MARRERO, District Judge:

[Plaintiff Christian Louboutin S.A sued Yves Saint Laurent America (YSL), asserting various claims under the Lanham Act and New York law. Louboutin sought a preliminary injunction. The court denied Louboutin's motion.]

I. BACKGROUND

Sometime around 1992 designer Christian Louboutin . . . began coloring glossy vivid red the outsoles of his high fashion women's shoes. . . . Louboutin deviated from industry custom. In his own words, this diversion was meant to give his line of shoes "energy," a purpose for which he chose a shade of red because he regarded it as "engaging, flirtatious, memorable and the color of passion," as well as "sexy." . . . In pursuit of the red sole's virtues, Louboutin invested substantial amounts of capital building a reputation and good will, as well as promoting and protecting Louboutin's claim to exclusive ownership of the mark as its signature in women's high fashion footwear.

[Louboutin succeeded to the point where the red outsole became closely associated with Louboutin. In 2008, the United States Patent and Trademark Office approved registration of the mark, as Registration No. 3,361,597 (the "Red Sole Mark")]. The issue now before the Court is whether, despite Christian Louboutin's acknowledged innovation and the broad association of the high fashion red outsole with him as its source, trademark protection should not have been granted to that registration.

[]The certificate of registration includes both a verbal description of the mark and a line drawing intended to show placement of the mark as indicated below.

The verbal description reads

> "For: Women's High Fashion Designer Footwear, In Class 25 (U.S. Cls. 22 and 39).
> First Use 0-0-1992; In Commerce 0-0-1992.
> The color(s) red is/are claimed as a feature of the mark. The mark consists of a lacquered red sole on footwear. The dotted lines are not part of the mark but are intended only to show placement of the mark."

. . .

[YSL] produces seasonal collections that include footwear. According to YSL, red outsoles have appeared occasionally in YSL collections dating back to the 1970s. Louboutin takes issue with four shoes from YSL's Cruise 2011 collection . . . Each of the challenged models bears a bright red outsole as part of a monochromatic design in which the shoe is entirely red (or entirely blue, or entirely yellow, etc.). . . . .

II. Discussion

. . .

Color alone "*sometimes*" may be protectable as a trademark, "where that color has attained 'secondary meaning' and therefore identifies and distinguishes a particular brand (and thus indicates its 'source')." Qualitex Co. v. Jacobson Prods. Co., 514 U.S. 159, 161, 163 (1995) (emphasis added) . . . . . Conversely, color may not be protectable where it is "functional," meaning that the color is essential to the use or purpose of the product, or affects the cost or quality of the product. Qualitex, 514 U.S. at 165. . . In short, color can meet the legal requirements for a trademark if it "act[s] as a symbol that distinguishes a firm's goods and identifies their source, *without serving any other significant function.*" Id. at 166 (emphasis added). As defined in the Restatement (Third) of Unfair Competition, a design is functional if its "aesthetic value" is able to "confe[r] a significant benefit that cannot practically be duplicated by the use of alternative designs." Id. at 170 (quoting Restatement (Third) of Unfair Competition § 17 cmt. c (1993)).

Applying these principles, courts have approved the use of a single color as a trademark for industrial products. . . . In some industrial markets the design, shape and general composition of the goods are relatively uniform, so as to conform to industry-wide standards. Steel bolts, fiber glass wall insulation and cleaning press pads, for example, are what they are regardless of which manufacturer produces them. The application of color to the product can be isolated to a single purpose: to change the article's external appearance so as to distinguish one source from another.

But, whatever commercial purposes may support extending trademark protection to a single color for industrial goods do not easily fit the unique characteristics and needs—the creativity, aesthetics, taste, and seasonal change—that define production of articles of fashion. That distinction may be readily visualized through an image of the incongruity presented by use of color in other industries in contrast to fashion. Can one imagine industrial models sashaying down the runways in displays of the designs and shades of the season's collections of wall insulation? The difference for Lanham Act purposes, as elaborated below, is that in fashion markets color serves not solely to identify sponsorship or source, but is used in designs primarily to advance expressive, ornamental and aesthetic purposes.

In the fashion industry, the Lanham Act has been upheld to permit the registration of the use of color in a trademark, but only in distinct patterns or combinations of shades that manifest a conscious effort to design a uniquely identifiable mark embedded in the goods. See, e.g., Louis Vuitton Malletier, 454 F.3d at 116 ("LV" monogram combined in a pattern of rows with 33 bright colors); Burberry Ltd. v. Euro Moda, Inc., No. 08 Civ. 5781, 2009 WL 1675080, at *5 (S.D.N.Y. June 10, 2009) (registered Burberry check pattern entitled to statutory presumption of validity). In these cases the courts clearly point out that the approved trademark applies to color not as an abstract concept, or to a specific single shade, but to the arrangement of different colors and thus their synergy to create a distinct recognizable image purposely intended to identify a source while at the same time serving as an expressive, ornamental or decorative concept.

The narrow question presented here is whether the Lanham Act extends protection to a trademark composed of a single color used as an expressive and defining quality of an article of wear produced in the fashion industry. In other words, the Court must decide whether there is something unique about the fashion world that militates against extending trademark protection to a single color, although such registrations have sometimes been upheld in other industries.

To answer this question, and recognizing the fanciful business from which this lawsuit arises, the Court begins with a fanciful hypothetical. Suppose that Monet, having just painted his water lilies, encounters a legal challenge from Picasso, who seeks by injunction to bar display or sale of those works. In his complaint, Picasso alleges that Monet, in depicting the color of water, used a distinctive indigo that Picasso claims was the same or too close to the exquisite shade that Picasso declares is "the color of melancholy," the hallmark of his Blue Period, and is the one Picasso applied in his images of water in paintings of that collection. By virtue of his longstanding prior use of that unique tinge of blue in context, affirmed by its registration by the trademark office, Picasso asserts exclusive ownership of the specific tone to portray that color of water in canvas painting. Should a court grant Picasso relief?

Putting aside the thousand technicalities lawyers would conjure and quibble about in arguing why the imagined case is inapposite or distinguishable from the real controversy before the Court, the example contains some analytic parallels perhaps helpful in resolving this actual dispute.

Painting and fashion design stem from related creative stock, and thus share many central features. Both find common ground and goals in two vital fields of human endeavor, art and commerce. For the ultimate ends they serve in these spheres, both integrally depend on creativity. Fashion designers and painters both regard themselves, and others regard them, as being engaged in labors for which artistic talent, as well as personal expression as a means to channel it, are vital. Moreover, the items generated by both painters and fashion designers acquire commercial value as they gain recognition. Louboutin himself would probably feel his sense of honneur wounded if he were considered merely a cobbler, rather than an artiste. But, as a matter differing only in degrees and order of priority, Louboutin and Picasso both may also be properly labeled as men of commerce, each in his particular market.

The creative energies of painter and fashion designer are devoted to appeal to the same sense in the beholder and wearer: aesthetics. Both strive to please patrons and markets by creating objects that not only serve a commercial purpose but also possess ornamental beauty (subjectively perceived and defined). Quintessentially, both painting and fashion embrace matters of taste. In consequence, they share vicissitudes natural to any matter of palate or palette. They change as the seasons change. Styles, features, whole lines come and go with passing likes and dislikes, to be replaced by new articles with origins from regions where genius charts a different course. Items fall in and out of fashion in all nuances of the word, conveying not only currency but seasonality and transience. Perhaps capturing something of that relative inconstancy, painting and fashion share a vocabulary. They speak in ethereal terms like fanciful, inventive, eccentric, whimsical, visionary, and, to quote Louboutin again, "engaging, flirtatious"—all words which also have in common an aim to evoke and affect things of the moment.

These creative means also share a dependence on color as an indispensable medium. Color constitutes a critical attribute of the goods each form designs. Alone, in combinations, in harmonious or even incongruous blends, in varying patterns and shapes, the whole spectrum of light serves as a primal ingredient without which neither painting nor fashion design as expressive and ornamental art would flourish. For, color depicts elemental properties. As it projects expression of the artist's mental world, it captures the mutability, the fancy, the moods of the visual world, in both spheres working as a means to execute singular concepts born of imagination for which not just any other shade will do. Hence, color in this context plays a unique role. It is a feature purposely given to an article of art or design to depict the idea as the creator conceived it, and to evoke an effect intended. In ornamenting, it draws attention to itself, and to the object for which its tone forms a distinct expressive feature. From these perspectives, color in turn elementally performs a creative function; it aims to please or be useful, not to identify and advertise a commercial source.

But, as an offshoot of color, perhaps most crucial among the features painting and fashion design share as commerce and art, are two interrelated qualities that both creative fields depend upon to thrive, and indeed to survive: artistic freedom and fair competition. In both forms, the greatest range for creative outlet exists with its highest, most vibrant and all-encompassing energies where every pigment of the spectrum is freely available for the creator to apply, where every painter and designer in producing artful works enjoys equal freedom to pick and choose color from every streak of the rainbow. The contrary also holds. Placing off limit signs on any given chromatic band by allowing one artist or designer to appropriate an entire shade and hang an ambiguous threatening cloud over a swath of other neighboring hues, thus delimiting zones where other imaginations may not veer or wander, would unduly hinder not just commerce and competition, but art as well.

The thrust and implications of the Court's analogy are clear. No one would argue that a painter should be barred from employing a color intended to convey a basic concept because another painter, while using that shade as an expressive feature of a similar work, also staked out a claim to it as a trademark in that context. If as a principle this proposition holds as applied to high art, it should extend with equal force to high fashion. The law should not countenance restraints that would interfere with creativity and stifle competition by one designer, while granting another a monopoly invested with the right to exclude use of an ornamental or functional medium necessary for freest and most productive artistic expression by all engaged in the same enterprise.

The question of whether the use of a single color in the fashion industry can constitute a valid mark necessarily raises another one: whether a single color may be "functional" in that context. "The functionality doctrine ... forbids the use of a product's feature as a trademark where doing so will put a competitor at a significant disadvantage because the feature is 'essential to the use or purpose of the article' or 'affects [its] cost or quality.' " . . . . Use of a single color has been held functional, and therefore not protectable under the Lanham Act, in other contexts. See, e.g., Brunswick Corp. v. British Seagull Ltd., 35 F.3d

1527, 1533 (Fed.Cir.1994) (black for marine outboard engines held functional because it is "compatib[le] with a wide variety of boat colors and [can] make objects appear smaller"); Deere & Co. v. Farmhand, Inc., 560 F.Supp. 85, 98 (S.D.Iowa 1982) (green for farm equipment held functional because farmers "prefer to match their loaders to their tractor"), aff'd, 721 F.2d 253 (8th Cir.1983). These cases illustrate the principle that "[a]esthetic appeal can be functional; often we value products for their looks." Eco Mfg. LLC v. Honeywell Int'l Inc., 357 F.3d 649, 653 (7th Cir.2003) (emphasis in original).

Christian Louboutin himself has acknowledged significant, nontrademark functions for choosing red for his outsoles. As already quoted above, he stated that he chose the color to give his shoe styles "energy" and because it is "engaging." He has also said that red is "sexy" and "attracts men to the women who wear my shoes." YSL, for its part, has used red to evoke Chinese design elements. For the Cruise 2011 collection, YSL employed the monochromatic style that it indicates is part of the brand's history, meaning that each of the challenged shoe models is entirely red. The shoes also coordinate with clothing items offered in the same collection. Color serves an additional significant nontrademark function: "to satisfy the 'noble instinct for giving the right touch of beauty to common and necessary things.'" Qualitex, 514 U.S. at 170 (quoting G. Chesterton, Simplicity and Tolstoy 61 (1912)). The outsole of a shoe is, almost literally, a pedestrian thing. Yet, coated in a bright and unexpected color, the outsole becomes decorative, an object of beauty. To attract, to reference, to stand out, to blend in, to beautify, to endow with sex appeal—all comprise nontrademark functions of color in fashion.

The red outsole also affects the cost of the shoe, although perhaps not in the way Qualitex envisioned. Arguably, adding the red lacquered finish to a plain raw leather sole is more expensive, not less, than producing shoes otherwise identical but without that extra ornamental finish. Yet, for high fashion designers such as Louboutin and YSL, the higher cost of production is desirable because it makes the final creation that much more exclusive, and costly.

Because the use of red outsoles serves nontrademark functions other than as a source identifier, and affects the cost and quality of the shoe, the Court must examine whether granting trademark rights for Louboutin's use of the color red as a brand would "significantly hinder competition," that is, "permit one competitor (or a group) to interfere with legitimate (nontrademark-related) competition through actual or potential exclusive use of an important product ingredient." Qualitex, 514 U.S. at 170. Here, Christian Louboutin singularly claimed "the color red" as a feature of the mark, and he registered a "lacquered red sole" for "women's high fashion designer footwear." Both components of the mark pose serious legal concerns as well as threats to legitimate competition in the designer shoe market.

Louboutin's claim to "the color red" is, without some limitation, overly broad and inconsistent with the scheme of trademark registration established by the Lanham Act. Awarding one participant in the designer shoe market a monopoly on the color red would impermissibly hinder competition among other participants. YSL has various reasons for seeking to use red on its outsoles—for example, to reference traditional Chinese lacquer ware, to create a monochromatic shoe, and to create a cohesive look consisting of color-coordinating shoes and garments. Presumably, if Louboutin were to succeed on its claim of trademark infringement, YSL and other designers would be prohibited from achieving those stylistic goals. In this respect, Louboutin's ownership claim to a red outsole would hinder competition not only in high fashion shoes, but potentially in the markets for other women's wear articles as well. Designers of dresses, coats, bags, hats and gloves who may conceive a red shade for those articles with matching monochromatic shoes would face the shadow or reality of litigation in choosing bands of red to give expression to their ideas.

The effects of this specter—the uncertainty and apprehension it generates—are especially acute in the fashion industry because of its grounding on the creative elements discussed above. Fashion is dependent on colors. It is subject to temporal change. It is susceptible to taste, to idiosyncrasies and whims and moods, both of designers and consumers. Thus, at any moment when the market and the deities of design, by whatever fancy they decide those things, proclaim that "passion" is in for a given season and must be expressed in reds in the year's various collections, Louboutin's claim would cast a red cloud over the whole industry, cramping what other designers could do, while allowing Louboutin to paint with a full palette. Louboutin would thus be able to market a total outfit in his red, while other designers would not. And this impediment would apply not just with respect to Louboutin's registered "the color red," but, on its theory as pressed in this litigation, to a broader band of various other shades of red which would be available to Louboutin but which it could bar others from using.

Louboutin asserts that it is the color depicted in the registration's drawing, and not the verbal reference to the "color red," that controls. In its reply brief, Louboutin identified that color for the first time as Pantone No. 18-1663 TP, or "Chinese Red," part of the PANTONE TEXTILE color system. Yet that identification raises additional issues. Louboutin cannot amend or augment its PTO registration by representations it makes in this litigation. Accordingly, the color that governs here remains, as Louboutin points out, the shade of red depicted in the registration's drawing. As Louboutin concedes, however, because of varying absorption and reflection qualities of the material to which it is applied, a color as it manifests on paper would appear quite different—some lighter, some darker hues—on other mediums such as leather and cloth. A competitor examining the Louboutin registration drawing for guidance as to what color it applies to may therefore remain unable to determine precisely which shade or shades it encompasses and which others are available for it to safely use.

Moreover, YSL has represented to the Court that the precise color of the styles Louboutin challenges is not Chinese Red, and that YSL has never used Pantone No. 18-1663 TP on its outsoles. Undaunted, Louboutin insists that YSL has nonetheless infringed the Red Sole Mark because its challenged shoe models use a shade confusingly too close to Chinese Red. Yet Louboutin cannot provide a satisfactory explanation as to why those models—but not others previously made by YSL that also bear a red outsole—are confusingly similar to its claimed mark. The larger question this conflict poses is how close to a protected single color used in an item of fashion can the next competitor approach without encountering legal challenge from the first claimant of a shade as a trademark.

In response to this legal dilemma, Louboutin proposes that the Court simply draw a designated range both above and below the borderlines of Pantone No. 18-1663 TP, and declare all other stripes of red within that zone forbidden to competitors. Its suggested metric references Olay Co., Inc. v. Cococare Prods., Inc. See 218 U.S.P.Q. 1028, 1045 (S.D.N.Y.1983) (issuing injunction requiring infringer to use "a discernibly different pink, at least 40% different in terms of [Pantone Matching System] tones" from that used by registrant). Louboutin's proposal would have the effect of appropriating more than a dozen shades of red-and perhaps other colors as well[6] — and goes far beyond the injunction upon which Louboutin relies. In *Olay*, the protectable interest was not "in the color pink alone," but rather in the color in combination with graphics and packaging. Here, Louboutin's claimed mark is, in essence, the color red alone when used on the soles of "high fashion" footwear. Moreover, although Louboutin attempts in these proceedings to limit the scope of the mark to high-heeled footwear, no such limitation appears on the face of the registration.

The other options Louboutin's claim would leave other competitors are no more practical or palatable. As YSL endeavored to do during a deposition of Christian Louboutin in connection with this action, other designers could seek advance clearance from Christian Louboutin himself, spreading the fan of shades before him to see at what tint his red light changes to amber. Or they could go to court and ask for declaratory relief holding that a proposed red sole is not close enough to Chinese Red to infringe Louboutin's mark, thereby turning the judge into an arbiter of fashion design. Though Qualitex points out that in trademark disputes courts routinely are called upon to decide difficult questions involving shades of differences in words or phrases or symbols, the commercial contexts in which the application of those judgments generally has arisen has not entailed use of a single color in the fashion industry, where distinctions in designs and ideas conveyed by single colors represent not just matters of degree but much finer qualitative and aesthetic calls.

Because Louboutin's registration specifies that it covers women's high fashion "designer footwear," the description is broad enough to encompass all styles of shoes, not just the high-heeled model illustrated in the PTO registration. Louboutin's argument that it would

---

[6] Louboutin's suggestion that the Court require other designers to stay some percentage away from Chinese Red raises the question: some percentage of what? Chinese Red, like any color, is made up of a certain combination of other colors. Based on the Court's research, this combination can be expressed in various metrics, such as a combination of RGB (red, green, blue) or CMYK (cyan, magenta, yellow, black), or HSB (hue, saturation, brightness). . . In Adobe Color Picker, a variance of just 10 percent in any of these inputs, in either direction, yields more than a dozen shades visibly different from Chinese Red, in some cases so different as to appear to the casual observer pink on one side of Chinese Red or orange on the other.

not pursue a claim of infringement based upon red outsoles on, for example, flat shoes, wedges or kitten heels, is cold comfort to competing designers. In fact, in one case in Paris, Louboutin sought to enforce its French trademark for a "shoe sole in the color red" against the company Zara France, S.A.R.I., which is not a high-end retailer.

Another dimension of uncertainty the Red Sole Mark creates pertains to its coating. Louboutin's claim extends not just to the base of "the color red," but also to its gloss. In the registration, it is described more specifically as "lacquered" red. Thus, it is not clear, for example, whether the protection of Louboutin's trademark would apply to a "Chinese Red" outsole that was not shiny, but entirely flat. In fact, that issue has surfaced in this case. YSL asserts that the color tone of some of the shoes Louboutin challenges is not lacquered at all but a flat red. By bringing this litigation, Louboutin is of course calling upon the Court to pass judgment as well on the degree of buffing that a competitor may give to a Chinese Red outsole before it begins to infringe on Louboutin's rights.

Finally, conferring legal recognition on Louboutin's claim raises the specter of fashion wars. If Louboutin owns Chinese Red for the outsole of high fashion women's shoes, another designer can just as well stake out a claim for exclusive use of another shade of red, or indeed even Louboutin's color, for the insole, while yet another could, like the world colonizers of eras past dividing conquered territories and markets, plant its flag on the entire heel for its Chinese Red. And who is to stop YSL, which declares it pioneered the monochrome shoe design, from trumping the whole footwear design industry by asserting rights to the single color shoe concept in all shades? And these imperial color wars in women's high fashion footwear would represent only the opening forays. What about hostile color grabs in the markets for low-fashion shoes? Or for sports shoes? Or expanding beyond footwear, what about inner linings, collars, or buttons on coats, jackets, or dresses in both women's and men's apparel?

In sum, the Court cannot conceive that the Lanham Act could serve as the source of the broad spectrum of absurdities that would follow recognition of a trademark for the use of a single color for fashion items. Because the Court has serious doubts that Louboutin possesses a protectable mark, the Court finds that Louboutin cannot establish a likelihood that it will succeed on its claims for trademark infringement and unfair competition under the Lanham Act. Thus there is no warrant to grant injunctive relief on those claims.

. . . .

At p. 222, Note 2, add the following:

Despite *Au-Tomotive Gold*, in *Fleischer Studios, Inc. v. A.V.E.L.A., Inc.*, 636 F.3d 1115 (9th Cir. 2011), a separate panel of the Ninth Circuit initially held inter alia that because the defendant was "not using Betty Boop as a trademark, but instead as a functional product", no trademark claim could lie. Thus, invocation of functionality did work to restrict merchandising rights. But note that the "functionality" being discussed by the court in *Fleischer Studios* is that of the *defendant's* use; the Betty Boop image was a functional aesthetic component of the defendant's product. Viewed as such this doctrine does not invalidate the plaintiff's mark. Rather, it provides a defense to the third party user, to be determined on a case-by-case basis depending upon the nature of the use challenged. As such, it begins to approximate the trademark use doctrine discussed in Chapter 7. *See* Graeme B. Dinwoodie and Mark D. Janis, *Confusion Over Use: Contextualism in Trademark Law*, 92 IOWA L. REV. 1597, 1654-55 (2007) (noting possible extension of trademark use theory to merchandising); Casebook, page 497 (noting litigation of question in the European Union). However, the court withdrew its opinion sua sponte.

At p. 223, add as Notes 3A and 3B:

3A. *Colour and the fashion industry.* Is *Louboutin* consistent with *Qualitex*? Has the court articulated a rule precluding the protection of color per se as a mark in the fashion industry? Would you support such a rule? *Cf. In re Clarke, supra*, Casebook p. 131.

3B. *Defining rights.* To what extent did the *Louboutin* court rely on the plaintiff's registration in defining its trademark rights? Would (and should) the scope of Louboutin's rights be different under section 43(a)? How would you define those rights, and why? Could you define Louboutin's trademark in a way that protects the distinctiveness of the red sole mark while permitting appropriate competition?

At p. 224, add as Note 8:

8. *Functionality and the Supplemental Register.* In *ERBE*, the plaintiff had also brought what the court denominated a "trademark" claim in addition to its "trade dress" claim based upon the fact that, in 2002, ERBE did register the color blue as applied to the tube portion of the APC probes on the *Supplemental* Register. (The effect of registration on the Principal and Supplemental Register is addressed in Chapter 5 of the Casebook.) This was another point of contention between the majority and Judge Newman. The majority simply noted that while "federal registration on the Principal Register provides a presumption of the mark's validity . . . [r]egistration of a mark on the Supplemental Register . . . does not." Thus, ERBE bore the burden of proving that it owned a valid mark. Judge Newman read the registration history in view of commentary from the Trademark Manual of Examining Procedure. Thus she took the view:

> Registration of the blue color for these products on the Supplemental Register required the applicant to show that the color is not functional. Trademark Manual of Examining Procedure § 1202.05(b) states:
>
>> A color mark is not registrable on the Principal Register under § 2(f), or the Supplemental Register, if the color is functional. Brunswick Corp. v. British Seagull Ltd., 35 F.3d 1527 (Fed. Cir. 1994), cert. denied, 514 U.S. 1050 (1995); In re Owens-Corning Fiberglas Corp., 774 F.2d 1116 (Fed. Cir. 1985).
>
> Thus the color mark passed the test of non-functionality, upon agency examination.
>
> The difference with respect to registration of a color on the Supplemental Register and the Principal Register does not relate to functionality, but to the need to establish secondary meaning for the particular color. Non-functionality does not of itself establish secondary meaning. . . .
>
> In accordance with the review procedures of the Administrative Procedure Act, the holding of the Patent and Trademark Office of non-functionality of the color blue for "flexible endoscopic probes for use in argon plasma coagulation," receives administrative deference. Although ERBE had not obtained registration on the Principal Register, ERBE was not required to do so in order to rely on its Supplemental registration for its statutory benefits . . . .

Judge Newman would thus have also relied on her reading of what the PTO must have decided in allowing registration on the Supplemental Register to support the argument that a genuine issue of material fact existed as to functionality. Section 43(a)(3) of the Lanham Act provides that "In a civil action for trade dress infringement under this chapter for trade dress not registered on the principal register, the person who asserts trade dress protection has the burden of proving that the matter sought to be protected is not functional." (*See* Casebook, p. 213 Note 13.) Does Judge Newman's view fit with this provision? Should it matter that the plaintiff claimed it was bringing a "trademark claim under Section 32 of the Lanham Act" based on its registration of the color blue on the Supplemental Register and a "trade dress" claim under Section 43(a) on the basis of the same (unregistered) mark?

At p. 225, line 2: the phrase "the color of ice cream is non-functional" should read "the color of ice cream is functional."

USE

4

At p. 246, Note 10, add the following:

See also Nat'l Pork Board v. Supreme Lobster & Seafood Co., 96 U.S.P.Q.2d (BNA) 1479 (TTAB 2010) (assessing whether slogan THE OTHER WHITE MEAT used in connection with pork industry promotional efforts functioned as a mark).

At p. 260, add as Note 1A:

1A. *Proving bona fide intent to use.* In *Spirits Int'l, B.V. v. S.S. Taris Zeytin Ve Zeytinyagi Tarim Satis Kooperatifleri Birligi*, 99 U.S.P.Q.2d (BNA) 1545 (TTAB 2011), the ITU applicant sought to register MOSKONISI for various alcoholic beverages. When challenged in an opposition, the applicant indicated that it had no documents corroborating its asserted intent to use, and the applicant submitted no other evidence on the point. The TTAB sustained the opposition, noting that if the applicant does not produce documentary evidence showing its intent to use, the burden shifts to the applicant to explain the lack of evidence. *Id.* at 1548-49; *see also Bobosky v. Adidas AG*, 2011 WL 6888688 (Dec. 29, 2011) (registration of WE NOT ME for various clothing items invalidated as void ab initio where registrant supplied no documentary corroboration of intent to use and admitted that his lawyer had created the list of goods in the registration application). If you were counseling an ITU applicant, what are some examples of documentary evidence that you would regard as sufficient to corroborate an intent to use? Is the TTAB's position in *Spirits* consistent with the goals of the ITU provisions? Does it reflect a view that the ITU provisions are too generous to applicants?

At p. 288, add the following to Problem 4-8:

For a more recent (and less dramatic) example, consider the Jeremy Lin phenomenon. In early February 2012, previously little-known professional basketball player Jeremy Lin of the NBA's New York Knicks played spectacularly in a string of games and became an instant sensation. Sports commentators, fans, and pretty much everyone else repeatedly used the term LINSANITY in reference to Jeremy Lin and his sudden rise to prominence. On February 13, 2012, Jeremy Lin applied to register LINSANITY for a wide variety of merchandise. Assume that a number of other applicants (none connected with Jeremy Lin) filed similar applications, both before and after February 13. How should the PTO rule on the priority issue—and why? For the answer to the first part of the question, see Ron Dicker, *'Linsanity' Trademark Fight Ends – Jeremy Lin Is Last Applicant Standing*, Huffington Post (May 24, 2012) < http://www.huffingtonpost.com/2012/05/24/linsanity-trademark-jeremy-lin_n_1543978.html?ir=Sports&ref=topbar>. Is this scenario analogous to the LET'S ROLL scenario?

At p. 307, add as Note 2A:

2A. *Controlling consistency of quality.* In *Eva's Bridal Ltd. v. Halanick Ent., Inc.,* 639 F.3d 788 (7th Cir. 2011), a mark owner licensed to another retailer the mark EVA'S BRIDAL for a bridal shop. The license contained no quality control provisions, and the mark owner admitted having made no attempt to exercise control over any aspect of the licensee's business. Faced with a claim that this constituted naked licensing, the mark owner argued that they never had any reason to doubt that the licensee adhered to high standards, and in any event, bridal shop consumers always demanded high quality. Judge Easterbrook pointed out that the assurance of "high" quality was not the point of the naked licensing inquiry:

> This argument that licensors may relinquish all control of licensees that operate "high quality" businesses misunderstands what judicial decisions and the *Restatement* mean when they speak about "quality." There is no rule that trademark proprietors must ensure "high quality" goods—or that "high quality" permits unsupervised licensing. "Kentucky Fried Chicken" is a valid mark, see *Kentucky Fried Chicken Corp. v. Diversified Packaging Corp.,* 549 F.2d 368 (5th Cir. 1977), though neither that chain nor any other fast-food franchise receives a star (or even a mention) in the *Guide Michelin.* The sort of supervision required for a trademark license is the sort that produces *consistent* quality. "Trademarks [are] indications of consistent and predictable quality assured through the trademark owner's control over the use of the designation." *Restatement* [*3d of Unfair Competition*] § 33 comment b. See also William M. Landes & Richard A. Posner, *The Economic Structure of Intellectual Property Law* 166–68, 184–86 (2003).

A person who visits one Kentucky Fried Chicken outlet finds that it has much the same ambiance and menu as any other. A visitor to any Burger King likewise enjoys a comforting familiarity and knows that the place will not be remotely like a Kentucky Fried Chicken outlet (and is sure to differ from Hardee's, Wendy's, and Applebee's too). The trademark's function is to tell shoppers what to expect—and whom to blame if a given outlet falls short. The licensor's reputation is at stake in every outlet, so it invests to the extent required to keep the consumer satisfied by ensuring a repeatable experience. See generally *Two Pesos, Inc. v. Taco Cabana, Inc.*, 505 U.S. 763 (1992).

How much control is enough? The licensor's self-interest largely determines the answer. Courts are apt to ask whether "the control retained by the licensor [is] sufficient under the circumstances to insure that the licensee's goods or services would meet the expectations created by the presence of the trademark." *Restatement* § 33 comment a (summarizing doctrine); see also *id* . at Reporter's Note comment c (collecting authority, which we need not set out). It isn't necessary to be more specific here, because plaintiffs did not retain *any* control— not via the license agreement, not via course of performance. A person who visited Eva's Bridal of Oak Lawn and then Eva's Bridal of Orland Park might not have found a common ambiance or means of doing business. And though the shops may have had many designers in common, this would not distinguish an "Eva's Bridal" shop from any other bridal shop; the trademark would not be doing any work if identical dresses could be purchased at Macy's or Nordstrom, and the "Eva's Bridal" shops were dissimilar except for some products that many retailers carried. Safeway could not license its marks to a corner grocery store, while retaining no control over inventory, appearance, or business methods, just because every grocery store is sure to have Coca-Cola and Wheaties on the shelf.

Id. at 790-91. According to Judge Easterbrook, the question of how much authority a mark owner had to exercise could not be answered at a general level, because both the nature of the business and consumer's particular expectations needed to be taken into account. *Id.* at 791. Applying those considerations to the case at hand, Judge Easterbrook concluded that this case was "the extreme case: plaintiffs had, and exercised, *no* authority over the appearance and operations of defendants' business, or even over what inventory to carry or avoid. That is the paradigm of a naked license." Do you agree that this is the paradigmatic case? If it was reasonable for the mark owner to rely on the licensee to maintain consistent quality, and there was no evidence of inconsistencies, is there a reason to invoke the naked licensing rule? Or should there be a no-harm, no-foul exception to that rule?

At p. 308, Note 4, add the following:

Consider another example. In March 2003, Deron Beal ("Beal") founded The Freecycle Network ("TFN"), a non-profit corporation dedicated to "freecycling" (giving an unwanted item away for continued use rather than disposing of it). TFN operates primarily through local volunteer member groups, led by volunteer moderators. Under the "Freecycle Ethos," TFN develops rules and policies in conjunction with the local moderators, but the moderators have flexibility in enforcement. One such rule, the "Keep it Free, Legal & Appropriate for All Ages" rule, expresses TFN's desire that members list only legal items. TFN permits member groups to identify their affiliation with TFN by using TFN's trademarks (*e.g.*, THE FREECYCLE NETWORK for services relating to freecycling). In October 2003, Lisanne Abraham ("Abraham") founded a local freecycling group, Freecycle Sunnyvale ("FS"). FS eventually was listed as a member group on TFN's website. Abraham e-mailed Beal to ask for a TFN logo to use on the FS website, and Beal responded by e-mail: "You can get the neutral logo from www.freecycle.org, just don't use it for commercial purposes. . ." After a dispute arose, FS challenged whether TFN had shown evidence of adequate quality control over its marks to avoid a finding of abandonment. What arguments would you make on behalf of TFN? How do you think that a court would resolve the quality control issue? *See FreecycleSunnyvale v. The Freecycle Network*, 626 F.3d 509 (9th Cir. 2010).

5

REGISTRATION

At p. 321, under the heading Principal Register v. Supplemental Register, add the following:

The Supplemental Register does also serve the additional function that its name implies: a parking place for applications that do not meet Lanham Act protectability standards, perhaps because the applicant is still in the process of attempting to establish secondary meaning, or perhaps because the applicant never really expects to establish it. Review the Lanham Act. Are there any substantial benefits to registering on the Supplemental Register? *See ERBE Electromedizin GmbH v. Canady Technology LLC*, 629 F.3d 1278 (Fed. Cir. 2010) (noting that registration on the Supplemental Register does not confer a presumption of validity); *see also Innovation Ventures, LLC v. N.V.E., Inc.*, 747 F.Supp.2d 853, 858-9 (E.D. Mich. 2010) (noting the argument that a supplemental registration confers no substantive rights and therefore cannot, as a matter of law, cause damages to a competitor). Consider also Judge Newman's dissent in *ERBE Electromedizin GmbH v. Canady Technology LLC*, 629 F.3d 1278 (Fed. Cir. 2010), excerpted and noted in Chapter 3 of this Supplement. Does this suggest benefits not apparent on the face of the statute?

At p. 322, add the following to the discussion of the specimen as a part of the application:

Responding to concerns about the accuracy of registrants' allegations of use, the PTO has amended its regulations to clarify that the PTO has the authority to require, upon request, information about the identified goods or services with which the mark is used. The information may include additional specimens, affidavits, or other exhibits. *See Changes in Requirements for Specimens and for Affidavits or Declarations of Continued Use or Excusable Nonuse in Trademark Cases*, 77 Fed. Reg. 30197 (May 22, 2012). Such requests might be made in a variety of settings – for example, in connection with an applicant's statement of use to perfect an ITU application, or in a registrant's declaration of continued use under Lanham Act Section 8.

At p. 325, add the following to the discussion of fraudulent procurement:

TTAB decisions applying *Bose* treat it as having adopted an intent standard, and some have restated the fraudulent procurement test as follows: (1) applicant/registrant made a false representation to the USPTO; (2) the false representation is material to the registrability of a mark; (3) applicant/registrant had knowledge of the falsity of the representation; and (4) applicant/registrant made the representation with intent to deceive the USPTO. *See ShutEmDown Sports, Inc. v. Carl Dean Lacy*, 102 U.S.P.Q.2d (BNA) 1036 (TTAB 2012).

The *Bose* decision did not specify how to assess materiality for fraudulent procurement. The Federal Circuit's jurisprudence on inequitable conduct in the patent area (an analog to fraudulent procurement in trademarks) specifies that a showing of inequitable conduct also requires evidence of intent and materiality. In a critical en banc ruling, the Federal Circuit decided that materiality for inequitable conduct is to be assessed under a but-for analysis: the misrepresentation or omission at issue is material if a patent would not have issued but for the misrepresentation or omission. *See Therasense, Inc. v. Becton, Dickinson & Co.*, 649 F.3d 1276 (Fed. Cir. 2011) (en banc). The court rejected more relaxed standards of materiality, such as the "reasonable examiner" standard (under which a materiality is satisfied simply by a showing that a reasonable examiner would have considered the information at issue to be important in deciding patentability), and the ground that it had led to a proliferation of dubious inequitable conduct charges. Should courts follow the *Therasense* ruling on materiality when assessing materiality in the context of fraudulent procurement of trademarks? For one approach, see *Fair Isaac Corp. v. Experian Information Solutions, Inc.*, 650 F.3d 1139, 1149-50 (8th Cir. 2011) (implicitly endorsing a "reasonable examiner" standard without discussing *Therasense* or the prospect of alternative standards).

At p. 337, Note 5, add the following:

For a separate cancellation proceeding brought on behalf of petitioners who had just reached the age of majority, see *Blackhorse v. Pro Football, Inc.*, Cancellation Proceeding No. 92046185, available at http://ttabvue.uspto.gov/ttabvue/v?qt=adv&pno=92046185. Petitioners argue that the clock for laches should begin to run only when the petitioner has reached the age of majority.

At p. 339, Note 11, add the following:

In addition, a separate set of much younger petitioners initiated a separate cancellation proceeding in *Blackhorse v. Pro Football, Inc.*, Cancellation Proceeding No. 92046185, available at http://ttabvue.uspto.gov/ttabvue/v?qt=adv&pno=92046185.

At p. 340, Note 13, add the following:

Suppose that the applicant is the government authority, seeking to protect its own symbols or other indicia. Should Section 2(b) still apply? Should the answer depend upon whether the authority seeks to register the mark for government services, as opposed to merchandise? *See In re City of Houston*, 101 U.S.P.Q.2d (BNA) 1588 (TTAB 2012) (ruling on the City of Houston's application to register its official seal for use in connection with "municipal services"); *In re The Government of the District of Columbia*, 101 U.S.P.Q.2d (BNA) 1588 (TTAB 2012) (ruling on the District of Columbia's application to register its official seal in connection with various merchandise such as clocks, memo pads, coasters, and sweat pants).

At pp. 359-60, Note 5, add the following:

See also Guantanamera Cigar Co. v. Corporacion Habanos, S.A., 729 F.Supp.2d 246, 254 (D.D.C. 2010) (overturning a TTAB determination on materiality rendered before *Spirits*; the TTAB had made no "substantial portion" determination, instead finding materiality based on Cuba's renown for cigars and the mark owner's subjective intent to deceive consumers through markings on its packaging). On remand, the TTAB found materiality, concluding that a substantial portion of consumers of cigars would be influenced in their purchase decision by the misdescriptive geographic connotation of GUANANAMERA for cigars not made in Guantanamo province, Cuba. *See Corporacion Habanos, S.A. v. Guantanamera Cigars Co.*, 102 U.S.P.Q.2d (BNA) 1085 (TTAB 2012). The TTAB noted that it was rejecting the proposition that direct evidence (presumably including survey or consumer testimony) is necessary to establish materiality. Indirect evidence such as "website evidence, and even expert testimony" may be used. *Id.* at 1099. The TTAB also expressed the view that "for goods, the PTO may raise an inference in favor of materiality with evidence that the placed named in the mark is famous as a source of the goods at issue," a position that the TTAB attributed to *California Innovations* and *Les Halles*. *Id.*

At p. 369, add the following new Problem:

PROBLEM 5-7A: CELEBRITY NAMES

Suppose that the celebrity recording artists Beyonce and Jay-Z are your clients. They inform you that they expect to become parents. (Actually, their people inform you of that. You wouldn't expect them to show up in person in your office, would you?) The blessed event is expected to occur in about three months. They intend to name the child Blue Ivy Carter and have spoken with their marketing people about launching a line of baby clothes under the BLUE IVY CARTER name. Their people tell you that Beyonce and Jay-Z insist on doing whatever they need to do to protect the baby's name from "exploitation by unscrupulous third parties." What is your advice? You might wish to consider a few of the following questions: (1) who owns the trademark rights in the baby's name? The parents? Beyonce alone? The baby? (2) Could the parents file an application now to register BLUE IVY CARTER for baby clothes? (3) If, as expected, others file applications for registration soon after the baby is born (and the name is publicly announced), what is the likely disposition of those other applications? (4) Suppose that, a few days after the baby is born, a Beyonce fan names her newborn baby Blue Ivy Carter. What if the fan reserves the domain name blueivycarter.com – would the fan be subject to suit for trademark infringement? (5) Suppose that a member of Beyonce's entourage hears about the baby's name long before the baby is born, and files an application to register BLUE IVY CARTER for fragrances, two months before Beyonce and Jay Z file their application. What effect would this have on Beyonce and Jay-Z's application?

At pp. 369-70, add the following to Problem 5-8:

(21) NUCKIN FUTS for prepared snacks made from nuts. (*See* Australian Registration No. 1408134. Australian trademark law prohibits the registration of marks that consist of "scandalous matter," which is to be judged from the perceptions of the "ordinary" Australian. This mystifies us because all (OK, most) of the Australians we know are extraordinary. In any event, the argument was apparently made that the term f**kin was part of the routine discourse of "ordinary" Australians, and thus wouldn't give offense.)

At p 378, Note 1, add the following:

Should the incontestable status of a registration foreclose challenges to the legality of later assignment agreements? Assume that the assignment documents are duly recorded in the PTO, which constitutes prima facie evidence of the execution of the assignment under Lanham Act § 10(3). *See Federal Treasury Enterprise Sojuzplodoimport v. Sprits Int'l N.V.*, 623 F.3d 61 (2d Cir. 2010).

SCOPE AND ENFORCEMENT OF TRADEMARK RIGHTS

GEOGRAPHIC LIMITS ON TRADEMARK RIGHTS

At p. 387, Note 8, add the following:

In a complex dispute between the respective operators of Patsy's Italian Restaurant and Patsy's Pizzeria, there was evidence of naked licensing of the PATSY'S PIZZERIA mark. Specifically, of the nine restaurants operating under the PATSY'S PIZZERIA name, there was evidence of inadequate quality control in connection with two—a restaurant located on Staten Island, and another located in Syosset. On appeal, the following question arose: did the finding of naked licensing result in the abandonment of all rights in the PATSY'S PIZZERIA mark, or only an abandonment in Staten Island and Syosset? In *Patsy's Italian Restaurant, Inc. v. Banas*, 658 F.3d 254 (2d Cir. 2011), the court endorsed a concept of geographically-limited abandonment:

> Appellants first argue that any finding of naked licensing necessarily acted as a total abandonment of all rights. We disagree. Although some forms of trademark abandonment may result in a loss of all rights in the mark, *see e.g., Feathercombs, Inc. v. Solo Prods. Co.,* 306 F.2d 251, 256 (2d Cir.1962), abandonment of a mark through naked licensing has different effects on the validity of the mark in different markets. *See Dawn Donut Co. v. Hart's Food Stores, Inc.,* 267 F.2d 358, 369 (2d Cir.1959) (a finding of naked licensing in the retail market would not result in the loss of trademark rights in the wholesale market). For example, if a restaurant operates in both New York and California, but engages in naked licensing only in California, the restaurant's registered mark may lose its significance in California while retaining its significance in New York. Thus, naked licensing will lead to an abandonment of a mark only where the mark loses its significance. 15 U.S.C. § 1127.

> As a result, we agree with the district court that a mark owner can abandon a mark through naked licensing in a particular geographic area without abandoning its rights throughout the entire United States. *See also*

Tumblebus Inc. v. Cranmer, 399 F.3d 754, 765–66 (6th Cir.2005) (recognizing that "there is considerable support for the concept that rights in a mark may be abandoned in certain geographic areas but not others"); [cit.].

Id. at 264-65. Do you agree with the proposition that the geographic scope of the loss of rights should match the geographic scope of the naked licensing activity?

At p. 396, add as Note 2A:

2A.   *Federal registration and local rights.* The Second Circuit in *Patsy's Italian Restaurant, Inc. v. Banas*, 658 F.3d 254 (2d Cir. 2011) emphasized that "local rights owned by another have been consistently viewed as sufficient to prevent a party from obtaining registration of a federal mark." *Id.* at 266. Why is this so? (Consider the scope of rights granted by federal registration). How local can those prior rights be and still constitute an impediment to federal registration? *See id.* at 266-68. Review Section 2(d) of the Lanham Act: does it impose any restriction on the type of use that might preclude federal registration?

At p. 399, Note 11, add the following:

Alternatively, does the ease with which marks cross borders mean that trademark law will have to adopt a greater range of doctrines that accommodate co-existence? *See* Max Planck Institute for Intellectual Property and Competition Law, Study on the Overall Functioning of the European Trade Mark System (Feb. 15, 2011) (proposing the introduction of a concept of co-existence within the unitary Community Trade Mark Regulation system).

At p. 420, Note 4, add the following:

See Fiat Group Automobiles SpA v. ISM Inc., 94 U.S.P.Q.2d (BNA) 1111, 1114-15 (TTAB 2010) (allowing understanding of what is a "famous" mark for purposes of opposition based on alleged dilution of well-known mark used only abroad to be informed by the statutory definition of "mark" including "the intent to use coupled with the filing of an application"). Should the intent of the foreign mark owner to use its mark in the United States be relevant to whether that mark should be protected in the United States under the well-known marks doctrine?

At p. 420, add as Note 5A;

If a mark is well-known in the United States, what should be the scope of protection it receives? Protection against confusion? Protection against dilution (as you will discover in Chapter 8, only "famous" marks receive protection against dilution under section 43(c)). See *Fiat Group Automobiles SpA v. ISM Inc.*, 94 U.S.P.Q.2d (BNA) 1111 (TTAB 2010). As a matter of international law, compare Article 6*bis* of the Paris Convention, Article 16(3) of TRIPS, and Article 4 of WIPO's Joint Recommendation Concerning Provisions on the Protection of Well-Known Marks (Sept. 1999).

At p. 424, add as Note 3:

3.   *Cuban embargo.* The Cuban Asset Control Regulations discussed in *Empresa Cubana* remain in place despite having been held by the WTO to violate the TRIPS Agreement. As a result, the United States continues to refuse a Cuban-owned export company to renew its trademark in HAVANA CLUB for rum. See *Empresa Cubana Exportadora de Alimentos y Productos Varios v. United States*, 638 F.3d 794 (D.C. Cir. 2011) (upholding the 1998 law by 2-1 against a challenge that it was impermissibly retroactive).

At p. 456, Note 4, add the following:

Although the Ninth Circuit test is regarded as less stringent, this does not mean that U.S. courts will always apply the Lanham Act extraterritorially. In *Love v. Associated Newspapers, Ltd.*, 611 F.3d 601 (9th Cir. 2010), the court applied the longstanding Ninth Circuit test, under which: (1) the alleged violations must create some effect on American foreign commerce; (2) the effect must be sufficiently great to present a cognizable injury to the plaintiffs under the Lanham Act; and (3) the interests of and links to American foreign commerce must be sufficiently strong in relation to those of other nations to justify an assertion of extraterritorial authority. The *Love* court noted that "the first two criteria may be met even where all of the challenged transactions occurred abroad, and where 'injury would seem to be limited to the deception of consumers' abroad, as long as 'there is monetary injury in the United States' to an American plaintiff." *Id.* at 613. However this was of no avail to the plaintiff (a former member of the musical group The Beach Boys), who could point only to a decrease in ticket sales for his U.S. performances after the allegedly infringing promotional CD was distributed abroad by a British newspaper. The Ninth Circuit concluded that "even if, as [plaintiff] argues, European purchasers of the Mail of Sunday [newspaper] would mistakenly associate the promotional CD [with the plaintiff or his new touring band] it is too great of a stretch to ask us, or a jury, to believe that such confusion overseas resulted in the decreased ticket sales in the United States."

CONFUSION-BASED TRADEMARK LIABILITY THEORIES   7

At p. 469, Note 5, add the following:

Also consider *Famous Horse Inc. v. 5th Avenue Photo Inc.*, 624 F.3d 106 (2d Cir. 2010). There, a clothing supplier (5th Avenue) sold jeans to a clothing retailer (Famous Horse). Although Famous Horse later discontinued sales of the jeans to its customers (having come to believe that the jeans were counterfeit), 5th Avenue allegedly represented to other retailers that Famous Horse was a "satisfied customer." Does confusion about whether Famous Horse was a satisfied customer of 5th Avenue constitute a type of confusion that is actionable under Lanham Act §§ 32 or 43(a)? If so, who should have standing to seek redress for likely confusion in such a case? Close questions on standing questions also arise in false advertising cases (*see* Problem 10-1, Chapter 10, p. 807) and in cases involving endorsement, attribution, and identity (*see* Chapter 11, p. 836, Note 2).

At p. 474, Note 1, add the following:

For a rare example of an actionable use discussion outside the context of the Internet, see *Ruggers, Inc. v. U.S.*, 736 F.Supp.2d 336 (D. Mass. 2010). Ruggers, an apparel supplier, had entered into an exclusive sponsorship agreement which provided that the USA RUGBY mark would appear exclusively on Ruggers' apparel, and that USA Rugby-sanctioned teams would wear, use, and promote only Ruggers' apparel. Ruggers claimed that Under Armour and other rival suppliers nevertheless "used" USA Rugby trademarks in such a way as to indicate falsely the sponsorship of the goods or sponsorship of USA Rugby and thus to confuse consumers. There was no allegation that Under Armour either sold or produced any item bearing the USA Rugby mark or that it attempted to exploit the mark in any of its advertising materials. Rather, Ruggers argued that on a number of occasions, members of the U.S. national rugby team wore Under Armour apparel "in close physical relation to the USA Rugby marks on other garments" during public appearances. Suppose that it is conceded that Under Armour (passively) received a benefit as a result of the players' sartorial choices. Has Under Armour made actionable use of the USA RUGBY mark?

At p. 475, add as Note 6:

6. *The use requirement and product substitution.* Suppose that a hotel places a soft drink dispenser in its lobby. The dispenser bears a COCA-COLA trademark and dispenses soft drink directly into the user's cup, free of charge. If the hotel begins to stock the dispenser with some nondescript, low-cost cola (probably made by Brother Billy in his basement), has the hotel engaged in an actionable use of the COCA COLA mark? *See Georgia-Pacific Consumer Prods., LP v. Von Drehle Corp.*, 618 F.3d 441, 452 (4th Cir. 2010) (discussing the hypothetical and applying it to a case involving substitution of paper towels in plaintiff's dispensers); *see also Georgia-Pacific Consumer Prods., LP v. Myers Supply, Inc.*, 621 F.3d 771 (8th Cir. 2010) (arising from a fact situation similar to that of the Fourth Circuit litigation). Suppose that a clothing retailer uses hangers bearing the HUGO BOSS mark to display for sale suits that are made by some anonymous third party (e,g., Cheap Suits, Inc.). Has the retailer engaged in actionable use of the HUGO BOSS mark? Does it matter that the HUGO BOSS mark is not actually affixed to the cheap suits? Would it matter if the evidence showed that the retailer had purchased genuine HUGO BOSS suits, sold the suits, and reused the hangers? You may wish to consider whether the material in Chapter 9 Part B (the first sale doctrine) is implicated.

At p. 492, Note 3:

See e.g., CJ Prods. LLC v. Snuggly Plushez LLC, 809 F.Supp.2d 127, 158 (E.D.N.Y. 2011) ("there is no dispute that defendant's use of the mark *to purchase* Adwords to advertise its products for sale on the Internet constitutes 'use in commerce'") (emphasis added).

At p. 495, Note 8, add the following:

Cf. Rosetta Stone Ltd. v. Google, Inc., 676 F.3d 144 (4th Cir. 2012) (noting allegation that defendant's use would "mislead Internet users into purchasing counterfeit ROSETTA STONE software"). In *Hearts on Fire, Co. LLC v. Blue Nile, Inc.*, 603 F.Supp.2d 274 (D. Mass. 2009), the district court adapted the conventional factors used in the First Circuit to the context of confusion alleged to have occurred by virtue of keyword searches. More particularly, it held that:

> "In addition to the[] familiar factors, under the circumstances here, the likelihood of confusion will ultimately turn on what the consumer saw on the screen and reasonably believed, given the context. This content and context includes: (1) the overall mechanics of web-browsing and internet navigation, in which a consumer can easily reverse course; (2) the mechanics of the specific consumer search at issue; (3) the content of the search results webpage that was displayed, including the content of the sponsored link itself; (4) downstream content on the Defendant's linked website likely to compound

any confusion; (5) the web-savvy and sophistication of the Plaintiff's potential customers; (6) the specific context of a consumer who has deliberately searched for trademarked diamonds only to find a sponsored link to a diamond retailer; and, in light of the foregoing factors, (7) the duration of any resulting confusion. This list is not exhaustive, but it identifies what the Court views as the most relevant elements to showing a likelihood of confusion in this case."

Id. at 289.   *Cf. CJ Prods. LLC v. Snuggly Plushez LLC*, 809 F.Supp.2d 127, 159 (E.D.N.Y. 2011) (declining to articulate any analysis beyond conventional *Polaroid* factors); *Network Automation, Inc. v. Advanced Systems Concepts, Inc.*, 638 F.3d 1137, 1153 n.6 (9th Cir. 2011) (declining to augment *Sleekcraft* factors with the *Hearts on Fire* multi-factor test).   Do you find the development of context-specific factors helpful? Should it help or hurt defendant that its advertisement was triggered by a search on the plaintiff's mark but that the defendant's ad text did *not* contain the plaintiff's trademark? *See Hearts on Fire, Co. LLC v. Blue Nile, Inc.*, 603 F.Supp.2d 274, 288-89 (D. Mass. 2009). Should the content of the web page linked to the ad matter? *See Network Automation, Inc. v. Advanced Systems Concepts, Inc.*, 638 F.3d 1137, 1154 (9th Cir. 2011)

At p. 495, add as Note 8A:

8A. *Doctrines analogous to trademark use?* Suppose that, in a keyword advertising case, a court does find actionable use within the meaning of existing case law. Rather than have to rebut claims of likely confusion, are there other doctrines that the defendant might invoke to withstand liability? One district court suggested that a defendant search engine ought to prevail in a keyword advertising case on the ground that "the functionality doctrine protects Google's use of the Rosetta Stone Marks as keyword triggers." *Rosetta Stone Ltd. v. Google, Inc.*, 730 F.Supp.2d 531 (E.D. Va. 2010). The *Rosetta Stone* court argued that "although *TrafFix* and *Qualitex* are cases where the functional element of the mark holder's product was present in both parties' products, the principal theory is the same—allowing competitors a monopoly on functional uses would inhibit legitimate competition." However, the Fourth Circuit disagreed, holding that the District Court misunderstood the doctrine of functionality: "Once it is determined that the product feature—the word mark ROSETTA STONE in this case—is not functional, then the functionality doctrine has no application, and it is irrelevant whether Google's computer program functions better by use of Rosetta Stone's nonfunctional mark." Was the District Court or the Court of Appeals correct? Even if the policy analysis is persuasive, is the functionality doctrine a useful doctrinal vehicle? How is it different from the trademark use doctrine? In what ways is this functionality determination different from those discussed in Chapter 3? *See* Dan L. Burk, *Cybermarks*, 94 MINN. L. REV. 1375 (2010).

At p. 492, Note 3, add the following:

In *Sensient Technologies Corp. v. Sensory Effects Flavor Co.*, 613 F.3d 754 (8th Cir. 2010), the plaintiff used the mark SENSIENT FLAVORS in connection with "flavor delivery systems." Defendant adopted SENSORY FLAVORS for the same products. As of the time when plaintiff sued defendant for trademark infringement, defendant had sent out announcements featuring the mark to contacts in the food ingredient industry, and had distributed a media release, likewise featuring the mark. Defendant had reserved the domain name sensoryflavors.com, but the website associated with the domain was "under construction." Defendant apparently had made no sales of products bearing the mark, and had sent out no packages labeled with the mark. Do defendant's activities constitute actionable use under the Section 45 definition? Do they constitute actionable use under the approach of *Rescuecom?* Cf. *Network Automation, Inc. v. Advanced Systems Concepts, Inc.*, 638 F.3d 1137 (9th Cir. 2011) (finding that declaratory plaintiff Network's purchase of keywords constituted actionable use and endorsing the *Rescuecom* standard); *Rosetta Stone Ltd. v. Google, Inc.*, 676 F.3d 144, 152 n.4 (4th Cir. 2012) (not deciding issue).

At p. 495, Note 8, add the following:

See also Network Automation, Inc. v. Advanced Systems Concepts, Inc., 638 F.3d 1137 (9th Cir. 2011) (finding no likelihood of success on the merits of the trademark owner's claim that the defendant's purchase of keywords was likely to give rise to initial interest confusion, and therefore reversing the grant of a preliminary injunction).

At p. 495, Note 9, add the following:

The Court of Justice has now issued its judgment in the *Interflora* case. *See Interflora Inc v Marks & Spencer Plc* (C-323/09), [2012] E.T.M.R. 1 (CJEU 2011). Unlike *Google France*, this was an action by the mark owner (Interflora) against the *purchaser* of the advertising, a rival online flower delivery service operated by a leading British retailer (M&S). The defendant's ad text used its own mark, but not that of the plaintiff. Rather, the plaintiff's mark was used only to trigger the defendant's ad. The clarity of the language in the opinion is not helped by the Court being compelled to work within the rubric of recent CJEU judgments, which have set the boundaries of protection by reference to various "functions" of trademarks about which the Court has given little guidance. However, a few basic points are clear from the opinion: (1) despite endorsing the apparently strict standard imposed by *Google France* on purchasers of keyword advertising, the Court appeared to backtrack slightly, noting that because "the relevant public comprises reasonably well-informed and reasonably observant internet users, . . . the fact that some internet users may have had difficulty grasping that the service provided by M&S is independent from that of Interflora is not a sufficient basis for a finding that the function of indicating origin has been adversely affected", *id..* at ¶ 50, and thus that the defendant is liable; (2) the awareness of consumers that the defendant was not part of the plaintiff's network could be shown either on the basis of general knowledge of the market, or through the defendant's ad, *id.* at ¶ 51; (3) that in light of the fact that "the commercial network of the trade mark proprietor is composed of a large number of retailers which vary greatly in terms of size and commercial profile . . .it may be particularly difficult for the reasonably well-informed and reasonably observant internet user to determine, in the absence of any indication from the advertiser, whether or not the advertiser . . . is part of that network," *id.* at ¶ 52. The Court did not explore in as much detail as the Advocate-General the variables that might affect the analysis by the national court on remand. In particular, despite endorsing the relevance of the "network" nature of the plaintiff's online flower business, the Court did not address the Advocate-General's general argument that "if the trade mark is not mentioned in the ad, [liability] depends . . . on the nature of goods and services protected by the trade mark . . ." (AG opinion, ¶ 43) and that the purchase of keyword advertising would be less likely to attract liability if the goods offered by the advertiser were different (AG opinion, ¶ 45). In discussing the advertising and investment functions (an effect on which might give rise to liability under EU law), the Court appeared to recognize the social value of rival third party uses: "the mere fact that the [third party] use . . . obliges the proprietor of that mark to intensify its advertising in order to maintain or enhance its profile with consumers is not a sufficient basis, in every case, for concluding that the trade mark's advertising function is adversely affected. In that regard, although the trade mark is an essential element in the system of undistorted competition which European law seeks to establish its purpose is not, however, to protect its proprietor against practices inherent in competition. Internet advertising on the basis of keywords corresponding to trade marks constitutes such a practice in that its aim, as a general rule, is merely to offer internet users alternatives to the goods or services of the proprietors of those trade marks." *Id.* at ¶¶ 57-58. The *Interflora* case also involved claims under the EU equivalent of dilution law. In that regard, the Court suggested a test that came very close to that announced in the context of marks without a reputation. *See id.* at ¶¶ 81-82. Again, the Court did not engage fully with the reasoning of the Advocate-General, who had suggested that a claim for blurring would at the very least require that the mark be mentioned in the advertisement (though that would not be sufficient in and of itself to establish blurring). *See* AG opinion, ¶ 91. More generally, the Court endorsed the value of keyword advertising, bringing much of it within the doctrinal safety-value of "due cause" which is an element of EU dilution claims and thus not a violation of the "unfair advantage"/free-riding cause of action. *See id.* at ¶ 90 (though perhaps more conditionally than did the Advocate-General, see AG opinion ¶ 99). How close is the Court of Justice to the position in the United States?

At p. 496, Note 10, add the following:

Since *Google France*, Google has further modified its policy, bringing its European policy closer to the one that was already in place with respect to google.co.uk. The new policy came into effect on September 14, 2010. At the same time, Google also made some changes to its UK policy, explicitly permitting use of the trademarks of others in ad text in specific circumstances (namely, descriptive uses, and nominatively in connection with the resale of trademarked goods, sale of component parts or compatible products, or in informational sites about the products, provided the landing page from the ad actually does sell the goods in question). Details of this change are at https://adwords.google.com/support/aw/bin/answer.py?hl=en&answer=145626. In March 2011, Microsoft announced changes to the policy it operates with respect to keyword advertising on its Bing search engine. Microsoft will no longer review trademark keyword complaints absent use of marks in ad text, bringing it closer to the position adopted by Google.

At p. 496-97, Note 11, add the following:

In April 2012, the Australian Federal Court found (reversing the lower court) that Google had engaged in misleading or deceptive conduct. The ruling did not, however, depend upon the failure of Google to adequately distinguish between organic results and sponsored links; Google had prevailed on that issue before the lower court, and that ruling was not appealed. Rather, liability rested on the fact that Google published ads headlined with a trademark in circumstances where users clicking on the ad were taken to the advertiser's website which contained no information about the competitor mark owner. *See Australian Competition and Consumer Commission v Google Inc* [2012] FCAFC 49 (FCA) (Aust.). Google has sought to leave to appeal to the High Court of Australia.

At p. 526, at end of sixth line of page:

See also Network Automation, Inc. v. Advanced Systems Concepts, Inc., 638 F.3d 1137 (9th Cir. 2011) (noting that the factors are "intended as an adaptable proxy for consumer confusion, not a rote checklist" and that in determining likely confusion, "we adhere to two long-standing principles: . . . the factors are non-exhaustive and . . . should be applied flexibly"); *Rosetta Stone Ltd. v. Google, Inc.*, 676 F.3d 144 (4th Cir. 2012) (noting that "this judicially created list of factors is not intended to be exhaustive or mandatory").

At p 526, first full paragraph, add the following:

In *Sabinsa Corp. v. Creative Compounds, Inc.*, 609 F.3d 175 (3d Cir. 2010), after a bench trial, the trial court found that Creative's use of FORSTHIN for a weight-loss supplement did not infringe Sabinsa's mark FORSLEAN for a competing product. On appeal, the Third Circuit reversed, and then decided that "because the undisputed facts weigh heavily in favor of Sabinsa so that any reasonable fact finder, weighing the [likelihood of confusion] factors properly, would find that Sabinsa had demonstrated a likelihood of confusion, we conclude that there is no need to remand for a re-weighing by the District Court of the [likelihood of confusion] factors." Accordingly, the appellate court entered judgment for Sabinsa. Should appellate courts routinely consider using this approach as a matter of efficient adjudication, or is there too great a danger that the appellate judges will invade the province of the trial court?

At p. 527, before first full paragraph, add the following:

Should courts be permitted to add factors to the likelihood of confusion test to customize the test for particular fact situations? In *Tana v. Dan Tanna's*, 611 F.3d 767 (11th Cir. 2010), the trial court had considered the fact that the plaintiff's restaurant (DAN TANA'S in West Hollywood, California) and the defendant's restaurant (DANTANNA'S in Atlanta, Georgia) were far apart geographically, even though geographic proximity was not explicitly recognized as a separate factor in the Eleventh Circuit's likelihood of confusion test. Is this an appropriate fine-tuning of the factors test? *Cf. Network Automation, Inc. v. Advanced Systems Concepts, Inc.*, 638 F.3d 1137, 1153 n. 6 (9th Cir. 2011) (declining to augment *Sleekcraft* factors with another multi-factor test).

At p. 528, Note 1, add the following at the end of the Note:

Cf. Facebook, Inc. v. Teachbook.com LLC, 819 F.Supp.2d 764, 780-81 (N.D. Cal. 2011) (declining to apply the truncated approach of *Top Tobacco*). The court reasoned that Top Tobacco involved "consumer goods sitting next to one another on a store shelf." By contrast, in cases involving websites, the textual and aural similarities between marks will be likely to matter more than the visual similarities because in the online context, consumers are likely to be attracted "through word-of-mouth, hyperlinks, and search engine results." *Id.* at 781. Do you agree?

Whether the ultimate question of likelihood of confusion in any given case can be resolved on summary judgment surely depends in part upon whether the court approaches the similarity of marks factor as suggested by the Ninth Circuit in *Jada*, or as suggested by the Seventh Circuit in *Top Tobacco*. Should summary judgment generally be disfavored in likelihood of confusion cases? *See Fortune Dynamic, Inc. v. Victoria's Secret Stores Brand Mgmt., Inc.*, 618 F.3d 1025, 1031 (9th Cir. 2010) ("This case is yet another example of the wisdom of the well-established principle that '[b]ecause of the intensely factual nature of trademark disputes, summary judgment is generally disfavored in the trademark arena,'" *quoting Entrepreneur Media, Inc. v. Smith*, 279 F.3d 1135, 1140 (9th Cir. 2002)); *but cf. General*

Conference Corp. of Seventh-Day Adventists v. McGill, 617 F.3d 402 (6th Cir. 2010) (affirming the grant of summary judgment in favor of plaintiff on likelihood of confusion).

At pp. 529-30, Note 3, add the following after the *TGI Friday's* cite:

COACH for standardized test preparation materials versus COACH for luxury handbags; *see Coach Services, Inc. v. Triumph Learning LLC*, 668 F.3d 1356 (Fed. Cir. 2012).

PEOPLES FEDERAL SAVINGS BANK for a bank versus PEOPLE'S UNITED BANK for a bank. Note that the marks as actually use appear as follows:

Peoples Federal Sav. Bank v. People's United Bank, 672 F.3d 1 (1st Cir. 2012).

At p. 530, add the following new Note 3A:

3A. *Similarity and online automated corrections.* Suppose that the marks at issue in a confusion factors analysis are BLACKBERRY for mobile communications and CRACKBERRY for, inter alia, a website catering to users of BLACKBERRY mobile devices. In assessing the similarity of marks factor, what weight would you give to the fact that Google auto-corrects defendant's mark to plaintiff and vice-versa?

At p. 535, Note 2, add the following:

Does your answer depend upon the procedural context? For example, should the market strength aspect of mark strength weigh less if the question is whether to grant the mark owner's motion for preliminary injunction, which is likely to involve accelerated proceedings and very limited discovery? *See Network Automation, Inc. v. Advanced Systems Concepts, Inc.*, 638 F.3d 1137, 1154 (9th Cir. 2011)

At pp. 535-36, Note 3, add the following:

Should the test for fame for the confusion analysis under Section 2(d) be different from the test for fame for the dilution analysis? The Federal Circuit has differentiated between the two, describing fame in the confusion analysis as a matter of degree and fame in the dilution analysis as binary. *See Coach Services, Inc. v. Triumph Learning LLC*, 668 F.3d 1356, 1373 (Fed. Cir. 2012) ("While fame for dilution 'is an either/or proposition'—it either exists or does not—fame for likelihood of confusion is a matter of degree along a continuum.") (internal citation omitted). Is this a plausible distinction? The court upheld a determination that the mark COACH for luxury handbags was famous for purposes of a confusion analysis, but not famous for purposes of a dilution analysis. Would it not simply make more sense to jettison reference to fame in the context of Section 2(d) and use the language of distinctiveness?

At p. 537, add the following to Note 6:

Should intent play a greater role in some forms of confusion than it does in others? For example, should it play a greater role in initial interest confusion (discussed in Chapter 7, Part E.1.)?   Should it play a greater role in cases involving allegations of online infringement (including allegations of online initial interest confusion)? Consider that question in view of *Facebook, Inc. v. Teachbook.com LLC*, 819 F.Supp.2d 764 (N.D. Ill. 2011), involving the marks FACEBOOK for a social networking site and TEACHBOOK for a social networking site aimed at teachers. In assessing the intent factor, how much weight would you give to the following language appearing on the TEACHBOOK site: "Many schools forbid their teachers to maintain Facebook and MySpace accounts because of the danger that students might learn personal information about their teachers. With Teachbook, you can manage your profile so that only other teachers and/or school administrators can see your personal information, blogs, posts, and so on. Teachbook is all about community, utility, and communication for teachers"?

At p. 538, add as Note 8:

8.   *Presence of accompanying house mark—effect on strength.*   Suppose that a mark owner regularly uses a mark in conjunction with its house mark. For example, tire maker

Bridgestone's advertisements for its POTENZA tires usually included the BRIDGESTONE logo. Does the presence of the house mark invariably diminish the strength of the mark at issue? Or does it sometimes diminish it, depending upon the relative prominence given the house mark? Depending upon other variables? Cf. *Bridgestone America Tire Operations, LLC v. Federal Corp.*, 673 F.3d 1330 (Fed. Cir. 2012) (discussing the issue and providing examples of relevant Bridgestone advertisements in the context of a Section 2(d) analysis).

At p. 539, Note 5, add the following:

See also Atomic Energy of Canada, Ltd. v. Areva NP Canada Ltd., 2009 F.C. 980 (Fed. Ct. Canada 2009) (in a case involving logos used in connection with nuclear reactor parts, the level of care and sophistication among relevant consumers was high, and "the fact that Homer Simpson may be confused is insufficient to find confusion").

At p. 540, Note 2, add the following:

But cf. Master's v. UHS of Delaware, Inc., 631 F.3d 434 (8th Cir. 2011) (declining to impose a requirement for evidence of actual confusion where the defendant was a former licensee of the plaintiff, the alleged infringement involved uses allegedly outside the scope of the license, and the remedy sought was disgorgement of profits).

At p. 541, Note 3, add the following:

In *Fortune Dynamic, Inc. v. Victoria's Secret Stores Brand Mgmt., Inc.*, 618 F.3d 1025, 1036 (9th Cir. 2010), the Ninth Circuit pointed out that "technical inadequacies" in survey methodology are unlikely to render a survey inadmissible, although they certainly may be taken into account when deciding how much weight to accord the survey results. The district court had excluded a survey from evidence on the grounds that "the survey compared the products side-by-side, failed to replicate real world conditions, failed to properly screen participants, and was 'highly suggestive.'" *Id.* at 1037. The Ninth Circuit agreed that the survey had some shortcomings — it was "conducted over the internet (thereby failing to replicate real world conditions), may have been suggestive, and quite possibly produced counterintuitive results." *Id.* at 1037-38. However, these problems went to the weight to be given to the survey; it was error for the district court to refuse to admit it.

At p. 556, after the *Majestic* cite, add the following:

If an applicant seeks to register a mark in standard characters (e.g. CAPITAL CITY BANK for banking services), how would you assess the similarity of the mark compared to an earlier registered mark that is in a stylized form – for example, CITIBANK shown as below? Suppose that Citibank argues that the applicant might actually begin to use the mark in any of a number of stylized forms, some of which could conceivably be reminiscent of CITIBANK in its stylized form. Should that be relevant to the similarity analysis? Should this question be answered by assuming that the applicant would adopt only a "reasonable range" of stylized forms? *See Citigroup Inc. v. Capital City Bank Group*, 637 F.3d 1344 (Fed. Cir. 2011).

citibank

Prior to the Federal Circuit's decision in *Citigroup*, the TTAB had used a "reasonable manners" test for assessing similarity of marks, meaning that if an applicant sought to register a word mark in standard characters, the PTO would consider all reasonable manners in which those words could be depicted. In *Citigroup*, the Federal Circuit rejected the reasonable manners test. The Federal Circuit concluded that "[t]he T.T.A.B. should not first determine whether certain depictions are 'reasonable' and then apply the *DuPont* analysis to only a subset of variations of a standard character mark." *Id.* at 1353. Instead, the TTAB should "simply use the *DuPont* factors to determine the likelihood of confusion between depictions of standard character marks that vary in font, style, size and color and the other mark." *Id.* Moreover, "illustrations of the mark as actually used may assist the T.T.A.B. in visualizing other forms in which the mark might appear." *Id. See also In re Viterra Inc.*, 671 F.3d 1358, 1364 (Fed. Cir. 2012) (noting that the *Citigroup* decision "discarded the Board's 'reasonable manners' standard in favor of a standard that allows a broader range of marks to be considered in the *DuPont* analysis when a standard character mark is at issue.") In *Viterra*, the court concluded that its holding in *Citigroup* rejecting the reasonable manners test was not limited to *inter partes* proceedings (the procedural context in which *Citigroup* arose) but also applied in *ex parte* examination. *Id.* at 1364-65.   The court also refused to limit *Citigroup* to its facts; the *Citigroup* holding applied to cases like this one, in which a standard character mark (XCEED for agricultural seeds) was being rejected under Section 2(d) on the basis of a composite word and design mark:

The court did leave some room for future argument, noting that "[i]n rejecting the 'reasonable manners' test, we are not suggesting that a standard character mark encompasses all possible design elements of the mark. We leave for future cases to determine the appropriate method of comparing design marks with standard character marks." *Id.* at 1365 (proceeding to uphold the rejection).

Suppose that an applicant seeks to register the word mark JUST JESU IT for various clothing items, but actually uses the phrase JUST JESU IT set against a graphic of a "crown of thorns." Should the similarity of marks analysis consider the mark strictly as it appears on the application, or as it appears in actual use? *See Nike, Inc. v. Maher*, 100 U.S.P.Q.2d (BNA) 1018 (TTAB 2011). Note that *Nike* was decided before *Viterra*. Would the TTAB have been compelled to change its similarity of marks analysis had the case arisen after *Viterra*? What of the similarity of goods factor: is the proper comparison between the goods as specified in the parties' respective registrations and applications, or between the goods that the parties actually sell? *See Coach Services, Inc. v. Triumph Learning LLC*, 668 F.3d 1356, 1369 (Fed. Cir. 2012) (declining to take into account the applicant's use on goods beyond those listed in its application, which would have arguably made the parties' goods more similar).

At p. 564, move the discussion of *Designer Skin* to the following new Note 4A, *Intentional deception as a limiting factor*, and after the *Designer Skin* discussion, add the following:

See also CJ Prods. LLC v. Snuggly Plushez LLC, 809 F.Supp.2d 127, 158 (E.D.N.Y. 2011) (likewise requiring a showing of deceptive conduct, but finding that the mark owner succeeded in making the showing). In view of this focus on deceptive conduct, is initial interest confusion less about consumer harm, and more about harm to competition?

At p. 564, Note 5, add the following:

See Network Automation, Inc. v. Advanced Systems Concepts, Inc., 638 F.3d 1137 (9th Cir. 2011) (largely endorsing Judge Berzon's comments and emphasizing that the *Playboy* holding reflected the fact that the linked banner advertisement were "unlabeled").

At p. 580, Note 4, add the following:

Although General Motors did not succeed in obtaining a preliminary injunction, it fared better after full trial. *See General Motors Co. v. Urban Gorilla, LLC*, 2010 WL 5395065 (D. Utah Dec. 27, 2010) (finding liability for trade dress infringement and dilution, and noting that the degree of purchase care factor deserved less weight in a case involving post-sale confusion).

At p. 594, in the *eBay* case heading, add the following:

cert. denied, 131 S.Ct. 647 (2010).

At p. 600, add as Note 1A:

1A. *Willful blindness in patent law.* In *Global-Tech Applicances, Inc. v. SEB, S.A.*, 131 S.Ct. 2060 (2011), a case involving allegations of induced patent infringement under 35 U.S.C. § 271(b), the Supreme Court that evidence of willful blindness as to the existence of patent rights sufficed to show that the alleged inducer knew of those rights. How important, if at all, should that ruling be for application of the *Inwood* standard in trademark law?

At p. 603, Note 5, add the following:

In *Gucci America, Inc. v. Frontline Processing Corp.*, 721 F.Supp.2d 228 (S.D.N.Y. 2010), Gucci alleged that an online merchant had sold counterfeit Gucci products, and Gucci sued three credit card processing companies that had serviced the online merchant. Gucci's claims of contributory infringement survived a motion to dismiss. All of the companies allegedly advertised for "high risk" merchants and charged them higher fees, but this alone was not sufficient to establish intentional inducement. However, that evidence, along with additional facts, sufficiently supported allegations under *Inwood*'s second prong because those facts collectively established either knowledge or willful blindness, and sufficient control. The additional facts included evidence that the companies knew that the online merchant's goods were supplied from China, and that the companies had reviewed the merchant's descriptions of its goods, which indicated that the goods were "replicas." For another case analyzing the sufficiency of allegations of indirect infringement in an online context (in particular, Amazon.com's "associates" program), see *Sellify Inc. v. Amazon.com, Inc.*, 2010 WL 4455830 (S.D.N.Y. Nov. 4, 2010) (granting Amazon.com's motion to dismiss).

In *Louis Vuitton Malletier, S.A. v. Akanoc Solutions, Inc.*, 658 F.3d 936 (9th Cir. 2011), the defendants ran a web-hosting business in which they operated servers and provided server space and IP addresses to its customers. Some of defendants' customers operated websites advertising Louis Vuitton merchandise and listing email addresses that interested parties could use to initiate a purchase transaction. Should the defendants prevail on an argument that the "instrumentalities" used for infringement were solely the websites, and not the defendants' hosting services or its servers? Or should the defendant be deemed to hold the "master switch" that controls whether the websites are online and available? Suppose that defendant concedes that it holds the master switch, but argues that this merely shows that the defendant had "direct control," whereas the test from cases such as *eBay* requires evidence of direct control *and* monitoring. Should the defendant withstand the contributory infringement charge on the ground that it was not "monitoring"? In view of *Akanoc* and *eBay*, does the trademark law effectively contain a judicially-developed "notice-and-takedown" regime (analogous to the statutory notice-and-takedown regime that exists in the U.S. Copyright Act?)

At p. 603, Note 6, add the following:

Cf. Rescuecom Corp. v. Google Inc., 562 F.3d 123 (2d Cir. 2009) (noting relevance of Google's Keyword Suggestion Tool to the question whether it had engaged in actionable use).

At pp. 603-04, Note 7, add the following:

The court distinguished *eBay* in *Rosetta Stone Ltd. v. Google, Inc.*, 676 F.3d 144, 163-65 (4th Cir. 2012). Rosetta Stone alleged that it had notified Google of approximately 200 instances in which a website associated with a keyword-triggered "sponsored link" was advertising counterfeit Rosetta Stone products, but that Google had allowed the same advertisers to continue to use Rosetta Stone's marks for sponsored links connected with those advertisers' other websites. The Fourth Circuit found this evidence sufficient to allow Rosetta Stone to withstand summary judgment on the question of whether Google had knowledge or reason to know of the alleged infringements. The *eBay* case had been decided after full trial, not on summary judgment. The fact that the *eBay* court had found mere generalized knowledge on the record before it was of only "limited application" in deciding whether a grant of summary judgment against the trademark owner should be upheld, according to the court in *Rosetta Stone*.

At p. 604, add as Note 9A:

9A. *Immunity for domain name registrars.* Under what circumstances should a domain name registrar be contributorily liable for registering or maintaining a domain name for another? The Lanham Act supplies an answer in Section 32(2)(D)(iii) (no liability for damages absent a showing of bad faith intent to profit from such registration or maintenance), an element of the Anticybersquatting Consumer Protection Act, enacted in 1999. *See Baidu, Inc. v. Register.com*, 760 F.Supp.2d 312 (S.D.N.Y. 2010) (discussing this provision). We discuss the ACPA in more detail in Chapter 8.

At p. 607, add new Problem 7-12A:

PROBLEM 7-12A: BROTHER BILLY AND THE BAPTISTS' BATHROOMS

Suppose that the Northwest Kentucky Paper Co. ("P") manufactures disposable paper towels (e.g. for use in public restrooms), and also manufactures dispensers that hold and dispense the towels. The dispensers bear P's "Kentuckian" logo, the exact appearance of which doesn't matter for purposes of this Problem and is best left to your imagination anyway. The towels aren't marked with the logo, but they come in a bulk package that is marked. Suppose that P sells a dispenser and a bulk package of towels to the Tick Ridge Separate Baptist Church of Tick Ridge, Kentucky. Brother Billy, as chair of the church's Board of Trustees, is in charge of ensuring that the dispenser is full of towels, which he does by tearing open the bulk package wrapper and discarding it, stuffing the dispenser full of towels, and leaving the extras in a stack near the dispenser. A lot of towels get used. Soon, the supply dwindles. Brother Billy (acting on behalf of the church) decides to buy a new supply of towels from Cousin Clem's Cut-Rate Janitorial Emporium. Cousin Clem's towels don't bear any trademark, and they come packaged in a plain brown wrapper. The towels are of generally lousy quality, although the people at church tend not to complain. Suppose that P finds out about Brother Billy's purchases and threatens action for trademark infringement. What's the possibility that Cousin Clem's Cut-Rate Janitorial Emporium is liable? What about the Tick Ridge Separate Baptist Church? Does it matter to your analysis whether the Baptists who attend regularly and use the towels are likely to be confused? (For that matter, what about those who don't attend religiously but sometimes use the towels?) *See Georgia-Pacific Consumer Prods., LP v. Von Drehle Corp.*, 618 F.3d 441, 452 (4th Cir. 2010) and *Georgia-Pacific Consumer Prods., LP v. Myers Supply, Inc.*, 621 F.3d 771 (8th Cir. 2010).

NON-CONFUSION-BASED TRADEMARK LIABILITY THEORIES

At p. 620, Note 3, add the following:

The Federal Circuit has characterized dilution fame as follows:

> It is well-established that dilution fame is difficult to prove. *See Toro Co. v. ToroHead Inc.*, 61 U.S.P.Q.2d 1164,1180 (T.T.A.B. 2001) ("Fame for dilution purposes is difficult to prove."); *Everest Capital, Ltd. v. Everest Funds Mgmt. LLC*, 393 F.3d 755, 763 (8th Cir. 2005) ("The judicial consensus is that 'famous' is a rigorous standard."); *see also* 4 *McCarthy*, § 24:104 at 24-286, 24-293 (noting that fame for dilution is "a difficult and demanding requirement" and that, although "all 'trademarks' are 'distinctive' – very few are 'famous'"). This is particularly true where, as here, the mark is a common English word that has different meanings in different contexts. . . .
>
> As noted, fame for dilution requires widespread recognition by the general public. 15 U.S.C. § 1125(c)(2)(A). To establish the requisite level of fame, the "mark's owner must demonstrate that the common or proper noun uses of the term and third-party uses of the mark are now eclipsed by the owner's use of the mark." *Toro*, 61U.S.P.Q.2d at 1180. An opposer must show that, when the general public encounters the mark "in almost any context, it associates the term, at least initially, with the mark's owner." *Id.* at 1181. In other words, a famous mark is one that has become a "household name." *Nissan Motor Co. v. Nissan Computer Corp.*, 378 F.3d 1002, 1012 (9th Cir. 2004) (quoting *Thane Int'l, Inc. v. Trek Bicycle Corp.*, 305 F.3d 894, 911 (9th Cir. 2002)).

Coach Services, Inc. v. Triumph Learning LLC, 668 F.3d 1356, 1373 (Fed. Cir. 2012) (footnote omitted). Do you agree with this interpretation of the fame requirement? Note that much of the authority that the court cites predates the 2006 legislation. Does this matter? The court proceeded to uphold the TTAB's determination that the mark COACH for various luxury goods had not been proven famous as of December 2004 (when Triumph filed its applications). Coach's annual reports had not been authenticated; its evidence of attention in the media came mainly after 2004; its brand awareness study likewise came after 2004, and showed only high brand awareness among women ages 13-24, not women generally (or men, at all); and the bare fact that Coach had registrations was not sufficient to show fame.

At p. 621, Note 7, add the following:

Mark fame for purposes of Section 43(c) must be measured as of the time when the defendant's alleged diluting use began. *See Rosetta Stone Ltd. v. Google, Inc.*, 676 F.3d 144, 171-73 (4th Cir. 2012); *Nissan Motor Co. v. Nissan Computer Corp.*, 378 F.3d 1002, 1013 (9th Cir. 2004). Suppose that a defendant begins using plaintiff's mark in 2006 and continues to the present. Suppose that the evidence shows that the plaintiff's mark became famous at least by 2010. Should the plaintiff be permitted to argue that the defendant's uses from 2006-2010 were not diluting uses, such that the plaintiff's mark was famous as of the time when the diluting uses commenced? How should the phrase "commences use" in Section 43(c) be interpreted?

At p. 621-22, Note 8, add the following:

In *National Business Forms & Printing, Inc. v. Ford Motor Co.*, 671F.3d 526 (5th Cir. 2012), a commercial printer (NBFP) printed advertising materials bearing Ford's marks for used car dealers that had no affiliation with Ford. In response to Ford's claim of dilution, NBFP argued that it was not using the Ford marks as contemplated by Section 43(c)(1) because NBFP was not adopting the marks to identify or distinguish its own goods or services. The Fifth Circuit agreed with the notion that Section 43(c)(1) includes a requirement for "trademark use." Does such a result square with the legislative history? The Fifth Circuit also invoked Lanham Act § 32(2)(A). That provision specifies that where an infringer under Section 43(a) (or a cybersquatter under Section 43(d)) is "engaged solely in the business of printing the mark. . .for others and establishes that he or she was an innocent infringer," the printer is liable only to the extent of injunctive relief. The court reasoned that because this provision did not mention Section 43(c), Congress must have meant to exclude dilution liability altogether for printers. Does this make sense in light of Section 43(c)(5), which limits relief in *all* dilution cases to injunctive relief unless willfulness is shown? *Cf. Rosetta Stone Ltd. v. Google, Inc.*, 676 F.3d 144, 168-69 (4th Cir. 2012) (concluding that the district court had erred by requiring the mark owner to demonstrate that the defendant's use was a trademark use as part of the prima facie case of trademark dilution).

At pp. 622-3, Note 10, add the following:

See also General Motors Co. v. Urban Gorilla, LLC, 2010 WL 5395065 (D. Utah Dec. 27, 2010) (finding dilution by blurring in a case involving product design trade dress).

At pp. 643-44, Note 8, add the following:

For an example of a successful effort to establish actual association (and, ultimately, a success in showing likelihood of dilution by blurring), see *Louis Vuitton Malletier, S.A. v. Hyundai Motor America*, 2012 WL 1022247 (S.D.N.Y. 2012). Hyundai had aired an advertisement called "Luxury" which depicted "policemen eating caviar in a patrol car; large yachts parked beside modest homes; blue-collar workers eating lobster during their lunch break; a four-second scene of an inner-city basketball game played on a lavish marble court with a gold hoop; and a ten-second scene of the Sonata driving down a street lined with chandeliers and red-carpet crosswalks." (quoting Hyundai's brief). The idea, according to Hyundai, was to "pok[e] fun at the silliness of luxury-as-exclusivity by juxtaposing symbols of luxury with everyday life," *id.*, communicating that the modestly-priced Hyundai Sonata automobile offered "luxury for all." The advertisement aired during the post-game show of the 2010 Super Bowl. (Professor Janis was too busy mourning the Indianapolis Colts' loss to notice it, and he wouldn't have gotten Hyundai's message anyway.) The advertisement's basketball scene included a one-second shot of a basketball bearing "a distinctive pattern resembling the famous trademarks" of Louis Vuitton. So, Louis Vuitton sued, claiming dilution. Study the district court's discussion of the dilution evidence, particularly the actual association evidence. Would you have found a likelihood of dilution by blurring? Are you satisfied that you have a clearer understanding of what dilution by blurring is, and how it differs from confusion, after studying the evidence in this case? Or not? For another case containing a discussion of actual association evidence, see *Rolex Watch U.S.A., Inc. v. AFP Imaging Corp.*, 101 U.S.P.Q.2d (BNA) 1188, 1196 (TTAB 2011).

At p. 641-44, add the following as Notes 2A and 10A:

2A. *Other blurring factors.* The list of statutory blurring factors is open-ended. Which additional factors (if any) beyond those expressly listed should be considered in a blurring analysis? For example, if the allegedly diluting mark is owned by a small business, and the allegedly diluted mark is owned by a multinational company, should this factor be given weight in a blurring analysis? *See Nike, Inc. v. Maher*, 100 U.S.P.Q.2d (BNA) 1018 (TTAB 2011).

10A. *Starbuck's on remand (again).* In the main case excerpted above, the Second Circuit remanded (again) to the district court. On remand, the district court (again) found no likelihood of dilution by blurring. *See Starbucks Corp. v. Wolfe's Borough Coffee, Inc.*, 101 U.S.P.Q.2d (BNA) 1212 (S.D.N.Y. 2011). The district court acknowledged that the distinctiveness, recognition, and exclusivity of use factors weighed in Starbucks' favor. However, the district court found that these factors were "not informative" because they did not require any "consideration of the nature of the challenged marks or any defendant's use of any challenged mark." Is this analysis legal error requiring reversal on appeal? As to similarity, the court found that the marks were only minimally similar as actually used (because, for example, the defendant always used CHARBUCKS with terms such as "Mister" and depicted the term with a black bear logo). The court also deemed the actual association evidence to be weak. Reviewing the survey evidence (which the Second Circuit had also discussed), the district court found fault with the survey methodology, pointing out that the survey presented the terms CHARBUCKS and STARBUCKS in isolation. Even then, the survey drew "only a 30.5% association response," far less than the 73% response in the *Visa* case, for example. Regarding the 3.1% response to the confusion survey (also mentioned in the Second Circuit's opinion), the district court declared that this mere "single-digit source confusion indicator" did not establish actual association for blurring. Reversible error or proper remand analysis?

At p. 645, add the following case before Problem 8-2:

VISA INT'L SERVICE ASSOC. v. JSL CORP.
610 F.3d 1088 (9th Cir. 2010)

KOZINSKI, Chief Judge:

She sells sea shells by the sea shore. That's swell, but how about Shell espresso, Tide motor oil, Apple bicycles and Playboy computers? We consider the application of anti-dilution law to trademarks that are also common English words.

Facts

Joseph Orr runs eVisa, a "multilingual education and information business that exists and operates exclusively on the Internet," at www.evisa.com. At least he did, until the district court enjoined him. Orr traces the name eVisa back to an English language tutoring service called "Eikaiwa Visa" that he ran while living in Japan. "Eikaiwa" is Japanese for English conversation, and the "e" in eVisa is short for Eikaiwa. The use of the word "visa" in both eVisa and Eikaiwa Visa is meant to suggest "the ability to travel, both linguistically and physically, through the English-speaking world." Orr founded eVisa shortly before his return to America, where he started running it out of his apartment in Brooklyn, New York.

Visa International Service Association sued JSL Corporation, through which Orr operates eVisa, claiming that eVisa is likely to dilute the Visa trademark. The district court granted summary judgment for Visa, and JSL appeals.

Analysis

A plaintiff seeking relief under federal anti-dilution law must show that its mark is famous and distinctive, that defendant began using its mark in commerce after plaintiff's mark became famous and distinctive, and that defendant's mark is likely to dilute plaintiff's mark. See *Jada Toys, Inc. v. Mattel, Inc.*, 518 F.3d 628, 634 (9th Cir. 2008). JSL does not dispute that the Visa mark is famous and distinctive or that JSL began using the eVisa mark in commerce after Visa achieved its renown. JSL claims only that the district court erred when it found as a matter of law that eVisa was likely to dilute the Visa trademark.

There are two types of dilution, but here we are concerned only with dilution by blurring, which occurs when a mark previously associated with one product also becomes associated with a second. [cit.] This weakens the mark's ability to evoke the first product in the minds of consumers. "For example, Tylenol snowboards, Netscape sex shops and Harry Potter dry cleaners would all weaken the 'commercial magnetism' of these marks and diminish their ability to evoke their original associations." *Mattel*, 296 F.3d at 903. Dilution isn't confusion; quite the contrary. Dilution occurs when consumers form new and different associations with the plaintiff's mark. "Even if no one suspects that the maker of analgesics has entered into the snowboard business, the Tylenol mark will now bring to mind two products, not one." *Id.*

Whether a defendant's mark creates a likelihood of dilution is a factual question generally not appropriate for decision on summary judgment. See *Jada Toys, Inc.*, 518 F.3d at 632. Nevertheless, summary judgment may be granted in a dilution case, as in any other, if no reasonable fact-finder could fail to find a likelihood of dilution. Congress has enumerated factors courts may use to analyze the likelihood of dilution, including the similarity between the two marks and the distinctiveness and recognition of the plaintiff's mark. 15 U.S.C. § 1125(c)(2)(B)(i), (ii), (iv); [cit.]. And, in an appropriate case, the district court may conclusively determine one or more of these factors before trial.

The marks here are effectively identical; the only difference is the prefix "e," which is commonly used to refer to the electronic or online version of a brand. That prefix does no more to distinguish the two marks than would the words "Corp." or "Inc." tacked onto the end. See *Horphag Research Ltd. v. Garcia*, 475 F.3d 1029, 1036 (9th Cir. 2007) (use of identical mark provides "circumstantial evidence" of dilution).

And Visa is a strong trademark. "In general, the more unique or arbitrary a mark, the more protection a court will afford it." *Nutri/System, Inc. v. Con-Stan Indus., Inc.*, 809 F.2d 601, 605 (9th Cir. 1987). The Visa mark draws on positive mental associations with travel visas, which make potentially difficult transactions relatively simple and facilitate new opportunities and experiences. Those are good attributes for a credit card. But those associations are sufficiently remote that the word visa wouldn't make people think of credit cards if it weren't for the Visa brand. "This suggests that any association is the result of goodwill and deserves broad protection from potential infringers." *Dreamwerks Prod. Grp., Inc. v. SKG Studio*, 142 F.3d 1127, 1130 n. 7 (9th Cir. 1998). Visa also introduced uncontroverted evidence that Visa is the world's top brand in financial services and is used for online purchases almost as often as all other credit cards combined. This was enough to support the district court's summary judgment.

JSL vigorously contests the validity of market surveys and expert testimony introduced by Visa to show that eVisa dilutes the Visa mark, and it claims that evidence should have been excluded under *Daubert v. Merrell Dow Pharm., Inc.*, 509 U.S. 579 (1993). But a plaintiff seeking to establish a likelihood of dilution is not required to go to the expense of producing expert testimony or market surveys; it may rely entirely on the characteristics of the marks at issue. See 15 U.S.C. § 1125(c)(2)(B) (listing relevant factors). Expert testimony and survey evidence may be necessary in marginal cases, or where a defendant introduces significant evidence to show that dilution is unlikely. But JSL presented nothing, other than Orr's statement that he did not intend to dilute the Visa mark, to rebut the inference of likely dilution created by the strength and similarity of the marks. Good intentions alone do not negate a showing of a likelihood of dilution. We therefore need not reach the admissibility of Visa's expert testimony and market survey evidence.

JSL claims the eVisa mark cannot cause dilution because, in addition to being an electronic payment network that's everywhere you want to be, a visa is a travel document authorizing the bearer to enter a country's territory. When a trademark is also a word with a dictionary definition, it may be difficult to show that the trademark holder's use of the word is sufficiently distinctive to deserve anti-dilution protection because such a word is likely to be descriptive or suggestive of an essential attribute of the trademarked good. Moreover, such a word may already be in use as a mark by third parties. For example, we rejected a dilution claim by Trek Bicycle Corporation for its "Trek" mark in part because it played heavily off the dictionary meaning of "trek," suggesting that the bicycles were designed for long or arduous journeys. *Thane Int'l, Inc. v. Trek Bicycle Corp.*, 305 F.3d 894, 912 n. 14 (9th Cir. 2002). Additionally, the creators of the Star Trek series had already "incorporated this common English language word into their trademark," and the "glow of this celebrity ma[de] it difficult for Trek to obtain fame using the same word." *Id.* In our case, Visa's use of the word visa is sufficiently distinctive because it plays only weakly off the dictionary meaning of the term and JSL presented no evidence that a third party has used the word as a mark.

It's true that the word visa is used countless times every day for its common English definition, but the prevalence of such non-trademark use does not undermine the uniqueness of Visa as a trademark. See 2 McCarthy on Trademarks and Unfair Competition § 11:87 (4th ed. 2010). "The significant factor is not whether the word itself is common, but whether the way the word is used in a particular context is unique enough to warrant trademark protection." *Wynn Oil Co. v. Thomas*, 839 F.2d 1183, 1190 n. 4 (6th Cir. 1988). In the context of anti-dilution law, the "particular context" that matters is use of the word in commerce to identify a good or service. There are, for instance, many camels, but just one Camel; many tides, but just one Tide. Camel cupcakes and Tide calculators would dilute the value of those marks. Likewise, despite widespread use of the word visa for its common English meaning, the introduction of the eVisa mark to the marketplace means that there are now two products, and not just one, competing for association with that word. This is the quintessential harm addressed by anti-dilution law.

JSL is not using the word visa for its literal dictionary definition, and this would be a different case if it were. Visa does not claim that it could enforce its Visa trademark to prevent JSL from opening "Orr's Visa Services," any more than Apple could shut down Orr's Apple Orchard or Camel could fold up Orr's Camel Breeders. Visa doesn't own the word "visa" and may not "deplete the stock of useful words" by asserting otherwise. *New Kids on the Block v. News America Publ'g, Inc.*, 971 F.2d 302, 306 (9th Cir .1992); *cf. Kellogg Co. v. Nat'l Biscuit Co.*, 305 U.S. 111, 116-17 (1938). Conferring anti-dilution rights to common English words would otherwise be untenable, as whole swaths of the dictionary could be taken out of circulation. Nor would a suit against Orr's Visa Services advance the purpose of anti-dilution law. Such use of the word would not create a new association for the word with a product; it would merely evoke the word's existing dictionary meaning, as to which no one may claim exclusivity.

JSL argues that its use of the word "visa" is akin to Orr's Visa Services because the eVisa mark is meant to "connote the ability to travel, both linguistically and physically, through the English-speaking world" and therefore employs the word's common English meaning. JSL's site depicted the eVisa mark next to a booklet that looks like a passport, and it divided the services offered into the categories "Travel Passport," "Language Passport" and "Technology Passport." But these allusions to the dictionary definition of the word visa do not change the fact that JSL has created a novel meaning for the word: to identify a "multilingual education and information business." This multiplication of meanings is the essence of dilution by blurring. Use of the word "visa" to refer to travel visas is permissible because it doesn't have this effect; the word elicits only the standard dictionary definition. Use of the word visa in a trademark to refer to a good or service other than a travel visa, as in this case, undoubtedly does have this effect; the word becomes associated with two products, rather than one. This is true even when use of the word also gestures at the word's dictionary definition.

JSL's allusions to international travel are more obvious and heavy-handed than Visa's, and JSL claims that its use of the word is therefore "different" from Visa's. That's true; Visa plays only weakly off the word's association with international travel, whereas JSL embraced the metaphor with gusto. But dilution always involves use of a mark by a defendant that is "different" from the plaintiff's use; the injury addressed by anti-dilution law in fact occurs when marks are placed in new and different contexts, thereby weakening the mark's ability to bring to mind the plaintiff's goods or services. See *Mattel*, 296 F.3d at 903. The only context that matters is that the marks are both used in commerce as trademarks to identify a good or service, as they undoubtedly are in this case.

The district court was quite right in granting summary judgment to Visa and enjoining JSL's use of the mark.

Affirmed.

NOTES AND QUESTIONS

1. *Confusingly similar?* Does *Visa* seem to be an "easy" case of likely dilution by blurring? Do you think it might even be an easy case of likely confusion? Do you think that the two causes of action are as separable in practice as the structure of the Lanham Act would seem to suggest?

2. *The quintessential harm.* According to the *Visa* opinion, the "quintessential harm addressed by anti-dilution law" occurs here, because "the introduction of the eVisa mark to the marketplace means that there are now two products, and not just one, competing for association with that word." Do you agree that this is the quintessential harm that Section 43(c) addresses? Is this the harm that Schechter identified? Elsewhere, the opinion refers to the "multiplication of meanings" as constituting "the essence of dilution by blurring." Is it? Consider another approach to harm: suppose that a mark owner claims dilution by blurring, and the evidence shows that during the time period of the alleged blurring, the mark owner's brand recognition actually increased. Should a court conclude that there is no harm, and no dilution by blurring? Can you think of a good counterargument?

3. *Blurring and fair use.* Judge Kozinski suggests that the use of the word "visa" in connection with travel visas cannot amount to dilution by blurring because it evokes only the common dictionary meaning. Do you agree? Or is Judge Kozinski actually suggesting that such a use might dilute, but should nonetheless be shielded from liability for policy reasons as a fair use? We discuss fair use in Chapter 9.

4. *An identity requirement?* Judge Kozinski mentions that the plaintiff's and defendant's marks are "effectively identical." Is this a prerequisite for dilution under the post-2006 version of Section 43(c), or is it merely helpful? Under the pre-2006 Section 43(c), the Ninth Circuit had developed a line of cases that arguably did impose a threshold requirement of identity. Applying those cases post-2006, a trial judge found that the plaintiff's mark (Levi's "arcuate" design, below left) was not identical to, and could not be diluted by, the defendant's mark (Abercrombie & Fitch's "Ruehl" design, below right). Suppose that Levi's appeals, contesting whether, as a matter of law, the post-2006 version of Section 43(c) requires identity. How would you decide the question? *See Levi Strauss & Co. v. Abercrombie & Fitch Trading Co.*, 633 F.3d 1158 (9th Cir. 2011). *See also Rolex Watch U.S.A., Inc. v. AFP Imaging Corp.*, 101 U.S.P.Q.2d (BNA) 1188, 1194 (TTAB 2011) (analyzing the issue in the context of Section 2(f) dilution, rejecting any requirement for identity or even "substantial" similarity, concluding that "the test we employ is the *degree* of similarity or dissimilarity of the marks in their entireties. . .") (emphasis supplied); *Nike, Inc. v. Maher*, 100 U.S.P.Q.2d (BNA) 1018 (TTAB 2011) (adopting the same approach).

At p. 647, after the *7-Eleven* cite, add the following:

See also Nat'l Pork Board v. Supreme Lobster & Seafood Co., 96 U.S.P.Q.2d(BNA) 1479 (TTAB 2010) (analyzing whether applicant's slogan THE OTHER RED MEAT for salmon should be refused registration for a likelihood of blurring in view of opposer's slogan THE OTHER WHITE MEAT used in connection with promoting the pork industry).

At p. 656, add the following two cases after *Sporty's Farm*:

DSPT INT'L, INC. v. NAHUM
624 F.3d 1213 (9th Cir. 2010)

KLEINFELD, Circuit Judge:

We address the scope of the Anticybersquatting Consumer Protection Act.

I. Facts

. . . .

DSPT, founded and owned by Paolo Dorigo, designs, manufactures, and imports men's clothing. The company sells clothes to between 500 and 700 retailers. It sells mostly shirts, but also some knitwear, trousers, and t-shirts. Its brand name since 1988 had been

Equilibrio. To serve a younger market with somewhat "trendier, tighter fitting fashion," the company created the EQ brand name in 1999.

At about that time, Dorigo brought his friend Lucky Nahum into the business. Dorigo lived in Los Angeles, Nahum in Rochester, New York. They decided to set up a site on what was then the fledgling internet, and Nahum's brother, a hairdresser, was doing part-time website design, so DSPT had Nahum arrange to have his brother prepare the site. The website, "www.eq-Italy.com" (eq for the brand, Italy for Dorigo's and the style's origin), was created solely for DSPT for the purpose of showing DSPT clothes. Nahum's brother designed the website in consultation with Dorigo, though Nahum registered the site to himself. This seemed trivial at the time, since Nahum was working exclusively for DSPT and registration cost only $25. Dorigo, who was not knowledgeable or interested in computer matters, was unaware that the registration was in Nahum's name.

The importance of the website grew with the importance of the internet. By 2005, the website served as DSPT's catalog. Customers accessed it 24 hours a day, chose designs from it, and sent in orders through it. DSPT e-mailed them about new items on the site. Salesmen sold DSPT clothes to retailers by referring them to pictures on the website and soliciting their orders based on the pictures.

Unfortunately, during the same period, the friendship between Dorigo and Nahum soured. Nahum's DSPT contract was up for renewal August 31, 2005, so Dorigo sent him a proposal in mid-August. At the same time, DSPT paid Nahum's airfare, hotel, and meals for a trip to Las Vegas for the West Coast Exclusive Wear show, an offshoot of the largest menswear show in the world (MAGIC, Men's Apparel Guild in California) which was taking place in Las Vegas. But while there, Nahum spent time in a competitor's booth, and arranged employment with that DSPT competitor. Though Dorigo was also at the show and asked Nahum whether he would be renewing his contract, Nahum only informed Dorigo by e-mail after the show that he was not renewing his contract.

At the beginning of October, DSPT's website mysteriously disappeared. If a customer typed "eq-Italy.com" into his web browser, instead of seeing DSPT's clothing line, all he saw was a screen saying "All fashion related questions to be referred to Lucky Nahum at: lnahum@yahoo.com." Nahum had no use for the website, but he told his new boss at DSPT's competitor that "he had inserted that sentence in order to get Equilibrio [DSPT's older brand] to pay him funds that were due to him." DSPT repeatedly but unsuccessfully asked Nahum to give back the website.

This created a crisis for DSPT. Retailers do around three fourths of their business during the last quarter of the year, so wholesalers and manufacturers, like DSPT, do a large percentage of their business supplying retailers during October, November, and the first part of December. DSPT's website in the fall also generated the orders for the upcoming spring. Without its website, DSPT could not sell anything in a manner approaching its previous efficiency. It was forced to go back to the old way of sending out samples, but retailers did not want to deal with DSPT using the old method. Sales plummeted and inventory was left over in the spring from the very bad fall. 2004 had been good, and the first quarter of 2005 was the best ever, but the last quarter of 2005, and all of 2006, were disastrous. A lot of inventory had to be sold below cost. DSPT spent $31,572.72, plus a great deal of time, writing to customers to explain the situation and replacing its website and the stationery that referred customers to "eq-Italy.com."

DSPT sued Nahum [inter alia] for "cybersquatting" . . . in violation of the Lanham Act. . . .

The case was tried to a jury. The jury returned a special verdict, finding, among other things, that "EQ" and "Equilibrio" were valid trademarks owned by DSPT; that "Lucky Nahum registered, trafficked in, or used the www.eq-Italy.com domain name"; that the name was identical or confusingly similar to DSPT's distinctive trademark; and that "Lucky Nahum commit[ed] the acts with a bad faith intent to profit from DSPT's mark." The jury found that DSPT's damages were $152,000. . . . [Nahum appealed].

II. Analysis

. . .

The Anti-Cybersquatting Consumer Protection Act establishes civil liability for "cyberpiracy" where a plaintiff proves that (1) the defendant registered, trafficked in, or used a domain name; (2) the domain name is identical or confusingly similar to a protected mark owned by the plaintiff; and (3) the defendant acted "with bad faith intent to profit from that mark."

Nahum first argues that as a matter of law, this statute does not apply to what he did. He argues that the statute applies only to one who registers a well-known trademark as a domain name, and then attempts to profit in bad faith by either (1) selling the domain name back to the trademark holder, or (2) using the domain name to divert business from the trademark holder. He argues that he cannot owe damages under the statute because the evidence shows only that he used DSPT's mark to gain leverage over DSPT in bargaining for money he claimed he was owed, not to sell under DSPT's mark or sell the mark to DSPT. He argues that even if in some sense he had a bad-faith intent to profit, any "intent to profit" under the act must be an intent to profit from the goodwill associated with the mark rather than to gain some other benefit. The core of his argument is that he did not register the domain name in bad faith, and used it only to get what he was entitled to.

His arguments are not implausible, but we conclude that they are mistaken. True, the statute was intended to prevent cybersquatters from registering well-known brand names as internet domain names in order to make the trademark owners buy the ability to do business under their own names. Nahum cites a remark in a Senate Committee report mentioning the intent to profit from the goodwill associated with someone else's trademark. And the Sixth Circuit noted that "[t]he paradigmatic harm that the

[Anticybersquatting Consumer Protection Act] was enacted to eradicate [was] the practice of cybersquatters registering several hundred domain names in an effort to sell them to the legitimate owners of the mark."

But the statute, like so many, is written more broadly than what may have been the political catalyst that got it passed. As in Bosley Medical Institute v. Kremer, we conclude that the words of the statute are broader than this political stimulus that led to its enactment. Though there was no evidence of anything wrong with Nahum's registration of the domain name to himself, the evidence supported a verdict that Nahum subsequently, years later, used the domain name to get leverage for his claim for commissions. The statute says "registers, traffics in, or uses," with "or" between the terms, so use alone is enough to support a verdict, even in the absence of violative registration or trafficking.

As for whether use to get leverage in a business dispute can establish a violation, the statutory factors for "bad faith intent" establish that it can. "Evidence of bad faith may arise well after registration of the domain name."[16] The statute contains a safe harbor provision, excluding a finding of "bad faith intent" for persons who reasonably believed that use of the domain name was fair use or otherwise lawful,[17] but that safe harbor has no application here. Nahum could not have reasonably believed that he could lawfully use "eq-Italy" when he no longer worked for DSPT. The safe harbor protects uses such as parody and comment,[18] and use by persons ignorant of another's superior right to the mark.[19]

The statute provides that a court "may consider factors such as, but not limited to" the . . . enumerated list of nine. Nahum does not challenge the jury instruction, which listed all of the factors, even though some have no bearing on this case, and some do not offer either side much support. One of the factors, number VI in the statute, strongly supports DSPT's claim. That factor notes that it is "indicative" of a bad faith intent to profit" from the mark if the person offering to transfer the domain name to the owner of the mark has never actually used or intended to use the domain name for bona fide sales of goods.

Factor VI may fairly be read to mean that it is bad faith to hold a domain name for ransom,[22] where the holder uses it to get money from the owner of the trademark rather than to sell goods. The jury had evidence that Nahum was using the "eq-Italy.com" domain name as leverage to get DSPT to pay him the disputed commissions, not for the bona fide

---

[16] Lahoti v. VeriCheck, Inc., 586 F.3d 1190, 1202 (9th Cir.2009) (citation omitted).

[17] 15 U.S.C. § 1125(d)(1)(B)(ii).

[18] See, e.g., Mattel, Inc. v. MCA Records, Inc., 296 F.3d 894, 906-07 (9th Cir.2002)

[19] See, e.g., 15 U.S.C. § 1114 (innocent infringement by publishers); 15 U.S.C. § 1115 (innocent infringement as a defense to right to use a mark).

[22] See Bosley Med. Inst., Inc. v. Kremer, 403 F.3d 672, 680 (9th Cir.2005) (stating that cybersquatting "occurs when a person other than the trademark holder registers the domain name of a well known trademark and then attempts to profit from this by either *ransoming the domain name back* to the trademark holder or by using the domain name to divert business from the trademark holder to the domain name holder." (emphasis added) (quoting DaimlerChrysler v. The Net Inc., 388 F.3d 201, 204 (6th Cir.2004))).

sale of clothes. Though there was no direct evidence of an explicit offer to sell the domain to DSPT for a specified amount, the jury could infer the intent to give back the site to DSPT only if DSPT paid Nahum the disputed commissions.

The "intent to profit," as factor VI shows, means simply the intent to get money or other valuable consideration. "Profit" does not require that Nahum receive more than he is owed on his disputed claim. Rather, "[p]rofit includes an attempt to procure an advantageous gain or return." Thus, it does not matter that, as the jury concluded, Nahum's claim for unpaid commissions was meritless, because he could not hold the domain name for ransom even if he had been owed commissions.

In this case, shortly after DSPT's content disappeared from eq-Italy.com, Nahum e-mailed Dorigo stating that the eq-Italy.com website would be back up under a new format. Nahum testified that he would transfer the domain to DSPT after Nahum and DSPT were able to resolve the "monetary issues regarding [Nahum's] commissions." Nahum's subsequent employer testified that Nahum told him that DSPT wanted the website returned to them, but Nahum was keeping it to use it as leverage in order to get the money he said DSPT owed him. This is evidence of an "intent to profit" under the Act.

C. Distinctive and Confusingly Similar

Nahum's second argument is that there was no evidence from which a jury could conclude that "www. eq- Italy. com" was a distinctive mark, or that it was confusingly similar to DSPT's "EQ" mark. The latter point is meritless, since the evidence showed that only DSPT used the mark "EQ" for a men's shirts line, and used the Italian fashion connection as a selling point. Even though DSPT had not registered the "EQ" mark, ownership of common law trademark "is obtained by actual use of a symbol to identify the goods or services of one seller and distinguish them from those offered by others." The evidence shows that DSPT used the mark in commerce in fall 1999, when it exhibited EQ at the New York fashion shows[25] and thereafter used the "EQ" symbol. Although Nahum showed that others used an "EQ" mark in subsequent years for other sorts of goods, such as online publications, engine cylinder heads, and bicycles, no one would likely confuse these goods with DSPT's. The only other use that was even arguably confusingly similar was EQ equestrian clothing, but the jury could conclude that retailers shopping for men's shirts are unlikely to be confused by a mark also used for equestrian clothing, and that the style in which the marks were displayed was too different to foster confusion. The shirts were marked by the letters EQ, whereas the equestrian apparel was marked by a rectangle inside another rectangle.

---

[25] See Chance [v. Pac-Tel Teletrac Inc., 242 F.3d 1151, 1156-59 (9th Cir.2001)] (applying totality of the circumstances test and determining that pre-sales activity could qualify mark for trademark protection); New West Corp. v. NYM Co. of Cal., Inc., 595 F.2d 1194, 1199 (9th Cir.1979) (holding "that appellee established a prior use of the mark without an actual sale"); [see generally 2 J.T. McCarthy, Trademarks and Unfair Competition § 16:12-14 (4th ed. 2010).]

As for whether "eq-Italy.com" is "confusingly similar" to EQ, a jury could reasonably conclude that in the context of men's shirts, it was. The jury could have concluded that, at the time Nahum used it, the mark was distinctive and his use of the site after leaving DSPT would confuse retailers trying to shop DSPT's catalog at the website where they had done so before.[28] In fact, as Dorigo testified, several customers were actually confused by the alteration of the website. "Now, people would still call and say, what happened? Where is it? You know, they wanted to know what's this screen?" By 2005, eq-Italy.com was identified with EQ and Equilibrio. The similarity of "EQ" and "eq-Italy" is considerably greater than "perfumebay.com" and "ebay.com," which we held were similar, and thus the jury's finding should be upheld.

. . . .

III. Conclusion

Even if a domain name was put up innocently and used properly for years, a person is liable under 15 U.S.C. § 1125(d) if he subsequently uses the domain name with a bad faith intent to profit from the protected mark by holding the domain name for ransom. The evidence sufficiently supported the jury's verdict that Nahum did so, causing $152,000 in damages to DSPT.

NEWPORT NEWS HOLDINGS CORP. v. VIRTUAL CITY VISION, INC.
650 F.3d 423 (4th Cir. 2011)

DUNCAN, Circuit Judge:

This appeal raises numerous issues arising out of the grant of summary judgment to Newport News Holdings Corporation ("NNHC") on its claims against Virtual City Vision and its owner Van James Bond Tran (collectively, "VCV") under the Anticybersquatting Consumer Protection Act ("ACPA"). . .

I.

A.

. . . . NNHC is a women's clothing and accessories company that has been in existence for over twenty years. It owns five federally registered trademarks for the mark "Newport News." These trademarks cover the sale of women's clothing and accessories and the offering of these items for sale through catalogs and the Internet. The trademarks also cover the domain name newport-news.com, which NNHC purchased in November 1997. NNHC attempted to acquire the domain name newportnews.com as well, but VCV had already purchased that domain name in October 1997. NNHC began offering its goods for sale over the Internet in 1999 using the newport-news.com domain name.

---

[28] The usual eight factors from AMF Inc. v. Sleekcraft Boats for determining whether passing off one's goods as another is "confusingly similar" are a poor fit in this context, because they are designed to address a different social harm than the cybersquatting statute. 599 F.2d 341, 348-49 (9th Cir.1979).

VCV, an Alabama corporation, owns at least thirty-one domain names that incorporate the names of geographic locations. Newportnews.com, which initially focused on Newport News, Virginia, is one such example. VCV's "original intent . . . was to create websites . . . where residents of, and visitors to, these cities could find information and advertising related to th[e] cities."

VCV's organization is skeletal. Tran is its president, sole employee, and the only participating member of its board of directors. He operates the business from his home.

NNHC and VCV first clashed in a private dispute resolution forum. In 2000, NNHC brought a complaint against VCV under the Uniform Domain Name Dispute Resolution Policy of the Internet Corporation for Assigned Names and Numbers ("ICANN"). NNHC alleged that VCV's newportnews.com website was "confusingly similar to [NNHC's] family of registered trademarks for the mark 'Newport News'"; that "any rights [VCV] has in the domain name in contention are illegitimate"; and that VCV "registered this domain name in bad faith."

The ICANN panel rejected NNHC's arguments and dismissed its complaint. In doing so, it found that, although the mark and the domain name are identical, "visitors to [NNHC's] branded web site, who seek out the latest women's clothing and home fashions would clearly not be confused when seeing a home page of another web site, bearing an identical mark, that explicitly provides city information . . . with no connection whatsoever to women's and home fashions." The panel further held that VCV's website provided "bona fide service offerings," which included "disseminat[ing] city information in an effort to increase tourism and other visitor traffic to the city." Significantly, with respect to NNHC's claim of bad faith, the panel noted that "given the total absence of competition between the businesses of [NNHC and VCV] . . . [VCV] did not register the contested domain name in an effort to cause any likelihood of confusion."

Between 2000 and 2004, newportnews.com remained relatively unchanged. It continued to provide information about the city of Newport News and link visitors to local businesses, such as hotels, movie theaters, real estate companies, and entertainment venues. In 2004, the website began running occasional advertisements for women's clothing.

In the summer of 2007, NNHC made an offer to purchase the newportnews.com domain name, which VCV rejected. VCV responded that it would sell the domain name for a "seven-figure" amount, or, in the alternative, sell NNHC goods on its website for a commission.

A substantive evolution in the VCV website began in the fall of 2007. The site shifted from a city focus, similar to that of VCV's other locality sites, to one emphasizing women's fashions. By February of 2008, the homepage was dominated by advertisements for women's apparel.

At about the same time, the management of the site changed as well. Tran began managing the newportnews.com website personally, taking control away from Local Matters, the company that ran VCV's locality sites. The changes to the website were lucrative. Tran would later testify that most of VCV's revenue during that time came from the newportnews.com website instead of the locality sites, either individually or in total. . . .

II

[VCV challenged the district court's grant of summary judgment in favor of NNHC on its claim under the ACPA.]

1.

[The court first considered the issue of bad faith under the ACPA.] VCV challenges the district court's finding of bad faith in several respects. It attacks the court's determination that VCV did not provide legitimate services that would constitute a fair use of the domain name. VCV also asserts that the evidence does not support a finding that it intended to create a likelihood of confusion. Finally, it challenges the court's reliance on the ICANN ruling as evidence that VCV knew it was acting unlawfully when it changed its website.

a.

VCV claims that, contrary to the district court's conclusion, its website offered a legitimate service by providing information about the city of Newport News.

The ACPA permits a registered trademark to be used by someone other than the mark owner if it is a "use, otherwise than as a mark, . . . of a term or device which is descriptive of and used fairly and in good faith only to describe the goods or services of such party, or their geographic origin." 15 U.S.C. § 1115(b)(4). The district court found that this provision did not apply here because "[o]n VCV's website, Newport News is no longer used to describe VCV's goods or services, or their geographic origin, because the site is dedicated primarily to women's fashion." VCV disputes this characterization, contending to the contrary that its website offered the legitimate service of providing information about the city of Newport News. We disagree.

The record conclusively shows that in making changes to its website in 2007, VCV shifted its focus away from the legitimate service of providing information related to the city of Newport News and became instead a website devoted primarily to women's fashion. Most of the items on its homepage, as well as those most prominently placed, related to women's attire. Not only was the site dominated by advertisements for apparel, it also contained dozens of links to shopping websites. The website's references to the city of Newport News became minor in comparison to the fashion-related content. VCV cannot escape the consequences of its deliberate metamorphosis. VCV would apparently have us hold that as long as it provided any information about the city of Newport News, it continued to provide a "bona fide" service. Such a formalistic approach would allow a cybersquatter seeking to profit from another company's trademark to avoid liability by ensuring that it provides some minimal amount of information about a legitimate subject. It would also undermine the purpose of the ACPA, which seeks to prevent "the bad-faith and abusive registration of distinctive marks as Internet domain names with the intent to profit from the goodwill associated with such marks." Barcelona.com, Inc. v. Excelentisimo Ayuntamiento de Barcelona, 330 F.3d 617, 624 (4th Cir. 2003) (quoting S.Rep. No. 106–140, at 4 (1999)).

As we have noted, in analyzing bad faith, we "view the totality of the circumstances." [Virtual Works, Inc. v. Volkswagen of Am., Inc., 238 F.3d 264, 270 (4th Cir. 2001)]. Here, even drawing all reasonable inferences in favor of VCV, the record is clear that after November 2007, VCV was no longer in the business of providing information about the city of Newport News. The contrast between the newportnews.com website and VCV's other locality websites, which were dominated by links and advertisements for businesses and activities in those cities, is stark. Unlike those websites, newportnews.com went from being a website about a city that happened to have some apparel advertisements to a website about women's apparel that happened to include minimal references to the city of Newport News. The district court correctly held that, once VCV largely abandoned its city information service, it ceased to have a right to use the name of Newport News to describe such service.

b.

VCV argues that the district court failed to properly analyze whether there was a likelihood of confusion between NNHC's website and VCV's website. Its argument, however, mischaracterizes the nature of an ACPA claim. The standard under the ACPA is not whether there is a likelihood of confusion between the two websites but rather whether the allegedly offending website "creat[es] a likelihood of confusion as to the source, sponsorship, affiliation, or endorsement of the site." 15 U.S.C. § 1125(d)(1)(B)(v). The ACPA provides for liability "without regard to the goods or services of the parties." Id. § 1125(d)(1)(A).

VCV argues that, under our precedent in Lamparello v. Falwell, 420 F.3d 309 (4th Cir. 2005), we must "determine whether a likelihood of confusion exists by 'examin[ing] the allegedly infringing use in the context in which it is seen by the ordinary consumer.'" Id. at 316 (alteration in original). However, the court in Lamparello made that statement in the context of trademark infringement, not the ACPA. See id. As the Eighth Circuit court has noted, "[t]he inquiry under the ACPA is . . . narrower than the traditional multifactor likelihood of confusion test for trademark infringement." Coca–Cola Co. v. Purdy, 382 F.3d 774, 783 (8th Cir. 2004); see also N. Light Tech., Inc. v. N. Lights Club, 236 F.3d 57, 66 n. 14 (1st Cir. 2001) ("[T]he likelihood of confusion test of trademark infringement is more comprehensive than the identical or confusingly similar requirement of ACPA, as it requires considering factors beyond the facial similarity of the two marks." (internal quotations omitted)). "The question under the ACPA is . . . whether the domain names which [the defendant] registered . . . are identical or confusingly similar to a plaintiff's mark." Coca-Cola Co., 382 F.3d at 783. Here VCV's domain name was identical to NNHC's mark.

VCV further alleges that its disclaimer, "We are Newport News, Virginia," which appeared near the top of the new version of the website, eliminated any likelihood of confusion. Again, VCV misinterprets the applicable law. For ACPA purposes, "[t]he fact that confusion about a website's source or sponsorship could be resolved by visiting the website is not relevant to whether the domain name itself is identical or confusingly similar to a plaintiff's mark." Id.; see also Virtual Works, 238 F.3d at 271 (finding that the domain name vw.net was confusingly similar to the Volkswagen "VW" mark for purposes of the ACPA, even though the domain name was being used as an internet service provider's website); . . . Given that VCV's domain name was identical to NNHC's mark, we find that the district court correctly held that VCV created a likelihood of confusion as to the source of the site.

c.

VCV argues that the district court erred in finding that the ICANN decision was further proof of VCV's bad faith in making the November 2008 changes to its website. It asserts that, because the ICANN decision did not prohibit any of the changes made by VCV, VCV's awareness of the decision does not support a finding that it made the changes in bad faith.

VCV's argument misses the mark here as well. What the court deemed most significant was that the ICANN decision found VCV's use proper precisely because its business of providing city information was unrelated to NNHC's clothing business. The ICANN decision found that VCV was not in competition with NNHC precisely because of their disparate business models. Indeed, in holding that there was no evidence of bad faith on the part of VCV, the ICANN relied on "*the total absence of competition between the businesses of [NNHC and VCV].*" (emphasis added). The fact that, in the face of this cautionary language, VCV later purposefully transformed its website into one that competed with NNHC by advertising women's apparel is a legitimate factor within the totality of the circumstances supporting the district court's finding of bad faith.[9]

---

[9] VCV's argument that the district court failed to consider the safe-harbor fair use defense fails as well. Under the ACPA's safe-harbor provision, "[b]ad faith intent . . . shall not be found in any case in which the court determines that the person believed and had reasonable grounds to believe that the use of the domain name was a fair use or otherwise lawful." 15 U.S.C. § 1125(d)(1)(B)(ii). The district court's specific finding that "VCV knew or should have known" that the November 2007 changes to its website "would give rise to some type of liability," defeats any contention that VCV "believed and had reasonable grounds to believe" that its use of the domain name was lawful.

[Affirmed].

At p. 660, Note 4, add the following after the *Harrods* cite in line 6:

Should legitimate ownership of one domain name registration (*e.g.*, gopetc.com) count in favor of a finding of good faith when the registrant registers additional related domain names (*e.g.*, gopet.org) in order to increase the selling price of the legitimate domain name registration? *See GoPets Ltd. v. Hise*, 657 F.3d 1024, 1032-33 (9th Cir. 2011).

At p. 660, Note 6, add the following at the end of the Note:

See contra GoPets Ltd. v. Hise, 657 F.3d 1024 (9th Cir. 2011) (registration does not include re-registration). To what extent should the answer to the re-registration question depend on whether initial registrations that predate the ACPA are covered by the Act? *See id.* at 1031-32.

At p. 662, add the following case after Note 10:

<u>MICROSOFT CORP. v. SHAH</u>
98 U.S.P.Q.2d (BNA) 1404 (D. Wash. 2011)

MARTINEZ, District Judge:

. . .

II. BACKGROUND

Defendants are alleged to have registered domain names containing Microsoft trademarks in order to drive traffic to their website. Consumers seeking a Microsoft website or product are mistakenly drawn to Defendants' website through Defendants' alleged use of Microsoft trademarks. Consumers who believe they are downloading a Microsoft product are then allegedly tricked into interacting with Defendants, who in turn solicit users to download emoticons. Defendants allegedly receive payment when a visitor clicks on links or advertisements displayed on their website, or when a visitor downloads or installs a product such as the emoticon toolbar.

Moreover, Defendants are alleged to have induced others to engage in infringement and cybersquatting by providing instruction on how to misleadingly use Microsoft marks to increase website traffic. Further, Defendants also allegedly sold a product that contained software to allow buyers to easily create websites incorporating Microsoft marks. This product allegedly included a video narrated by Defendant Shah.

III. DISCUSSION

A. Contributory Cybersquatting

1. Case Precedent

The first issue is determining whether Plaintiff may bring a novel cause of action for contributory cybersquatting. The Anti-Cybersquatting Consumer Protection Act ("ACPA") creates liability for certain forms of cyberpiracy. Under the ACPA, a plaintiff must show that "(1) the defendant registered, trafficked in, or used a domain name; (2) the domain name is identical or confusingly similar to a protected mark owned by the plaintiff; and (3) the defendant acted with 'bad faith intent to profit from that mark.'" DSPT International v. Nahum, [624 F.3d 1213 (9th Cir. 2010)]; 15 U.S.C. § 1125(d)(1)(A).

It is well established that the theory of contributory liability, as found in the context of tort law, is applicable to trademark infringement. Fonovisa, Inc. v. Cherry Auction, Inc., 76 F.3d 259, 264 (9th Cir. 1996). Contributory trademark liability applies where a defendant (1) intentionally induces another to infringe on a trademark or (2) continues to supply a product knowing that the recipient is using the product to engage in trademark infringement. Id. (citing Inwood Laboratories v. Ives Laboratories, 456 U.S. 844, 854-855 (1982)).

In the case at hand, Plaintiff makes a claim for contributory cybersquatting, along with a claim for cybersquatting. The cause of action of contributory (or induced) cybersquatting has neither been explicitly addressed by an appellate court nor by statute. However, several federal district court cases have at least discussed the notional cause of action. In *Ford Motor Co. v. Greatdomains.com*, plaintiff brought claims for direct and contributory liability for cybersquatting, trademark infringement, and dilution against the owner of a website that auctioned domain names. 177 F.Supp.2d 635 (E.D. Mich. 2001). In addressing the contributory liability of the domain name auctioneer, the Ford court discussed the familiar "flea market" analysis. This analysis states that a flea market that exercises "direct control and monitoring" over its vendors may be liable for contributory infringement if it "suppl[ied] the necessary marketplace." Id. at 646 (quoting Lockheed Martin Corp. v. Network Solutions, Inc., 194 F.3d 980, 984-985 (9th Cir. 1999)). The court noted that the analysis, while traditionally applied to trademark infringement, could potentially be applied to allegations of cybersquatting. Id. at 647.

However, the ACPA requires a showing of "bad faith intent," which is not a requisite element under traditional trademark infringement, unfair competition, and dilution causes of action. Therefore, the Ford court reasoned that a claim for contributory cybersquatting would require a somewhat heightened standard. Id. Ford explained that it was insufficient for defendant Greatdomains.com to have a mere awareness that the infringing domain names were being sold over its website. Instead, a plaintiff must show that the defendant "cyber-landlord" knew or should have known that its vendors had no legitimate reason for having registered the disputed domain names. Ultimately, the court concluded that a claim for contributory liability could not be maintained against the owner of the domain-name auctioning website. Id. A defendant such as Greatdomains.com that creates a marketplace for domain names "could not be expected to ascertain the good or bad faith intent of its vendors." Id. Therefore, contributory liability for cybersquatting could apply to "cyber-landlords" only in exceptional circumstances.

The Ford court declined to find the defendant liable not because the court did not recognize a cause of action for contributory liability in the context of cybersquatting, but rather because the requisite bad faith could not be shown with respect to a "cyber-landlord" who could not have known that vendors utilizing the marketplace for domain names had no legitimate purpose. However, the decision recognized the applicability of a potential cause of action for contributory cybersquatting under the facts of the case.

The conduct of the Ford defendant differed significantly from the alleged conduct of Defendants in the case before this Court. Plaintiff's claim for contributory liability in the context of cybersquatting focuses on Defendants allegedly providing instructions and their alleged sales of a method known as the "Magic Bullet System," which is meant to teach buyers how to use Microsoft marks in order to sell the emoticon-related software. In essence, the contributory cybersquatting claim alleges that Defendants induced others to use domain names incorporating Microsoft marks. Defendants did not simply provide a marketplace where a trade in domain names may take place, as was the case in Ford. Rather, Defendants allegedly developed and marketed a method, the sole purpose of which was to allow purchasers to profit from the illicit use of Microsoft marks. Unlike the defendant in Ford, the Defendants in the case at hand either knew or should have known that the purchasers of the "Magic Bullet System" could not have had a legitimate reason for purchasing the method. Therefore, it is likely that Plaintiff has made a sufficient showing of Defendants' bad faith under the heightened standard employed by the Ford court.

In addition, another district court decision recognized the cause of action for contributory cybersquatting in its refusal to dismiss plaintiff's claim for contributory cybersquatting. Solid Host, NL v. Namecheap, Inc., 652 F.Supp.2d 1092, 1117 (C.D. Cal. 2009). These two decisions, along with the case at hand, reveal the relevance of the cause of action for contributory cybersqatting. Moreover, the Ford decision has provided a simple framework that addresses the ACPA's additional element requiring bad faith.

2. Interpreting the ACPA

The Lanham Act itself does not expressly address causes of action for contributory liability. Nonetheless, the court-made doctrine of contributory liability for trademark infringement is well-established. Fonovisa, Inc.,76 F.3d 259. Courts have simply applied the traditional principles of tort law to impose liability on those who have assisted with or contributed to infringement. Id. Both trademark infringement and cybersquatting are tort-like causes of actions to which the theory of contributory liability would appear to be naturally suited. A recent Ninth Circuit decision interprets the ACPA broadly, and therefore lends support to allowing claims for contributory cybersquatting. DSPT International v. Nahum, [624 F.3d 1213 (9th Cir. 2010)]. . . .

In the current case, Defendants' alleged conduct falls squarely within the statute's goal of imposing liability on those who seek to profit in bad faith by means of registering, trafficking, or using domain names that contain identical or confusingly similar marks. Defendants allegedly sought to profit in bad faith by teaching others how to trade off the widespread recognition of Plaintiff's mark in order to drive traffic to a given website. A defendant who seeks to profit by selling a method that teaches others how to benefit from violating the ACPA should not be able to escape liability by interpreting the statute so narrowly. The practice of instructing others on how to engage in cybersquatting runs counter to the purpose of the ACPA. Finally, "it is a well-established canon of statutory construction that a court should go beyond the literal language of a statute if reliance on that language would defeat the plain purpose of the statute." Bob Jones Univ. v. United States, 461 U.S. 574, 586 (1983). As DSPT International makes clear, the ACPA should not be read so narrowly as to unduly constrain the protections the statute is meant to afford against cybersquatters.

B. Contributory Trademark Dilution

The second issue is whether Plaintiff may bring a novel cause of action for contributory dilution. Owners of famous marks are afforded a cause of action under the Trademark Dilution Act. Dilution can occur by blurring of the famous mark, which weakens the connection between the good and the mark in the minds of consumers. Dilution can also occur by tarnishment, where a defendant makes use of the mark in an unwholesome manner or connects it to inferior goods. Like contributory cybersquatting, a cause of action for contributory trademark dilution has never been directly addressed by statute or by appellate courts.

However there has been some discussion of the cause of action in preceding cases. The only appellate treatment of the issue came in Lockheed Martin v. Network Solutions, Inc., where the Ninth Circuit denied leave to amend a complaint to state a claim for contributory dilution. 194 F.3d 980, 986 (9th Cir. 1999). While the Lockheed court acknowledged that contributory dilution was not an established cause of action, the court's denial of leave to amend was predicated on the plaintiff's failure to meet the standard necessary to show contributory liability. The Ninth Circuit recognized the cause of action as potentially viable and cited Kegan v. Apple Computer for its definition of contributory dilution as the encouragement of others to dilute. No. 95 C 1339, 1996 WL 667808. (N.D.Ill. Nov. 15, 1996). Other more recent decisions have declined to dismiss the cause of action, without [a]ffirmatively reaching the issue of the cause of action's actual existence. See Google, Inc. v. American Blind & Wallpaper Factory, Inc., No. C03-05340, 2005 WL 832398 (N.D. Cal. Mar. 30, 2005); Steinway, Inc. v. Ashley, No. 01 CIV 9703, 2002 WL 122929 (S.D.N.Y. Jan.29, 2002); Perfect 10, Inc. v. Cybernet Ventures, Inc., 167 F.Supp 2d 1114 (C.D. Cal. 2001).

As with contributory cybersquatting, contributory dilution is a tort-like cause of action which naturally lends itself to the theory of contributory liability. In the case at hand, Defendants are alleged to have encouraged others to utilize the famous Microsoft mark in such a way that could cause dilution of the Microsoft mark. The Trademark Dilution Act seeks to provide a mechanism through which owners of famous marks may seek protection against exactly the kind of harm-in the form of blurring or tarnishing-that is alleged in the present case. It would be inconsistent with the Trademark Dilution Act to prohibit a cause of action for contributory dilution. . . .

[Defendant's Motion to Dismiss Denied].

At p. 675, add as Note 11:

In footnote 15, the *Harrods* court references the safe harbor in Section 43(d)(1)(B)(ii). However, the courts have stressed that this should be used "very sparingly and only in the most unusual cases." *See GoPets Ltd. v. Hise*, 657 F.3d 1024 (9th Cir. 2011); *Lahoti v. VeriCheck, Inc.*, 586 F.3d 1190, 1123 (9th Cir. 2009).

At p. 684, Note 2, add the following:

For a summary of decisions under the UDRP, *see* WIPO Overview of WIPO Panel Views on Selected UDRP Questions, Second Edition (2011) ("WIPO Overview 2.0"), available at http://wipo.int/amc/en/domains/search/overview2.0/index.html

At p. 684, Note 7, add the following:

In 2010, trademark owners filed a record number of UDRP cases (2,696 cases) with the WIPO Arbitration and Media Center. 82% of cases involved registrations in the .com domain.

At p. 695, the reference to Section 34(c) before the *Gabbanelli* cite should be to Section 35(c).

At p. 695, after the *Gabbanelli* cite, add the following:

Unlike Section 35(b), Section 35(c) does not, however, make express reference to an award of attorneys' fees. If a trademark owner elects statutory damages under Section 35(c), may the trademark owner still argue that the case is exceptional and attorneys' fees should be awarded? *See Louis Vuitton Malletier S.A. v. Ly USA, Inc.*, 676 F.3d 83 (2d Cir. 2012) (yes). The court reasoned that an election under Section 35(c) in a trademark counterfeiting case should not preclude the trademark owner from invoking the same attorneys' fees remedy that other prevailing plaintiffs would have in any trademark infringement case that is deemed to be exceptional. (That remedy is provided for in Section 35(a)). Two of the three panel judges found it useful to consult the legislative history to arrive at this conclusion:

> Before 1996, trademark remedies were governed by sections 1117(a) and (b) alone. Section 1117(a) provided as remedies—then as now—profits, actual damages, and costs, plus attorney's fees in an "exceptional" case. Section 1117(b) provided—in cases of willful counterfeiting—for treble damages, a "reasonable attorney's fee," and prejudgment interest.
>
> In 1996, Congress passed the Anticounterfeiting Consumer Protection Act (the "Act"), which amended section 1117 to add subsection (c), providing

for the alternative of statutory damages. Anticounterfeiting Consumer Protection Act of 1996, § 7, Pub.L. No. 104–153, 110 Stat. 1386 (codified at 15 U.S.C. § 1117(c)). Congress appears to have been motivated by a gap in the law: Plaintiffs who were victorious on their civil counterfeiting claims were often unable to obtain an adequate recovery in actual damages because counterfeiters often maintain sparse business records, if any at all. *See* S. Rep. 104–177, at 10 (1995).[27]   In passing the Act, which allows trademark plaintiffs to elect to recover statutory damages in counterfeit cases in lieu of actual damages, Congress apparently sought to ensure that plaintiffs would receive more than *de minimis* compensation for the injury caused by counterfeiting as a result of the unprovability of actual damages despite the plain inference of damages to the plaintiff from the defendant's unlawful behavior. The Act was thus apparently designed to provide an alternative to the type of recovery provided in section 1117(a); not to all of the remedies provided for in that section. The Act was meant to expand the range of remedies available to a trademark plaintiff, not restrict them.

In light of that history, it seems to us unlikely that Congress intended to prevent a plaintiff who opts to recover statutory damages from also receiving attorney's fees. If Congress's purpose in enacting section 1117(c) was to address the problem facing a plaintiff unable to prove actual damages, denying an attorney's fee award to those plaintiffs making use of the new statutory-damages election would be inconsistent with that remedial purpose. The key legislative-history sources—the House and Senate Reports—do not indicate that Congress intended a tradeoff between statutory damages and both actual damages and attorney's fees. *See* H.R. Rep. 104–556 (2005); S. Rep. 104–177.

This case is illustrative. The district court concluded that the defendants were responsible for a "massive counterfeiting enterprise" based at least in

---

[27] The Senate Report provides, with respect to section 7 of the Act:

This section amends section 35 of the Lanham Act, allowing civil litigants the option of obtaining discretionary, judicially imposed damages in trademark counterfeiting cases, instead of actual damages. The committee recognizes that under current law, a civil litigant may not be able to prove actual damages if a sophisticated, large-scale counterfeiter has hidden or destroyed information about his counterfeiting.

Moreover, counterfeiters' records are frequently nonexistent, inadequate or deceptively kept in order to willfully deflate the level of counterfeiting activity actually engaged in, making proving actual damages in these cases extremely difficult if not impossible. Enabling trademark owners to elect statutory damages is both necessary and appropriate in light of the deception routinely practiced by counterfeiters. The amounts are appropriate given the extent of damage done to business goodwill by infringement of trademarks.

S. Rep. 104-177, at 10.

part on plaintiff's allegations and the unavailability of records suggesting otherwise. As we have explained, a defendant facing a statutory damage award less than the actual amount of the damages he or she caused has the incentive to frustrate ascertainment of the actual amount of the damages. It makes little sense, we think, to further reward a defendant successful in defeating the plaintiff's and the court's attempts to fix the actual amount of damages by allowing him or her to avoid an award of attorney's fees. Such a scheme would only further incentivize the defendant to avoid making, keeping, or producing sales records.

Id. at 110-11.

At p. 695, after the insert above, add the following:

Should Section 35(c) be available in cases where the defendant is a contributory infringer? *See Louis Vuitton Malletier, S.A. v. Akanoc Solutions, Inc.*, 658 F.3d 936, 944-45 (9th Cir. 2011). Can you develop a statutory interpretation argument that supports this outcome?

At pp. 698-99, Note 1, add the following:

Section 2320 was amended again, effective December 31, 2011, as part of the National Defense Authorization Act of 2012. The amendments appear in this Statutory Supplement. For background, see James Klaiber, *Uncovering Enhanced Trademark Protections In the NDAA*, Law360 Mar. 6, 2012 (explaining that the amendments to the anti-counterfeiting legislation arose from concerns about counterfeit electronic goods used by the military). Two of the primary changes are (1) in a charge of conspiracy to commit trademark counterfeiting, there is no longer any requirement to prove that at least one alleged co-conspirator carried out an "overt act" in furtherance of the conspiracy and (2) increased penalties, including imprisonment, for trademark counterfeiting violations. *Id.* Because of the elimination of the overt act requirement, one who agrees to commit trademark counterfeiting but never carries it out could still be guilty of a criminal offense.

At p. 698, add the following as Note 1A:

1A. *"Substantially indistinguishable from. . .?"* Section 2320 defines "counterfeit mark" as a "spurious" mark that is either identical to, "or substantially indistinguishable from," a registered mark. Suppose that a defendant is accused of counterfeiting the Burberry "check" mark (a well-known plaid pattern, as you are probably aware). Suppose that the defendant's goods include a similar plaid pattern, with an equestrian figure superimposed over it. Is the defendant's mark "substantially indistinguishable" from the registered Burberry check even if the registration does not include any equestrian figure? Would it matter if Burberry had separately registered an equestrian figure and sometimes sold products having both the check pattern and the equestrian figure? (Would you need to know how similar the respective equestrian figures were?) *See U.S. v. Chong Lam,* 677 F.3d 190 (4th Cir. 2012).

At p. 699, add the following as Note 6 :

6. *Void for vagueness?* Would you uphold Section 2320 against a constitutional challenge that the definition of "counterfeit" is void for vagueness? As noted in Note 1A above, a "counterfeit mark" under Section 2320 is defined as a "spurious" mark that is either identical to, "or substantially indistinguishable from," a registered mark. Is the phrase "substantially indistinguishable from" void for vagueness? *See U.S. v. Chong Lam,* 677 F.3d 190 (4th Cir. 2012). The relevant standard requires an assessment as to whether the relevant criminal offense is defined (1) with enough definiteness that ordinary people can understand what conduct is prohibited, and (2) in a manner that does not encourage arbitrary and discriminatory enforcement.

PERMISSIBLE USES OF ANOTHER'S TRADEMARK

At p. 718, add the following case before Problem 9-1:

FORTUNE DYNAMIC, INC. v. VICTORIA'S SECRET STORES BRAND MGM'T, INC.
618 F.3d 1025 (9th Cir. 2010)

BYBEE, Circuit Judge:

I

Since 1987 Fortune has been in the business of designing and selling footwear for women, young women, and children. In 1997, Fortune began using DELICIOUS as a trademark on its footwear for young women. Two years later, in 1999, Fortune registered the DELICIOUS trademark for footwear on the principal register of the U.S. Patent and Trademark Office. For most of the time relevant to this appeal, Fortune depicted DELICIOUS in standard block lettering with a capital "D."[1]

Fortune spends approximately $350,000 a year advertising its footwear. In the three-year period from 2005 to 2007, Fortune sold more than 12 million pairs of DELICIOUS shoes. DELICIOUS shoes are featured on Fortune's website and in its catalogs, and have appeared in fashion magazines directed specifically to young women, including *Cosmo girl, Elle girl, Teen People, Twist, In Touch, Seventeen, Latina, ym, Shop, CB, marie claire,* and *Life & Style.* DELICIOUS footwear is available in authorized retail outlets throughout the United States.

Victoria's Secret is a well-known company specializing in intimate apparel. It sells a wide variety of lingerie, beauty products, and personal care products in its 900 retail stores. In February 2007, Victoria's Secret launched a line of personal care products under the trademark BEAUTY RUSH. At the same time, it started a promotion that included giving away a gift package of BEAUTY RUSH lip gloss and-most importantly for our case-a pink

---

[1] In June 2007 (after this lawsuit was filed), Fortune applied to register DELICIOUS in a stylized font for use on clothing.

tank top to anyone who purchased $35 of beauty product.[3] The tank top was folded inside a clear plastic pouch with the lip gloss and a coupon for a future BEAUTY RUSH purchase. Across the chest of the tank top was written, in silver typescript, the word "Delicious" with a capital "D." On the back, in much smaller lettering, there appeared the word "yum," and the phrase "beauty rush" was written in the back collar. Victoria's Secret models were featured wearing the tank top, as were mannequins on in-store display tables. Victoria's Secret distributed 602,723 "Delicious" tank tops in connection with its BEAUTY RUSH promotion, which lasted until March 2007. Those tank tops not sold or given away during the promotion were sold at Victoria's Secret's semi-annual sale a few months later.

Victoria's Secret executives offered two explanations for using the word "Delicious" on the tank top. First, they suggested that it accurately described the taste of the BEAUTY RUSH lip glosses and the smell of the BEAUTY RUSH body care. Second, they thought that the word served as a "playful self-descriptor," as if the woman wearing the top is saying, "I'm delicious." No one at Victoria's Secret conducted a search to determine whether DELICIOUS was a registered trademark, but Victoria's Secret had run a very similar promotion several months earlier, this one in conjunction with the launch of its VERY SEXY makeup. That promotion also included a tank top, but that tank top was "black ribbed" with "Very Sexy" written in hot pink crystals across the chest. VERY SEXY is a Victoria's Secret trademark.

. . .

III

[The court analyzed confusion under the *Sleekcraft* factors, finding multiple fact issues that should have precluded the grant of summary judgment.]

B

We next turn to Victoria's Secret's argument that its use of the word "Delicious" was protected by the Lanham Act's fair use defense. 15 U.S.C. § 1115(b)(4). Long before the Lanham Act was enacted, the Supreme Court explained that "[t]he use of a similar name by another to truthfully describe his own product does not constitute a legal or moral wrong, even if its effect be to cause the public to mistake the origin . . . of the product." *William R. Warner & Co. v. Eli Lilly & Co.*, 265 U.S. 526, 529 (1924). Congress codified this common law principle in the Lanham Act's fair use defense, which allows a party to use a descriptive word "otherwise than as a mark . . . [and] fairly and in good faith only to describe the goods or services of such party, or their geographic origin." 15 U.S.C. § 1115(b)(4). In establishing that its use was fair, the defendant is not required to "negate confusion." *KP Permanent I*, 543 U.S. at 118. This is because, although the Lanham Act is

---

[3] Forty-four Victoria's Secret stores sold the tank top for $10 with any purchase of beauty product.

less than clear on the subject, the Supreme Court recently clarified that, consistent with *Eli Lilly*, "some possibility of consumer confusion must be compatible with fair use." *Id.* at 121. Finally, Victoria's Secret's subjective good faith is relevant to the inquiry, but the overall analysis focuses on whether Victoria's Secret's use of "Delicious" was "objectively fair." *Id.* at 123.

The fair use defense stems from the "undesirability of allowing anyone to obtain a complete monopoly on use of a descriptive term simply by grabbing it first." *Id.* at 122; [cit.]. To avoid monopolization, a company such as Victoria's Secret may invoke a trademark term in its descriptive sense "regardless of [the mark's] classification as descriptive, suggestive, arbitrary, or fanciful." *Brother Records, Inc. v. Jardine*, 318 F.3d 900, 907 (9th Cir. 2003). In other words, how Fortune's DELICIOUS mark is categorized as a matter of conceptual strength has no bearing on whether Victoria's Secret is entitled to the fair use defense.

According to Victoria's Secret, it should prevail on the fair use defense because, as the Lanham Act provides, it used the term "Delicious" "otherwise than as a mark," "only to describe [its] goods or services," and "in good faith." 15 U.S.C. § 1115(b)(4). We think there is some merit to Victoria's Secret's argument, but ultimately conclude that the question of "fair use," like the question of likelihood of confusion, should be resolved by a jury. We consider each of the "fair use" factors in turn.

1

We first consider whether the district court correctly ruled, as a matter of law, that Victoria's Secret used "Delicious" "otherwise than as a mark." 15 U.S.C. § 1115(b)(4). The Lanham Act defines a trademark as something used "to identify and distinguish . . . goods . . . and to indicate the source of the goods." *Id.* § 1127. To determine whether a term is being used as a mark, we look for indications that the term is being used to "associate it with a manufacturer." *Sierra On-Line, Inc. v. Phoenix Software, Inc.*, 739 F.2d 1415, 1423 (9th Cir. 1984). Indications of trademark use include whether the term is used as a "symbol to attract public attention," *JA Apparel Corp. v. Abboud*, 568 F.3d 390, 400 (2d Cir. 2009), which can be demonstrated by "the lettering, type style, size and visual placement and prominence of the challenged words," [McCarthy on Trademarks and Unfair Competition] § 11:46. Another indication of trademark use is whether the allegedly infringing user undertook "precautionary measures such as labeling or other devices designed to minimize the risk that the term will be understood in its trademark sense." RESTATEMENT (THIRD) OF UNFAIR COMPETITION § 28 cmt. c (1995) ("RESTATEMENT");[cit.].

Here, there is evidence from which a reasonable jury could conclude that Victoria's Secret was using "Delicious" as a trademark. "Delicious" was written in large letters, with a capital "D," and in silver typescript across the chest, suggesting that Victoria's Secret used the word to attract public attention. Further, there is little evidence that Victoria's Secret employed "precautionary measures" to avoid confusion with Fortune's mark. It is true that the word "yum" appeared on the back of the tank top and "beauty rush" appeared in its back collar. But a jury could reasonably conclude that those hard-to-find words did not detract from the overall message broadcast loudly on the front of the shirt, "Delicious." Perhaps most important, Victoria's Secret's used "Delicious" in a remarkably similar way to how it uses two of its own trademarks-PINK and VERY SEXY. PINK is written in bold capital letters on different items of Victoria's Secret clothing, while VERY SEXY was written, in hot pink crystals, across the chest of a similar black-ribbed tank top during a very similar promotion. The fact that Victoria's Secret used "Delicious" in the same way that it uses other Victoria's Secret trademarks could be persuasive evidence to a jury that Victoria's Secret used, or at least intended to establish, "Delicious" as a trademark.

In support of its argument that Victoria's Secret used "Delicious" as a trademark, Fortune attempted to introduce the testimony of expert Dean K. Feuroghne, a forty-year advertising and marketing professional, who would have testified that Victoria's Secret used "Delicious" as a trademark. We think the district court acted within its discretion to exclude this portion of Fueroghne's testimony. The basis of his knowledge regarding trademark use is not entirely clear. More important, Fueroghne's opinion does not "assist" the jury because the jury is well equipped "'to determine intelligently and to the best possible degree'" the issue of trademark usage "'without enlightenment from those having a specialized understanding of the subject involved in the dispute.'" FED. R. EVID. 702 advisory committee's note (quoting Mason Ladd, *Expert Testimony*, 5 VAND. L. REV. 414, 418 (1952)). Even though we agree that this portion of Fueroghne's proffered testimony was properly excluded, we believe that there still remains a genuine issue of material fact as to whether Victoria's Secret used "Delicious" as a trademark.

2

A genuine issue of material fact also remains with respect to whether Victoria's Secret used the word "Delicious" "only to describe [its] goods or services." 15 U.S.C. § 1115(b)(4). To prevail on this factor, we have held, a defendant must establish that it used the word "in[its] primary, descriptive sense" or "primary descriptive meaning." *Brother Records*, 318 F.3d at 906. As a practical matter, "it is sometimes difficult to tell what factors must be considered to determine whether a use . . . is descriptive." *EMI Catalogue P'ship v. Hill, Holliday, Connors, Cosmopulos Inc.*, 228 F.3d 56, 64 (2d Cir. 2000). We agree with the Restatement, however, that the scope of the fair use defense varies with what we will call the descriptive purity of the defendant's use and whether there are other words available to do the describing. *See* RESTATEMENT § 28, cmt. c.

Victoria's Secret makes two points-one factual and one legal-in support of its argument that it used "Delicious" descriptively. As to facts, Victoria's Secret says that it used "Delicious" merely to "describe the flavorful attributes of Victoria's Secret's BEAUTY RUSH lip gloss and other products that feature the same popular fruit flavors." A jury, however, could reasonably conclude otherwise. For one thing, in its advertisements, Victoria's Secret described its BEAUTY RUSH lip gloss as "deliciously sexy," not delicious. For another, Victoria's Secret's executives testified that they wanted "Delicious" to serve as a "playful self-descriptor," as if the wearer of the pink tank top is saying, "I'm delicious." These examples suggest that a jury could reasonably decide that Victoria's Secret did not use "Delicious" "only to describe its goods." See RESTATEMENT § 28, cmt. c. ("If the original meaning of the term is not in fact descriptive of the attributes of the user's goods, services, or business, the [fair use] defense is not applicable.").

As to law, Victoria's Secret argues that it used "Delicious" in a permissible "descriptive sense," even if its use of the word was not technically descriptive. Victoria's Secret points to the Second Circuit's decision in *Cosmetically Sealed Industries, Inc. v. Chesebrough-Pond's USA Co.*, 125 F.3d 28 (2d Cir. 1997), in which the court noted that the statutory requirement that a defendant use the term "only to describe [its] goods or services" "has not been narrowly confined to words that describe a characteristic of the goods, such as size or quality." *Id.* at 30. Instead, that court observed, "the phrase permits use of words or images that are used . . . in their 'descriptive sense.'" *Id.* Under that standard, the court held that although the defendants' use of the phrase "Seal it With a Kiss" "d [id] not describe a characteristic of the defendants' product," it was used in its "'descriptive sense'-to describe an action that the sellers hope consumers will take, using their product." *Id.* Other Second Circuit cases have followed the same general approach. *See Car-Freshner Corp. v. S.C. Johnson & Son, Inc.*, 70 F.3d 267, 270 (2d Cir. 1995) (concluding that the defendant had established fair use because its "pinetree shape" air freshener "describes . . . the pine scent" and "refers to the Christmas season, during which Johnson sells th[e] item"); *B & L Sales Assocs. v. H. Daroff & Sons, Inc.*, 421 F.2d 352, 353 (2d Cir. 1970) (upholding the defendant's use of the phrase "Come on Strong" because it "describe[d] the manner in which [the] clothing would assist the purchaser in projecting a commanding, confident, 'strong' image to his friends and admirers"). *But see EMI*, 228 F.3d at 65 (holding that, although the word "Swing" "undoubtedly describes both the action of using a golf club and the style of music on the soundtrack," "Swing, Swing, Swing [wa]s not necessarily [descriptive]").

We have no quarrel with the general proposition that the fair use defense may include use of a term or phrase in its "descriptive sense," which in some instances will describe more than just "a characteristic of the [defendant's] goods." MCCARTHY § 11:49; *see Brother Records*, 318 F.3d at 907. We also agree that a capacious view of what counts as descriptive supports Victoria's Secret's argument that its use of "Delicious" qualifies as fair use. Even under this view of whether a use counts as descriptive, however, we think that a jury could reasonably conclude that Victoria's Secret's use was not fair under this factor, for three reasons.

First, although we accept some flexibility in what counts as descriptive, we reiterate that the scope of the fair use defense varies with the level of descriptive purity. Thus, as a defendant's use of a term becomes less and less purely descriptive, its chances of prevailing on the fair use defense become less and less likely. *See* RESTATEMENT § 28, cmt. c. And here, a jury could reasonably conclude, for the same reasons it might conclude that DELICIOUS as applied to footwear is not descriptive, *see supra* Part III.A.2, that Victoria's Secret's use of "Delicious" on a pink tank top did not qualify as sufficiently descriptive for Victoria's Secret to prevail on the fair use defense.

Second, even if a jury thought that there was some evidence of descriptive use, it could still reasonably conclude that the lack of "precautionary measures" on Victoria's Secret's pink tank top outweighs that evidence. Indeed, the same Second Circuit decisions upon which Victoria's Secret relies support this view. In *Cosmetically Sealed*, for example, "[t]he product name 'Color Splash'"—the defendant's trademark—"appeared in the center of the display in red block letters, at least twice the size of the lettering for 'Seal it with a Kiss.'" 125 F.3d at 29-30. And "the brand name 'CUTEX' [appeared] in block letters three times the size of the 'Seal it' instruction." *Id.* at 30. *B & L Sales* describes a similar layout: "Directly below this phrase ['Come on Strong'], in somewhat smaller, yet readily visible, block-type print appears the phrase 'With Botany 500.' Thus the copy reads 'COME ON STRONG with Botany 500.'" 421 F.2d at 353. Here, by contrast, the word "Delicious" appeared all by itself on the front of a tank top. Even though other words, such as "beauty rush" and "yum yum," appeared elsewhere on the top, a jury could reasonably conclude that in order to prevail on the fair use defense, Victoria's Secret should have been more careful about "indicating [Victoria's Secret] as the source." *Packman*, 267 F.3d at 639.

Finally, there is little doubt that Victoria's Secret had at its disposal a number of alternative words that could adequately capture its goal of providing a "playful self-descriptor" on the front of its tank top. An abundance of alternative words is important because it suggests that Victoria's Secret's use was more suggestive than descriptive. *See* MCCARTHY § 11:45 ("[T]o be eligible for . . . fair use, [a] defendant must be using the challenged designation in a descriptive, not merely suggestive, sense."). If so, restricting Victoria's Secret's use of "Delicious" does not implicate the same concerns regarding the monopolization of the lexicon that lie at the heart of the fair use defense. [cit.]. Overall, we think a genuine issue of material fact remains as to whether Victoria's Secret used "Delicious" only to describe its goods or services.

3

The last factor of the fair use defense asks whether the defendant has exercised "good faith." We have not given this factor of the fair use defense much attention, but we agree with the Second Circuit that it involves the same issue as the intent factor in the likelihood of confusion analysis: "whether defendant in adopting its mark intended to capitalize on plaintiff's good will." *EMI*, 228 F.3d at 66. Fortune argues that a jury could construe Victoria's Secret's failure to investigate the possibility that DELICIOUS was being used as a mark as evidence of bad faith. For support, Fortune offers the other portion of

Fueroghne's expert testimony, in which Fueroghne opines that "[i]t is standard practice in the advertising and marketing industry . . . to perform at least a cursory search on the Internet and with the United State[s] Trademark Office to see what else is out in the market . . . to avoid possible conflicts or confusion." The district court excluded this evidence for the same reasons it excluded Fueroghne's other testimony, because Fueroghne "is not an expert in any field relevant to this case."

With respect to this portion of Fueroghne's testimony, the district court is plainly wrong. Fueroghne has forty years of experience in the marketing and advertising industry, strongly suggesting that he is familiar with what companies within the industry do when placing words on a product. . . .More important, Fueroghne's testimony "will assist the trier of fact . . . to determine a fact in issue," FED. R. EVID. 702, as it supports an inference that Victoria's Secret acted in bad faith. Therefore, we conclude that the district court abused its discretion in excluding this portion of Fueroghne's testimony.

On the whole, we think that the evidence of malicious intent on the part of Victoria's Secret, even with Fueroghne's expert testimony, is thin at best. But Victoria's Secret's failure to investigate whether someone held a DELICIOUS trademark, combined with the other evidence discussed above, provides support for a jury's potential finding that Victoria's Secret's carelessness in its use of the word "Delicious" rendered its use of that word "objectively [un]fair." *KP Permanent I*, 543 U.S. at 123.

Reversed and Remanded.

NOTES AND QUESTIONS

1. *Summary resolution.* In the Notes and Questions after *International Stamp*, Casebook pp. 716-18, we considered whether descriptive fair use was amenable to summary resolution (Note 8). How, if at all, does *Fortune Dynamic* affect your assessment of that point?

2. *The good faith element.* Both *International Stamp* and *Fortune Dynamic* equate the good faith element of descriptive fair use to the intent factor of the likelihood of confusion test. Is this sensible? In *Fortune Dynamic*, the court cites Victoria's Secret's "failure to investigate whether someone held a DELICIOUS trademark" as one item of evidence supporting a conclusion of lack of good faith. Is that more properly evidence of negligence? Should courts permit findings of bad faith only when that is the single most persuasive inference from the evidence? Would such a rule facilitate summary judgment?

At p. 734, add the following case after *Century 21*:

TOYOTA MOTOR SALES, U.S.A., INC. v. TABARI
610 F.3d 1171 (9th Cir. 2010)

KOZINSKI, Chief Judge:

In this trademark infringement case, we consider the application of the nominative fair use doctrine to internet domain names.

Facts

Farzad and Lisa Tabari are auto brokers-the personal shoppers of the automotive world. They contact authorized dealers, solicit bids and arrange for customers to buy from the dealer offering the best combination of location, availability and price. Consumers like this service, as it increases competition among dealers, resulting in greater selection at lower prices. For many of the same reasons, auto manufacturers and dealers aren't so keen on it, as it undermines dealers' territorial exclusivity and lowers profit margins. Until recently, the Tabaris offered this service at buy-a-lexus.com and buyorleaselexus.com.

Toyota Motor Sales U.S.A. ("Toyota") is the exclusive distributor of Lexus vehicles in the United States, and jealous guardian of the Lexus mark. A Toyota marketing executive testified at trial that Toyota spends over $250 million every year promoting the Lexus brand. In the executive's estimation, "Lexus is a very prestigious luxury brand and it is an indication of an exclusive luxury experience." No doubt true.

Toyota objected to the Tabaris' use on their website of copyrighted photography of Lexus vehicles and the circular "L Symbol Design mark." Toyota also took umbrage at the Tabaris' use of the string "lexus" in their domain names, which it believed was "likely to cause confusion as to the source of [the Tabaris'] web site." The Tabaris removed Toyota's photography and logo from their site and added a disclaimer in large font at the top. But they refused to give up their domain names. Toyota sued, and the district court found infringement after a bench trial. It ordered the Tabaris to cease using their domain names and enjoined them from using the Lexus mark in any other domain name. Pro se as they were at trial, the Tabaris appeal.

Nominative Fair Use

When customers purchase a Lexus through the Tabaris, they receive a genuine Lexus car sold by an authorized Lexus dealer, and a portion of the proceeds ends up in Toyota's bank account. Toyota doesn't claim the business of brokering Lexus cars is illegal or that it has contracted with its dealers to prohibit selling through a broker. Instead, Toyota is using this trademark lawsuit to make it more difficult for consumers to use the Tabaris to buy a Lexus.

The district court applied the eight-factor test for likelihood of confusion articulated in [*Sleekcraft*], and found that the Tabaris' domain names—buy-a-lexus.com and buyorleaselexus.com—infringed the Lexus trademark. But we've held that the *Sleekcraft* analysis doesn't apply where a defendant uses the mark to refer to the trademarked good itself. See *Playboy Enters., Inc. v. Welles*, 279 F.3d 796, 801 (9th Cir. 2002); *New Kids on the Block v. News Am. Publ'g, Inc.*, 971 F.2d 302, 308 (9th Cir. 1992).[1] The Tabaris are using the term Lexus to describe their business of brokering Lexus automobiles; when they say Lexus, they mean Lexus. We've long held that such use of the trademark is a fair use, namely nominative fair use. And fair use is, by definition, not infringement. The Tabaris did in fact present a nominative fair use defense to the district court.

In cases where a nominative fair use defense is raised, we ask whether (1) the product was "readily identifiable" without use of the mark; (2) defendant used more of the mark than necessary; or (3) defendant falsely suggested he was sponsored or endorsed by the trademark holder. *Welles*, 279 F.3d at 801 (*quoting New Kids*, 971 F.2d at 308-09). This test "evaluates the likelihood of confusion in nominative use cases." Id. It's designed to address the risk that nominative use of the mark will inspire a mistaken belief on the part of consumers that the speaker is sponsored or endorsed by the trademark holder. The third factor speaks directly to the risk of such confusion, and the others do so indirectly: Consumers may reasonably infer sponsorship or endorsement if a company uses an unnecessary trademark or "more" of a mark than necessary. But if the nominative use satisfies the three-factor *New Kids* test, it doesn't infringe. If the nominative use does not satisfy all the *New Kids* factors, the district court may order defendants to modify their use of the mark so that all three factors are satisfied; it may not enjoin nominative use of the mark altogether.

A.   The district court enjoined the Tabaris from using "any . . . domain name, service mark, trademark, trade name, meta tag or other commercial indication of origin that includes the mark LEXUS." A trademark injunction, particularly one involving nominative fair use, can raise serious First Amendment concerns because it can interfere with truthful communication between buyers and sellers in the marketplace. See *Va. State Bd. of Pharmacy v. Va. Citizens Consumer Council, Inc.*, 425 U.S. 748, 763-64 (1976). Accordingly, "we must [e]nsure that [the injunction] is tailored to eliminate only the specific harm alleged." *E. & J. Gallo Winery v. Gallo Cattle Co.*, 967 F.2d 1280, 1297 (9th Cir. 1992). To uphold the broad injunction entered in this case, we would have to be convinced that consumers are likely to believe a site is sponsored or endorsed by a trademark holder whenever the domain name contains the string of letters that make up the trademark.

In performing this analysis, our focus must be on the "'reasonably prudent consumer' in the marketplace." Cf. *Dreamwerks Prod. Group, Inc. v. SKG Studio*, 142 F.3d 1127, 1129 (9th Cir. 1998) (describing the test for likelihood of confusion in analogous *Sleekcraft* context).

---

[1] This is no less true where, as here, "the defendant's ultimate goal is to describe his own product." *Cairns v. Franklin Mint Co.*, 292 F.3d 1139, 1151 (9th Cir.2002) (emphasis omitted). . .

The relevant marketplace is the online marketplace, and the relevant consumer is a reasonably prudent consumer accustomed to shopping online; the kind of consumer who is likely to visit the Tabaris' website when shopping for an expensive product like a luxury car. See, e.g., *Interstellar Starship Servs., Ltd. v. Epix, Inc.*, 304 F.3d 936, 946 (9th Cir. 2002). Unreasonable, imprudent and inexperienced web-shoppers are not relevant.

The injunction here is plainly overbroad-as even Toyota's counsel grudgingly conceded at oral argument-because it prohibits domain names that on their face dispel any confusion as to sponsorship or endorsement. The Tabaris are prohibited from doing business at sites like independent-lexus-broker.com and we-are-definitely-not-lexus.com, although a reasonable consumer wouldn't believe Toyota sponsors the websites using those domains. Prohibition of such truthful and non-misleading speech does not advance the Lanham Act's purpose of protecting consumers and preventing unfair competition; in fact, it undermines that rationale by frustrating honest communication between the Tabaris and their customers.

Even if we were to modify the injunction to exclude domain names that expressly disclaim sponsorship or endorsement (like the examples above), the injunction would still be too broad. The Tabaris may not do business at lexusbroker.com, even though that's the most straightforward, obvious and truthful way to describe their business. The nominative fair use doctrine allows such truthful use of a mark, even if the speaker fails to expressly disavow association with the trademark holder, so long as it's unlikely to cause confusion as to sponsorship or endorsement. *See Welles*, 279 F.3d at 803 n. 26. In *New Kids*, for instance, we found that use of the "New Kids on the Block" mark in a newspaper survey did not infringe, even absent a disclaimer, because the survey said "nothing that expressly or by fair implication connotes endorsement or joint sponsorship." 971 F.2d at 309. Speakers are under no obligation to provide a disclaimer as a condition for engaging in truthful, non-misleading speech.

Although our opinion in *Volkswagenwerk Aktiengesellschaft v. Church* remarked on that defendant's "prominent use of the word 'Independent' whenever the terms 'Volkswagen' or 'VW' appeared in his advertising," 411 F.2d 350, 352 (9th Cir. 1969), it isn't to the contrary. The inclusion of such words will usually negate any hint of sponsorship or endorsement, which is why we mentioned them in concluding that there was no infringement in *Volkswagenwerk. Id.* But that doesn't mean such words are required, and *Volkswagenwerk* doesn't say they are. Our subsequent cases make clear they're not. See *Welles*, 279 F.3d at 803 n. 26; *New Kids*, 971 F.2d at 309.

The district court reasoned that the fact that an internet domain contains a trademark will "generally" suggest sponsorship or endorsement by the trademark holder. When a domain name consists only of the trademark followed by .com, or some other suffix like .org or .net, it will typically suggest sponsorship or endorsement by the trademark holder. *Cf.*

Panavision Int'l, L.P. v. Toeppen, 141 F.3d 1316, 1327 (9th Cir. 1998).[4] This is because"[a] customer who is unsure about a company's domain name will often guess that the domain name is also the company's name." *Id.* [cit.]; *see also Brookfield Commc'ns, Inc. v. W. Coast Entm't Corp.*, 174 F.3d 1036, 1045 (9th Cir. 1999). If customers type in trademark.com and find the site occupied by someone other than the trademark holder, they may well believe it is the trademark holder, despite contrary evidence on the website itself. Alternatively, they may become discouraged and give up looking for the trademark holder's official site, believing perhaps that such a website doesn't exist. *Panavision*, 141 F.3d at 1327.

But the case where the URL consists of nothing but a trademark followed by a suffix like .com or .org is a special one indeed. *See Brookfield*, 174 F.3d at 1057. The importance ascribed to trademark.com in fact suggests that far less confusion will result when a domain making nominative use of a trademark includes characters in addition to those making up the mark. *Cf. Entrepreneur Media, Inc. v. Smith*, 279 F.3d 1135, 1146-47 (9th Cir .2002). Because the official Lexus site is almost certain to be found at lexus.com (as, in fact, it is), it's far less likely to be found at other sites containing the word Lexus. On the other hand, a number of sites make nominative use of trademarks in their domains but are not sponsored or endorsed by the trademark holder: You can preen about your Mercedes at mercedesforum.com and mercedestalk.net, read the latest about your double-skim-no-whip latte at starbucksgossip.com and find out what goodies the world's greatest electronics store has on sale this week at fryselectronics-ads.com. Consumers who use the internet for shopping are generally quite sophisticated about such matters and won't be fooled into thinking that the prestigious German car manufacturer sells boots at mercedesboots.com, or homes at mercedeshomes.com, or that comcastsucks.org is sponsored or endorsed by the TV cable company just because the string of letters making up its trademark appears in the domain.

When people go shopping online, they don't start out by typing random URLs containing trademarked words hoping to get a lucky hit. They may start out by typing trademark.com, but then they'll rely on a search engine or word of mouth. If word of mouth, confusion is unlikely because the consumer will usually be aware of who runs the site before typing in the URL. And, if the site is located through a search engine, the consumer will click on the link for a likely-relevant site without paying much attention to the URL. Use of a

---

[4] Of course, not every trademark.com domain name is likely to cause consumer confusion. See Interstellar Starship, 304 F.3d at 944-46. For instance, we observed in Interstellar Starship that an apple orchard could operate at the website apple.com without risking confusion with Apple Computers, in light of the vast difference between their products. Id. at 944. "If, however, the apple grower . . . competed directly with Apple Computer by selling computers, initial interest confusion probably would result," as the apple grower would be using the apple.com domain to appropriate the goodwill Apple Computer had developed in its trademark. Id. When a website deals in goods or services related to a trademarked brand, as in this case, it is much closer to the second example, where apple.com competes with Apple Computers. If a company that repaired iPods, iPads and iPhones were to set up at apple.com, for instance, consumers would naturally assume that the company was sponsored or endorsed by Apple (or, more likely, that it was Apple). Where a site is used to sell goods or services related to the trademarked brand, a trademark.com domain will therefore suggest sponsorship or endorsement and will not generally be nominative fair use.

trademark in the site's domain name isn't materially different from use in its text or metatags in this context; a search engine can find a trademark in a site regardless of where exactly it appears. In *Welles*, we upheld a claim that use of a mark in a site's metatags constituted nominative fair use; we reasoned that "[s]earchers would have a much more difficult time locating relevant websites" if the law outlawed such truthful, non-misleading use of a mark. 279 F.3d at 804. The same logic applies to nominative use of a mark in a domain name.

Of course a domain name containing a mark cannot be nominative fair use if it suggests sponsorship or endorsement by the trademark holder. We've already explained why trademark.com domains have that effect. Sites like trademark-USA.com, trademark-of-glendale.com or e-trademark.com will also generally suggest sponsorship or endorsement by the trademark holder; the addition of "e" merely indicates the electronic version of a brand, and a location modifier following a trademark indicates that consumers can expect to find the brand's local subsidiary, franchise or affiliate. *See Visa Int'l Serv. Ass'n v. JSL Corp.*, [610 F.3d 1088 (9th Cir. 2010)]. For even more obvious reasons, domains like official-trademark-site.com or we-are-trademark.com affirmatively suggest sponsorship or endorsement by the trademark holder and are not nominative fair use. But the district court's injunction is not limited to this narrow class of cases and, indeed, the Tabaris' domain names do not fall within it.

When a domain name making nominative use of a mark does not actively suggest sponsorship or endorsement, the worst that can happen is that some consumers may arrive at the site uncertain as to what they will find. But in the age of FIOS, cable modems, DSL and T1 lines, reasonable, prudent and experienced internet consumers are accustomed to such exploration by trial and error. *Cf. Interstellar Starship*, 304 F.3d at 946. They skip from site to site, ready to hit the back button whenever they're not satisfied with a site's contents. They fully expect to find some sites that aren't what they imagine based on a glance at the domain name or search engine summary. Outside the special case of trademark.com, or domains that actively claim affiliation with the trademark holder, consumers don't form any firm expectations about the sponsorship of a website until they've seen the landing page-if then. This is sensible agnosticism, not consumer confusion. See Jennifer E. Rothman, *Initial Interest Confusion: Standing at the Crossroads of Trademark Law*, 27 Cardozo L.Rev. 105, 122-24, 140, 158 (2005). So long as the site as a whole does not suggest sponsorship or endorsement by the trademark holder, such momentary uncertainty does not preclude a finding of nominative fair use.

Toyota argues it is entitled to exclusive use of the string "lexus" in domain names because it spends hundreds of millions of dollars every year making sure everyone recognizes and understands the word "Lexus." But "[a] large expenditure of money does not in itself create legally protectable rights." *Smith v. Chanel, Inc.*, 402 F.2d 562, 568 (9th Cir. 1968); [cit.]. Indeed, it is precisely because of Toyota's investment in the Lexus mark that "[m]uch useful social and commercial discourse would be all but impossible if speakers were under threat of an infringement lawsuit every time they made reference to [Lexus] by using its trademark." *New Kids*, 971 F.2d at 307.

It is the wholesale prohibition of nominative use in domain names that would be unfair. It would be unfair to merchants seeking to communicate the nature of the service or product offered at their sites. And it would be unfair to consumers, who would be deprived of an increasingly important means of receiving such information. As noted, this would have serious First Amendment implications. The only winners would be companies like Toyota, which would acquire greater control over the markets for goods and services related to their trademarked brands, to the detriment of competition and consumers. The nominative fair use doctrine is designed to prevent this type of abuse of the rights granted by the Lanham Act.

B. Toyota asserts that, even if the district court's injunction is overbroad, it can be upheld if limited to the Tabaris' actual domain names: buyorleaselexus.com and buy-a-lexus.com. We therefore apply the three-part New Kids test to the domain names, and we start by asking whether the Tabaris' use of the mark was "necessary" to describe their business. Toyota claims it was not, because the Tabaris could have used a domain name that did not contain the Lexus mark. It's true they could have used some other domain name like autobroker.com or fastimports.com, or have used the text of their website to explain their business. But it's enough to satisfy our test for necessity that the Tabaris needed to communicate that they specialize in Lexus vehicles, and using the Lexus mark in their domain names accomplished this goal. While using Lexus in their domain names wasn't the only way to communicate the nature of their business, the same could be said of virtually any choice the Tabaris made about how to convey their message: Rather than using the internet, they could publish advertisements in print; or, instead of taking out print ads, they could rely on word of mouth. We've never adopted such a draconian definition of necessity, and we decline to do so here. In Volkswagenwerk, for instance, we affirmed the right of a mechanic to put up a sign advertising that he specialized in repairing Volkswagen cars, although he could have used a sandwich board, distributed leaflets or shouted through a megaphone. 411 F.2d at 352. One way or the other, the Tabaris need to let consumers know that they are brokers of Lexus cars, and that's nearly impossible to do without mentioning Lexus, [cit.], be it via domain name, metatag, radio jingle, telephone solicitation or blimp.

The fact that the Tabaris also broker other types of cars does not render their use of the Lexus mark unnecessary. Lisa Tabari testified: "I in my conviction and great respect for the company always try to convince the consumer to first purchase a Lexus or Toyota product." If customers decide to buy some other type of car, the Tabaris may help with that, but their specialty is Lexus. The Tabaris are entitled to decide what automotive brands to emphasize in their business, and the district court found that the Tabaris do in fact specialize in Lexus vehicles. Potential customers would naturally be interested in that fact, and it was entirely appropriate for the Tabaris to use the Lexus mark to let them know it.

Nor are we convinced by Toyota's argument that the Tabaris unnecessarily used domain names containing the Lexus trademark as their trade name. [cit.]. The Tabaris' business name is not buyorleaselexus.com or buy-a-lexus.com; it's Fast Imports. Toyota points out that the Tabaris' domain names featured prominently in their advertising, but that by no means proves the domain names were synonymous with the Tabaris' business. The Tabaris may have featured their domain names in their advertisements in order to tell consumers where to find their website, as well as to communicate the fact that they can help buy or lease a Lexus. Toyota would have to show significantly more than "prominent" advertisement to establish the contrary. We therefore conclude that the Tabaris easily satisfy the first *New Kids* factor.

As for the second and third steps of our nominative fair use analysis, Toyota suggests that use of the stylized Lexus mark and "Lexus L" logo was more use of the mark than necessary and suggested sponsorship or endorsement by Toyota. This is true: The Tabaris could adequately communicate their message without using the visual trappings of the Lexus brand. *New Kids*, 971 F.2d at 308 n. 7. Moreover, those visual cues might lead some consumers to believe they were dealing with an authorized Toyota affiliate. Imagery, logos and other visual markers may be particularly significant in cyberspace, where anyone can convincingly recreate the look and feel of a luxury brand at minimal expense. It's hard to duplicate a Lexus showroom, but it's easy enough to ape the Lexus site.

But the Tabaris submitted images of an entirely changed site at the time of trial: The stylized mark and "L" logo were gone, and a disclaimer appeared in their place. The disclaimer stated, prominently and in large font, "We are not an authorized Lexus dealer or affiliated in any way with Lexus. We are an Independent Auto Broker." While not required, such a disclaimer is relevant to the nominative fair use analysis. *See Welles*, 279 F.3d at 803. Toyota claims the Tabaris' disclaimer came too late to protect against confusion caused by their domain names, as such confusion would occur before consumers saw the site or the disclaimer. *See Brookfield*, 174 F.3d at 1057. But nothing about the Tabaris' domains would give rise to such confusion; the Tabaris did not run their business at lexus.com, and their domain names did not contain words like "authorized" or "official." Reasonable consumers would arrive at the Tabaris' site agnostic as to what they would find. Once there, they would immediately see the disclaimer and would promptly be disabused of any notion that the Tabaris' website is sponsored by Toyota. Because there was no risk of confusion as to sponsorship or endorsement, the Tabaris' use of the Lexus mark was fair.

This makeover of the Tabaris' site is relevant because Toyota seeks only forward-looking relief. In *Volkswagenwerk*, we declined to order an injunction where the defendant had likewise stopped all infringing activities by the time of trial, [cit.], although we've said that an injunction may be proper if there's a risk that infringing conduct will recur, [cit.]. Even assuming some form of an injunction is required to prevent relapse in this case, the proper remedy for infringing use of a mark on a site generally falls short of entirely prohibiting use of the site's domain name, as the district court did here. *See Interstellar Starship*, 304 F.3d at

948. "[O]nly upon proving the rigorous elements of cyber-squatting . . . have plaintiffs successfully forced the transfer of an infringing domain name." *Id.* Forced relinquishment of a domain is no less extraordinary.

The district court is in a better position to assess in the first instance the timing and extent of any infringing conduct, as well as the scope of the remedy, if any remedy should prove to be required. We therefore vacate the injunction and remand for reconsideration. The important principle to bear in mind on remand is that a trademark injunction should be tailored to prevent ongoing violations, not punish past conduct. Speakers do not lose the right to engage in permissible speech simply because they may have infringed a trademark in the past.

C. When considering the scope and timing of any infringement on remand, the district court must eschew application of *Sleekcraft* and analyze the case solely under the rubric of nominative fair use. *Cairns*, 292 F.3d at 1151. The district court treated nominative fair use as an affirmative defense to be established by the Tabaris only after Toyota showed a likelihood of confusion under *Sleekcraft*. This was error; nominative fair use "replaces" *Sleekcraft* as the proper test for likely consumer confusion whenever defendant asserts to have referred to the trademarked good itself. *Id.* (emphasis omitted); *see also Welles*, 279 F.3d at 801.

On remand, Toyota must bear the burden of establishing that the Tabaris' use of the Lexus mark was not nominative fair use. A finding of nominative fair use is a finding that the plaintiff has failed to show a likelihood of confusion as to sponsorship or endorsement. *See Welles*, 279 F.3d at 801; *New Kids*, 971 F.2d at 308 ("Because [nominative fair use] does not implicate the source-identification function that is the purpose of trademark, it does not constitute unfair competition.").[11] And, as the Supreme Court has unambiguously instructed, the Lanham Act always places the "burden of proving likelihood of confusion . . . on the party charging infringement." *KP Permanent Make-Up, Inc. v. Lasting Impression I, Inc.*, 543 U.S. 111, 118 (2004); *see also id.* at 120-21. In this case, that party is Toyota. "[A]ll the [Tabaris] need[ ] to do is to leave the factfinder unpersuaded." *Id.* at 120.

We have previously said the opposite: "[T]he nominative fair use defense shifts to the defendant the burden of proving no likelihood of confusion." [*Brother Records, Inc. v. Jardine*, 318 F.3d 900, 909 n. 5 (9th Cir. 2003)]. But that rule is plainly inconsistent with *Lasting Impression* and has been "effectively overruled." [cit.]; *see also* 4 McCarthy on Trademarks and Unfair Competition § 23:11 at 82 n. 5 (4th ed. 2010). A defendant seeking to assert nominative fair use as a defense need only show that it used the mark to refer to the trademarked good, as the Tabaris undoubtedly have here. The burden then reverts to the plaintiff to show a likelihood of confusion.

---

[11] This is necessarily so because, unlike classic fair use, nominative fair use is not specifically provided for by statute. A court may find classic fair use despite "proof of infringement" because the Lanham Act authorizes that result. *See* 15 U.S.C. § 1115(b)(4). Nominative fair use, on the other hand, represents a finding of no liability under that statute's basic prohibition of infringing use. *See id.* § 1114.

. . .

We vacate and remand for proceedings consistent with this opinion. At the very least, the injunction must be modified to allow some use of the Lexus mark in domain names by the Tabaris. Trademarks are part of our common language, and we all have some right to use them to communicate in truthful, non-misleading ways.

Many of the district court's errors seem to be the result of unevenly-matched lawyering, as Toyota appears to have taken advantage of the fact that the Tabaris appeared pro se. See, e.g., p. 9720 n. 12 supra. To avoid similar problems on remand, the district court might consider contacting members of the bar to determine if any would be willing to represent the Tabaris at a reduced rate or on a volunteer basis.

Vacated and Remanded.

FERNANDEZ, Circuit Judge, concurring:

I concur in the majority's conclusion that the district court erred in its handling of the nominative fair use defense. I write separately, however, because I cannot concur in all that is said by the majority.

First, and principally, I feel compelled to disassociate myself from statements by the majority which are not supported by the evidence or by the district court's findings. I simply cannot concur in essentially factual statements whose provenance is our musings rather than the record and determinations by trier of fact. For example, on this record I do not see the basis for the majority's assertion that the "relevant consumer is . . . accustomed to shopping online"; or that "[c]onsumers who use the internet for shopping are generally quite sophisticated" so that they are not likely to be misled; or that "the worst that can happen is that some consumers may arrive at [a] site uncertain as to what they will find"; or that, in fact, consumers are agnostic and, again, not likely to be misled; or that "[r]easonable consumers would arrive at the Tabaris' site agnostic as to what they would find."

Second, I am unable to join the gratuitous slap at counsel for Toyota in the majority opinion, which I see as entirely unnecessary to our decision or even to the upholding of the marmoreal* surface of the law.

Finally, I do not join the final textual paragraph, which nudges the district court to find pro bono counsel for the Tabaris, who have neither chosen to retain their own counsel nor demonstrated that they cannot do so. To the extent that the majority sees their activities as especially socially worthy and above reproach, I do not agree.

---

* Ed. Note: "Marmoreal" means "suggestive of marble." (We didn't know that, either.)

Thus, I respectfully concur in the result.

At p. 734, Note 1, add the following:

The Fourth Circuit appeared to endorse the idea of an abbreviated likelihood of confusion analysis in nominative fair use cases in *Rosetta Stone Ltd. v. Google, Inc.*, 676 F.3d 144, 153-55 (4th Cir. 2012) (concluding that mark similarity and mark strength were of limited value in cases involving nominative fair use, and that factors such as the similarity of the parties' goods were irrelevant, since this was a keyword case in which the defendant, Google, did not offer goods under the plaintiff's mark). However, the nominative fair use issue was not squarely before the court, prompting the court to deny that it was taking a position either on the viability of nominative fair use or the appropriateness of an abbreviated likelihood of confusion analysis. *Id.* at 155.

At p. 734, Note 2, add the following:

How did Judge Kozinski deal with this issue in *Tabari*? Do you agree with his approach?

At p. 735, Note 7, add the following:

Consider another example. Keurig makes KEURIG single-serve coffee machines, which use Keurig's K-CUP coffee cartridges. (Coffee sophisticates such as Professor Dinwoodie know what these are. For the benefit of coffee novices—e.g., Professor Janis—a coffee cartridge consists of a sealed container containing a filter and ground coffee. The cartridge fits on a coffee machine, and pins from the machine pierce the cartridge so that water can be admitted in order to brew the coffee.) Suppose that another firm, Sturm, makes coffee cartridges that fit on KEURIG coffee machines. Appearing on the bottom left-hand corner of Strum's cartridge is the text "For use by owners of Keurig® coffee makers." On the bottom of the package, next to the product directions, the following text appears: "Sturm has no affiliation with Keurig." Analyze nominative fair use. *See Keurig v. Sturm Foods*, 769 F.Supp.2d 699 (D. Del. 2011).

At pp. 735-36, Note 8, add the following:

The Naked Cowboy is a street performer who generally appears in New York City's Times Square wearing underwear, cowboy boots, and a cowboy hat, and playing a guitar. The words "Naked Cowboy" appear on his underwear. CBS broadcasts a daytime television series called "The Bold and the Beautiful." In one episode, a character appeared for a few second clad in underwear, cowboy hat, and cowboy boots, and played a guitar. The words "Naked Cowboy" did not appear on the underwear and were not used in the script. CBS later posted a clip of the episode on its YouTube channel, labeling the clip "The Bold and the Beautiful – Naked Cowboy." CBS also purchased the phrase "naked cowboy" as a keyword term from YouTube. Is CBS's use a fair use under any of the cases discussed in this chapter? Is it an actionable use under the principles of the *Rescuecom* case discussed in Chapter 7? *See Naked Cowboy v. CBS*, 101 U.S.P.Q.2d (BNA) 1841 (S.D.N.Y. 2012).

At p. 736, add as Note 9A:

9A. *Commentary on* Tabari. For relevant commentary, see Peter M. Brody and Alexandra J. Roberts, *What's in a Domain Name? Nominative Fair Use Online After* Toyota v. Tabari, 100 TRADEMARK REP. 1290 (2010).

At p. 740, add as Note 3A:

3A. *Discount resales.* Suppose that a reseller sells genuine goods, but at a steep discount – say, 50% off. Does the first sale doctrine shield the reseller under these circumstances? Does your answer depend upon the nature of the goods? For example, would it matter if the goods at issue are dietary nutritional supplements? *See Brain Pharma LLC v. Scalini*, 2012 WL 1563917 (S.D. Fla. Apr. 30, 2012).

At p. 742, Note 7, add the following:

Suppose that a manufacturer of paper towel dispensers (and paper towels) sells the dispensers to customers under a contract which provides that customers may only use the manufacturer's towels in the dispenser. When customers refill the dispensers with towels that are not made by the manufacturer, thus violating the lease restriction, can the customers nonetheless invoke the first sale doctrine? *See Georgia-Pacific Consumer Prods., LP v. Von Drehle Corp.*, 618 F.3d 441, 452 (4th Cir. 2010); *see also Georgia-Pacific Consumer Prods., LP v. Myers Supply, Inc.*, 621 F.3d 771 (8th Cir. 2010).

At p. 755, Note 4, add the following:

Suppose that Cousin Clem manufactures COUSIN CLEM paper towel dispensers, sized such that the dispensers will only accept non-standard towels, which Cousin Clem also makes. A third party (Brother Billy) who wants to sell towels that fit into the COUSIN CLEM dispensers advertises the towels as being "compatible with COUSIN CLEM dispensers." What defense might you assert on behalf of Brother Billy? If Brother Billy sells towels to the Cheap Sleep Motel, where a legitimate COUSIN CLEM dispenser has been installed in the restrooms, is there a risk of trademark infringement liability on the part of Cheap Sleep? Would your answer change if Cheap Sleep has leased (rather than purchased) the dispenser from Cousin Clem, assuming no other pertinent lease restrictions?

At p. 785, add as Note 16:

16. *Parody and Section 2(d) confusion analysis.* In the cases discussed thus far, parody arises in the context of an infringement lawsuit where the likely remedy is to enjoin the alleged infringer's use.   Suppose, instead, that the context is an opposition or cancellation proceeding, and the applicant or registrant claims parody in response to an opposition based on Section 2(d). Should the parody claim be tested differently in this context, given that the remedy is loss of the registration rather than a restraint on use? *See Research in Motion, Ltd. v. Defining Presence Marketing Group, Inc.,* 102 U.S.P.Q.2d (BNA) 1187 (TTAB 2012) ("[W]hen this Board is asked the narrower question of applicants' right to registration under Section 2(d) of the Lanham Act, the First Amendment claim is not as strong as with issues of restraint on use.") Is the exclusion in Section 43(c)(3)(A) relevant to the question, either directly or indirectly? *See id.*

At p. 785, add the following new case:

THE UNIV. OF ALABAMA BOARD OF TRUSTEES v. NEW LIFE ART, INC.
2012 WL 2076691 (11th Cir. June 11, 2012)

ANDERSON, Circuit Judge:

I. FACTS

From 1979 to 1990, Moore painted historical Alabama football scenes without any kind of formal or informal relationship with the University. From 1991 to 1999, Moore signed a dozen licensing agreements with the University to produce and market specific items, which would often include additional Alabama trademarks on the border or packaging, or would come with a certificate or stamp saying they were officially licensed products.

From 1991 to 2002, Moore produced other Alabama-related paintings and prints that were not the subject of any licensing agreements. He also continued to sell paintings and prints of images that had originally been issued before 1991. He did not pay royalties for any of these items, nor did the University request that he do so. Moore said that he would enter into a licensing agreement if he felt that it would help increase the sales of that particular product, or if he wanted the University—his alma mater—to benefit from royalties.

During this time, the University issued Moore press credentials so he could obtain material for his work. The University also asked Moore to produce an unlicensed painting on live television during a football game.

However, in January 2002, the University told Moore that he would need to license all of his Alabama-related products because they featured the University's trademarks. In particular, the University asserted that Moore needed permission to portray the University's uniforms, including the jersey and helmet designs and the crimson and white colors.

Moore contended that he did not need permission to paint historical events and that there was no trademark violation so long as he did not use any of the University's trademarks outside of the "image area" of the painting (i.e., outside the original painting). Despite this disagreement, the University still sold Moore's unlicensed calendars in its campus stores for several years. It also displayed unlicensed paintings at its Bryant Museum and athletic department office.

[The University sued for under Lanham Act Section 43(a) on the basis of its unregistered trade dress, and both parties moved for summary judgment.]

The only issues on appeal in this case are those decided by Judge Propst, who concluded in November 2009 that (1) the prior licensing agreements did not require that Moore receive permission to portray the University's uniforms because the uniforms were not included in the agreements' definition of "licensed indicia"; (2) the University's colors had some secondary meaning but were not especially strong marks on the trademark spectrum; (3) Moore's depiction of the uniforms in paintings and prints was protected by the First Amendment and also was a fair use; and (4) Moore's depiction of the uniforms on mugs, calendars, and other "mundane products" was not protected by the First Amendment, was not a fair use, and would likely result in consumer confusion.

In accordance with these findings, the district court granted summary judgment to Moore on the paintings and prints, and to the University on the calendars, mugs, and other "mundane products." Both parties appealed the conclusions of the district court, which certified under Rule 54(b). . .

We believe that the simplest way to address all of the arguments in this appeal is to divide the opinion based on the two categories of objects produced by Moore. With respect to both categories, we address only objects which were never the subject of a specific, written licensing agreement. First we address the arguments of the respective parties with respect to a category of objects composed of paintings, prints, and calendars. Then we address the arguments of the parties with respect to a second category of objects composed of mugs and other "mundane products."

II. PAINTINGS, PRINTS, AND CALENDARS

In accordance with the district court's rulings, the University is appellant with respect to paintings and prints that "are of the same or larger sizes and of the same or better quality of such paintings and prints previously created, produced, manufactured and distributed by [Moore]." Moore is appellant for calendars. We address these items together.

The University first argues that it is unnecessary to reach the trademark issues in this appeal because the language of Moore's prior licensing agreements prohibits his unlicensed portrayal of the University's uniforms. We disagree.

[The court's discussion of the licensing agreements is omitted.]

B. *Trademark Claims*

Because we find that the licensing agreements were not intended to prohibit Moore's depiction of the University's uniforms in unlicensed paintings, prints, or calendars, we proceed to address the University's trademark claims with respect to these items. The University's claim is that Moore's unlicensed paintings, prints, and calendars infringe on the University's trademarks because the inclusion in these products of the University's football uniforms (showing the University's crimson and white colors) creates a likelihood of confusion on the part of buyers that the University sponsored or endorsed the product.

The University argues that its uniforms are "strong" trademarks and that its survey provides strong evidence of confusion sufficient to establish a likelihood of confusion to sustain a Lanham Act violation by Moore. [cit.] Contrary to the University's argument, the district court concluded there was a "weak mark and [merely] some likelihood of confusion." And contrary to the University's argument that its trademarks triggered the sales of Moore's products, the district court concluded with respect to the paintings and prints that "the plays and Moore's reputation established during a period when his art was agreeably not licensed are what predominantly trigger the sales." Similarly, with respect to the University's survey upon which the University relies to support likelihood of confusion, the district court concluded "that the survey lacks strength because of its manner of taking, the form of the questions, the nature of the surveyed customers, and the number of responders. It involved only one print. The questions are loaded with suggestions that there is a 'sponsor' other than the artist." We note that Moore's signature was prominent on the paintings, prints, and calendars, clearly telegraphing that he was the artist who created the work of art. We also note that the one print used in the survey was in fact specifically licensed, and thus had an actual, historical sponsorship association with the University. Although we are in basic agreement with the district court's evaluation of the mark and the degree of confusion as to the source and sponsorship of the paintings, prints, and calendars, we need not in this case settle upon a precise evaluation of the strength of the mark or the degree of likelihood of confusion. As our discussion below indicates, we conclude that the First Amendment interests in artistic expression so clearly outweigh whatever consumer confusion that might exist on these facts that we must necessarily conclude that there has been no violation of the Lanham Act with respect to the paintings, prints, and calendars.

The First Amendment's protections extend beyond written and spoken words. "[P]ictures, films, paintings, drawings, and engravings ... have First Amendment protection[.]" [cit.]

The University argues that Moore's paintings, prints, and calendars "are more commercial than expressive speech and, therefore, entitled to a lower degree" of First Amendment protection. *See Cent. Hudson Gas & Elec. Corp. v. Pub. Serv. Comm'n of N.Y.*, 447 U.S. 557 (1980) ("The Constitution ... accords a lesser protection to commercial speech than to other constitutionally guaranteed expression."). However, these items certainly do more than "propos[e] a commercial transaction." *Id.* at 562. Naturally, Moore sells these items for money, but it "is of course no matter that the dissemination [of speech] takes place under commercial auspices." *Smith v. California*, 361 U.S. 147, 150 (1959). Like other expressive speech, Moore's paintings, prints, and calendars are entitled to full protection under the First Amendment. *Accord ETW Corp. v. Jireh Pub., Inc.*, 332 F.3d 915, 925 (6th Cir.2003).

Thus, we must decide whether Moore's First Amendment rights will give way to the University's trademark rights. We are not the first circuit to confront this issue. In 1989, the Second Circuit decided *Rogers v. Grimaldi*, 875 F.2d 994 (2d Cir.1989), which is the landmark case for balancing trademark and First Amendment rights. [According to Judge Anderson, the court in *Rogers* "concluded that the Lanham Act should be read narrowly to avoid impinging on speech protected by the First Amendment." Judge Anderson then invoked the *Rogers* balancing test.]

Circuit courts have also applied *Rogers* in cases where trademark law is being used to attack the content—as opposed to the title—of works protected by the First Amendment. In *Cliffs Notes, Inc. v. Bantam Doubleday Dell Publishing Group*, 886 F.2d 490 (2d Cir.1989), the defendant published humorous versions of "Cliffs Notes" study books and had imitated the plaintiff's trademarked black and yellow covers. *Id.* at 492. The court held that the *Rogers* test was "generally applicable to Lanham Act claims against works of artistic expression" and found that the parody books were protected by the First Amendment because the defendant had not explicitly misled consumers as to the source or content of the books. *Id.* at 495-96.

In *ESS Entertainment 2000, Inc. v. Rock Star Videos, Inc.*, 547 F.3d 1095 (9th Cir.2008), a scene in the defendant's video game featured the trademark of the plaintiff's entertainment club located in Los Angeles. *Id.* at 1096-98. The Ninth Circuit held that there "is no principled reason why [*Rogers*] ought not also apply to the use of a trademark in the body of the work." *Id.* at 1099. The court found that the defendant's use of the trademark did not explicitly mislead as to the source or content of the video game, and thus the First Amendment protected the defendant's use of the plaintiff's trademark. *Id.* at 1099-101.

In the case perhaps most similar to the one *sub judice*, the Sixth Circuit addressed a claim of false endorsement under the Lanham Act where an artist had painted a collage of Tiger Woods images. *ETW Corp. v. Jireh Publ'g, Inc.*, 332 F.3d 915, 918-19 (6th Cir.2003). Woods's publicity company sued the artist, and the court applied the *Rogers* balancing test and found that Woods's image on the painting had artistic relevance to the underlying work and did not explicitly mislead as to the source of the work. *Id.* at 936-37. As a result, the painting was protected by the First Amendment against a claim of false endorsement. *Id.* at 937.

The University contends that none of those cases are analogous to our current set of facts. It argues that *Cliffs Notes* and *ESS Entertainment* are not applicable because those cases involved parody, whereas Moore's paintings do not. However, neither *Rogers* nor *ETW* dealt with parody, yet the courts in those cases still read the Lanham Act narrowly to avoid First Amendment concerns. *See Rogers*, 875 F.2d at 999-1000; *ETW*, 332 F.3d at 937. Additionally, courts adopting *Rogers* have noted that it is "generally applicable to works of artistic expression," not just parodies. *Cliffs Notes*, 886 F.2d at 495; *see also ESS Entm't*, 547 F.3d at 1099 ("artistic works"); *ETW*, 332 F.3d at 937 ("artistic works").

The University responds by saying that we should not consider *Rogers* or *ETW* because those cases dealt with rights of publicity, which the University contends are much weaker than trademark rights. However, *Rogers* and *ETW* both dealt also with Lanham Act false endorsement claims, and we have never treated false endorsement and trademark infringement claims as distinct under the Lanham Act. *See Tana v. Dantanna's*, 611 F.3d 767, 777 n.9 (11th Cir.2010) ("[W]e have ... never recognized a separate claim of false endorsement, distinct from trademark infringement under § 43(a) ...."); *see also Landham v. Lewis Galoob Toys, Inc.*, 227 F.3d 619, 626 (6th Cir.2000) ("A false designation of origin claim ... under § 43(a) of the Lanham Act ... is equivalent to a false association or endorsement claim....").

Therefore, we have no hesitation in joining our sister circuits by holding that we should construe the Lanham Act narrowly when deciding whether an artistically expressive work infringes a trademark. This requires that we carefully "weigh the public interest in free expression against the public interest in avoiding consumer confusion." *Cliffs Notes*, 886 F.2d at 494. An artistically expressive use of a trademark will not violate the Lanham Act "unless the use of the mark has no artistic relevance to the underlying work whatsoever, or, if it has some artistic relevance, unless it explicitly misleads as to the source or the content of the work." *ESS Entm't*, 547 F.3d at 1099 (quotations and alterations omitted); *see also Rogers*, 875 F.2d at 999.

In this case, we readily conclude that Moore's paintings, prints, and calendars are protected under the *Rogers* test. The depiction of the University's uniforms in the content of these items is artistically relevant to the expressive underlying works because the uniforms' colors and designs are needed for a realistic portrayal of famous scenes from Alabama football history. Also there is no evidence that Moore ever marketed an unlicensed item as "endorsed" or "sponsored" by the University, or otherwise explicitly stated that such items were affiliated with the University. Moore's paintings, prints, and calendars very clearly are embodiments of artistic expression, and are entitled to full First Amendment protection. The extent of his use of the University's trademarks is their mere inclusion (their necessary inclusion) in the body of the image which Moore creates to memorialize and enhance a particular play or event in the University's football history. Even if "some members of the public would draw the incorrect inference that [the University] had some involvement with [Moore's paintings, prints, and calendars,] ... that risk of misunderstanding, not engendered by any overt [or in this case even implicit] claim ... is so outweighed by the interest in artistic expression as to preclude" any violation of the Lanham Act. *Rogers*, 875 F.2d at 1001.

Because Moore's depiction of the University's uniforms in the content of his paintings, prints, and calendars results in no violation of the Lanham Act, we affirm the district court with respect to paintings and prints, and reverse with respect to calendars.

III. MUGS AND OTHER "MUNDANE PRODUCTS"

We now proceed to the issues related to Moore's depiction of the University's uniforms on "mini-prints, mugs, cups, ... flags, towels, t-shirts, or any other mundane products." Moore is appellant for these items, which we will refer to as "mugs and other 'mundane products.'"

[The court's discussion of the trademark licensing agreements is omitted.]

B. Moore's Copyright Argument

Moore argues that because his original paintings do not infringe the University's trademarks, he has an unfettered right to produce derivative works featuring those paintings. We disagree with this broad contention. "[T]he defendant's ownership of or license to use a copyrighted image is no defense to a charge of trademark infringement. It should be remembered that a copyright is not a 'right' to use: it is a right to exclude *others* from using the copyrighted work." 1 J. Thomas McCarthy, *McCarthy on Trademarks and Unfair Competition* § 6:14 (4th ed.2011) (emphasis added); [cit.]

If it were otherwise, a person could easily circumvent trademark law by drawing another's trademark and then placing that drawing on various products with impunity. Selling the copyrighted drawing itself may not amount to a trademark infringement, but its placement on certain products very well might. *See, e.g., Nova Wines, Inc. v. Adler Fels Winery LLC,* 467 F.Supp.2d 965, 983 (N.D.Cal.2006) (holding that the copyright holder of a Marilyn Monroe photograph could not use the photo on wine bottles because it would infringe the trademark rights of another winery that sold wine in bottles that prominently featured images of Monroe); McCarthy, *supra,* § 6:14. Thus, we reject Moore's argument that his copyright in the paintings gives him an automatic defense to any trademark claims made by the University.

C. Trademark Claims

Because the district court ruled against Moore with respect to the mugs and other "mundane products," Moore is appellant for these items. However, he has waived any challenge to the district court's conclusions that his use of the uniforms on these products was not a fair use and was not protected by the First Amendment. . .

Acquiescence is the only remaining trademark argument that Moore has preserved on appeal for these items. Acquiescence is a statutory defense under 15 U.S.C. § 1115(b)(9). "The defense of acquiescence requires proof of three elements: (1) the plaintiff actively represented it would not assert a right or claim; (2) the delay between the active representation and assertion of the right or claim was not excusable; and (3) the delay caused the defendant undue prejudice." *Angel Flight of Ga., Inc. v. Angel Flight Am., Inc.,* 522 F.3d 1200, 1207 (11th Cir.2008) (citation and quotation omitted). "The difference between acquiescence and laches is that laches denotes passive consent and acquiescence denotes active consent." *Id.* Thus, the relevant evidence for acquiescence would be active behavior by the University during the time that Moore has been portraying the University's uniforms (i.e., since 1979).

"Active consent" does not necessarily mean an explicit promise not to sue. It only requires "conduct on the plaintiff's part that amounted to an assurance to the defendant, express or implied, that plaintiff would not assert his trademark rights against the defendant." *Creative Gifts, Inc. v. UFO,* 235 F.3d 540, 547–48 (10th Cir.2000); [cit.].

Here, a finding of acquiescence on the mugs or other "mundane products" would estop the University from prosecuting its action against Moore with respect to those items, [cit.], unless the University can show that " 'inevitable confusion' arises from the continued dual use of the marks." *SunAmerica Corp. v. Sun Life Assurance Co. of Can.*, 77 F.3d 1325, 1334 (11th Cir.1996). As we noted in our discussion *supra* at Part III.A, the record is not clear with respect to the parties' course of conduct towards Moore's sale of mugs and other "mundane products." The record relevant to acquiescence on these items is similarly undeveloped. Accordingly, we remand this acquiescence issue for the district court to conduct further proceedings, if necessary.

IV. CONCLUSION

As evidenced by the parties' course of conduct, Moore's depiction of the University's uniforms in his unlicensed paintings, prints, and calendars is not prohibited by the prior licensing agreements. Additionally, the paintings, prints, and calendars do not violate the Lanham Act because these artistically expressive objects are protected by the First Amendment, by virtue of our application of the *Rogers* balancing test. The uniforms in these works of art are artistically relevant to the underlying works, Moore never explicitly misled consumers as to the source of the items, and the interests in artistic expression outweigh the risk of confusion as to endorsement. Accordingly, we affirm the judgment of the district court with respect to the paintings and prints, and reverse with respect to the prints as replicated on calendars.

With respect to the licensing agreements' coverage of the mugs and other "mundane products," we reverse the district court because disputed issues of fact remain. [cit.] Moore has not argued on appeal that his actions with respect to these items constituted fair use or were protected by the First Amendment, and therefore any such protection has been waived, and we need not address those issues with respect to the mugs and other "mundane products." We remand this case to the district court for further proceedings, consistent with this opinion.

Affirmed in part, reversed in part, and remanded.

NOTES AND QUESTIONS

1. *Applying the* Rogers *test to the "mundane" products.* Suppose that the court had decided that Moore had not waived the First Amendment challenge with regards to the "mundane" products. How should the court have decided the First Amendment question applying the *Rogers* test? Or should some other test apply to such products?

2. *Other arguments.* Consider, and evaluate, alternative arguments that you might formulate on behalf of Moore.   Should the court invalidate the University's marks on grounds of functionality? Should Moore have a defense based on *Dastar*?

At p. 794, after *Louis Vuitton*, add the following new case:

ROSETTA STONE LTD. v. GOOGLE, INC.
676 F.3d 144 (4th Cir. 2012)

TRAXLER, Chief Judge:

I. Background

Rosetta Stone began in 1992 as a small, family-owned business that marketed its language-learning software under the brand name "Rosetta Stone."   By 2006, Rosetta Stone had become an industry leader in technology-based language-learning products and online services, and, by January 2010, it had become a publicly traded corporation with 1,738 employees and gross revenues of approximately $252 million. Its products consist of "software, online services and audio practice tools" available in over thirty languages.

Rosetta Stone owns and uses several registered marks in connection with its products and services: ROSETTA STONE, ROSETTA STONE LANGUAGE LEARNING SUCCESS, ROSETTASTONE.COM, and ROSETTA WORLD. Using this family of registered marks, Rosetta Stone markets its brand through various types of media, including the Internet, television, radio, magazines and other print media, and kiosks in public venues. From 2003 through 2009, Rosetta Stone spent approximately $57 million for television and radio advertising, $40 million for print media marketing, and $12.5 million to advertise on the Internet. In 2009, Rosetta Stone's marks enjoyed the highest level of brand recognition by far in the domestic language-learning market.[4] Rosetta Stone has achieved international success as well, with its products in use in over 150 countries.

Rosetta Stone began advertising in connection with Google's website and online services in 2002 and has continued to do so since that time. Google operates one of the world's most popular Internet search engines—programs that enable individuals to find websites and online content, generally through the use of a "keyword" search. [cit.] [The court discussed Google's AdWords platform and related keyword practices.   Review the discussion in the

---

[4] Rosetta Stone conducted a brand equity study in February 2009 showing a substantial gap in actual recognition of the Rosetta Stone mark and the closest competing brand. When asked to identify without prompting "all brand names that come to mind when you think of language learning," almost 45% of the respondents were able to recall "Rosetta Stone," while only about 6% thought of "Berlitz," the second-place finisher.   When prompted, 74% indicated they had heard of Rosetta Stone language products. Berlitz, again the closest competitor, was familiar to only 23% of the respondents when prompted.

Rescuecom decision in Chapter 7 if you need to a reminder about the details of those practices.]

Prior to 2004, Google's policy precluded both the use of trademarks in the text of an advertisement and the use of trademarks as keywords upon request of the trademark owner. In 2004, Google loosened its trademark usage policy to allow the use of third-party trademarks as keywords even over the objection of the trademark owner. Google later even introduced a trademark-specific keyword tool that suggested relevant trademarks for Google's advertising clients to bid on as keywords. Google, however, continued to block the use of trademarks in the actual advertisement text at the request of a trademark owner. At that time, Google's internal studies suggested the unrestricted use of trademarks in the text of an advertisement might confuse Internet users.

Finally, in 2009, Google changed its policy to permit the limited use of trademarks in advertising text in four situations: (1) the sponsor is a reseller of a genuine trademarked product; (2) the sponsor makes or sells component parts for a trademarked product; (3) the sponsor offers compatible parts or goods for use with the trademarked product; or (4) the sponsor provides information about or reviews a trademarked product. Google's policy shift came after it developed the technology to automatically check the linked websites to determine if the sponsor's use of the trademark in the ad text was legitimate.[5]

Rosetta Stone contends that Google's policies concerning the use of trademarks as keywords and in ad text created not only a likelihood of confusion but also actual confusion as well, misleading Internet users into purchasing counterfeit ROSETTA STONE software. Moreover, Rosetta Stone alleges that it has been plagued with counterfeiters since Google announced its policy shift in 2009. According to Rosetta Stone, between September 3, 2009, and March 1, 2010, it was forced to report 190 instances to Google in which one of Google's sponsored links was marketing counterfeit ROSETTA STONE products.

[Rosetta Stone sued Google, alleging, *inter alia*, various Lanham Act causes of action. The district court granted Google's summary judgment motion as to the Lanham Act claims, and Rosetta Stone appealed. The Fourth Circuit vacated the grant of summary judgment as to the direct infringement and contributory infringement claims, finding that Rosetta Stone had raised triable issues of fact. The court then turned to the dilution claim.]

VI. Trademark Dilution

. . . .

---

[5] This automated tool checks the "landing page"— *i.e.*, the page linked to the ad referring to the trademark—and determines whether the page uses the trademark prominently; whether the page contains commercial information suggesting the sponsor is a reseller; and whether the landing page is a review site.

To state a prima facie dilution claim under the FTDA, the plaintiff must show the following:

(1) that the plaintiff owns a famous mark that is distinctive;

(2) that the defendant has commenced using a mark in commerce that allegedly is diluting the famous mark;

(3) that a similarity between the defendant's mark and the famous mark gives rise to an association between the marks; and

(4) that the association is likely to impair the distinctiveness of the famous mark or likely to harm the reputation of the famous mark.

[*Louis Vuitton Malletier S.A. v. Haute Diggity Dog, LLC*, 507 F.3d 252, 264-65 (4th Cir. 2007).]

The district court granted summary judgment for Google on the dilution claim on two bases. First, the district court held that Rosetta Stone was required but failed to present evidence that Google was "us[ing] the Rosetta Stone Marks to identify its *own* goods and services." [cit.]   To support its conclusion, the district court relied on the text of the statutory "fair use" defense that shields a person's "fair use" of plaintiff's mark so long as such use is not as "a designation of source for the person's own goods or services." 15 U.S.C. § 1125(c)(3)(A).

Second, the district court concluded that Rosetta Stone failed to show that Google's use of the mark was likely to impair the distinctiveness of or harm the reputation of the ROSETTA STONE marks. Specifically, the district court indicated that there was "no evidence of dilution by blurring when Rosetta Stone's brand awareness has only increased since Google revised its trademark policy in 2004," and the court noted evidence that Rosetta Stone's "brand awareness equity also increased from 19% in 2005 to 95% in 2009." [cit.]   In support of this conclusion, the district court read our decision in *Louis Vuitton* to establish the proposition that "no claim for dilution by blurring exists where a defendants' product only increases public identification of the plaintiffs' marks." *Id.*

A. Google's Non-Trademark Use of Rosetta Stone's Marks

We first consider the district court's grant of summary judgment based on the lack of evidence that Google used the ROSETTA STONE marks "to identify its *own* goods and services." The district court held that Rosetta Stone could not establish its dilution claim, specifically, the third element, without showing that Google used the mark as a source identifier for its products and services. In support of this conclusion, however, the district court relied upon the "fair use" defense available under the FTDA. *See* 15 U.S.C. §

1125(c)(3)(A) ("Any fair use, including a nominative or descriptive fair use, or facilitation of such fair use, of a famous mark by another person other than as a designation of source for the person's own goods or services" is not "actionable as dilution by blurring or dilution by tarnishment.") Thus, the district court apparently concluded that Rosetta Stone was required, as part of its prima facie showing of dilution under the FTDA, to demonstrate that Google was using the mark as a source identifier for Google's own goods.

We view § 1125(c)(3)(A) as affording a fair use *defense* to defendants in dilution actions. *See Louis Vuitton*, 507 F.3d at 265-66. In our view, once the owner of a famous mark establishes a prima facie case of dilution by blurring or tarnishment, it falls to the defendant to demonstrate that its use constituted a "fair use ... other than as a designation of source for the [defendant's] own goods or services," 15 U.S.C. § 1125(c)(3)(A). Whether Google used the mark other than as a source identifier and in good faith is an issue that Google, not Rosetta Stone, is obligated to establish. Thus, the district court erroneously required Rosetta Stone to demonstrate that Google was using the ROSETTA STONE mark as a source identifier for Google's own products.

More importantly, the district court erred when it ruled that Google was not liable for dilution simply because there was no evidence that Google uses the Rosetta Stone marks to identify Google's own goods and services. In essence, the district court made nontrademark use coextensive with the "fair use" defense under the FTDA. The statute, however, requires more than showing that defendant's use was "other than as a designation of source"—the defendant's use must also qualify as a "fair use." 15 U.S.C. § 1125(c)(3)(A). Indeed, if the district court's analysis is correct—that is, if a federal trademark dilution claim is doomed solely by the lack of proof showing that the defendant used the famous mark as a trademark—then the term "fair use" as set forth in § 1125(c)(3)(A) would be superfluous.

The district court failed to determine whether this was "fair use". Although the FTDA does not expressly define "fair use," the classic concept of "fair use" is well-established and incorporated as an affirmative defense to a claim of trademark infringement. *See* 15 U.S.C. § 1115(b)(4). The contours of the fair-use defense in the infringement context are therefore instructive on the classic or descriptive fair-use defense to a dilution claim. [cit.]

Descriptive, or classic, fair use applies when the defendant is using a trademark "in its primary, descriptive sense" *to describe* the defendant's goods or services. [cit.] The FTDA also expressly includes "nominative" fair use as a defense. *See* 15 U.S.C. § 1125(c)(3)(A). Typically, nominative fair use comes into play when the defendant uses the famous mark to identify or compare *the trademark owner's* product. [cit.] Regardless of the type of fair use claimed by a defendant, a common component of fair use is good faith. *See, e.g., JA Apparel Corp. v. Abboud*, 568 F.3d 390, 401 (2d Cir.2009) ("Assessment of this defense thus requires analysis of whether a given use was (1) other than as a mark, (2) in a descriptive sense, and (3) in good faith." (internal quotation marks omitted)). . .

[T]he court's summary judgment order omitted this analysis, impermissibly omitting the question of good faith and collapsing the fair-use defense into one question—whether or not Google uses the ROSETTA STONE mark as a source identifier for its own products. Accordingly, we vacate the district court's summary judgment order and remand for reconsideration of Rosetta Stone's dilution claim. If the district court determines that Rosetta Stone has made a prima facie showing under the elements set forth in *Louis Vuitton*, 507 F.3d at 264–65, it should reexamine the nominative fair-use defense in light of this opinion.

B. Likelihood of Dilution

Alternatively, the district court held that Rosetta Stone failed to satisfy the fourth and final element of its trademark dilution claim requiring that the plaintiff show defendant's use is "likely to impair the distinctiveness of the famous mark or likely to harm the reputation of the famous mark." The court based its conclusion solely on the fact that "Rosetta Stone's brand awareness ha[d] only increased since Google revised its trademark policy in 2004." On the strength of this evidence, the district court concluded that "the distinctiveness of the Rosetta Stone Marks has not been impaired" and therefore that "Rosetta Stone cannot show that Google's trademark policy likely caused dilution by blurring."

To determine whether the defendant's use is likely to impair the distinctiveness of the plaintiff's famous mark, the FTDA enumerates a non-exhaustive list of six factors that are to be considered by the courts [citing 15 U.S.C. § 1125(c)(2)(B) and listing the factors]. Although "[n]ot every factor will be relevant in every case, and not every blurring claim will require extensive discussion of the factors[,] ... a trial court must offer a sufficient indication of which factors it has found persuasive and explain why they are persuasive." *Louis Vuitton*, 507 F.3d at 266.

The district court addressed only one factor—the degree of recognition of Rosetta Stone's mark—and did not mention any other remaining statutory factor. The court's reliance on Louis Vuitton for the proposition that no claim for dilution by blurring exists when there is evidence that public recognition of the defendants' product increased was error. *Louis Vuitton* addressed a far different fact pattern, where the defendant's fair use claim was based on parody, which Congress expressly included as a protected fair use under the FTDA so long as the mark being parodied is not being "used as a designation of source for the person's own goods or services." *See* 15 U.S.C.A. § 1125(c)(3)(A)(ii). We concluded that a successful parody "might actually enhance the famous mark's distinctiveness by making it an icon. The brunt of the joke becomes *yet more famous*." *Louis Vuitton*, 507 F.3d at 267(emphasis added). We disagree, therefore, the district court's reading of *Louis Vuitton*. Under the FTDA, Rosetta Stone must show only a *likelihood* of dilution and need not prove actual economic loss or reputational injury. *See id.* at 264 n. 2. The decision below employed a truncated analysis that placed a very heavy emphasis upon whether there had been any actual injury suffered by Rosetta Stone's brand. On remand, the court should address whichever additional factors might apply to inform its determination of whether Google's use is likely to impair the distinctiveness of Rosetta Stone's mark. *See* 15 U.S.C. § 1125(c)(2)(B).

[The court also found triable issues of fact about whether Rosetta Stone's marks had become famous before Google commenced the allegedly dilutive use.]

[Affirmed in part, vacated in part, and remanded.]

At p. 797, add as Note 7:

7. *The* Louis Vuitton *Analysis in the context of Section 2(f).* Suppose that dispute between Louis Vuitton and Haute Diggity Dog had arisen in a different context: assume that Haute Diggity Dog had sought to register CHEWY VUITON for dog toys, and Louis Vuitton had opposed registration under Section 2(f) on dilution grounds. How, if at all, would this have changed the dilution analysis? First, are any of the exclusions in Section 43(c)(3)(A) relevant to the analysis? Would they allow Haute Diggity Dog to withstand an opposition? Second, consider the claim of parody and its effect on the blurring factors. How would that analysis change—or would it? *See Research in Motion, Ltd. v. Defining Presence Marketing Group, Inc.,* 102 U.S.P.Q.2d (BNA) 1187 (TTAB 2012).

FALSE ADVERTISING

At p. 806, Problem 10-1, add the following after the *Conte Bros.* cite:

See also Harold H. Huggins Realty, Inc. v. FNC, Inc., 634 F.3d 787 (5th Cir. 2011) (engaging in an extensive analysis of the *Conte Bros.* factors and concluding that the trial court had erred in denying prudential standing). The plaintiffs were real estate appraisers and defendants provide software used in the mortgage industry. Plaintiffs alleged that defendant encouraged appraisers to enter appraisal data using defendant's software, while also representing falsely to plaintiffs that the appraisal data would be kept private and would not be used to develop a database that could be used as an alternative to appraisal services.

For a discussion of the Ninth Circuit's approach to Lanham Act standing, and a reminder that there is a separate requirement to show Article III standing, see *Trafficschool.com v. EDriver, Inc.*, 653 F.3d 820 (9th Cir. 2011), excerpted in this Supplement, at the end of this chapter.

At p. 809, insert the following as Problem 10-3A:

PROBLEM 10-3A: LANHAM ACT FALSE ADVERTISING VERSUS OTHER FEDERAL LABELING REGULATIONS

The U.S. Food and Drug Administration (FDA) regulates the labels that may appear on many food and beverage products under the Food, Drug, and Cosmetic Act (FDCA), 21 U.S.C. §§ 301 *et seq.* For example, food and beverage labels that are "false or misleading in any particular" violate 21 U.S.C. §343(a)(1), and may trigger action by the FDA or Department of Justice. The FDA has promulgated regulations that address in detail the content of labels for many products. *See, e.g.*, 21 C.F.R. 102.33(c), (d) (labels for juice beverages).

Suppose that Coca-Cola distributes a juice product that is labeled, as shown below, as "Pomegranate Blueberry Blend of 5 Juices." The product actually contains 99.4% apple and grape juices, 0.3% pomegranate juice, 0.2% blueberry juice, and 0.1% raspberry juice. Assume that the content and size of the text on the labels comply with the applicable FDA regulations for juice labels (which do specify how juice blends may be labeled, among other things). Should a competitor of Coca-Cola still be able to assert a Lanham Act false advertising cause of action based on the labeling? If a court permits the Lanham Act allegation to go forward, does this undermine the FDA's regulatory authority? If a wide array of products are subject to various federal labeling regulations, should a Lanham Act false advertising cause of action be barred in all of these circumstances? See *Pom Wonderful LLC v. Coca-Cola Co.*, 2012 WL 1739704 (9th Cir. May 17, 2012).

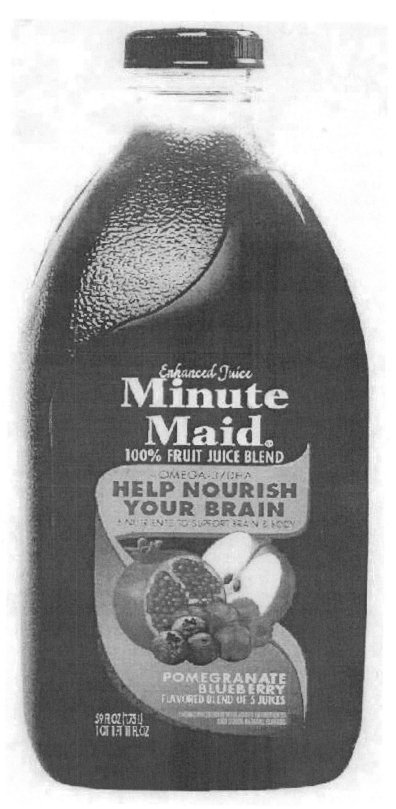

At p. 813, Note 1, add the following:

On the question of whether consumer survey evidence is important to the threshold determination of what message an advertisement conveys (especially when the allegation is that the statement is literally true but misleading), see *Pernod Ricard USA, LLC v. Bacardi U.S.A., Inc.*, 653 F.3d 241 (3d Cir. 2011). The case involved Bacardi's HAVANA CLUB rum. The bottle's label says "Puerto Rican Rum" on the front, and elsewhere says that the rum is "distilled and crafted in Puerto Rico," which, we understand, is a literally true statement. Pernod sued for false advertising, claiming that the label misleadingly implied that the rum was made in Havana (when, in fact, the rum was made in Puerto Rico, albeit from a recipe that originated in Havana). Pernod submitted a consumer survey that allegedly supported its view. The district court determined that it need not consider the survey, and the Third Circuit agreed. The court endorsed the "general proposition that there are circumstances under which the meaning of a factually accurate and facially unambiguous statement is not open to attack through a consumer survey. In other words, there may be cases, and this is one, in which a court can properly say that no reasonable person could be misled by the advertisement in question." *Id.* at 252. According to the Third Circuit, when the words "Havana Club" were read in the context of the entire label, including the references to Puerto Rico, no reasonable consumer could be misled into thinking that the rum was manufactured in Havana. Under such circumstances, "a district court can properly disregard survey evidence as immaterial, because, by definition, § 43(a)(1) does not forbid language that reasonable people would have to acknowledge is not false or misleading. . . . A contrary holding would not only be out of keeping with the language of § 43(a)(1), it would undermine the purpose of subsection (a)(1)(B) by subjecting advertisers to a level of risk at odds with consumer protection." A similar rationale animates the doctrine of puffery, according to the court. Do you agree with the court's approach? The court acknowledged that its rule might appear to give "license to lightly disregard survey evidence about consumer reactions to challenged advertisements." *Id.* at 254. The court cautioned that "[b]efore a defendant or a district judge decides that an advertisement could not mislead a reasonable person, serious care must be exercised to avoid the temptation of thinking, 'my way of seeing this is naturally the only reasonable way.' Thoughtful reflection on potential ambiguities in an advertisement, which can be revealed by surveys and will certainly be pointed out by plaintiffs, will regularly make it the wisest course to consider survey evidence." *Id.* at 254-55. Does this allay any concerns you might have about the court's rule – or does it magnify them?

At pp. 830-31, Note 5, add the following:

In *Skydive Arizona, Inc. v. Quattrocchi*, 673 F.3d 1105 (9th Cir. 2012), plaintiff did not submit survey evidence as proof of materiality. Instead, plaintiff relied on a declaration from a disgruntled consumer. Apparently the declaration stated that the declarant "had personally bought [defendant's] SKYRIDE certificates based on the [defendant's] online representations and advertisements that he could redeem the certificates at Skydive Arizona [the plaintiff's business]." Should this alone suffice to establish materiality? The Ninth Circuit also looked to evidence concerning "numerous consumers who had telephoned or came to Skydive Arizona's facility after having been deceived into believing there was an affiliation between Skydive Arizona and [defendant]." Is this evidence probative as to materiality? Or as to deception? Or both? How likely is it that materiality will serve a significant role in filtering out unwarranted claims of false advertising?

The court in *Cashmere* notes that one method of establishing materiality is to show that the false or misleading statement relates to an inherent quality of the product at issue. Suppose that the plaintiff produces plush toys called PILLOW PETS that fold out flat into pillows. Suppose that the defendant produces similar goods under a similar name, and represents (falsely) that its goods are "As Seen on TV." Is that misrepresentation material? Does it relate to an "inherent quality" of the goods? *See CJ Prods. LLC v. Snuggly Plushez LLC*, 809 F.Supp.2d 127, 147-48 (E.D.N.Y. 2011).

At p. 831, Note 6, add the following after the phrase "Lanham Act remedies.":

Regarding the grant of injunctive relief for false advertising, see *PBM Prods., LLC v. Mead Johnson & Co.*, 639 F.3d 111 (4th Cir. 2011) (applying the factors from the Supreme Court's patent decision on injunctive relief, *eBay, Inc. v. MercExchange*, 547 U.S. 388, 391 (2006)). Should the plaintiff in a false advertising case be required to show an actual diversion of sales in order to make out a showing of irreparable harm under the *eBay* factors? We return to the issue of injunctive relief, and remedies more generally, in Chapter 12.

At p. 831, Note 6, add the following:

In *Skydive Arizona, Inc. v. Quattrocchi*, 673 F.3d 1105 (9th Cir. 2012), a divided panel of the Ninth Circuit upheld an award of $1 million in actual damages for false advertising. The damages evidence (which was offered to support damages claims for both trademark infringement and false advertising) consisted of exhibits showing "the hundreds of thousands of dollars Skydive Arizona spent in developing and advertising its business, and "multiple declarations and witness testimony proving that customers were very angry with, and blamed Skydive Arizona for, problems caused by [defendant]," along with an argument that corrective advertising was needed. The panel majority found this showing sufficient; plaintiff did not need to provide a "specific mathematical formula" for the jury to use in calculating actual damage to the plaintiff's goodwill. Judge Noonan, dissenting as to the damages judgment, called for a more rigorous quantitative approach to measuring goodwill, and asserted that Skydive Arizona's expenditures might be relevant to computing the value of its goodwill, but did not provide a measure of the damage to that goodwill that defendant's activities had caused. *Id.* at 1116–17 (Noonan, J., dissenting-in-part).

At p. 831, after Note 6, add the following case:

TRAFFICSCHOOL.COM, INC. v. EDRIVER, INC.
653 F.3d 820 (9th Cir. 2011)

KOZINSKI, Chief Judge:

Defendants own and manage DMV.org, a for-profit website with a mission to save you "time, money and even a trip to the DMV!" DMV.org, Home Page, http://www.dmv.org (last visited Feb. 28, 2011). Consumers visit DMV.org for help renewing driver's licenses, buying car insurance, viewing driving records, beating traffic tickets, registering vehicles, even finding DUI/DWI attorneys. The more eyeballs DMV.org attracts, the more money defendants earn from selling sponsored links and collecting fees for referring site visitors to vendors of traffic school courses, driver's ed lessons and other driver-related services. This seems like a legitimate and useful business, except that some visitors mistakenly believe the site is run by their state's department of motor vehicles (DMV).

Plaintiffs TrafficSchool.com, Inc. and Drivers Ed Direct, LLC market and sell traffic school and driver's ed courses directly to consumers. They also compete with DMV.org for referral revenue. Plaintiffs claim that defendants violated federal and state unfair competition and false advertising laws by actively fostering the belief that DMV.org is an official state DMV website, or is affiliated or endorsed by a state DMV.

After a trial, the district court held that defendants violated section 43(a) of the Lanham Act, 15 U.S.C. § 1125(a), but rejected plaintiffs' claim under California's unfair competition statute, Cal. Bus. & Prof.Code § 17200. The court issued an injunction ordering DMV.org to present every site visitor with a splash screen bearing a disclaimer. Unhappily for plaintiffs, the court denied monetary relief and declined to award attorney's fees. Both sides appeal.

[Judge Kozinski first discussed whether plaintiffs had standing to bring their claims. He noted that a standing analysis for a Lanham Act false advertising claim should include two independent components: (1) an analysis of Article III standing, implicating the federal court's subject matter jurisdiction (and requiring a showing of injury-in-fact, causation, and redressability); and (2) an analysis of standing under the Lanham Act false advertising provision (requiring a showing of *likely* injury), which determines whether the plaintiff has the ability to recover a remedy under the Lanham Act. As to the Article III analysis, Judge Kozinski concluded that evidence of direct competition between plaintiff and defendant (in this case for revenue from referrals) was "strong proof that plaintiffs have a stake in the outcome of the suit" sufficient to justify Article III standing. False advertising plaintiffs were not required to produce evidence of actual lost sales to satisfy Article III; plaintiffs merely needed to create "chain of inferences showing how defendant's false advertising could harm plaintiff's business."

Turning to Lanham Act standing, Judge Kozinski invoked the Ninth Circuit's standing analysis from Jack Russell Terrier Network of Northern California v. American Kennel Club, Inc., 407 F.3d 1027, 1037 (9th Cir.2005), where the court held that "a plaintiff must show: (1) a commercial injury based upon a misrepresentation about a product; and (2) that the injury is 'competitive,' or harmful to the plaintiff's ability to compete with the defendant." The parties had disputed whether the evidence demonstrated a "commercial injury" as called for in the first prong. Judge Kozinski ruled that when (as here) defendant and plaintiff are direct competitors and defendant's misrepresentation has a tendency to mislead consumers, commercial injury will be presumed. He left for future cases whether the presumption was conclusive or rebuttable. Judge Kozinski also observed that proof of a commercial injury did not require the plaintiff to show an identifiable injury to itself. Regarding the evidence that established the requisite "tendency to mislead," Judge Kozinski pointed to plaintiff's evidence of actual confusion, which included "two declarations from individuals who confused DMV.org with an official DMV site and hundreds of emails sent by consumers who contacted DMV.org thinking it was their state's DMV." Some of the emails contained "sensitive personal information that the typical consumer wouldn't share with a commercial website," while others came from law enforcement officials and state DMV employees. The plaintiff also introduced survey evidence. As to the defendants website itself, "DMV.org's site design also mimicked an actual DMV site by copying slogans and state symbols, and by linking to web pages elsewhere on the site that helped consumers complete DMV-related transactions like applying for a license, registering a car and signing up for traffic school. DMV .org did disclaim connection with state DMVs, but this disclaimer was easy to miss because it was displayed in small font at the bottom of each page, where many consumers would never scroll." In addition, defendant had affiliated "ca.dmv.org" or "california.dmv.org," respectively with its website, which "obviously was designed to suggest an affiliation with the State of California." Judge Kozinski concluded that the plaintiff had Lanham Act standing. He then turned to the merits.]

False Advertising

A. To succeed on an Internet false advertising claim, a plaintiff must show that a statement made in a commercial advertisement or promotion is false or misleading, that it actually deceives or has the tendency to deceive a substantial segment of its audience, that it's likely to influence purchasing decisions and that the plaintiff has been or is likely to be injured by the false advertisement. [cit.].[3] As we explained. . .the district court made extensive findings in support of its conclusion that the DMV.org URL, defendants' search engine marketing strategy and the design of DMV.org were likely to, and did, confuse consumers. None of these findings was clearly erroneous, and they establish that the DMV.org site deceives a substantial segment of its audience. Plaintiffs' evidence also shows that a "recommended by DMV" endorsement will affect purchase decisions, and that plaintiffs are likely to suffer injury when consumers visit DMV.org instead of their

---

[3] A plaintiff bringing a false advertising claim must also show that defendant caused its false or misleading statement to enter interstate commerce, [cit.], but this is virtually automatic for websites.

competing sites. The district court committed no error in holding that defendants violated the Lanham Act.

B. By way of a remedy, the district court ordered DMV.org to present every site visitor with a splash screen stating, "YOU ARE ABOUT TO ENTER A PRIVATELY OWNED WEBSITE THAT IS NOT OWNED OR OPERATED BY ANY STATE GOVERNMENT AGENCY." Visitors can't access DMV.org's content without clicking a "CONTINUE" button on the splash screen [reproduced at the end of this excerpt]. Defendants argue that the district court abused its discretion by fashioning a "blanket injunction" that's overbroad—i.e., restrains conduct not at issue in plaintiffs' complaint—and violates the First Amendment.

Overbreadth. The district court reasoned that the splash screen was necessary to: (1) "remedy any confusion that consumers have already developed before visiting DMV.ORG for the first time," (2) "remedy the public interest concerns associated with [confused visitors'] transfer of sensitive information to Defendants," and (3) "prevent confusion among DMV.ORG's consumers." Defendants argue that the splash screen doesn't effectuate these stated goals. But their only evidence is a declaration from DMV.org's CEO stating that defendants tested several alternative disclaimers and found them to be more effective than the splash screen in preventing consumers from emailing DMV.org with sensitive personal information. To the extent we credit a self-serving declaration, [cit.], defendants' evidence doesn't prove that the splash screen is ineffective in this respect, and says nothing about whether the alternative disclaimers serve the other two interests identified by the district court. Defendants haven't carried their "heavy burden" of showing that their alternative disclaimers reduce DMV.org's likelihood of confusing consumers. [cit.] The scope of an injunction is within the broad discretion of the district court, [cit.], and the district court here didn't abuse that discretion when it concluded that the splash screen was the optimal means of correcting defendants' false advertising.

First Amendment. Courts routinely grant permanent injunctions prohibiting deceptive advertising. See 1 Charles E. McKenney & George F. Long III, Federal Unfair Competition: Lanham Act § 43(a) § 10:5 (17th ed.2010). Because false or misleading commercial statements aren't constitutionally protected, see *Cent. Hudson Gas & Elec. Corp. v. Pub. Serv. Comm'n of N.Y.*, 447 U.S. 557, 563 (1980); [cit.], such injunctions rarely raise First Amendment concerns.

The permanent injunction here does raise such concerns because it erects a barrier to all content on the DMV.org website, not merely that which is deceptive. Some of the website's content is informational and thus fully protected, such as guides to applying for a driver's license, buying insurance and beating traffic tickets. See *Mattel, Inc. v. MCA Records, Inc.*, 296 F.3d 894, 906 (9th Cir. 2002). The informational content is commingled with truthful commercial speech, which is entitled to significant First Amendment protection. See *Cent. Hudson*, 447 U.S. at 564. The district court was required to tailor the injunction so as to burden no more protected speech than necessary. [cit.]

The district court does not appear to have considered that its injunction would permanently and unnecessarily burden access to DMV.org's First Amendment-protected content. The splash screen forces potential visitors to take an additional navigational step, deterring some consumers from entering the website altogether.[5] It also precludes defendants from tailoring DMV.org's landing page to make it welcoming to visitors, and interferes with the operation of search engines, making it more difficult for consumers to find the website and its protected content.[6] All of these burdens on protected speech are, under the current injunction, permanent.

The district court premised its injunction on its findings that defendants' "search engine marketing" and "non-sponsored natural listings, including the DMV.ORG domain name," caused consumers to be confused even before they viewed DMV.org's content. The court also identified specific misleading statements on the website. The splash screen is justified to remedy the harm caused by such practices so long as they continue. But website content and advertising practices can and do change over time. Indeed, the court found that defendants had already "made some changes to DMV.ORG and how they marketed it."

The splash screen is also justified so long as it helps to remedy lingering confusion caused by defendants' past deception. But the splash screen will continue to burden DMV.org's protected content, even if all remaining harm has dissipated. At that point, the injunction will burden protected speech without justification, thus burdening more speech than necessary. [cit.]; see also *E. & J. Gallo Winery v. Gallo Cattle Co.*, 967 F.2d 1280, 1298 (9th Cir.1992) (permanent injunction can't burden future non-misleading business practices); *U–Haul Int'l, Inc. v. Jartran, Inc.*, 793 F.2d 1034, 1042–43 (9th Cir.1986) ("U–Haul II") (permanent injunction can't burden future truthful advertising).

---

[5] Defendants' website usability expert submitted a declaration stating that splash screens typically drive away up to a quarter of potential site visitors. Plaintiffs cite nothing to rebut this evidence.

[6] Defendants introduced unrebutted evidence that splash screens commonly interfere with the automated "spiders" that search engines deploy to "crawl" the Internet and compile the indexes of web pages they use to determine every page's search ranking. And splash screens themselves don't have high search rankings: Search engines commonly base these rankings on the web page's content and the number of other pages linking to it, and splash screens lack both content and links.

On remand, the district court shall reconsider the duration of the splash screen in light of any intervening changes in the website's content and marketing practices, as well as the dissipation of the deception resulting from past practices. If the district court continues to require the splash screen, it shall explain the continuing justification for burdening the website's protected content and what conditions defendants must satisfy in order to remove the splash screen in the future. In the alternative, or in addition, the court may permanently enjoin defendants from engaging in deceptive marketing or placing misleading statements on DMV.org. See *U–Haul II*, 793 F.2d at 1043 (modifying injunction to prohibit only false or misleading advertising).

C. The district court denied plaintiffs' request for an award of profits because they provided "no evidence [of causation or evidence] quantifying the extent of any ... harm" they suffered as a result of DMV.org's actions. Nothing in the Lanham Act conditions an award of profits on plaintiff's proof of harm, and we've held that profits may be awarded in the absence of such proof. [cit.]; *U–Haul II*, 793 F .2d at 1040–42. But an award of profits with no proof of harm is an uncommon remedy in a false advertising suit. It's appropriate in false comparative advertising cases, where it's reasonable to presume that every dollar defendant makes has come directly out of plaintiff's pocket. [cit.] It's also appropriate where ordinary damages won't deter unlawful conduct: for example, when defendant associates its product with plaintiff's noncompetitive product to appropriate good will or brand value. See, e.g., *Maier Brewing Co. v. Fleischmann Distilling Corp.*, 390 F.2d 117, 120, 123–24 (9th Cir.1968) (brewer of Black & White beer forced to pay profits to distiller of Black & White scotch). The reason there is that plaintiff is unlikely to have lost any sales or sale contracts to defendant, and the damages must be measured by defendant's gains from the illicit use.

But neither the comparative advertising nor good will cases are relevant here, where plaintiffs claim that "defendant[s] advertised a different (and allegedly better) product than they delivered." Harper House, Inc. v. Thomas Nelson, Inc., 889 F.2d 197, 209 n. 8 (9th Cir. 1989). The Lanham Act allows an award of profits only to the extent the award "shall constitute compensation and not a penalty." 15 U.S.C. § 1117(a). But "when advertising does not directly compare defendant's and plaintiff's products," the injury to plaintiff "may be a small fraction of the defendant's sales, profits, or advertising expenses." *Harper House, Inc.*, 889 F.2d at 209 n. 8. Plaintiffs didn't produce any proof of past injury or causation, so the district court had no way to determine with any degree of certainty what award would be compensatory. [cit.] The district court didn't err in denying damages.

[The court then determined that the district court abused its discretion by denying the plaintiff's motion for attorney's fees. The discussion of that issue is omitted.]

[*Affirmed in part, reversed in part, and remanded.*]

NOTES AND QUESTIONS

1. *Injunctive relief and the requirement to use a "splash screen."* The court remands so that the trial court can determine how long the defendant should be required to use the splash screen. But if it's the dmv.org domain name that lies at the root of the defendant's deception of consumers, then it would seem that the splash screen would always be needed, unless the defendant stops using the domain name. Thus is may be a little odd to suggest that the splash screen only need be in place for as long as the deception continues. Professor Rebecca Tushnet has pointed this out. *See* Rebecca Tushnet & Eric Goldman, Joint post: Kozinski on DMV.org, http://tushnet.blogspot.com/2011/08/joint-post-kozinski-on-dmvorg.html (Aug. 2 2011). Defendant's dmv.org website currently (as of May 2012) includes no splash screen, but does include a banner stating in capital letters that "DMV.ORG IS A **PRIVATELY OWNED** WEBSITE THAT IS NOT OWNED OR OPERATED BY ANY STATE GOVERNMENT AGENCY." Is this adequate to dispel consumer deception?

11

Trade Identity Rights in One's Persona: Endorsement, Attribution, and Publicity

At p. 836, Note 2, add the following:

See also Stayart v. Yahoo! Inc., 623 F.3d 436 (7th Cir. 2010) (concluding that private individual lacked standing to bring a Section 43(a) action absent evidence of a commercial interest in her name). The plaintiff complained that when she conducted internet searches on her name using the Yahoo! search engine, the search results included links to websites that the plaintiff considered undesirable.

At p. 852, Note 6, add the following:

If courts recognize a post-mortem right of publicity in a common law jurisdiction, should they require evidence that the personality exploited the right during the personality's lifetime? For a discussion applying New Jersey law (as embodied in the *McFarland* case cited in the note), see *Hebrew Univ. of Jerusalem v. General Motors LLC.*, 2012 WL 907497 (C.D. Cal. Mar. 12, 2012) (involving use of Albert Einstein image in an automobile advertisement).

At p. 853, add as Note 10A:

10A. *Choice of law.* Even if it is proper for a court in a particular state to exercise jurisdiction in a right of publicity case, the court must engage in a separate analysis to determine which state's law should apply — or which country's law, for that matter. For a case analyzing a conflict between California and English law, see *Love v. Associated Newspapers, Ltd.*, 611 F.3d 601 (9th Cir. 2010).

At p. 860, add the following to Problem 11-3:

Suppose that NISU contracts with a video game manufacturer to permit the use of NISU trademarks, and likenesses of NISU players (including Billie), to appear in a video game, "NCAA Softball 2012." Suppose that Billie sues the video game manufacturer to enforce her right of publicity. As a policy matter, how should a court balance (1) Billie's interest in being compensated for portrayals of her likeness under a right of publicity theory; and (2) the video game manufacturer's First Amendment interests? To understand how courts might reduce this policy discussion into more concrete doctrinal terms, review the cases in part B.3 of Chapter 11, discussing limitations on the right of publicity. Consider how you would apply both the transformative test of the *Comedy III* case and the *Rogers v. Grimaldi* balancing test (introduced in Chapter 9). *See Hart v. Electronic Arts, Inc.*, 808 F.Supp.2d 757 (D.N.J. 2011); *cf. Keller v. Electronic Arts, Inc.*, 94 U.S.P.Q.2d (BNA) 1130 (N.D. Cal. 2010). Both cases were on appeal at the time of this writing.

12

REMEDIES

At p. 902, add the following case after *Axiom Worldwide*:

VOICE OF THE ARAB WORLD v. MDTV MEDICAL NEWS NOW, INC.
645 F.3d 26 (1st Cir. 2011)

TORRUELLA, Circuit Judge:

In this appeal, plaintiff-appellant Voice of the Arab World, Inc. ("VOAW") challenges the district court's interlocutory order granting defendant-appellee MDTV Medical News Now, Inc.'s ("Medical News Now") motion to preliminarily enjoin VOAW from the use, sale, or promotion of the mark "MDTV," or formative versions of that mark on the Internet, in connection with medical-related informational or educational programming or services. . .

. . .

On August 15, 2009, Medical News Now sent VOAW a letter threatening to file an action for trademark infringement and domain name cybersquatting unless VOAW agreed to transfer the "mdtv" domain names to Medical News Now in exchange for a nominal sum. Thereafter, on September 10, 2009, VOAW filed an action in the district court seeking declaratory judgment (1) that it had a right to use and register the "MDTV" mark, and (2) that its activities did not infringe upon Medical News Now's purported rights in the "MDTV" mark, or constitute domain name cybersquatting.

Medical News Now responded on November 24, 2009, by bringing counterclaims against VOAW for trademark infringement, unfair competition and cybersquatting. In addition, on November 25, 2009, Medical News Now moved to preliminarily enjoin VOAW from using the "MDTV" mark. On February 25, 2010, the district court granted Medical News Now's motion and issued an order preliminarily enjoining VOAW from the use, sale or promotion of the "MDTV" mark or formative versions thereof on the Internet, in connection with medical-related information or educational programming or services. VOAW appeals the district court's preliminary injunction order. . . .

III. Discussion

[VOAW challenged the district court's preliminary injunction order inter alia on the ground that the district court erred as a matter of law by presuming that Medical News Now would likely suffer irreparable harm in the absence of preliminary injunctive relief, and not requiring Medical News Now to actually demonstrate such likelihood of irreparable harm.]

VOAW's argument on the irreparable harm issue is two-fold. First, VOAW maintains that presuming irreparable harm in trademark infringement cases where preliminary injunctive relief is sought is inconsistent with the Supreme Court's opinion in eBay Inc. v. MercExchange, L.L.C., 547 U.S. 388 (2006). Second, VOAW contends in the alternative that, even if irreparable harm may be presumed in certain trademark infringement cases, such presumption cannot apply here, in light of Medical News Now's excessive delay in seeking injunctive relief.

As discussed below, we agree that the traditional equitable principles discussed by the Supreme Court in eBay apply in the present case. See N. Am. Med. Corp. v. Axiom Worldwide, Inc., 522 F.3d 1211, 1228 (11th Cir. 2008) . . . . However, it is unnecessary to decide at this time whether the rule relied upon by the district court (i.e., irreparable harm is presumed upon a finding of likelihood of success on the merits of a trademark infringement claim) is consistent with such principles, because—even if we assume without deciding that such rule is good law—we still find that the district court abused its discretion in applying such a presumption here. This is due to the fact that such presumption has been held inapplicable in cases where, as here, the plaintiff delays excessively in seeking injunctive relief.

Accordingly, . . . we vacate the district court's preliminary injunction order and remand the case.

We begin our discussion by delineating the applicable preliminary injunction standard. In doing so, because there seems to be confusion in some district courts as to whether the principles of eBay apply to preliminary injunctions of alleged trademark infringement, see, e.g., Operation Able of Greater Bos., Inc. v. Nat'l Able Network, Inc., 646 F.Supp.2d 166, 176-77 (D. Mass. 2009), we clarify certain aspects concerning the application of eBay in this context.

A. Preliminary Injunction Standard

"A preliminary injunction is an 'extraordinary and drastic remedy,'" Munaf v. Geren, 553 U.S. 674, 689-90 (2008) (quoting 11A Charles Alan Wright, Arthur R. Miller & Mary Kay Kane, Federal Practice and Procedure § 2948, at 129 (2d ed. 1995) [hereinafter "Wright & Miller"]), that "is never awarded as of right." Id. at 690. Rather, as the Supreme Court recently reaffirmed, "[a] plaintiff seeking a preliminary injunction must establish that he is likely to succeed on the merits, that he is likely to suffer irreparable harm in the absence of preliminary relief, that the balance of equities tips in his favor, and that an injunction is in the public interest." Winter v. Natural Res. Def. Council, Inc., 555 U.S. 7 (2008).

"The [Supreme] Court has repeatedly held that the basis for injunctive relief in the federal courts has always been irreparable injury and the inadequacy of legal remedies." Weinberger v. Romero–Barceló, 456 U.S. 305, 312 (1982); . . .

This circuit has previously held that "a trademark plaintiff who demonstrates a likelihood of success on the merits creates a presumption of irreparable harm." [cit]. However, the validity of this rule has been called into question by the Supreme Court's recent opinion in eBay. . . . . .

Although eBay dealt with the Patent Act, in the context of a request for permanent injunctive relief, we see no principled reason why it should not apply in the present case. See N. Am. Med. Corp., 522 F.3d at 1228.

First, the text and logic of eBay strongly suggest that the traditional principles of equity it discussed should be presumed to apply whenever a court must determine whether to issue an injunction, whether the case is a patent case or any other type of case. In this regard, it is significant that the Court in eBay supported its formulation of the traditional four-factor permanent injunction standard by citing cases that were unrelated to patent law. . . . The Court then analyzed whether the traditional equitable principles set forth in these cases applied in the patent law context and answered in the affirmative, noting that "'a major departure from the long tradition of equity practice should not be lightly implied,'" id. (quoting Romero–Barceló, 456 U.S. at 320), and finding that "[n]othing in the Patent Act indicate[d] that Congress intended such a departure," id. at 391–92. Similarly, nothing in the Lanham Act indicates that Congress intended to depart from traditional equitable principles. Rather, like the Patent Act, the Lanham Act provides a court the "power to grant injunctions, *according to the principles of equity* and upon such terms as the court may deem reasonable, to prevent [,]" among other things, trademark infringement and domain name cybersquatting. 15 U.S.C. § 1116(a) (emphasis added). This provision codifies the traditional equitable remedy of injunction. . . .

Second, the fact that *eBay* dealt with a permanent injunction does not change our conclusion that its principles are equally applicable in the context of preliminary injunctions. This conclusion is buttressed by the logic and language of eBay, which, as previously mentioned, supported its formulation of the traditional four-factor test by citing Amoco Production Co., a case that involved a request for a preliminary injunction. See eBay, 547 U.S. at 391. Our conclusion is also consistent with Supreme Court precedent, which has repeatedly recognized that "[t]he standard for a preliminary injunction is essentially the same as for a permanent injunction with the exception that the plaintiff must show a likelihood of success on the merits rather than actual success." Amoco Prod. Co., 480 U.S. at 546 n. 12, cited with approval in Winter, 129 S.Ct. at 381.

Based on the above, we conclude that a request to preliminarily enjoin alleged trademark infringement is subject to traditional equitable principles, as set forth by the Supreme Court in eBay, and more recently in Winter, which also discusses such principles. We, however, decline to address at this time the full impact of eBay and Winter in this area. For example, we do not address whether our previous rule, relied upon by the district court, i.e., "that a trademark plaintiff who demonstrates a likelihood of success on the merits creates a presumption of irreparable harm," [cit.], is consistent with traditional equitable principles. In other words, we decline to decide whether the aforementioned presumption is analogous to the "general" or "categorical" rules rejected by the Supreme Court in eBay[8] . . . . [I]t is unnecessary to decide this question here because—even if we assume without deciding that said presumption is good law—we still find that the district court abused its discretion in applying the presumption here, in light of the fact that such presumption has been held inapplicable in cases where the party seeking injunctive relief excessively delays in seeking such relief. . . . .

[*Vacated and remanded.*]

At p. 903, add as Note 2A:

2A.   *eBay and Preliminary Injunctions.* A number of courts have now extended *eBay* to the trademark context. *See, e.g., CJ Prods. v. Snuggly Plushez LLC,* 809 F. Supp. 2d 127 (E.D.N.Y. 2011). Suppose that a trademark owner attempts to license the trademark widely, beyond goods and services that the trademark owner itself provides. Taken to an extreme, this behavior might resemble the non-practicing entity or "troll" behavior to which Justice Kennedy alluded in *eBay*. To what extent does trademark law already contain doctrinal devices to preclude trademark "troll" behavior? That is, will these doctrines operate to prevent assertions of likely success on the merits, before the analysis even reaches the question of irreparable harm?

---

[8] The Supreme Court has still not determined whether it is consistent with traditional equitable principles for a court to presume irreparable harm once it concludes that a trademark infringement claim is likely to succeed on the merits. At least two courts of appeal (the Fifth and Eleventh Circuits) have questioned whether such a presumption is consistent with these principles, in light of eBay, but have declined to conclusively answer the question. See Paulsson Geophysical Servs., Inc. v. Sigmar, 529 F.3d 303, 313 (5th Cir. 2008); N. Am. Med. Corp., 522 F.3d at 1228. Furthermore, although the Ninth Circuit applied the presumption in Marlyn Nutraceuticals, Inc. v. Mucos Pharma GmbH & Co., 571 F.3d 873, 877 (9th Cir. 2009), it did so without discussing the impact of eBay. In addition, district courts have split on the issue. Compare Marks Org., Inc. v. Joles, No. 09 CV 10629 (KMW), 2011 WL 1044386, at *8 (S.D.N.Y. Mar. 16, 2011) (finding that "courts may not presume irreparable injury from a showing of likelihood of success on merits" of a trademark infringement claim), with TMX Funding, Inc. v. Impero Techs., Inc., No. C 10-00202 JF (PVT), 2010 WL 2745484, at *7 (N.D .Cal. July 8, 2010) (finding that courts may validly presume irreparable harm upon a showing of likelihood of success on the merits of a trademark infringement claim).

At p. 905, Note 10, add the following:

What should be the scope of an injunction where different regional circuits reach differing results on questions of liability? *Compare Georgia-Pacific Consumer Prods., LP v. Von Drehle Corp.*, 618 F.3d 441 (4th Cir. 2010) (vacating a grant of summary judgment to defendant competitor of paper towel manufacturer on trademark claims arising from supply of paper towels compatible with plaintiff's dispenser) *with Georgia-Pacific Consumer Prods., LP v. Myers Supply, Inc.*, 621 F.3d 771 (8th Cir. 2010) (affirming judgment for defendant in case brought by same plaintiff against towel distributor, as opposed to manufacturer). How should the principle of non-mutual offensive collateral estoppel work to resolve such questions?

At p. 907, Note 15, add the following:

See also Green Edge Enters., LLC v. Rubber Mulch, LLC, 620 F.3d 1287 (Fed. Cir. 2010) (applying *MedImmune* to trademark counterclaims seeking declarations of noninfringement and invalidity).

Nike sued Already (doing business as "Yums") over trademarks relating to Nike's AIR FORCE 1 shoe. Yums filed counterclaims seeking a declaratory judgment that Nike's marks were invalid and one of its registrations should be cancelled. (Lanham Act Section 37 gives courts the power to order cancellation of a registration "[i]n any action involving a registered mark.") Subsequently, Nike covenanted not to sue Yums "based on the appearance of any of [Yums]'s current and/or previous footwear product designs, and any colorable imitations thereof, regardless of whether that footwear is produced, distributed, offered for sale, advertised, sold, or otherwise used in commerce before or after the Effective Date of this Covenant." Nike then voluntarily dismissed its claims and sought to have Yums' counterclaims dismissed on the ground that the court had been divested of jurisdiction. The district court dismissed the claims, invoking *Medimmune, Inc. v. Genentech, Inc.*, 549 U.S. 118 (2007), a patent case dealing with the requirement for a justiciable controversy in declaratory judgment actions. The Second Circuit affirmed, relying on *Medimmune* and also holding that Lanham Act Section 37 did not provide an independent basis for jurisdiction. *Nike, Inc. v. Already, LLC*, 663 F.3d 89 (2d Cir. 2011); *but cf. Bancroft & Masters, Inc. v. Augusta National Inc.*, 223 F.3d 1082 (9th Cir. 2000) (commenting that Section 37 cancellation claim would have provided independent basis for jurisdiction). How should the U.S. Supreme Court rule if the Court takes up the case? Consider the interests at stake. How is Yums affected by a dismissal, especially given that the covenant covers both current and previous designs, even if those designs are sold in the future? How would Nike be affected by a decision finding jurisdiction (denying dismissal)? Where does the public interest lie – in facilitating challenges to the validity of registrations? In encouraging settlement? Both?

At p. 925, add the following case after *Green*:

NIGHTINGALE HOME HEALTHCARE, INC. v. ANODYNE THERAPY, LLC,
626 F.3d 958 (7th Cir. 2010)

POSNER, Circuit Judge:

After Anodyne successfully defended against Nightingale's suit, the district judge granted the defendant's request for an award of attorneys' fees in the amount of $72,747. The award was based on 15 U.S.C. § 1117(a), which allows attorneys' fees to be awarded to prevailing parties in Lanham Act suits-but only in "exceptional cases," a term we shall try to clarify in this opinion because of the surprising lack of agreement among the federal courts of appeals concerning its meaning in the Act. . . . The judge had granted summary judgment in favor of Anodyne on Nightingale's Lanham Act claim early in the litigation. Nightingale, which had not appealed that ruling, contends that no award of attorneys' fees is justified, because the case is not "exceptional."

The Fourth, Sixth, Tenth, and D.C. Circuits apply different tests of exceptionality depending on whether it was the plaintiff or the defendant who prevailed. In the Fourth and D.C. Circuits a prevailing plaintiff is entitled to an award of attorneys' fees if the defendant's infringement (most cases under the Lanham Act charge trademark infringement) was willful or in bad faith (these terms being regarded as synonyms), while a prevailing defendant "can qualify for an award of attorney fees upon a showing of 'something less than bad faith' by the plaintiff," such as "economic coercion, groundless arguments, and failure to cite controlling law." Retail Services Inc. v. Freebies Publishing, 364 F.3d 535, 550 (4th Cir. 2004); Reader's Digest Ass'n, Inc. v. Conservative Digest, Inc., 821 F.2d 800, 808-09 (D.C. Cir. 1987).

In the Tenth Circuit the prevailing plaintiff has to prove that the defendant acted in bad faith, while the prevailing defendant need only show "(1) . . . lack of any foundation [of the lawsuit], (2) the plaintiff's bad faith in bringing the suit, (3) the unusually vexatious and oppressive manner in which it is prosecuted, or (4) perhaps for other reasons as well." National Ass'n of Professional Baseball Leagues, Inc. v. Very Minor Leagues, Inc., 223 F.3d 1143, 1147 (10th Cir. 2000). Given the fourth item in this list, the Tenth Circuit can hardly be said to have a test.

The Sixth Circuit asks in the case of a prevailing plaintiff whether the defendant's infringement of the plaintiff's trademark was "malicious, fraudulent, willful, or deliberate," and in the case of a prevailing defendant whether the plaintiff's suit was "oppressive." Eagles, Ltd. v. American Eagle Foundation, 356 F.3d 724, 728 (6th Cir. 2004). As factors indicating oppressiveness, Eagles quotes the Tenth Circuit's list but states in the alternative, quoting (see id. at 729) our opinion in S Industries, Inc. v. Centra 2000, Inc.,

249 F.3d 625, 627 (7th Cir. 2001), that "a suit is oppressive if it lacked merit, had elements of an abuse of process claim, and plaintiff's conduct unreasonably increased the cost of defending against the suit."

The Second, Fifth, and Eleventh Circuits require prevailing defendants, as well as prevailing plaintiffs, to prove that their opponent litigated in bad faith, or (when the defendant is the prevailing party) that the suit was a fraud. Patsy's Brand, Inc. v. I.O.B. Realty, Inc., 317 F.3d 209, 221-22 (2d Cir. 2003); Procter & Gamble Co. v. Amway Corp., 280 F.3d 519, 527-28 (5th Cir. 2002); Lipscher v. LRP Publications, Inc., 266 F.3d 1305, 1320 (11th Cir. 2001); Tire Kingdom, Inc. v. Morgan Tire & Auto, Inc., 253 F.3d 1332, 1335-36 (11th Cir. 2001) (per curiam). The Fifth Circuit adds that a court considering a prevailing defendant's application for an award of attorneys' fees should "consider the merits and substance of the civil action when examining the plaintiffs' good or bad faith." Procter & Gamble Co. v. Amway Corp., supra, 280 F.3d at 528.

The First, Third, Eighth, and Ninth Circuits, like the Second and the Eleventh, do not distinguish between prevailing plaintiffs and prevailing defendants; neither do they require a showing of bad faith. Tamko Roofing Products, Inc. v. Ideal Roofing Co., 282 F.3d 23, 32 (1st Cir. 2002) ("willfulness short of bad faith or fraud will suffice when equitable considerations justify an award and the district court supportably finds the case exceptional"); Securacomm Consulting, Inc. v. Securacom Inc., 224 F.3d 273, 280 (3d Cir. 2000) ("culpable conduct on the part of the losing party" is required but "comes in a variety of forms and may vary depending on the circumstances of a particular case"); Stephen W. Boney, Inc. v. Boney Services, Inc., 127 F.3d 821, 827 (9th Cir. 1997) ("a finding that the losing party has acted in bad faith may provide evidence that the case is exceptional" but "other exceptional circumstances may [also] warrant a fee award"); Hartman v. Hallmark Cards, Inc., 833 F.2d 117, 123 (8th Cir. 1987) ("bad faith is not a prerequisite" to an award). Yet a later Ninth Circuit decision interprets "exceptional" to mean "the defendant acted maliciously, fraudulently, deliberately, or willfully" (note the echo of the Sixth Circuit's Eagles decision) or the plaintiff's case was "groundless, unreasonable, vexatious, or pursued in bad faith." Love v. Associated Newspapers, Ltd., 611 F.3d 601, 615 (9th Cir. 2010).

And where are we, the Seventh Circuit, in this jumble? In Door Systems, Inc. v. Pro-Line Door Systems, Inc., 126 F.3d 1028, 1031 (7th Cir. 1997), we said that the test was whether the conduct of the party from which the payment of attorneys' fees was sought had been "oppressive," and that "whether the plaintiff's suit was oppressive" turned on whether the suit "was something that might be described not just as a losing suit but as a suit that had elements of an abuse of process, whether or not it had all the elements of the tort." But that, we said, "would not be the right question if the plaintiff had prevailed and was seeking the award of attorneys' fees. In such a case the focus would be on whether the defendant had lacked a solid justification for the defense or had put the plaintiff to an unreasonable expense in suing." Id. The quoted passage was actually discussing the award of attorneys' fees under the Illinois Consumer Fraud and Deceptive Business Practices Act.

But fees were also sought under the Lanham Act, and the opinion-seeking to make sense of one of the definitions of "exceptional" (namely, "malicious, fraudulent, deliberate, or willful") that is found, as we noted earlier, in the cases-suggests that the test is the same under both statutes: "oppressive," in the sense expounded in Door Systems. Id. at 1031-32.

In later cases we said that oppressive conduct by a plaintiff that might justify an award of reasonable attorneys' fees to the defendant would be conduct that "lacked merit, had elements of an abuse of process claim, and plaintiff's conduct in the litigation unreasonably increased the cost of defending against the suit," S Industries, Inc. v. Centra 2000, Inc., supra, 249 F.3d at 627; see also Central Mfg., Inc. v. Brett, 492 F.3d 876, 883-84 (7th Cir. 2007); that oppressive conduct by defendants included not only willful infringement of the plaintiff's trademark but also "vexatious litigation conduct," TE-TAMA Truth Foundation-Family of URI, Inc. v. World Church of the Creator, 392 F.3d 248, 261-63 (7th Cir. 2004); and that a finding that a suit was oppressive could be "based solely on the weakness" of the plaintiff's claims, S Industries, Inc. v. Centra 2000, Inc., supra, 249 F.3d at 627, or the plaintiff's "vexatious litigation conduct." TE-TA-MA Truth Foundation-Family of URI, Inc. v. World Church of the Creator, supra, 392 F.3d at 263. So "vexatious litigation conduct" by the losing party can justify the award of attorneys' fees to the winner, regardless of which side engages in such conduct, as long as it's the losing side.

It is surprising to find so many different standards for awarding attorneys' fees in Lanham Act cases. The failure to converge may be an illustration of "circuit drift": the heavy caseloads and large accumulations of precedent in each circuit induce courts of appeals to rely on their own "circuit law," as if each circuit were a separate jurisdiction rather than all being part of a single national judiciary enforcing a uniform body of federal law. But whether the difference in standards generates actual differences in result is unclear because the opinions avoid commitment by using vague words and explicit escape clauses, with the Tenth Circuit's catchall ("perhaps for other reasons as well") taking the prize. To decide whether the standards differ more than semantically would require a close study of the facts of each case.

It may be helpful in the interest of clarity, simplicity, and uniformity to start with first principles, by asking why the Lanham Act makes an exception, albeit a narrow one (if "exceptional" is to be given proper force), to the "American" rule that forbids shifting the litigation expenses of the prevailing party to the loser.

The reason has been said to be that "the public interest in the integrity of marks as a measure of quality of products" is so great that it would be "unconscionable not to provide a complete remedy including attorney fees for acts which courts have characterized as malicious, fraudulent, deliberate, and willful," and the award of fees "would make a trademark owner's remedy complete in enforcing his mark against willful infringers, and would give defendants a remedy against unfounded suits." S.Rep. No. 1400, 93d Cong., 2d Sess. 5-6 (1974). In addition, the patent and copyright statutes authorize the award of attorneys' fees, id. at 5, and trademark law protects an analogous form of intellectual property.

A more practical concern is the potential for businesses to use Lanham Act litigation for strategic purposes-not to obtain a judgment or defeat a claim but to obtain a competitive advantage independent of the outcome of the case by piling litigation costs on a competitor. Almost all cases under the Act (this one, as we'll see, is a rare exception), whether they are suits for trademark infringement or for false advertising, 15 U.S.C. §§ 1114, 1125(a), are between competitors. The owner of a trademark might bring a Lanham Act suit against a new entrant into his market, alleging trademark infringement but really just hoping to drive out the entrant by imposing heavy litigation costs on him. See, e.g., Peaceable Planet, Inc. v. Ty, Inc., 362 F.3d 986, 987 (7th Cir. 2004). "Trademark suits, like much other commercial litigation, often are characterized by firms' desire to heap costs on their rivals, imposing marketplace losses out of proportion to the legal merits." Mead Johnson & Co. v. Abbott Laboratories, 201 F.3d 883, 888 (7th Cir. 2000). "The increased ease of bringing suit in federal court and the greater availability of remedies may extend the competitive battlefield beyond the 'shelves of the supermarket' and into the halls of the courthouse. Commentators have already suggested that the availability of large damage awards will motivate firms to litigate false advertising suits aggressively in the hope of winning large damage awards and impairing the competitiveness of a business rival, particularly a new entrant." James B. Kobak Jr. & Mary K. Fleck, "Commercial Defamation Claim Added to Revised Lanham Act," Nat'l L.J., Oct. 30, 1989, p. 33. Similarly, a large firm sued for trademark infringement by a small one might mount a scorched-earth defense to a meritorious claim in the hope of imposing prohibitive litigation costs on the plaintiff.

These, then, are the types of suit rightly adjudged "exceptional"; for in a battle of equals each contestant can bear his own litigation costs without impairing competition.

When the plaintiff is the oppressor, the concept of abuse of process provides a helpful characterization of his conduct. Unlike malicious prosecution, which involves filing a baseless suit to harass or intimidate an antagonist, abuse of process is the use of the litigation process for an improper purpose, whether or not the claim is colorable. "The gist of the abuse of process tort is said to be misuse of legal process primarily to accomplish a purpose for which it was not designed, usually to compel the victim to yield on some matter not involved in the suit. . . .. If the plaintiff can show instigation of a suit for an improper purpose without probable cause and with a termination favorable to the now plaintiff, she has a malicious prosecution or a wrongful litigation claim, not a claim for abuse of process. . . .. [T]he abuse of process claim permits the plaintiff to recover without showing the traditional want of probable cause for the original suit and without showing termination of that suit." 2 Dan B. Dobbs, The Law of Torts § 438 (2001). Abuse of process is a prime example of litigating in bad faith.

The term "abuse of process" is not used to describe behavior by defendants. Id. It has been said that "while it is obvious that the torts of abuse of process and malicious prosecution are prevalent and damaging to both innocent defendants as well as the judicial process, it is not so obvious where the line is that separates an attorney's zealous advocacy from his tortious interference with the litigation processes." Leah J. Pollema, "Beyond the Bounds of Zealous Advocacy: The Prevalence of Abusive Litigation in Family Law and the Need for Tort Remedies," 75 U. Mo.-Kan. City L.Rev. 1107, 1117 (2007). But the need to draw that line is the same whether the plaintiff is attacking or the defendant is defending. If a defendant's trademark infringement or false advertising is blatant, his insistence on mounting a costly defense is the same misconduct as a plaintiff's bringing a case (frivolous or not) not in order to obtain a favorable judgment but instead to burden the defendant with costs likely to drive it out of the market. Predatory initiation of suit is mirrored in predatory resistance to valid claims.

We conclude that a case under the Lanham Act is "exceptional," in the sense of warranting an award of reasonable attorneys' fees to the winning party, if the losing party was the plaintiff and was guilty of abuse of process in suing, or if the losing party was the defendant and had no defense yet persisted in the trademark infringement or false advertising for which he was being sued, in order to impose costs on his opponent.

This approach captures the concerns that underlie the various tests and offers a pathway through the semantic jungle. It can account for most of the case outcomes in the various circuits with the exception of those that make it easier for prevailing defendants to obtain attorneys' fees than prevailing plaintiffs. The usual rule, notably in civil rights cases, is the reverse: a prevailing plaintiff is presumptively entitled to an award of attorneys' fees, while a prevailing defendant is entitled to such an award only if the plaintiff's suit was frivolous. [cit.] But those are cases in which the plaintiff is an individual and the defendant a corporation or other institution, implying an asymmetry of resources for litigation. Plaintiffs and defendants in Lanham Act cases usually are symmetrically situated: they are businesses. Of course they may be very different in size, but this is not a reason for a general rule favoring prevailing plaintiffs or prevailing defendants, for there is no correlation between the size of a party and which side of the litigation he's on. Big businesses sue big and small businesses for trademark infringement and false advertising, and small businesses sue big and small businesses for the same torts. Disparity in size will often be relevant in evaluating the legitimacy of the suit or defense, but it is as likely to favor the defendant as the plaintiff.

But there's a puzzle: cases such as Chambers v. NASCO, Inc., 501 U.S. 32, 45-46 (1991), state that one of the inherent powers of a federal court is to "assess attorney's fees when a party has acted in bad faith, vexatiously, wantonly, or for oppressive reasons." [cit.] That sounds a lot like the abuse of process test that we think best describes the exceptional case that merits an award of attorneys' fees under the Lanham Act. But if we are right about our interpretation of "exceptional case," the question arises why Congress bothered to include a fee-shifting provision in the Act; for didn't the courts already have inherent power to award fees for abuse of process in Lanham Act cases?

Although the fee provision of the Lanham Act dates only from 1975, already by then the courts' inherent power to assess fees for abusive litigation was recognized. [cit]. But in Fleischmann Distilling Corp. v. Maier Brewing Co., 386 U.S. 714, 719-20 (1967), decided eight years before the fee provision was added to the Lanham Act, the Supreme Court held that attorneys' fees could not be awarded in cases under the Act; it was that decision which prompted Congress to add the fee-shifting provision. *Fleischmann* rejected the proposition that courts could award fees in cases under the Act without explicit statutory authorization. "The recognized exceptions to the general rule [of no fee shifting] were not . . . developed in the context of statutory causes of action for which the legislature had prescribed intricate remedies. . . . [I]n the Lanham Act, Congress meticulously detailed the remedies available to a plaintiff who proves that his valid trademark has been infringed. It provided not only for injunctive relief, but also for compensatory recovery measured by the profits that accrued to the defendant by virtue of his infringement, the costs of the action, and damages which may be trebled in appropriate circumstances. . . . When a cause of action has been created by a statute which expressly provides the remedies for vindication of the cause, other remedies should not readily be implied." Id. This reasoning is consistent with interpreting the Lanham Act's "exceptional case" provision as having the same substantive content as the inherent power held inapplicable to Lanham Act cases. The puzzle is solved.

A procedural issue remains to be considered. Abuse of process is the name of a tort. A tort is proved in a tort suit. But a proceeding for an award of attorneys' fees is not a suit; it is a tail dangling from a suit. We don't want the tail to wag the dog, and this means that an elaborate inquiry into the state of mind of the party from whom reimbursement of attorneys' fees is sought should be avoided. It should be enough to justify the award if the party seeking it can show that his opponent's claim or defense was objectively unreasonable—was a claim or defense that a rational litigant would pursue only because it would impose disproportionate costs on his opponent—in other words only because it was extortionate in character if not necessarily in provable intention. That should be enough to make a case "exceptional."

In this case, however, there is more. Nightingale, a provider of home healthcare services, had bought several infrared lamps from Anodyne that were designed to relieve pain and improve circulation, paying $6,000 for each lamp. Its Lanham Act claim was that Anodyne's sales representative had falsely represented that the lamp had been approved by the Food and Drug Administration for treatment of peripheral neuropathy. The device was FDA-approved and was intended for the treatment of peripheral neuropathy, and though the FDA had not approved it for that purpose this did not preclude a physician or other healthcare provider, such as Nightingale, from prescribing the device to patients as a treatment for that condition. The decision to prescribe such "off-label usage," as it is called, is deemed a professional judgment for the healthcare provider to make. [cit].

Nightingale told its patients that Anodyne's device was intended for treating peripheral neuropathy, but as far as appears did not tell them that it had been approved by the FDA for the treatment of that condition-a representation that could have gotten Nightingale into trouble with the agency. And when it replaced Anodyne's lamps with the virtually identical lamps of another company (apparently for reasons of price, unrelated to the scope of the FDA's approval), it advertised them just as it had advertised Anodyne's lamps-as devices for the treatment of peripheral neuropathy.

Not only had the Lanham Act claim no possible merit (which would not by itself demonstrate an abuse of process), but the district judge found that Nightingale had made the claim in an attempt to coerce a price reduction from Anodyne. Nightingale would have been content to continue buying Anodyne's lamps, as indicated by its purchasing lamps that were subject to the same limited FDA approval and advertising them the same way. The fact that the FDA had not approved Anodyne's lamps for treatment of peripheral neuropathy was thus of no consequence, for neither had it approved for that purpose the lamps that Nightingale bought to replace Anodyne's. To bring a frivolous claim in order to obtain an advantage unrelated to obtaining a favorable judgment is to commit an abuse of process.

Nightingale continues its frivolous litigation tactics in this court by arguing that Anodyne has "unclean hands" because it failed to turn over certain documents during discovery. It is apparent that the documents are not within the scope of Nightingale's discovery demand once omitted matter indicated by an ellipsis in Nightingale's quotation from the demand is restored.

Nightingale argues that even if Anodyne is entitled to reimbursement for some of the attorneys' fees that it incurred, the district court's award is excessive because it includes fees for defending against claims . . . that were based on state law rather than the Lanham Act. But Anodyne showed that the work that its lawyers had performed in defending against the Lanham Act claim could not be separated from their work in defending against the other claims, and Nightingale presented no rebuttal.

We not only affirm the judgment of the district court but also grant Anodyne's motion for fees and costs pursuant to Rule 38 of the appellate rules . . . .

At p. 930, Note 13, add the following:

See also La Quinta Corp. v. Heartland Properties LLC, 603 F.3d 327 (6th Cir. 2010) (affirming award of treble damages).

At p. 932, Note 14, add the following:

See also Louis Vuitton Malletier S.A. v. Ly USA, Inc., 676 F.3d 83 (2d Cir. 2012) (claim for attorney's fees permissible when mark owner elects statutory damages in counterfeiting case).

At p. 932, Note 19, add the following:

In *Newport News Holdings Corp. v. Virtual City Vision*, 650 F.3d 423 (4th Cir. 2011), the Court of Appeal for the Fourth Circuit indicated that, in determining whether an award of statutory damages under the ACPA was excessive, it would be guided in part by considerations developed by courts applying similar provisions under the Copyright Act. To what extent does the Seventh Amendment confer a right to jury trial on the question of statutory damages? *See GoPets Ltd. v. Hise*, 657 F.3d 1024, 1034 (9th Cir. 2011).

IV

EXPLOITATION OF TRADEMARKS

13 TRADEMARK TRANSACTIONS

At p. 990, Note 4, add the following:

See also Georgia-Pacific Consumer Prods., LP v. Von Drehle Corp., 618 F.3d 441, 458 (4th Cir. 2010) (Wilson, J., concurring) (alluding to a tying allegation in which Georgia Pacific's trademarked towel dispensers was the alleged tying product and towels for use in the dispensers were the alleged tied products).

At p. 993, Note 8, add the following:

See also Fair Isaac Corp. v. Experian Information Solutions, Inc., 650 F.3d 1139, 1150-51 (8th Cir. 2011) (analyzing a claim of licensee estoppel and concluding that the party challenging validity was neither a licensee nor in privity with one, and therefore was not estopped under the doctrine).

STATUTORY MATERIALS

U.S. – Federal Law

TRADEMARK ACT OF 1946 ("LANHAM ACT")

Trademark Act of 1946 ("Lanham Act")

As Amended

15 U.S.C.A. §§ 1051-1141 (§§ 1-74)
Table of Contents

Chapter 22 - Trademarks
Subchapter I - The Principal Register

1051.	(§ 1)	Application for registration; verification
1052.	(§ 2)	Trademarks registrable on principal register; concurrent registration
1053.	(§ 3)	Service marks registrable
1054.	(§ 4)	Collective marks and certification marks registrable
1055.	(§ 5)	Use by related companies affecting validity and registration
1056.	(§ 6)	Disclaimer of unregistrable matter
1057.	(§ 7)	Certificates of registration
1058.	(§ 8)	Duration
1059.	(§ 9)	Renewal of registration
1060.	(§ 10)	Assignment
1061.	(§ 11)	Execution of acknowledgments and verifications
1062.	(§ 12)	Publication
1063.	(§ 13)	Opposition to registration
1064.	(§ 14)	Cancellation of registration
1065.	(§ 15)	Incontestability of right to use mark under certain conditions
1066.	(§ 16)	Interference; declaration by Director
1067.	(§ 17)	Interference, opposition, and proceedings for concurrent use registration or for cancellation; notice; Trademark Trial and Appeal Board
1068.	(§ 18)	Action of Director in interference, opposition, and proceedings for concurrent use registration or for cancellation
1069.	(§ 19)	Application of equitable principles in inter partes proceedings
1070.	(§ 20)	Appeals to Trademark Trial and Appeal Board from decisions of examiners
1071.	(§ 21)	Appeals to courts
1072.	(§ 22)	Registration as constructive notice of claim of ownership

Subchapter II - The Supplemental Register

1091.	(§ 23)	Supplemental register
1092.	(§ 24)	Publication; not subject to opposition; cancellation
1093.	(§ 25)	Registration certificates for marks on principal and supplemental registers to be different
1094.	(§ 26)	Provisions of chapter applicable to registrations on supplemental register
1095.	(§ 27)	Registration on principal register not precluded
1096.	(§ 28)	Registration on supplemental register not used to stop importations

SUBCHAPTER III - GENERAL PROVISIONS

1111. (§ 29)   Notice of registration; display with mark; recovery of profits and damages in infringement suit

1112. (§ 30)   Classification of goods and services; registration in plurality of classes

1113. (§ 31)   Fees

1114. (§ 32)   Remedies; infringement; innocent infringement by printers and publishers

1115. (§ 33)   Registration on principal register as evidence of exclusive right to use mark; defenses

1116. (§ 34)   Injunctive relief

1117. (§ 35)   Recovery for violation of rights

1118. (§ 36)   Destruction of infringing articles

1119. (§ 37)   Power of court over registration

1120. (§ 38)   Civil liability for false or fraudulent registration

1121. (§ 39)   Jurisdiction of Federal courts; State and local requirements that registered trademarks be altered or displayed differently; prohibition

1122. (§ 40)   Liability of United States and States, instrumentalities and officials thereof

1123. (§ 41)   Rules and regulations for conduct of proceedings in Patent and Trademark Office

1124. (§ 42)   Importation of goods bearing infringing marks or names forbidden

1125. (§ 43)   False designations of origin and false descriptions and dilution forbidden

1126. (§ 44)   International conventions

1127. (§ 45)   Construction and definitions; intent of chapter

1128. (§ 46)   National Intellectual Property Law Enforcement Coordination Council

1129. (§ 47)   Cyberpiracy protections for individuals

SUBCHAPTER IV - THE MADRID PROTOCOL

1141. (§ 60)   Definitions

1141a. (§ 61)   International applications based on United States applications or registrations

1141b. (§ 62)   Certification of the international application

1141c. (§ 63)   Restriction, abandonment, cancellation, or expiration of a basic application or basic registration

1141d. (§ 64)   Request for extension of protection subsequent to international registration

1141e. (§ 65)   Extension of protection of an international registration to the United States under the Madrid Protocol

1141f. (§ 66)   Effect of filing a request for extension of protection of an international registration to the United States

1141g. (§ 67)   Right of priority for request for extension of protection to the United

States

1141h. (§ 68)   Examination of and opposition to request for extension of protection; notification of refusal

1141i. (§ 69)   Effect of extension of protection

1141j. (§ 70)   Dependence of extension of protection to the United States on the underlying international registration

1141k. (§ 71)   Affidavits and fees

1141l. (§ 72)   Assignment of an extension of protection

1141m. (§ 73)   Incontestability

1141n. (§ 74)   Rights of extension of protection

SUBCHAPTER I – PRINCIPAL REGISTER

§ 1051. (§ 1) Application for registration; verification
(a) Application for use of trademark

(1)   The owner of a trademark used in commerce may request registration of its trademark on the principal register hereby established by paying the prescribed fee and filing in the Patent and Trademark Office an application and a verified statement, in such form as may be prescribed by the Director, and such number of specimens or facsimiles of the mark as used as may be required by the Director.

(2)   The application shall include specification of the applicant's domicile and citizenship, the date of the applicant's first use of the mark, the date of the applicant's first use of the mark in commerce, the goods in connection with which the mark is used, and a drawing of the mark.

(3)   The statement shall be verified by the applicant and specify that –

(A)   the person making the verification believes that he or she, or the juristic person in whose behalf he or she makes the verification, to be the owner of the mark sought to be registered;

(B)   to the best of the verifier's knowledge and belief, the facts recited in the application are accurate;

(C)   the mark is in use in commerce; and

(D)   to the best of the verifier's knowledge and belief, no other person has the right to use such mark in commerce either in the identical form thereof or in such near resemblance thereto as to be likely, when used on or in connection with the goods of such other person, to cause confusion, or to cause mistake, or to deceive, except that, in the case of every application claiming concurrent use, the applicant shall –

(i) state exceptions to the claim of exclusive use; and

(ii) shall specify, to the extent of the verifier's knowledge –

(I) any concurrent use by others;

(II) the goods on or in connection with which and the areas in which each concurrent use exists;

(III) the periods of each use; and

(IV) the goods and area for which the applicant desires registration.

(4)   The applicant shall comply with such rules or regulations as may be prescribed by the Director. The Director shall promulgate rules prescribing the requirements for the application and for obtaining a filing date herein.

(b) Application for bona fide intention to use trademark

(1)   A person who has a bona fide intention, under circumstances showing the good faith of such person, to use a trademark in commerce may request registration of its trademark on the principal register hereby established by paying the prescribed fee and filing in the Patent and Trademark Office an application and a verified statement, in such form as may be prescribed by the Director.

(2)   The application shall include specification of the applicant's domicile and citizenship, the goods in connection with which the applicant has a bona fide intention to use the mark, and a drawing of the mark.

(3)   The statement shall be verified by the applicant and specify —

(A)   that the person making the verification believes that he or she, or the juristic person in whose behalf he or she makes the verification, to be entitled to use the mark in commerce;

(B)   the applicant's bona fide intention to use the mark in commerce;

(C)   that, to the best of the verifier's knowledge and belief, the facts recited in the application are accurate; and

(D)   that, to the best of the verifier's knowledge and belief, no other person has the right to use such mark in commerce either in the identical form thereof or in such near resemblance thereto as to be likely, when used on or in connection with the goods of such other person, to cause confusion, or to cause mistake, or to deceive.

Except for applications filed pursuant to section 44 [15 USC §1126] of this title, no mark shall be registered until the applicant has met the requirements of subsections (c) and (d) of this section.

(4)   The applicant shall comply with such rules or regulations as may be prescribed by the Director. The Director shall promulgate rules prescribing the requirements for the application and for obtaining a filing date herein.

(c) Amendment of application under subsection (b) to conform to requirements under subsection (a).

At any time during examination of an application filed under subsection (b) of this section, an applicant who has made use of the mark in commerce may claim the benefits of such use for purposes of this chapter, by amending his or her application to bring it into conformity with the requirements of subsection (a) of this section.

(d) Verified statement that trademark is used in commerce.

(1) Within six months after the date on which the notice of allowance with respect to a mark is issued under section 13(b)(2) [15 USC §1063(b)(2)] of this title to an applicant under subsection (b) of this section, the applicant shall file in the Patent and Trademark Office, together with such number of specimens or facsimiles of the mark as used in commerce as may be required by the Director and payment of the prescribed fee, a verified statement that the mark is in use in commerce and specifying the date of the applicant's first use of the mark in commerce and those goods or services specified in the notice of allowance on or in connection with which the mark is used in commerce. Subject to examination and acceptance of the statement of use, the mark shall be registered in the Patent and Trademark Office, a certificate of registration shall be issued for those goods or services recited in the statement of use for which the mark is entitled to registration, and notice of registration shall be published in the Official Gazette of the Patent and Trademark Office. Such examination may include an examination of the factors set forth

in subsections (a) through (e) of section 2 [15 USC §1052] of this title. The notice of registration shall specify the goods or services for which the mark is registered.

(2) The Director shall extend, for one additional 6-month period, the time for filing the statement of use under paragraph (1), upon written request of the applicant before the expiration of the 6-month period provided in paragraph (1). In addition to an extension under the preceding sentence, the Director may, upon a showing of good cause by the applicant, further extend the time for filing the statement of use under paragraph (1) for periods aggregating not more than 24 months, pursuant to written request of the applicant made before the expiration of the last extension granted under this paragraph. Any request for an extension under this paragraph shall be accompanied by a verified statement that the applicant has a continued bona fide intention to use the mark in commerce and specifying those goods or services identified in the notice of allowance on or in connection with which the applicant has a continued bona fide intention to use the mark in commerce. Any request for an extension under this paragraph shall be accompanied by payment of the prescribed fee. The Director shall issue regulations setting forth guidelines for determining what constitutes good cause for purposes of this paragraph.

(3) The Director shall notify any applicant who files a statement of use of the acceptance or refusal thereof and, if the statement of use is refused, the reasons for the refusal. An applicant may amend the statement of use.

(4) The failure to timely file a verified statement of use under paragraph (1) or an extension request under paragraph (2) shall result in abandonment of the application, unless it can be shown to the satisfaction of the Director that the delay in responding was unintentional, in which case the time for filing may be extended, but for a period not to exceed the period specified in paragraphs (1) and (2) for filing a statement of use.

(e) Designation of resident for service of process and notices.

If the applicant is not domiciled in the United States the applicant may designate, by a document filed in the United States Patent and Trademark Office, the name and address of a person resident in the United States on whom may be served notices or process in proceedings affecting the mark. Such notices or process may be served upon the person so designated by leaving with that person or mailing to that person a copy thereof at the address specified in the last designation so filed. If the person so designated cannot be found at the address given in the last designation, or if the registrant does not designate by a document filed in the United States Patent and Trademark Office the name and address of a person resident in the United States on whom may be served notices or process in proceedings affecting the mark, such notices or process may be served on the Director.

§ 1052. (§ 2) Trademarks registrable on principal register;
concurrent registration

No trademark by which the goods of the applicant may be distinguished from the goods of others shall be refused registration on the principal register on account of its nature unless it—

(a) Consists of or comprises immoral, deceptive, or scandalous matter; or matter which may disparage or falsely suggest a connection with persons, living or dead, institutions, beliefs, or national symbols, or bring them into contempt, or disrepute; or a geographical indication which, when used on or in connection with wines or spirits, identifies a place other than the origin of the goods and is first used on or in connection with wines or spirits by the applicant on or after one year after the date on which the WTO Agreement (as defined in section 3501(9) of title 19) enters into force with respect to the United States.

(b) Consists of or comprises the flag or coat of arms or other insignia of the United States, or of any State or municipality, or of any foreign nation, or any simulation thereof.

(c) Consists of or comprises a name, portrait, or signature identifying a particular living individual except by his written consent, or the name, signature, or portrait of a deceased President of the United States during the life of his widow, if any, except by the written consent of the widow.

(d) Consists of or comprises a mark which so resembles a mark registered in the Patent and Trademark Office, or a mark or trade name previously used in the United States by another and not abandoned, as to be likely, when used on or in connection with the goods of the applicant, to cause confusion, or to cause mistake, or to deceive: *Provided*, That if the Director determines that confusion, mistake, or deception is not likely to result from the continued use by more than one person of the same or similar marks under conditions and limitations as to the mode or place of use of the marks or the goods on or in connection with which such marks are used, concurrent registrations may be issued to such persons when they have become entitled to use such marks as a result of their concurrent lawful use in commerce prior to (1) the earliest of the filing dates of the applications pending or of any registration issued under this chapter; (2) July 5, 1947, in the case of registrations previously issued under the Act of March 3, 1881, or February 20, 1905, and continuing in full force and effect on that date; or (3) July 5, 1947, in the case of applications filed under the Act of February 20, 1905, and registered after July 5, 1947. Use prior to the filing date of any pending application or a registration shall not be required when the owner of such application or registration consents to the grant of a concurrent registration to the applicant. Concurrent registrations may also be issued by the Director when a court of competent jurisdiction has finally determined that more than one person is entitled to use the same or similar marks in commerce. In issuing concurrent registrations, the Director shall prescribe conditions and limitations as to the mode or place of use of the mark or the goods on or in connection with which such mark is registered to the respective persons.

(e) Consists of a mark which (1) when used on or in connection with the goods of the applicant is merely descriptive or deceptively misdescriptive of them, (2) when used on or in connection with the goods of the applicant is primarily geographically descriptive of them, except as indications of regional origin may be registrable under section 4 [15 USC §1054] of this title, (3) when used on or in connection with the goods of the applicant is primarily geographically deceptively misdescriptive of them, (4) is primarily merely a surname, or (5) comprises any matter that, as a whole, is functional.

(f) Except as expressly excluded in subsections (a), (b), (c), (d), (e)(3), and (e)(5) of this section, nothing in this chapter shall prevent the registration of a mark used by the applicant which has become distinctive of the applicant's goods in commerce. The Director may accept as prima facie evidence that the mark has become distinctive, as used on or in connection with the applicant's goods in commerce, proof of substantially exclusive and continuous use thereof as a mark by the applicant in commerce for the five years before the date on which the claim of distinctiveness is made. Nothing in this section shall prevent the registration of a mark which, when used on or in connection with the goods of the applicant, is primarily geographically deceptively misdescriptive of them, and which became distinctive of the applicant's goods in commerce before the date of the enactment of the North American Free Trade Agreement Implementation Act [enacted Dec. 8, 1993].

A mark which would be likely to cause dilution by blurring or dilution by tarnishment under section 43(c) [15 USC §1125(c)] of this title, may be refused registration only pursuant to a proceeding brought under section 13 [15 USC §1063] of this title. A registration for a mark which would be likely to cause dilution by blurring or dilution by tarnishment under section 43(c) [15 USC §1125(c)] of this title, may be canceled pursuant to a proceeding brought under either section 14 [15 USC §1064] of this title or section 24 [15 USC §1092] of this title.

§ 1053. (§ 3) Service marks registrable

Subject to the provisions relating to the registration of trademarks, so far as they are applicable, service marks shall be registrable, in the same manner and with the same effect as are trademarks, and when registered they shall be entitled to the protection provided in this chapter in the case of trademarks. Applications and procedure under this section shall conform as nearly as practicable to those prescribed for the registration of trademarks.

§ 1054. (§ 4) Collective marks and certification marks registrable

Subject to the provisions relating to the registration of trademarks, so far as they are applicable, collective and certification marks, including indications of regional origin, shall be registrable under this chapter, in the same manner and with the same effect as are trademarks, by persons, and nations, States, municipalities, and the like, exercising legitimate control over the use of the marks sought to be registered, even though not possessing an industrial or commercial establishment, and when registered they shall be entitled to the protection provided in this chapter in the case of trademarks, except in the case of certification marks when used so as to represent falsely that the owner or a user thereof makes or sells the goods or performs the services on or in connection with which such mark is used. Applications and procedure under this section shall conform as nearly as practicable to those prescribed for the registration of trademarks.

§ 1055. (§ 5) Use by related companies affecting validity and registration

Where a registered mark or a mark sought to be registered is or may be used legitimately by related companies, such use shall inure to the benefit of the registrant or applicant for registration, and such use shall not affect the validity of such mark or of its registration, provided such mark is not used in such manner as to deceive the public. If first use of a mark by a person is controlled by the registrant or applicant for registration of the mark with respect to the nature and quality of the goods or services, such first use shall inure to the benefit of the registrant or applicant, as the case may be.

§ 1056. (§ 6) Disclaimer of unregistrable matter
(a) Compulsory and voluntary disclaimers

The Director may require the applicant to disclaim an unregistrable component of a mark otherwise registrable. An applicant may voluntarily disclaim a component of a mark sought to be registered.

(b) Prejudice of rights

No disclaimer, including those made under subsection (e) of section 7 of this Act [15 USC §1057(e)] of this title, shall prejudice or affect the applicant's or registrant's rights then existing or thereafter arising in the disclaimed matter, or his right of registration on another application if the disclaimed matter be or shall have become distinctive of his goods or services.

§ 1057. (§ 7) Certificates of registration
(a) Issuance and form

Certificates of registration of marks registered upon the principal register shall be issued in the name of the United States of America, under the seal of the United States Patent and Trademark Office, and shall be signed by the Director or have his signature placed thereon, and a record thereof shall be kept in the United States Patent and Trademark Office. The registration shall reproduce the mark, and state that the mark is registered on the principal register under this chapter, the date of the first use of the mark, the date of the first use of the mark in commerce, the particular goods or services for which it is registered, the number and date of the registration, the term thereof, the date on which the application for registration was received in the United States Patent and Trademark Office, and any conditions and limitations that may be imposed in the registration.

(b) Certificate as prima facie evidence

A certificate of registration of a mark upon the principal register provided by this chapter shall be prima facie evidence of the validity of the registered mark and of the registration of the mark, of the owner's ownership of the mark, and of the owner's exclusive right to use the registered mark in commerce on or in connection with the goods or services specified in the certificate, subject to any conditions or limitations stated in the certificate.

(c) Application to register mark considered constructive use

Contingent on the registration of a mark on the principal register provided by this chapter, the filing of the application to register such mark shall constitute constructive use of the mark, conferring a right of priority, nationwide in effect, on or in connection with the goods or services specified in the registration against any other person except for a person whose mark has not been abandoned and who, prior to such filing —

(1) has used the mark;

(2) has filed an application to register the mark which is pending or has resulted in registration of the mark; or

(3) has filed a foreign application to register the mark on the basis of which he or she has acquired a right of priority, and timely files an application under section 44(d) [15 USC §1126(d)] of this title to register the mark which is pending or has resulted in registration of the mark.

(d) Issuance to assignee

A certificate of registration of a mark may be issued to the assignee of the applicant, but the assignment must first be recorded in the United States Patent and Trademark Office. In case of change of ownership the Director shall, at the request of the owner and upon a proper showing and the payment of the prescribed fee, issue to such assignee a new certificate of registration of the said mark in the name of such assignee, and for the unexpired part of the original period.

(e) Surrender, cancellation, or amendment by registrant

Upon application of the owner the Director may permit any registration to be surrendered for cancellation, and upon cancellation appropriate entry shall be made in the records of the United States Patent and Trademark Office. Upon application of the owner and payment of the prescribed fee, the Director for good cause may permit any registration to be amended or to be disclaimed in part: *Provided*, That the amendment or disclaimer does not alter materially the character of the mark. Appropriate entry shall be made in the records of the United States Patent and Trademark Office and upon the certificate of registration.

(f) Copies of Patent and Trademark Office records as evidence

Copies of any records, books, papers, or drawings belonging to the United States Patent and Trademark Office relating to marks, and copies of registrations, when authenticated by the seal of the United States Patent and Trademark Office and certified by the Director, or in his name by an employee of the Office duly designated by the Director, shall be evidence in all cases wherein the originals would be evidence; and any person making application therefor and paying the prescribed fee shall have such copies.

(g) Correction of Patent and Trademark Office mistake

Whenever a material mistake in a registration, incurred through the fault of the United States Patent and Trademark Office, is clearly disclosed by the records of the Office a certificate stating the fact and nature of such mistake shall be issued without charge and recorded and a printed copy thereof shall be attached to each printed copy of the registration and such corrected registration shall thereafter have the same effect as if the same had been originally issued in such corrected form, or in the discretion of the Director a new certificate of registration may be issued without charge. All certificates of correction heretofore issued in accordance with the rules of the United States Patent and Trademark Office and the registrations to which they are attached shall have the same force and effect as if such certificates and their issue had been specifically authorized by statute.

(h) Correction of applicant's mistake

Whenever a mistake has been made in a registration and a showing has been made that such mistake occurred in good faith through the fault of the applicant, the Director is authorized to issue a certificate of correction or, in his discretion, a new certificate upon the payment of the prescribed fee: *Provided*, That the correction does not involve such changes in the registration as to require republication of the mark.

§ 1058. (§ 8) Duration, affidavits and fees.

(a) Time periods for required affidavits

Each registration shall remain in force for 10 years, except that the registration of any mark shall be canceled by the Director unless the owner of the registration files in the United States Patent and Trademark Office affidavits that meet the requirements of subsection (b), within the following time periods:

(1) Within the 1-year period immediately preceding the expiration of 6 years following the date of registration under this Act or the date of the publication under section 12(c) [15 USC §1062(c)].

(2) Within the 1-year period immediately preceding the expiration of 10 years following the date of registration, and each successive 10-year period following the date of registration.

(3) The owner may file the affidavit required under this section within the 6-month grace period immediately following the expiration of the periods established in paragraphs (1) and (2), together with the fee described in subsection (b) and the additional grace period surcharge prescribed by the Director.

(b) Requirements for affidavit

The affidavit referred to in subsection (a) shall —

(1)(A) state that the mark is in use in commerce;

(B) set forth the goods and services recited in the registration on or in connection with which the mark is in use in commerce;

(C) be accompanied by such number of specimens or facsimiles showing current use of the mark in commerce as may be required by the Director; and

(D) be accompanied by the fee prescribed by the Director; or

(2)(A) set forth the goods and services recited in the registration on or in connection with which the mark is not in use in commerce;

(B) include a showing that any nonuse is due to special circumstances which excuse such nonuse and is not due to any intention to abandon the mark; and

(C) be accompanied by the fee prescribed by the Director.

(c) Deficient affidavit

If any submission filed within the period set forth in subsection (a) is deficient, including that the affidavit was not filed in the name of the owner of the registration, the deficiency may be corrected after the statutory time period, within the time prescribed after notification of the deficiency. Such submission shall be accompanied by the additional deficiency surcharge prescribed by the Director.

(d) Notice of requirement

Special notice of the requirement for such affidavit shall be attached to each certificate of registration and notice of publication under section 12(c) [15 USC §1062(c)].

(e) Notification of acceptance or refusal

The Director shall notify any owner who files any affidavit required by this section of the Director's acceptance or refusal thereof and, in the case of a refusal, the reasons therefor.

(f) Designation of resident for service of process and notices

If the owner is not domiciled in the United States, the owner may designate, by a document filed in the United States Patent and Trademark Office, the name and address of a person resident in the United States on whom may be served notices or process in proceedings affecting the mark. Such notices or process may be served upon the person so designated by leaving with that person or mailing to that person a copy thereof at the address specified in the last designation so filed. If the person so designated cannot be found at the last designated address, or if the owner does not designate by a document filed in the United States Patent and Trademark Office the name and address of a person resident in the United States on whom may be served notices or process in proceedings affecting the mark, such notices or process may be served on the Director.

§ 1059. (§ 9) Renewal of registration
(a) Period of renewal; time for renewal

Subject to the provisions of section 8 [15 USC §1058] of this title, each registration may be renewed for periods of 10 years at the end of each successive 10-year period following the date of registration upon payment of the prescribed fee and the filing of a written application, in such form as may be prescribed by the Director. Such application may be made at any time within 1 year before the end of each successive 10-year period for which the registration was issued or renewed, or it may be made within a grace period of 6 months after the end of each successive 10-year period, upon payment of a fee and surcharge prescribed therefor. If any application filed under this section is deficient, the deficiency may be corrected within the time prescribed after notification of the deficiency, upon payment of a surcharge prescribed therefor.

(b) Notification of refusal of renewal

If the Director refuses to renew the registration, the Director shall notify the registrant of the Director's refusal and the reasons therefor.

(c) Designation of resident for service of process and notices

If the registrant is not domiciled in the United States, the registrant may designate, by a document filed in the United States Patent and Trademark Office, the name and address of a person resident in the United States on whom may be served notices or process in proceedings affecting the mark. Such notices or process may be served upon the person so designated by leaving with that person or mailing to that person a copy thereof at the address specified in the last designation so filed. If the person so designated cannot be found at the address given in the last designation, or if the registrant does not designate by a document filed in the United States Patent and Trademark Office the name and address of a person resident in the United States on whom may be served notices or process in proceedings affecting the mark, such notices or process may be served on the Director.

§ 1060. (§ 10) Assignment

(a) (1) A registered mark or a mark for which an application to register has been filed shall be assignable with the good will of the business in which the mark is used, or with that part of the good will of the business connected with the use of and symbolized by the mark. Notwithstanding the preceding sentence, no application to register a mark under section 1(b) [15 USC §1051(b)] of this title shall be assignable prior to the filing of an amendment under section 1(c) [15 USC §1051(c)] to bring the application into conformity with section 1(a) [15 USC §1051(a)] of this title or the filing of the verified statement of use under section 1(d) [15 USC §1051(d)] of this title, except for an assignment to a successor to the business of the applicant, or portion thereof, to which the mark pertains, if that business is ongoing and existing.

(2) In any assignment authorized by this section, it shall not be necessary to include the good will of the business connected with the use of and symbolized by any other mark used in the business or by the name or style under which the business is conducted.

(3) Assignments shall be by instruments in writing duly executed. Acknowledgment shall be prima facie evidence of the execution of an assignment, and when the prescribed information reporting the assignment is recorded in the Patent and Trademark Office, the record shall be prima facie evidence of execution.

(4) An assignment shall be void against any subsequent purchaser for valuable consideration without notice, unless the prescribed information reporting the assignment is recorded in the Patent and Trademark Office within 3 months after the date of the assignment or prior to the subsequent purchase.

(5) The Patent and Trademark Office shall maintain a record of information on assignments, in such form as may be prescribed by the Director.

(b) An assignee not domiciled in the United States may designate by a document filed in the United States Patent and Trademark Office the name and address of a person resident in the United States on whom may be served notices or process in proceedings affecting the mark. Such notices or process may be served upon the person so designated by leaving with that person or mailing to that person a copy thereof at the address specified in the last designation so filed. If the person so designated cannot be found at the address given in the last designation, or if the assignee does not designate by a document filed in the United States Patent and Trademark Office the name and address of a person resident in the United States on whom my be served notices or process in proceedings affecting the mark, such notices or process may be served upon the Director.

§ 1061. (§ 11) Execution of acknowledgments and verifications

Acknowledgments and verifications required under this chapter may be made before any person within the United States authorized by law to administer oaths, or, when made in a foreign country, before any diplomatic or consular officer of the United States or before any official authorized to administer oaths in the foreign country concerned whose authority is proved by a certificate of a diplomatic or consular officer of the United States, or apostille of an official designated by a foreign country which, by treaty or convention, accords like effect to apostilles of designated officials in the United States, and shall be valid if they comply with the laws of the state or country where made.

§ 1062. (§ 12) Publication

(a) Examination and publication

Upon the filing of an application for registration and payment of the prescribed fee, the Director shall refer the application to the examiner in charge of the registration of marks, who shall cause an examination to be made and, if on such examination it shall appear that the applicant is entitled to registration, or would be entitled to registration upon the acceptance of the statement of use required by section 1(d)[15 USC §1051(d)] of this title, the Director shall cause the mark to be published in the Official Gazette of the Patent and Trademark Office: *Provided*, That in the case of an applicant claiming concurrent use, or in the case of an application to be placed in an interference as provided in section 16 of this Act [15 USC §1066] of this title the mark, if otherwise registrable, may be published subject to the determination of the rights of the parties to such proceedings.

(b) Refusal of registration; amendment of application; abandonment

If the applicant is found not entitled to registration, the examiner shall advise the applicant thereof and of the reasons therefor. The applicant shall have a period of six months in which to reply or amend his application, which shall then be reexamined. This procedure may be repeated until (1) the examiner finally refuses registration of the mark or (2) the applicant fails for a period of six months to reply or amend or appeal, whereupon the application shall be deemed to have been abandoned, unless it can be shown to the satisfaction of the Director that the delay in responding was unintentional, whereupon such time may be extended.

(c) Republication of marks registered under prior acts

A registrant of a mark registered under the provisions of the Act of March 3, 1881, or the Act of February 20, 1905, may, at any time prior to the expiration of the registration thereof, upon the payment of the prescribed fee file with the Director an affidavit setting forth those goods stated in the registration on which said mark is in use in commerce and that the registrant claims the benefits of this chapter for said mark. The Director shall publish notice thereof with a reproduction of said mark in the Official Gazette, and notify the registrant of such publication and of the requirement for the affidavit of use or nonuse as provided for in subsection (b) of Section 8[15 USC §1058(b)] of this title. Marks published under this subsection shall not be subject to the provisions of section 13 [15 USC §1063] of this title.

§ 1063. (§ 13) Opposition to registration

(a) Any person who believes that he would be damaged by the registration of a mark upon the principal register, including the registration of any mark which would be likely to cause dilution by blurring or dilution by tarnishment under section 43(c) [15 USC §1125(c)] of this title, may, upon payment of the prescribed fee, file an opposition in the Patent and Trademark Office, stating the grounds therefor, within thirty days after the publication under subsection (a) of section 12[15 USC §1062] of this title of the mark sought to be registered. Upon written request prior to the expiration of the thirty-day period, the time for filing opposition shall be extended for an additional thirty days, and further extensions of time for filing opposition may be granted by the Director for good cause when requested prior to the expiration of an extension. The Director shall notify the applicant of each extension of the time for filing opposition. An opposition may be amended under such conditions as may be prescribed by the Director.

(b) Unless registration is successfully opposed —

(1) a mark entitled to registration on the principal register based on an application filed under section 1(a) [15 USC §1051(a)] of this title or pursuant to section 44 [15 USC §1126] of this title shall be registered in the Patent and Trademark Office, a certificate of registration shall be issued, and notice of the registration shall be published in the Official Gazette of the Patent and Trademark Office; or

(2) a notice of allowance shall be issued to the applicant if the applicant applied for registration under section 1(b) [15 USC §1051(b)] of this title.

§ 1064. (§ 14) Cancellation of registration

A petition to cancel a registration of a mark, stating the grounds relied upon, may, upon payment of the prescribed fee, be filed as follows by any person who believes that he is or will be damaged, including as a result of likelihood of dilution by blurring or dilution by tarnishment under section 43(c) [15 USC §1125(c)], by the registration of a mark on the principal register established by this chapter, or under the Act of March 3, 1881, or the Act of February 20, 1905:

(1) Within five years from the date of the registration of the mark under this Act.

(2) Within five years from the date of publication under section 12(c) [15 USC §1062(c)] of this title of a mark registered under the Act of March 3, 1881, or the Act of February 20, 1905.

(3) At any time if the registered mark becomes the generic name for the goods or services, or a portion thereof, for which it is registered, or is functional, or has been abandoned, or its registration was obtained fraudulently or contrary to the provisions of section 4 [15 USC §1054] of this title or of subsection (a), (b), or (c) of section 2 [15 USC §1052] of this title for a registration under this chapter, or contrary to similar prohibitory provisions of such prior Acts for a registration under

such Acts, or if the registered mark is being used by, or with the permission of, the registrant so as to misrepresent the source of the goods or services on or in connection with which the mark is used. If the registered mark becomes the generic name for less than all of the goods or services for which it is registered, a petition to cancel the registration for only those goods or services may be filed. A registered mark shall not be deemed to be the generic name of goods or services solely because such mark is also used as a name of or to identify a unique product or service. The primary significance of the registered mark to the relevant public rather than purchaser motivation shall be the test for determining whether the registered mark has become the generic name of goods or services on or in connection with which it has been used.

(4) At any time if the mark is registered under the Act of March 3, 1881, or the Act of February 20, 1905, and has not been published under the provisions of subsection (c) of section 12[15 USC §1062] of this title.

(5) At any time in the case of a certification mark on the ground that the registrant (A) does not control, or is not able legitimately to exercise control over, the use of such mark, or (B) engages in the production or marketing of any goods or services to which the certification mark is applied, or (C) permits the use of the certification mark for purposes other than to certify, or (D) discriminately refuses to certify or to continue to certify the goods or services of any person who maintains the standards or conditions which such mark certifies:

Provided, That the Federal Trade Commission may apply to cancel on the grounds specified in paragraphs (3) and (5) of this section any mark registered on the principal register established by this chapter, and the prescribed fee shall not be required.

Nothing in paragraph (5) shall be deemed to prohibit the registrant from using its certification mark in advertising or promoting recognition of the certification program or of the goods or services meeting the certification standards of the registrant. Such uses of the certification mark shall not be grounds for cancellation under paragraph (5), so long as the registrant does not itself produce, manufacture, or sell any of the certified goods or services to which its identical certification mark is applied.

§ 1065. (§ 15) Incontestability of right to use mark under certain conditions

Except on a ground for which application to cancel may be filed at any time under paragraphs (3) and (5) of section 14[15 USC §1064(3), (5)] of this title, and except to the extent, if any, to which the use of a mark registered on the principal register infringes a valid right acquired under the law of any State or Territory by use of a mark or trade name continuing from a date prior to the date of registration under this chapter of such registered mark, the right of the owner to use such registered mark in commerce for the goods or services on or in connection with which such registered mark has been in continuous use for five consecutive years subsequent to the date of such registration and is still in use in commerce, shall be incontestable: *Provided*, That —

(1) there has been no final decision adverse to the owner's claim of ownership of such mark for such goods or services, or to the owner's right to register the same or to keep the same on the register; and

(2) there is no proceeding involving said rights pending in the United States Patent and Trademark Office or in a court and not finally disposed of; and

(3) an affidavit is filed with the Director within one year after the expiration of any such five-year period setting forth those goods or services stated in the registration on or in connection with which such mark has been in continuous use for such five consecutive years and is still in use in commerce, and the other matters specified in paragraphs (1) and (2) of this section; and

(4) no incontestable right shall be acquired in a mark which is the generic name for the goods or services or a portion thereof, for which it is registered.

Subject to the conditions above specified in this section, the incontestable right with reference to a mark registered under this chapter shall apply to a mark registered under the Act of March 3, 1881, or the Act of February 20, 1905, upon the filing of the required affidavit with the Director within one year after the expiration of any period of five consecutive years after the date of publication of a mark under the provisions of subsection (c) of section 12[15 USC §1062(c)] of this title.

The Director shall notify any registrant who files the above-prescribed affidavit of the filing thereof.

§ 1066. (§ 16) Interference; declaration by Director

Upon petition showing extraordinary circumstances, the Director may declare that an interference exists when application is made for the registration of a mark which so resembles a mark previously registered by another, or for the registration of which another has previously made application, as to be likely when used on or in connection with the goods or services of the applicant to cause confusion or mistake or to deceive. No interference shall be declared between an application and the registration of a mark the right to the use of which has become incontestable.

§1067. (§ 17) Interference, opposition, and proceedings for concurrent use registration or for cancellation; notice; Trademark Trial and Appeal Board

(a) In every case of interference, opposition to registration, application to register as a lawful concurrent user, or application to cancel the registration of a mark, the Director shall give notice to all parties and shall direct a Trademark Trial and Appeal Board to determine and decide the respective rights of registration.

(b) The Trademark Trial and Appeal Board shall include the Director, the Commissioner for Patents, the Commissioner for Trademarks, and administrative trademark judges who are appointed by the Director.

§1068. (§ 18) Action of Director in interference, opposition, and proceedings for concurrent use registration or for cancellation

In such proceedings the Director may refuse to register the opposed mark, may cancel the registration, in whole or in part, may modify the application or registration by limiting the goods or services specified therein, may otherwise restrict or rectify with respect to the register the registration of a registered mark, may refuse to register any or all of several interfering marks, or may register the mark or marks for the person or persons entitled thereto, as the rights of the parties under this chapter may be established in the proceedings: *Provided*, That in the case of the registration of any mark based on concurrent use, the Director shall determine and fix the conditions and limitations provided for in subsection (d) of section 2[15 USC §1052(d)] of this title. However, no final judgment shall be entered in favor of an applicant under section 1(b) [15 USC §1051(b)] of this title before the mark is registered, if such applicant cannot prevail without establishing constructive use pursuant to section 7(c) [15 USC §1057(c)] of this title.

§ 1069. (§ 19) Application of equitable principles in inter partes proceedings

In all inter partes proceedings equitable principles of laches, estoppel, and acquiescence, where applicable may be considered and applied.

§1070. (§ 20) Appeals to Trademark Trial and Appeal Board from decisions of examiners

An appeal may be taken to the Trademark Trial and Appeal Board from any final decision of the examiner in charge of the registration of marks upon the payment of the prescribed fee.

§ 1071. (§ 21) Appeal to courts

(a)   **Persons entitled to appeal; United States Court of Appeals for the Federal Circuit; waiver of civil action; election of civil action by adverse party; procedure**

(1) An applicant for registration of a mark, party to an interference proceeding, party to an opposition proceeding, party to an application to register as a lawful concurrent user, party to a cancellation proceeding, a registrant who has filed an affidavit as provided in section 8 [15 USC §1058] or section 71 [15 USC §1141k] of this title, or an applicant for renewal, who is dissatisfied with the decision of the Director or Trademark Trial and Appeal Board, may appeal to the United States Court of Appeals for the Federal Circuit thereby waiving his right to proceed under subsection (b) of this section: *Provided*, That such appeal shall be dismissed if any adverse party to the proceeding, other than the Director, shall, within twenty days after the appellant has filed notice of appeal according to paragraph (2) of this subsection, files notice with the Director that he elects to have all further proceedings conducted as provided in subsection (b) of this section. Thereupon the appellant shall have thirty days thereafter within which to file a civil action under subsection (b) of this section, in default of which the decision appealed from shall govern the further proceedings in the case.

(2) When an appeal is taken to the United States Court of Appeals for the Federal Circuit, the appellant shall file in the United States Patent and Trademark Office a written notice of appeal directed to the Director, within such time after the date of the decision from which the appeal is taken as the Director prescribes, but in no case less than 60 days after that date.

(3) The Director shall transmit to the United States Court of Appeals for the Federal Circuit a certified list of the documents comprising the record in the United States Patent

and Trademark Office. The court may request that the Director forward the original or certified copies of such documents during pendency of the appeal. In an ex parte case, the Director shall submit to that court a brief explaining the grounds for the decision of the United States Patent and Trademark Office, addressing all the issues involved in the appeal. The court shall, before hearing an appeal, give notice of the time and place of the hearing to the Director and the parties in the appeal.

(4) The United States Court of Appeals for the Federal Circuit shall review the decision from which the appeal is taken on the record before the United States Patent and Trademark Office. Upon its determination the court shall issue its mandate and opinion to the Director, which shall be entered of record in the United States Patent and Trademark Office and shall govern the further proceedings in the case. However, no final judgment shall be entered in favor of an applicant under section 1(b) [15 USC §1051(b)] of this title before the mark is registered, if such applicant cannot prevail without establishing constructive use pursuant to section 7(c) [15 USC §1057(c)] of this title.

(b) Civil action; persons entitled to; jurisdiction of court; status of Director; procedure

(1) Whenever a person authorized by subsection (a) of this section to appeal to the United States Court of Appeals for the Federal Circuit is dissatisfied with the decision of the Director or Trademark Trial and Appeal Board, said person may, unless appeal has been taken to said United States Court of Appeals for the Federal Circuit, have remedy by a civil action if commenced within such time after such decision, not less than sixty days, as the Director appoints or as provided in subsection (a) of this section. The court may adjudge that an applicant is entitled to a registration upon the application involved, that a registration involved should be canceled, or such other matter as the issues in the proceeding require, as the facts in the case may appear. Such adjudication shall authorize the Director to take any necessary action, upon compliance with the requirements of law. However, no final judgment shall be entered in favor of an applicant under section 1(b) [15 USC §1051(b)] of this title before the mark is registered, if such applicant cannot prevail without establishing constructive use pursuant to section 7(c) [15 USC §1057(c)] of this title.

(2) The Director shall not be made a party to an inter partes proceeding under this subsection, but he shall be notified of the filing of the complaint by the clerk of the court in which it is filed and shall have the right to intervene in the action.

(3) In any case where there is no adverse party, a copy of the complaint shall be served on the Director, and, unless the court finds the expenses to be unreasonable, all the expenses of the proceeding shall be paid by the party bringing the case, whether the final decision is in favor of such party or not. In suits brought hereunder, the record in the United States Patent and Trademark Office shall be admitted on motion of any party, upon such terms and conditions as to costs, expenses, and the further cross-examination of the witnesses as the court imposes, without prejudice to the right of any party to take further testimony. The testimony and exhibits of the record in the United States Patent and Trademark Office, when admitted, shall have the same effect as if originally taken and produced in the suit.

(4) Where there is an adverse party, such suit may be instituted against the party in interest as shown by the records of the United States Patent and Trademark Office at the time of the decision complained of, but any party in interest may become a party to the action. If there are adverse parties residing in a plurality of districts not embraced within the same State, or an adverse party residing in a foreign country, the United States District Court for the District of Columbia shall have jurisdiction and may issue summons against the adverse parties directed to the marshal of any district in which any adverse party resides. Summons against adverse parties residing in foreign countries may be served by publication or otherwise as the court directs.

§ 1072. (§ 22) Registration as constructive notice of claim of ownership

Registration of a mark on the principal register provided by this chapter or under the Act of March 3, 1881, or the Act of February 20, 1905, shall be constructive notice of the registrant's claim of ownership thereof.

SUBCHAPTER II - THE SUPPLEMENTAL REGISTER

§ 1091. (§ 23) Supplemental register
(a) Marks registrable

In addition to the principal register, the Director shall keep a continuation of the register provided in paragraph (b) of section 1 of the Act of March 19, 1920, entitled "An Act to give effect to certain provisions of the convention for the protection of trademarks and commercial names, made and signed in the city of Buenos Aires, in the Argentine Republic, August 20, 1910, and for other purposes", to be called the supplemental register. All marks capable of distinguishing applicant's goods or services and not registrable on the principal register provided in this chapter, except those declared to be unregistrable under subsections (a), (b), (c), (d), and (e)(3) of section 2[15 USC §1052] of this title, which are in lawful use in commerce by the owner thereof, on or in connection with any goods or services may be registered on the supplemental register upon the payment of the prescribed fee and compliance with the provisions of subsections (a) and (e) of section 1 [15 USC §1051] of this title so far as they are applicable. Nothing in this section shall prevent the registration on the supplemental register of a mark, capable of distinguishing the applicant's goods or services and not registrable on the principal register under this Act, that is declared to be unregistrable under section 2(e)(3) [15 USC §1052(e)(3)] of this title, if such mark has been in lawful use in commerce by the owner thereof, on or in connection with any goods or services, since before December 8, 1993.

(b) Application and proceedings for registration

Upon the filing of an application for registration on the supplemental register and payment of the prescribed fee the Director shall refer the application to the examiner in charge of the registration of marks, who shall cause an examination to be made and if on such examination it shall appear that the applicant is entitled to registration, the registration shall be granted. If the applicant is found not entitled to registration the provisions of subsection (b) of section 12 of this Act [15 USC §1062] of this title shall apply.

(c) Nature of mark

For the purposes of registration on the supplemental register, a mark may consist of any trademark, symbol, label, package, configuration of goods, name, word, slogan, phrase, surname, geographical name, numeral, device, any matter that as a whole is not functional, or any combination of any of the foregoing, but such mark must be capable of distinguishing the applicant's goods or services.

§ 1092. (§ 24) Publication; not subject to opposition; cancellation

Marks for the supplemental register shall not be published for or be subject to opposition, but shall be published on registration in the Official Gazette of the Patent and Trademark Office. Whenever any person believes that such person is or will be damaged by the registration of a mark on the supplemental register—

(1) for which the effective filing date is after the date on which such person's mark became famous and which would be likely to cause dilution by blurring or dilution by tarnishment under section 43(c); or

(2) on grounds other than dilution by blurring or dilution by tarnishment, such person may at any time, upon payment of the prescribed fee and the filing of a petition stating the ground therefor, apply to the Director to cancel such registration.

The Director shall refer such application to the Trademark Trial and Appeal Board which shall give notice thereof to the registrant. If it is found after a hearing before the Board that the registrant is not entitled to registration, or that the mark has been abandoned, the registration shall be canceled by the Director. However, no final judgment shall be entered in favor of an applicant under section 1(b) [15 USC §1051(b)] of this title before the mark is registered, if such applicant cannot prevail without establishing constructive use pursuant to section 7(c) [15 USC §1057(c)] of this title.

§ 1093. (§ 25) Registration certificates for marks on principal and supplemental registers to be different

The certificates of registration for marks registered on the supplemental register shall be conspicuously different from certificates issued for marks registered on the principal register.

§ 1094. (§ 26) Provisions of chapter applicable to registrations on supplemental register

The provisions of this chapter shall govern so far as applicable applications for registration and registrations on the supplemental register as well as those on the principal register, but applications for and registrations on the supplemental register shall not be subject to or receive the advantages of sections 1(b), 2(e), 2(f), 7(b), 7(c), 12(a), 13 to 18, inclusive, 22, 33, and 42[15 USC §§1051(b), 1052(e), 1052(f), 1057(b), 1057(c), 1062(a), 1063 to 1068, inclusive, 1072, 1115 and 1124] of this title.

§ 1095. (§ 27) Registration on principal register not precluded

Registration of a mark on the supplemental register, or under the Act of March 19, 1920, shall not preclude registration by the registrant on the principal register established by this chapter. Registration of a mark on the supplemental register shall not constitute an admission that the mark has not acquired distinctiveness.

§1096. (§ 28) Registration on supplemental register not used to stop importations

Registration on the supplemental register or under the Act of March 19, 1920, shall not be filed in the Department of the Treasury or be used to stop importations.

SUBCHAPTER III - GENERAL PROVISIONS

§ 1111. (§ 29) Notice of registration; display with mark; recovery of profits and damages in infringement suit

Notwithstanding the provisions of section 22 [15 USC §1072] of this title, a registrant of a mark registered in the Patent and Trademark Office, may give notice that his mark is registered by displaying with the mark the words "Registered in U. S. Patent and Trademark Office" or "Reg. U.S. Pat. & Tm. Off." or the letter R enclosed within a circle, thus ®; and in any suit for infringement under this chapter by such a registrant failing to give such notice of registration, no profits and no damages shall be recovered under the provisions of this chapter unless the defendant had actual notice of the registration.

§ 1112. (§ 30) Classification of goods and services; registration in plurality of classes

The Director may establish a classification of goods and services, for convenience of Patent and Trademark Office administration, but not to limit or extend the applicant's or registrant's rights. The applicant may apply to register a mark for any or all of the goods or services on or in connection with which he or she is using or has a bona fide intention to use the mark in commerce: *Provided*, That if the Director by regulation permits the filing of an application for the registration of a mark for goods or services which fall within a plurality of classes, a fee equaling the sum of the fees for filing an application in each class shall be paid, and the Director may issue a single certificate of registration for such mark.

§ 1113. (§ 31) Fees
(a) Applications; services; materials

The Director shall establish fees for the filing and processing of an application for the registration of a trademark or other mark and for all other services performed by and materials furnished by the Patent and Trademark Office related to trademarks and other marks. Fees established under this subsection may be adjusted by the Director once each year to reflect, in the aggregate, any fluctuations during the preceding 12 months in the Consumer Price Index, as determined by the Secretary of Labor. Changes of less than 1 percent may be ignored. No fee established under this section shall take effect until at least 30 days after notice of the fee has been published in the Federal Register and in the Official Gazette of the Patent and Trademark Office.

(b) Waiver; Indian products

The Director may waive the payment of any fee for any service or material related to trademarks or other marks in connection with an occasional request made by a department or agency of the Government, or any officer thereof. The Indian Arts and Crafts Board will not be charged any fee to register Government trademarks of genuineness and quality for Indian products or for products of particular Indian tribes and groups.

§ 1114. (§ 32) Remedies; infringement; innocent infringement by printers and publishers

(1) Any person who shall, without the consent of the registrant—

(a) use in commerce any reproduction, counterfeit, copy, or colorable imitation of a registered mark in connection with the sale, offering for sale, distribution, or advertising of any goods or services on or in connection with which such use is likely to cause confusion, or to cause mistake, or to deceive; or

(b) reproduce, counterfeit, copy, or colorably imitate a registered mark and apply such reproduction, counterfeit, copy, or colorable imitation to labels, signs, prints, packages, wrappers, receptacles or advertisements intended to be used in commerce upon or in connection with the sale, offering for sale, distribution, or advertising of goods or services on or in connection with which such use is likely to cause confusion, or to cause mistake, or to deceive,

shall be liable in a civil action by the registrant for the remedies hereinafter provided. Under subsection (b) hereof, the registrant shall not be entitled to recover profits or damages unless the acts have been committed with knowledge that such imitation is intended to be used to cause confusion, or to cause mistake, or to deceive.

As used in this paragraph, the term "any person" includes the United States, all agencies and instrumentalities thereof, and all individuals, firms, corporations, or other persons acting for the United States and with the authorization and consent of the United States, and any State, any instrumentality of a State, and any officer or employee of a State or instrumentality of a State acting in his or her official capacity. The United States, all agencies and instrumentalities thereof, and all individuals, firms, corporations, other persons acting for the United States and with the authorization and consent of the United States, and any State, and any such instrumentality, officer, or employee, shall be subject to the provisions of this chapter in the same manner and to the same extent as any nongovernmental entity.

(2) Notwithstanding any other provision of this chapter, the remedies given to the owner of a right infringed under this chapter or to a person bringing an action under section 43(a) or (d) [15 USC §1125(a) or (d)] of this title shall be limited as follows:

(A) Where an infringer or violator is engaged solely in the business of printing the mark or violating matter for others and establishes that he or she was an innocent infringer or innocent violator, the owner of the right infringed or person bringing the action under section 43(a) [15 USC §1125(a)] of this title shall be entitled as against such infringer or violator only to an injunction against future printing.

(B) Where the infringement or violation complained of is contained in or is part of paid advertising matter in a newspaper, magazine, or other similar periodical or in an electronic communication as defined in section 2510(12) of title 18, the remedies of the owner of the right infringed or person bringing the action under section 43(a) [15 USC §1125(a)] of this title as against the publisher or distributor of such newspaper, magazine, or other similar periodical or electronic communication shall be limited to an injunction against the presentation of such advertising matter in future issues of such newspapers, magazines, or other similar periodicals or in future transmissions of such electronic communications. The limitations of this subparagraph shall apply only to innocent infringers and innocent violators.

(C) Injunctive relief shall not be available to the owner of the right infringed or person bringing the action under section 43(a) [15 USC §1125(a)] with respect to an issue of a newspaper, magazine, or other similar periodical or an electronic communication containing infringing matter or violating matter where restraining the dissemination of such infringing matter or violating matter in any particular issue of such periodical or in an electronic communication would delay the delivery of such issue or transmission of such electronic communication after the regular time for such delivery or transmission, and such delay would be due to the method by which publication and distribution of such periodical or transmission of such electronic communication is customarily conducted in accordance with sound business practice, and not due to any method or device adopted to evade this section or to prevent or delay the issuance of an injunction or restraining order with respect to such infringing matter or violating matter.

(D) (i) (I) A domain name registrar, a domain name registry, or other domain name registration authority that takes any action described under clause (ii) affecting a domain name shall not be liable for monetary relief or, except as provided in subclause (II), for injunctive relief, to any person for such action, regardless of whether the domain name is finally determined to infringe or dilute the mark.

(II) A domain name registrar, domain name registry, or other domain name registration authority described in subclause (I) may be subject to injunctive relief only if such registrar, registry, or other registration authority has—

(aa) not expeditiously deposited with a court, in which an action has been filed regarding the disposition of the domain name, documents sufficient for the court to establish the court's control and authority regarding the disposition of the registration and use of the domain name;

(bb) transferred, suspended, or otherwise modified the domain name during the pendency of the action, except upon order of the court; or

(cc) willfully failed to comply with any such court order.

(ii) An action referred to under clause (i)(I) is any action of refusing to register, removing from registration, transferring, temporarily disabling, or permanently canceling a domain name—

(I) in compliance with a court order under section 43(d) [15 USC §1125(d)] of this title; or

(II) in the implementation of a reasonable policy by such registrar, registry, or authority prohibiting the registration of a domain name that is identical to, confusingly similar to, or dilutive of another's mark.

(iii) A domain name registrar, a domain name registry, or other domain name registration authority shall not be liable for damages under this section for the registration or maintenance of a domain name for another absent a showing of bad faith intent to profit from such registration or maintenance of the domain name.

(iv) If a registrar, registry, or other registration authority takes an action described under clause (ii) based on a knowing and material misrepresentation by any other person that a domain name is identical to, confusingly similar to, or dilutive of a mark, the person making the knowing and material misrepresentation shall be liable for any damages, including costs and attorney's fees, incurred by the domain name registrant as a result of such action. The court may also grant injunctive relief to the domain name registrant, including the reactivation of the domain name or the transfer of the domain name to the domain name registrant.

(v) A domain name registrant whose domain name has been suspended, disabled, or transferred under a policy described under clause (ii)(II) may, upon notice to the mark owner, file a civil action to establish that the registration or use of the domain name by such registrant is not unlawful under this Act. The court may grant injunctive relief to the domain name registrant, including the reactivation of the domain name or transfer of the domain name to the domain name registrant.

(E) As used in this paragraph—

(i) the term "violator" means a person who violates section 43(a) [15 USC §1125(a)] of this title; and

(ii) the term "violating matter" means matter that is the subject of a violation under section 43(a) [15 USC §1125(a)] of this title.

(3)(A) Any person who engages in the conduct described in paragraph (11) of section 110 of Title 17, and who complies with the requirements set forth in that paragraph is not liable on account of such conduct for a violation of any right under this chapter. This subparagraph does not preclude liability, nor shall it be construed to restrict the defenses or limitation on rights granted under this chapter, of a person for conduct not described in paragraph (11) of section 110 of Title 17, even if that person also engages in conduct described in paragraph (11) of section 110 of such title.

(B) A manufacturer, licensee, or licensor or technology that enables the making of limited portions of audio or video content of a motion picture imperceptible as described in subparagraph (A) is not liable on account of such manufacture or license for a violation of any right under this chapter, if such manufacturer, licensee, or licensor ensures that the technology provides a clear and conspicuous notice at the beginning of each performance that the performance of the motion picture is altered from the performance intended by the director or copyright holder of the motion picture. The limitations on liability in subparagraph (A) and this subparagraph shall not apply to a manufacturer, licensee, or licensor of technology that fails to comply with this paragraph.

(C) The requirement under subparagraph (B) to provide notice shall apply only with respect to technology manufactured after the end of the 180-day period beginning on April 27, 2005.

(D) Any failure by a manufacturer, licensee, or licensor of technology to qualify for the exemption under subparagraphs (A) and (B) shall not be construed to create an inference that any such party that engages in conduct described in paragraph (11) of section 110 of Title 17 is liable for trademark infringement by reason of such conduct.

§ 1115. (§ 33) Registration on principal register as evidence of exclusive right to use mark; defenses

(a) Evidentiary value; defenses

Any registration issued under the Act of March 3, 1881, or the Act of February 20, 1905, or of a mark registered on the principal register provided by this chapter and owned by a party to an action shall be admissible in evidence and shall be prima facie evidence of the validity of the registered mark and of the registration of the mark, of the registrant's ownership of the mark, and of the registrant's exclusive right to use the registered mark in commerce on or in connection with the goods or services specified in the registration subject to any conditions or limitations stated therein, but shall not preclude another person from proving any legal or equitable defense or defect, including those set forth in subsection (b) of this section, which might have been asserted if such mark had not been registered.

(b) Incontestability; defenses

To the extent that the right to use the registered mark has become incontestable under section 15 [15 USC §1065] of this title, the registration shall be conclusive evidence of the validity of the registered mark and of the registration of the mark, of the registrant's ownership of the mark, and of the registrant's exclusive right to use the registered mark in commerce. Such conclusive evidence shall relate to the exclusive right to use the mark on or in connection with the goods or services specified in the affidavit filed under the provisions of section 15 [15 USC §1065] of this title, or in the renewal application filed under the provisions of section 9 [15 USC §1059] of this title if the goods or services specified in the renewal are fewer in number, subject to any conditions or limitations in the registration or in such affidavit or renewal application. Such conclusive evidence of the right to use the registered mark shall be subject to proof of infringement as defined in section 32 [15 USC §1114] of this title, and shall be subject to the following defenses or defects:

(1) That the registration or the incontestable right to use the mark was obtained fraudulently; or

(2) That the mark has been abandoned by the registrant; or

(3) That the registered mark is being used, by or with the permission of the registrant or a person in privity with the registrant, so as to misrepresent the source of the goods or services on or in connection with which the mark is used; or

(4) That the use of the name, term, or device charged to be an infringement is a use, otherwise than as a mark, of the party's individual name in his own business, or of the individual name of anyone in privity with such party, or of a term or device which is descriptive of and used fairly and in good faith only to describe the goods or services of such party, or their geographic origin; or

(5) That the mark whose use by a party is charged as an infringement was adopted without knowledge of the registrant's prior use and has been continuously used by such party or those in privity with him from a date prior to (A) the date of constructive use of the mark established pursuant to section 7(c) [15 USC §1057(c)] of this title, (B) the registration of the mark under this chapter if the application for registration is filed before the effective date of the Trademark Law Revision Act of 1988, or (C) publication of the registered mark under subsection (c) of section 12 of this Act [15 USC §1062(c)] of this title: *Provided, however,* That this defense or defect shall apply only for the area in which such continuous prior use is proved; or

(6) That the mark whose use is charged as an infringement was registered and used prior to the registration under this chapter or publication under subsection (c) of section 12 of this Act [15 USC §1062(c)] of this title of the registered mark of the registrant, and not abandoned: *Provided, however,* That this defense or defect shall apply only for the area in which the mark was used prior to such registration or such publication of the registrant's mark; or

(7) That the mark has been or is being used to violate the antitrust laws of the United States; or

(8) That the mark is functional; or

(9) That equitable principles, including laches, estoppel, and acquiescence, are applicable.

§ 1116. (§ 34) Injunctive relief
(a) Jurisdiction; service

The several courts vested with jurisdiction of civil actions arising under this chapter shall have power to grant injunctions, according to the principles of equity and upon such terms as the court may deem reasonable, to prevent the violation of any right of the registrant of a mark registered in the Patent and Trademark Office or to prevent a violation under subsection (a), (c), or (d) of section 43 [15 USC §1125] of this title. Any such injunction may include a provision directing the defendant to file with the court and serve on the plaintiff within thirty days after the service on the defendant of such injunction, or such extended period as the court may direct, a report in writing under oath setting forth in detail the manner and form in which the defendant has complied with the injunction. Any such injunction granted upon hearing, after notice to the defendant, by any district court of the United States, may be served on the parties against whom such injunction is granted anywhere in the United States where they may be found, and shall be operative and may be enforced by proceedings to punish for contempt, or otherwise, by the court by which such injunction was granted, or by any other United States district court in whose jurisdiction the defendant may be found.

(b) Transfer of certified copies of court papers

The said courts shall have jurisdiction to enforce said injunction, as provided in this chapter, as fully as if the injunction had been granted by the district court in which it is sought to be enforced. The clerk of the court or judge granting the injunction shall, when required to do so by the court before which application to enforce said injunction is made, transfer without delay to said court a certified copy of all papers on file in his office upon which said injunction was granted.

(c) Notice to Director

It shall be the duty of the clerks of such courts within one month after the filing of any action, suit, or proceeding involving a mark registered under the provisions of this chapter to give notice thereof in writing to the Director setting forth in order so far as known the names and addresses of the litigants and the designating number or numbers of the registration or registrations upon which the action, suit, or proceeding has been brought, and in the event any other registration be subsequently included in the action, suit, or proceeding by amendment, answer, or other pleading, the clerk shall give like notice thereof to the Director, and within one month after the judgment is entered or an appeal is taken the clerk of the court shall give notice thereof to the Director, and it shall be the duty of the Director on receipt of such notice forthwith to endorse the same upon the file wrapper of the said registration or registrations and to incorporate the same as a part of the contents of said file wrapper.

(d) Civil actions arising out of use of counterfeit marks

(1)(A) In the case of a civil action arising under section 32(1)(a) [15 USC §1114(1)(a)] of this title or section 220506 of title 36 [section 110 of the Act entitled "An Act to incorporate the United States Olympic Association"] with respect to a violation that consists of using a counterfeit mark in connection with the sale, offering for sale, or distribution of goods or services, the court may, upon ex parte application, grant an order under subsection (a) of this section pursuant to this subsection providing for the seizure of goods and counterfeit marks involved in such violation and the means of making such marks, and records documenting the manufacture sale, or receipt of things involved in such violation.

(B) As used in this subsection the term "counterfeit mark" means—

(i) a counterfeit of a mark that is registered on the principal register in the United States Patent and Trademark Office for such goods or services sold, offered for sale, or distributed and that is in use, whether or not the person against whom relief is sought knew such mark was so registered; or

(ii) a spurious designation that is identical with, or substantially indistinguishable from, a designation as to which the remedies of this chapter are made available by reason of section 220506 of title 36 [section 110 of the Act entitled "An Act to incorporate the United States Olympic Association"];

but such term does not include any mark or designation used on or in connection with goods or services of which the manufacture or producer was, at the time of the manufacture or production in question authorized to use the mark or designation for the type of goods or services so manufactured or produced, by the holder of the right to use such mark or designation.

(2) The court shall not receive an application under this subsection unless the applicant has given such notice of the application as is reasonable under the circumstances to the United States attorney for the judicial district in which such order is sought. Such attorney may participate in the proceedings arising under such application if such proceedings may affect evidence of an offense against the United States. The court may deny such application if the court determines that the public interest in a potential prosecution so requires.

(3) The application for an order under this subsection shall—

(A) be based on an affidavit or the verified complaint establishing facts sufficient to support the findings of fact and conclusions of law required for such order; and

(B) contain the additional information required by paragraph (5) of this subsection to be set forth in such order.

(4) The court shall not grant such an application unless—

(A) the person obtaining an order under this subsection provides the security determined adequate by the court for the payment of such damages as any person may be entitled to recover as a result of a wrongful seizure or wrongful attempted seizure under this subsection; and

(B) the court finds that it clearly appears from specific facts that—

(i) an order other than an ex parte seizure order is not adequate to achieve the purposes of section 32[15 USC. §1114] of this title;

(ii) the applicant has not publicized the requested seizure;

(iii) the applicant is likely to succeed in showing that the person against whom seizure would be ordered used a counterfeit mark in connection with the sale, offering for sale, or distribution of goods or services;

(iv) an immediate and irreparable injury will occur if such seizure is not ordered;

(v) the matter to be seized will be located at the place identified in the application;

(vi) the harm to the applicant of denying the application outweighs the harm to the legitimate interests of the person against whom seizure would be ordered of granting the application; and

(vii) the person against whom seizure would be ordered, or persons acting in concert with such person, would destroy, move, hide, or otherwise make such matter inaccessible to the court, if the applicant were to proceed on notice to such person.

(5) An order under this subsection shall set forth—

(A) the findings of fact and conclusions of law required for the order;

(B) a particular description of the matter to be seized, and a description of each place at which such matter is to be seized;

(C) the time period, which shall end not later than seven days after the date on which such order is issued, during which the seizure is to be made;

(D) the amount of security required to be provided under this subsection; and

(E) a date for the hearing required under paragraph (10) of this subsection.

(6) The court shall take appropriate action to protect the person against whom an order under this subsection is directed from publicity, by or at the behest of the plaintiff, about such order and any seizure under such order.

(7) Any materials seized under this subsection shall be taken into the custody of the court. For seizures made under this section, the court shall enter an appropriate protective order with respect to discovery and use of any records or information that has been seized. The protective order shall provide for appropriate procedures to ensure that confidential, private, proprietary, or privileged information contained in such records is not improperly disclosed or used.

(8) An order under this subsection, together with the supporting documents, shall be sealed until the person against whom the order is directed has an opportunity to contest such order, except that any person against whom such order is issued shall have access to such order and supporting documents after the seizure has been carried out.

(9) The court shall order that service of a copy of the order under this subsection shall be made by a Federal law enforcement officer (such as a United States marshal or an officer or agent of the United States Customs Service, Secret Service, Federal Bureau of Investigation, or Post Office) or may be made by a State or local law enforcement officer, who, upon making service, shall carry out the seizure under the order. The court shall issue orders, when appropriate, to protect the defendant from undue damage from the disclosure of trade secrets or other confidential information during the course of the seizure, including, when appropriate, orders restricting the access of the applicant (or any agent or employee of the applicant) to such secrets or information.

(10) (A) The court shall hold a hearing, unless waived by all the parties, on the date set by the court in the order of seizure. That date shall be not sooner than ten days after the order is issued and not later than fifteen days after the order is issued, unless the applicant for the order shows good cause for another date or unless the party against whom such order is directed consents to another date for such hearing. At such hearing the party obtaining the order shall have the burden to prove that the facts supporting findings of fact and conclusions of law necessary to support such order are still in effect. If that party fails to meet that burden, the seizure order shall be dissolved or modified appropriately.

(B) In connection with a hearing under this paragraph, the court may make such orders modifying the time limits for discovery under the Rules of Civil Procedure as may be necessary to prevent the frustration of the purposes of such hearing.

(11) A person who suffers damage by reason of a wrongful seizure under this subsection has a cause of action against the applicant for the order under which such seizure was made, and shall be entitled to recover such relief as may be appropriate, including damages for lost profits, cost of materials, loss of good will, and punitive damages in instances where the seizure was sought in bad faith, and, unless the court finds extenuating circumstances, to recover a reasonable attorney's fee. The court in its discretion may award prejudgment interest on relief recovered under this paragraph, at an annual interest rate established under section 6621(a)(2) of Title 26, commencing on the date of service of the claimant's pleading setting forth the claim under this paragraph and

ending on the date such recovery is granted, or for such shorter time as the court deems appropriate.

§ 1117. (§ 35) Recovery for violation of rights
(a) Profits; damages and costs; attorney fees

When a violation of any right of the registrant of a mark registered in the Patent and Trademark Office, a violation under section 43(a), or (d) [15 USC §1125(a), or (d)] of this title, or a willful violation under section 43(c) [15 USC §1125(c)] of this title, shall have been established in any civil action arising under this Act, the plaintiff shall be entitled, subject to the provisions of sections 29 and 32 [15 USC §§1111 and 1114] of this title, and subject to the principles of equity, to recover (1) defendant's profits, (2) any damages sustained by the plaintiff, and (3) the costs of the action. The court shall assess such profits and damages or cause the same to be assessed under its direction. In assessing profits the plaintiff shall be required to prove defendant's sales only; defendant must prove all elements of cost or deduction claimed. In assessing damages the court may enter judgment, according to the circumstances of the case, for any sum above the amount found as actual damages, not exceeding three times such amount. If the court shall find that the amount of the recovery based on profits is either inadequate or excessive the court may in its discretion enter judgment for such sum as the court shall find to be just, according to the circumstances of the case. Such sum in either of the above circumstances shall constitute compensation and not a penalty. The court in exceptional cases may award reasonable attorney fees to the prevailing party.

(b) Treble damages for use of counterfeit mark

In assessing damages under subsection (a) for any violation of section 32(1)(a) of this Act or section 220506 of title 36, United States Code, in a case involving use of a counterfeit mark or designation (as defined in section 34(d) of this Act), the court shall, unless the court finds extenuating circumstances, enter judgment for three times such profits or damages, whichever amount is greater, together with a reasonable attorney's fee, if the violation consists of—

(1) intentionally using a mark or designation, knowing such mark or designation is a counterfeit mark (as defined in section 34(d) of this Act), in connection with the sale, offering for sale, or distribution of goods or services; or

(2) providing goods or services necessary to the commission of a violation specified in paragraph (1), with the intent that the recipient of the goods or services would put the goods or services to use in committing the violation.

In such a case, the court may award prejudgment interest on such amount at an annual interest rate established under section 6621(a)(2) of the Internal Revenue Code of 1986, beginning on the date of the service of the claimant's pleadings setting forth the claim for such entry of judgment and ending on the date such entry is made, or for such shorter time as the court considers appropriate.

(c) Statutory damages for use of counterfeit marks

In a case involving the use of a counterfeit mark (as defined in section 34(d) [15 U.S.C. 1116(d)] of this title in connection with the sale, offering for sale, or distribution of goods or services, the plaintiff may elect, at any time before final judgment is rendered by the trial court, to recover, instead of actual damages and profits under subsection (a) of this section, an award of statutory damages for any such use in connection with the sale, offering for sale, or distribution of goods or services in the amount of —

(1) not less than $ 1,000 or more than $ 200,000 per counterfeit mark per type of goods or services sold, offered for sale, or distributed, as the court considers just; or

(2) if the court finds that the use of the counterfeit mark was willful, not more than $ 2,000,000 per counterfeit mark per type of goods or services sold, offered for sale, or distributed, as the court considers just.

(d) Statutory damages for violation of section 43(d)(1) [15 USC § 1125(d)(1)]

In a case involving a violation of section 43(d)(1) [15 USC §1125(d)(1)] of this title, the plaintiff may elect, at any time before final judgment is rendered by the trial court, to recover, instead of actual damages and profits, an award of statutory damages in the amount of not less than $ 1,000 and not more than $ 100,000 per domain name, as the court considers just.

(e) [Rebuttable presumption of willful violation]

In the case of violation referred to in this section, it shall be a rebuttable presumption that the violation is willful for purposes of determining relief if the violator, or a person acting in concert with the violator, knowingly provided or knowingly cause to be provided materially false contact information to a domain name registrar, domain name registry, or other domain name registration authority in registering, maintaining, or renewing a domain name used in connection with the violation. Nothing in this subsection limits what may be considered a willful violation under this section.

§ 1118. (§ 36) Destruction of infringing articles

In any action arising under this chapter, in which a violation of any right of the registrant of a mark registered in the Patent and Trademark Office, a violation under section 43(a) [15 USC §1125(a)] of this title, or a willful violation under section 43(c) [15 USC §1125(c)] of this title, shall have been established, the court may order that all labels, signs, prints, packages, wrappers, receptacles, and advertisements in the possession of the defendant, bearing the registered mark or, in the case of a violation of section 43(a) [15 USC §1125(a)] of this title or a willful violation under section 43(c) [15 USC §1125(c)] of this title, the word, term, name, symbol, device, combination thereof, designation, description, or representation that is the subject of the violation, or any reproduction, counterfeit, copy, or colorable imitation thereof, and all plates, molds, matrices, and other means of making the same, shall be delivered up and destroyed. The party seeking an order under this section for destruction of articles seized under section 34(d) [15 U.S.C. 1116(d)] of this title shall give ten days' notice to the United States attorney for the judicial district in which such order is sought (unless good cause is shown for lesser notice) and such United States attorney may, if such destruction may affect evidence of an offense against the United States, seek a hearing on such destruction or participate in any hearing otherwise to be held with respect to such destruction.

§ 1119. (§ 37) Power of court over registration

In any action involving a registered mark the court may determine the right to registration, order the cancellation of registrations, in whole or in part, restore canceled registrations, and otherwise rectify the register with respect to the registrations of any party to the action. Decrees and orders shall be certified by the court to the Director, who shall make appropriate entry upon the records of the Patent and Trademark Office, and shall be controlled thereby.

§1120. (§ 38) Civil liability for false or fraudulent registration

Any person who shall procure registration in the Patent and Trademark Office of a mark by a false or fraudulent declaration or representation, oral or in writing, or by any false means, shall be liable in a civil action by any person injured thereby for any damages sustained in consequence thereof.

§1121. (§ 39) Jurisdiction of Federal courts; State and local requirements that registered trademarks be altered or displayed differently; prohibition

(a) The district and territorial courts of the United States shall have original jurisdiction and the courts of appeal of the United States (other than the United States Court of Appeals for the Federal Circuit) shall have appellate jurisdiction, of all actions arising under this chapter, without regard to the amount in controversy or to diversity or lack of diversity of the citizenship of the parties.

(b) No State or other jurisdiction of the United States or any political subdivision or any agency thereof may require alteration of a registered mark, or require that additional trademarks, service marks, trade names, or corporate names that may be associated with or incorporated into the registered mark be displayed in the mark in a manner differing from the display of such additional trademarks, service marks, trade names, or corporate names contemplated by the registered mark as exhibited in the certificate of registration issued by the United States Patent and Trademark Office.

§ 1121a. Transferred

§1122. (§ 40) Liability of States, instrumentalities of states and state officials

(a) Waiver of sovereign immunity by the United States

The United States, all agencies and instrumentalities thereof, and all individuals, firms, corporations, other persons acting for the United States and with the authorization and consent of the United States, shall not be immune from suit in Federal or State court by any person, including any governmental or nongovernmental entity, for any violation under this chapter.

(b) Waiver of sovereign immunity by States

Any State, instrumentality of a State or any officer or employee of a State or instrumentality of a State acting in his or her official capacity, shall not be immune, under the eleventh amendment of the Constitution of the United States or under any other doctrine of sovereign immunity, from suit in Federal court by any person, including any governmental or nongovernmental entity for any violation under this chapter.

(c) Remedies

In a suit described in subsection (a) or (b) of this section for a violation described therein, remedies (including remedies both at law and in equity) are available for the violation to the same extent as such remedies are available for such a violation in a suit against any person other than the United States or any agency or instrumentality thereof, or any individual, firm, corporation, or other person acting for the United States and with authorization and consent of the United States, or a State, instrumentality of a State, or officer or employee of a State or instrumentality of a State acting in his or her official capacity. Such remedies include injunctive relief under section 34 [15 USC §1116] of this title, actual damages, profits, costs and attorney's fees under section 35 [15 USC §1117] of this title, destruction of infringing articles under section 36 [15 USC §1118] of this title, the remedies provided for under sections 32, 37, 38, 42 and 43, [15 USC §§1114, 1119, 1120, 1124, and 1125] of this title, and for any other remedies provided under this chapter.

§ 1123. (§ 41) Rules and regulations for conduct of proceedings in Patent and Trademark Office

The Director shall make rules and regulations, not inconsistent with law, for the conduct of proceedings in the Patent and Trademark Office under this chapter.

§ 1124. (§ 42) Importation of goods bearing infringing marks or names forbidden

Except as provided in subsection (d) of section 1526 of title 19, no article of imported merchandise which shall copy or simulate the name of any domestic manufacture, or manufacturer, or trader, or of any manufacturer or trader located in any foreign country which, by treaty, convention, or law affords similar privileges to citizens of the United States, or which shall copy or simulate a trademark registered in accordance with the provisions of this chapter or shall bear a name or mark calculated to induce the public to believe that the article is manufactured in the United States, or that it is manufactured in any foreign country or locality other than the country or locality in which it is in fact manufactured, shall be admitted to entry at any customhouse of the United States; and, in order to aid the officers of the customs in enforcing this prohibition, any domestic manufacturer or trader, and any foreign manufacturer or trader, who is entitled under the provisions of a treaty, convention, declaration, or agreement between the United States and any foreign country to the advantages afforded by law to citizens of the United States in respect to trademarks and commercial names, may require his name and residence, and the name of the locality in which his goods are manufactured, and a copy of the certificate of registration of his trademark, issued in accordance with the provisions of this chapter, to be recorded in books which shall be kept for this purpose in the Department of the Treasury, under such regulations as the Secretary of the Treasury shall prescribe, and may furnish to the Department facsimiles of his name, the name of the locality in which his goods are manufactured, or of his registered trademark, and thereupon the Secretary of the Treasury shall cause one or more copies of the same to be transmitted to each collector or other proper officer of customs.

§ 1125. (§ 43) False designations of origin, false descriptions, and dilution forbidden
(a) Civil action

(1) Any person who, on or in connection with any goods or services, or any container for goods, uses in commerce any word, term, name, symbol, or device, or any combination thereof, or any false designation of origin, false or misleading description of fact, or false or misleading representation of fact, which—

(A) is likely to cause confusion, or to cause mistake, or to deceive as to the affiliation, connection, or association of such person with another person, or as to the origin, sponsorship, or approval of his or her goods, services, or commercial activities by another person, or

(B) in commercial advertising or promotion, misrepresents the nature, characteristics, qualities, or geographic origin of his or her or another person's goods, services, or commercial activities,

shall be liable in a civil action by any person who believes that he or she is or is likely to be damaged by such act.

(2) As used in this subsection, the term "any person" includes any State, instrumentality of a State or employee of a State or instrumentality of a State acting in his or her official capacity. Any State, and any such instrumentality, officer, or employee, shall be subject to the provisions of this chapter in the same manner and to the same extent as any nongovernmental entity.

(3) In a civil action for trade dress infringement under this chapter for trade dress not registered on the principal register, the person who asserts trade dress protection has the burden of proving that the matter sought to be protected is not functional.

(b) Importation

Any goods marked or labeled in contravention of the provisions of this section shall not be imported into the United States or admitted to entry at any customhouse of the United States. The owner, importer, or consignee of goods refused entry at any customhouse under this section may have any recourse by protest or appeal that is given under the customs revenue laws or may have the remedy given by this chapter in cases involving goods refused entry or seized.

(c) Dilution by blurring; dilution by tarnishment

(1) **Injunctive relief.** Subject to the principles of equity, the owner of a famous mark that is distinctive, inherently or through acquired distinctiveness, shall be entitled to an injunction against another person who, at any time after the owner's mark has become famous, commences use of a mark or trade name in commerce that is likely to cause dilution by blurring or dilution by tarnishment of the famous mark, regardless of the presence or absence of actual or likely confusion, of competition, or of actual economic injury.

(2) **Definitions.** (A) For purposes of paragraph (1), a mark is famous if it is widely recognized by the general consuming public of the United States as a designation of source of the goods or services of the mark's owner. In determining whether a mark possesses the requisite degree of recognition, the court may consider all relevant factors, including the following:

(i) The duration, extent, and geographic reach of advertising and publicity of the mark, whether advertised or publicized by the owner or third parties.

(ii) The amount, volume, and geographic extent of sales of goods or services offered under the mark.

(iii) The extent of actual recognition of the mark.

(iv) Whether the mark was registered under the Act of March 3, 1881, or the Act of February 20, 1905, or on the principal register.

(B) For purposes of paragraph (1), "dilution by blurring" is association arising from the similarity between a mark or trade name and a famous mark that impairs the distinctiveness of the famous mark. In determining whether a mark or trade name is likely to cause dilution by blurring, the court may consider all relevant factors, including the following:

(i) The degree of similarity between the mark or trade name and the famous mark.

(ii) The degree of inherent or acquired distinctiveness of the famous mark.

(iii) The extent to which the owner of the famous mark is engaging in substantially exclusive use of the mark.

(iv) The degree of recognition of the famous mark.

(v) Whether the user of the mark or trade name intended to create an association with the famous mark.

(vi) Any actual association between the mark or trade name and the famous mark.

(C) For purposes of paragraph (1), "dilution by tarnishment" is association arising from the similarity between a mark or trade name and a famous mark that harms the reputation of the famous mark.

(3) **Exclusions.** The following shall not be actionable as dilution by blurring or dilution by tarnishment under this subsection:

(A) Any fair use, including a nominative or descriptive fair use, or facilitation of such fair use, of a famous mark by another person other than as a designation of source for the person's own goods or services, including use in connection with—

(i) advertising or promotion that permits consumers to compare goods or services; or

(ii) identifying and parodying, criticizing, or commenting upon the famous mark owner or the goods or services of the famous mark owner.

(B) All forms of news reporting and news commentary.

(C) Any noncommercial use of a mark.

(4) Burden of proof. In a civil action for trade dress dilution under this [Chapter] for trade dress not registered on the principal register, the person who asserts trade dress protection has the burden of proving that—

(A) the claimed trade dress, taken as a whole, is not functional and is famous; and

(B) if the claimed trade dress includes any mark or marks registered on the principal register, the unregistered matter, taken as a whole, is famous separate and apart from any fame of such registered marks.

(5) Additional remedies. In an action brought under this subsection, the owner of the famous mark shall be entitled to injunctive relief as set forth in section 34 [15 USC §1116 of this title]. The owner of the famous mark shall also be entitled to the remedies set forth in sections 35(a) and 36 [15 USC §§1117(a) and 1118 of this title], subject to the discretion of the court and the principles of equity if—

(A) the mark or trade name that is likely to cause dilution by blurring or dilution by tarnishment was first used in commerce by the person against whom the injunction is sought after the date of enactment of the Trademark Dilution Revision Act of 2006 [Oct. 6, 2006]; and

(B) in a claim arising under this subsection—

(i) by reason of dilution by blurring, the person against whom the injunction is sought willfully intended to trade on the recognition of the famous mark; or

(ii) by reason of dilution by tarnishment, the person against whom the injunction is sought willfully intended to harm the reputation of the famous mark.

(6) Ownership of valid registration a complete bar to action. The ownership by a person of a valid registration under the Act of March 3, 1881, or the Act of February 20,1905, or on the principal register under this Act shall be a complete bar to an action against that person, with respect to that mark, that—

(A) (i) is brought by another person under the common law or a statute of a State; and

(B)(i)(ii) seeks to prevent dilution by blurring or dilution by tarnishment; or

(ii)(B) asserts any claim of actual or likely damage or harm to the distinctiveness or reputation of a mark, label, or form of advertisement.

(7) Savings clause. Nothing in this subsection shall be construed to impair, modify, or supersede the applicability of the patent laws of the United States.

(d) Cyberpiracy prevention

(1)(A) A person shall be liable in a civil action by the owner of a mark, including a personal name which is protected as a mark under this section, if, without regard to the goods or services of the parties, that person

(i) has a bad faith intent to profit from that mark, including a personal name which is protected as a mark under this section; and

(ii) registers, traffics in, or uses a domain name that—

(I) in the case of a mark that is distinctive at the time of registration of the domain name, is identical or confusingly similar to that mark;

(II) in the case of a famous mark that is famous at the time of registration of the domain name, is identical or confusingly similar to or dilutive of that mark; or

(III) is a trademark, word, or name protected by reason of section 706 of Title 18 or section 220506 of Title 36.

(B)(i) In determining whether a person has a bad faith intent described under subparagraph (a), a court may consider factors such as, but not limited to

(I) the trademark or other intellectual property rights of the person, if any, in the domain name;

(II) the extent to which the domain name consists of the legal name of the person or a name that is otherwise commonly used to identify that person;

(III) the person's prior use, if any, of the domain name in connection with the bona fide offering of any goods or services;

(IV) the person's bona fide noncommercial or fair use of the mark in a site accessible under the domain name;

(V) the person's intent to divert consumers from the mark owner's online location to a site accessible under the domain name that could harm the goodwill represented by the mark, either for commercial gain or with the intent to tarnish or disparage the mark, by creating a likelihood of confusion as to the source, sponsorship, affiliation, or endorsement of the site;

(VI) the person's offer to transfer, sell, or otherwise assign the domain name to the mark owner or any third party for financial gain without having used, or having an intent to use, the domain name in the bona fide offering of any goods or services, or the person's prior conduct indicating a pattern of such conduct;

(VII) the person's provision of material and misleading false contact information when applying for the registration of the domain name, the person's intentional failure to maintain accurate contact information, or the person's prior conduct indicating a pattern of such conduct;

(VIII) the person's registration or acquisition of multiple domain names which the person knows are identical or confusingly similar to marks of others that are distinctive at the time of registration of such domain names, or dilutive of famous marks of others that are famous at the time of registration of such domain names, without regard to the goods or services of the parties; and

(IX) the extent to which the mark incorporated in the person's domain name registration is or is not distinctive and famous within the meaning of subsection (c) of this section.

(ii) Bad faith intent described under subparagraph (A) shall not be found in any case in which the court determines that the person believed and had reasonable grounds to believe that the use of the domain name was a fair use or otherwise lawful.

(C) In any civil action involving the registration, trafficking, or use of a domain name under this paragraph, a court may order the forfeiture or cancellation of the domain name or the transfer of the domain name to the owner of the mark.

(D) A person shall be liable for using a domain name under subparagraph (A) only if that person is the domain name registrant or that registrant's authorized licensee.

(E) As used in this paragraph, the term "traffics in" refers to transactions that include, but are not limited to, sales, purchases, loans, pledges, licenses, exchanges of currency, and any other transfer for consideration or receipt in exchange for consideration.

(2)(A) The owner of a mark may file an in rem civil action against a domain name in the judicial district in which the domain name registrar, domain name registry, or other domain name authority that registered or assigned the domain name is located if

(i) the domain name violates any right of the owner of a mark registered in the Patent and Trademark Office, or protected under subsection (a) or (c) of this section; and

(ii) the court finds that the owner—

(I) is not able to obtain in personam jurisdiction over a person who would have been a defendant in a civil action under paragraph (1); or

(II) through due diligence was not able to find a person who would have been a defendant in a civil action under paragraph (1) by—

(aa) sending a notice of the alleged violation and intent to proceed under this paragraph to the registrant of the domain name at the postal and e-mail address provided by the registrant to the registrar; and

(bb) publishing notice of the action as the court may direct promptly after filing the action.

(B) The actions under subparagraph (A)(ii) shall constitute service of process.

(C) In an in rem action under this paragraph, a domain name shall be deemed to have its situs in the judicial district in which

(i) the domain name registrar, registry, or other domain name authority that registered or assigned the domain name is located; or

(ii) documents sufficient to establish control and authority regarding the disposition of the registration and use of the domain name are deposited with the court.

(D)(i) The remedies in an in rem action under this paragraph shall be limited to a court order for the forfeiture or cancellation of the domain name or the transfer of the domain name to the owner of the mark. upon receipt of written notification of a filed, stamped copy of a complaint filed by the owner of a mark in a United States district court under this paragraph, the domain name registrar, domain name registry, or other domain name authority shall

(I) expeditiously deposit with the court documents sufficient to establish the court's control and authority regarding the disposition of the registration and use of the domain name to the court; and

(II) not transfer, suspend, or otherwise modify the domain name during the pendency of the action, except upon order of the court.

(ii) The domain name registrar or registry or other domain name authority shall not be liable for injunctive or monetary relief under this paragraph except in the case of bad faith or reckless disregard, which includes a willful failure to comply with any such court order.

(3) The civil action established under paragraph (1) and the in rem action established under paragraph (2), and any remedy available under either such action, shall be in addition to any other civil action or remedy otherwise applicable.

(4) The in rem jurisdiction established under paragraph (2) shall be in addition to any other jurisdiction that otherwise exists, whether in rem or in personam.

§ 1126. (§ 44) International conventions

(a) Register of marks communicated by international bureaus

The Director shall keep a register of all marks communicated to him by the international bureaus provided for by the conventions for the protection of industrial property, trademarks, trade and commercial names, and the repression of unfair competition to which the United States is or may become a party, and upon the payment of the fees required by such conventions and the fees required in this chapter may place the marks so communicated upon such register. This register shall show a facsimile of the mark or trade or commercial name; the name, citizenship, and address of the registrant; the number, date, and place of the first registration of the mark, including the dates on which application for such registration was filed and granted and the term of such registration; a list of goods or services to which the mark is applied as shown by the registration in the country of origin, and such other data as may be useful concerning the mark. This register shall be a continuation of the register provided in section 1(a) of the Act of March 19, 1920.

(b) Benefits of section to persons whose country of origin is party to convention or treaty

Any person whose country of origin is a party to any convention or treaty relating to trademarks, trade or commercial names, or the repression of unfair competition, to which the United States is also a party, or extends reciprocal rights to nationals of the United States by law, shall be entitled to the benefits of this section under the conditions expressed herein to the extent necessary to give effect to any provision of such convention, treaty or reciprocal law, in addition to the rights to which any owner of a mark is otherwise entitled by this chapter.

(c) Prior registration in country of origin; country of origin defined

No registration of a mark in the United States by a person described in subsection (b) of this section shall be granted until such mark has been registered in the country of origin of the applicant, unless the applicant alleges use in commerce.

For the purposes of this section, the country of origin of the applicant is the country in which he has a bona fide and effective industrial or commercial establishment, or if he has not such an establishment the country in which he is domiciled, or if he has not a domicile in any of the countries described in subsection (b) of this section, the country of which he is a national.

(d) Right of priority

An application for registration of a mark under sections 1, 3, 4, or 23 of this Act [15 USC §§1051, 1053, 1054, or 1091] of this title or under subsection (e) of this section filed by a person described in subsection (b) of this section who has previously duly filed an application for registration of the same mark in one of the countries described in subsection (b) shall be accorded the same force and effect as would be accorded to the same application if filed in the United States on the same date on which the application was first filed in such foreign country: *Provided*, That—

(1) the application in the United States is filed within six months from the date on which the application was first filed in the foreign country;

(2) the application conforms as nearly as practicable to the requirements of this chapter, including a statement that the applicant has a bona fide intention to use the mark in commerce;

(3) the rights acquired by third parties before the date of the filing of the first application in the foreign country shall in no way be affected by a registration obtained on an application filed under this subsection;

(4) nothing in this subsection shall entitle the owner of a registration granted under this section to sue for acts committed prior to the date on which his mark was registered in this country unless the registration is based on use in commerce.

In like manner and subject to the same conditions and requirements, the right provided in this section may be based upon a subsequent regularly filed application in the same foreign country, instead of the first filed foreign application: *Provided*, That any foreign application filed prior to such subsequent application has been withdrawn, abandoned, or otherwise disposed of, without having been laid open to public inspection and without leaving any rights outstanding, and has not served, nor thereafter shall serve, as a basis for claiming a right of priority.

(e) Registration on principal or supplemental register; copy of foreign registration

A mark duly registered in the country of origin of the foreign applicant may be registered on the principal register if eligible, otherwise on the supplemental register herein provided. Such applicant shall submit, within such time period as may be prescribed by the Director, a true copy, a photocopy, a certification, or a certified copy of the registration in the country of origin of the applicant. The application must state the applicant's bona fide intention to use the mark in commerce, but use in commerce shall not be required prior to registration.

(f) Domestic registration independent of foreign registration

The registration of a mark under the provisions of subsections (c), (d), and (e) of this section by a person described in subsection (b) of this section shall be independent of the registration in the country of origin and the duration, validity, or transfer in the United States of such registration shall be governed by the provisions of this chapter.

(g) Trade or commercial names of foreign nationals protected without registration

Trade names or commercial names of persons described in subsection (b) of this section shall be protected without the obligation of filing or registration whether or not they form parts of marks.

(h) Protection of foreign nationals against unfair competition

Any person designated in subsection (b) of this section as entitled to the benefits and subject to the provisions of this chapter shall be entitled to effective protection against unfair competition, and the remedies provided in this chapter for infringement of marks shall be available so far as they may be appropriate in repressing acts of unfair competition.

(i) Citizens or residents of United States entitled to benefits of section

Citizens or residents of the United States shall have the same benefits as are granted by this section to persons described in subsection (b) of this section.

§ 1127. (§ 45) Construction and definitions; intent of chapter

In the construction of this chapter, unless the contrary is plainly apparent from the context—

The United States includes and embraces all territory which is under its jurisdiction and control.

The word "commerce" means all commerce which may lawfully be regulated by Congress.

The term "principal register" refers to the register provided for by sections 1 to 22 [15 USC §§1051 to 1072] of this title, and the term "supplemental register" refers to the register provided for by sections 23 to 28 [15 USC §§1091 to1096] of this title.

The term "person" and any other word or term used to designate the applicant or other entitled to a benefit or privilege or rendered liable under the provisions of this chapter includes a juristic person as well as a natural person. The term "juristic person" includes a firm, corporation, union, association, or other organization capable of suing and being sued in a court of law.

The term "person" also includes the United States, any agency or instrumentality thereof, or any individual, firm, or corporation acting for the United States and with the authorization and consent of the United States. The United States, any agency or instrumentality thereof, and any individual, firm, or corporation acting for the United States and with the authorization and consent of the United States, shall be subject to the provisions of this chapter in the same manner and to the same extent as any nongovernmental entity.

The term "person" also includes any State, any instrumentality of a State, and any officer or employee of a State or instrumentality of a State acting in his or her official capacity. Any State, and any such instrumentality, officer, or employee, shall be subject to the provisions of this chapter in the same manner and to the same extent as any nongovernmental entity.

The terms "applicant" and "registrant" embrace the legal representatives, predecessors, successors and assigns of such applicant or registrant.

The term "Director" means the Under Secretary of Commerce for Intellectual Property and Director of the United States Patent and Trademark Office.

The term "related company" means any person whose use of a mark is controlled by the owner of the mark with respect to the nature and quality of the goods or services on or in connection with which the mark is used.

The terms "trade name" and "commercial name" mean any name used by a person to identify his or her business or vocation.

The term "trademark" includes any word, name, symbol, or device, or any combination
thereof —

(1) used by a person, or

(2) which a person has a bona fide intention to use in commerce and applies to register on the principal register established by this chapter,

to identify and distinguish his or her goods, including a unique product, from those manufactured or sold by others and to indicate the source of the goods, even if that source is unknown.

The term "service mark" means any word, name, symbol, or device, or any combination
thereof

(1) used by a person, or

(2) which a person has a bona fide intention to use in commerce and applies to register on the principal register established by this chapter,

to identify and distinguish the services of one person, including a unique service, from the services of others and to indicate the source of the services, even if that source is unknown. Titles, character names, and other distinctive features of radio or television programs may be registered as service marks notwithstanding that they, or the programs, may advertise the goods of the sponsor.

The term "certification mark" means any word, name, symbol, or device, or any combination thereof—

(1) used by a person other than its owner, or

(2) which its owner has a bona fide intention to permit a person other than the owner to use in commerce and files an application to register on the principal register established by this chapter,

to certify regional or other origin, material, mode of manufacture, quality, accuracy, or other characteristics of such person's goods or services or that the work or labor on the goods or services was performed by members of a union or other organization.

The term "collective mark" means a trademark or service mark—

(1) used by the members of a cooperative, an association, or other collective group or organization, or

(2) which such cooperative, association, or other collective group or organization has a bona fide intention to use in commerce and applies to register on the principal register established by this chapter,

and includes marks indicating membership in a union, an association, or other organization.

The term "mark" includes any trademark, service mark, collective mark, or certification mark.

The term "use in commerce" means the bona fide use of a mark in the ordinary course of trade, and not made merely to reserve a right in a mark. For purposes of this chapter, a mark shall be deemed to be in use in commerce—

(1) on goods when—

(A) it is placed in any manner on the goods or their containers or the displays associated therewith or on the tags or labels affixed thereto, or if the nature of the goods makes such placement impracticable, then on documents associated with the goods or their sale, and

(B) the goods are sold or transported in commerce, and

(2) on services when it is used or displayed in the sale or advertising of services and the services are rendered in commerce, or the services are rendered in more than one State or in the United States and a foreign country and the person rendering the services is engaged in commerce in connection with the services.

A mark shall be deemed to be "abandoned" if either of the following occurs:

(1) When its use has been discontinued with intent not to resume such use. Intent not to resume may be inferred from circumstances. Nonuse for 3 consecutive years shall be prima facie evidence of abandonment. "Use" of a mark means the bona fide use of such mark made in the ordinary course of trade, and not made merely to reserve a right in a mark.

(2) When any course of conduct of the owner, including acts of omission as well as commission, causes the mark to become the generic name for the goods or services on or in connection with which it is used or otherwise to lose its significance as a mark. Purchaser motivation shall not be a test for determining abandonment under this paragraph.

The term "colorable imitation" includes any mark which so resembles a registered mark as to be likely to cause confusion or mistake or to deceive.

The term "registered mark" means a mark registered in the United States Patent and Trademark Office under this chapter or under the Act of March 3, 1881, or the Act of February 20, 1905, or the Act of March 19, 1920. The phrase "marks registered in the Patent and Trademark Office" means registered marks.

The term "Act of March 3, 1881," "Act of February 20, 1905," or "Act of March 19, 1920," means the respective Act as amended.

A "counterfeit" is a spurious mark which is identical with, or substantially indistinguishable from, a registered mark.

The term "domain name" means any alphanumeric designation which is registered with or assigned by any domain name registrar, domain name registry, or other domain name registration authority as part of an electronic address on the Internet.

The term "Internet" has the meaning given that term in section 230(f)(1) of Title 47.

Words used in the singular include the plural and vice versa.

The intent of this chapter is to regulate commerce within the control of Congress by making actionable the deceptive and misleading use of marks in such commerce; to protect registered marks used in such commerce from interference by State, or territorial legislation; to protect persons engaged in such commerce against unfair competition; to prevent fraud and deception in such commerce by the use of reproductions, copies, counterfeits, or colorable imitations of registered marks; and to provide rights and remedies stipulated by treaties and conventions respecting trademarks, trade names, and unfair competition entered into between the United States and foreign nations.

§ 1128. (§ 46) National Intellectual Property Law Enforcement Coordination Council

(a) Establishment

There is established the National Intellectual Property Law Enforcement Coordination Council (in this section referred to as the "Council"). The Council shall consist of the following members —

(1) The Under Secretary of Commerce for Intellectual Property and Director of the United States Patent and Trademark Office, who shall serve as co-chair of the Council.

(2) The Assistant Attorney General, Criminal Division, who shall serve as co-chair of the Council.

(3) The Under Secretary of State for Economic and Agricultural Affairs.

(4) The Ambassador, Deputy United States Trade Representative.

(5) The Commissioner of Customs.

(6) The Under Secretary of Commerce for International Trade.

(7) The Coordinator for International Intellectual Property Enforcement.

(b) Duties

The Council established in subsection (a) of this section shall coordinate domestic and international intellectual property law enforcement among federal and foreign entities.

(c) Consultation required

The Council shall consult with the Register of Copyrights on law enforcement matters relating to copyright and related rights and matters.

(d) Non-derogation

Nothing in this section shall derogate from the duties of the Secretary of State or from the duties of the United States Trade Representative as set forth in section 2171 of Title 19, or from the duties and functions of the Register of Copyrights, or otherwise alter current authorities relating to copyright matters.

(e) Report

The Council shall report annually on its coordination activities to the President, and to the Committees on Appropriations and on the Judiciary of the Senate and the House of Representatives.

(f) Funding

Notwithstanding section 1346 of title 31, or section 610 of this Act, funds made available for fiscal year 2000 and hereafter by this or any other Act shall be available for interagency funding of the National Intellectual Property Law Enforcement Coordination Council.

§ 1129. (§ 47) Cyberpiracy protections for individuals

(1) In general

(A) Civil liability

Any person who registers a domain name that consists of the name of another living person, or a name substantially and confusingly similar thereto, without that person's consent, with the specific intent to profit from such name by selling the domain name for financial gain to that person or any third party, shall be liable in a civil action by such person.

(B) Exception

A person who in good faith registers a domain name consisting of the name of another living person, or a name substantially and confusingly similar thereto, shall not be liable under this paragraph if such name is used in, affiliated with, or related to a work of authorship protected under Title 17, including a work made for hire as defined in section 101 of Title 17, and if the person registering the domain name is the copyright owner or licensee of the work, the person intends to sell the domain name in conjunction with the lawful exploitation of the work, and such registration is not prohibited by a contract between the registrant and the named person. The exception under this subparagraph shall apply only to a civil action brought under paragraph (1) and shall in no manner limit the protections afforded under the Trademark Act of 1946 (15 U.S.C. 1051 et seq.) or other provision of Federal or State law.

(2) Remedies

In any civil action brought under paragraph (1), a court may award injunctive relief, including the forfeiture or cancellation of the domain name or the transfer of the domain name to the plaintiff. The court may also, in its discretion, award costs and attorneys fees to the prevailing party.

(3) Definition

In this subsection, the term "domain name" has the meaning given that term in section 45 of the Trademark Act of 1946 (15 U.S.C. 1127).

(4) Effective date

This subsection shall apply to domain names registered on or after November 29, 1999.

SUBCHAPTER IV - THE MADRID PROTOCOL

§ 1141. (§ 60)   Definitions
In this subchapter:

(1) Basic application

The term "basic application" means the application for the registration of a mark that has been filed with an Office of a Contracting Party and that constitutes the basis for an application for the international registration of that mark.

(2) Basic registration

The term "basic registration" means the registration of a mark that has been granted by an Office of a Contracting Party and that constitutes the basis for an application for the international registration of that mark.

(3) Contracting Party

The term "Contracting Party" means any country or inter-governmental organization that is a party to the Madrid Protocol.

(4) Date of recordal

The term "date of recordal" means the date on which a request for extension of protection, filed after an international registration is granted, is recorded on the International Register.

(5) Declaration of bona fide intention to use the mark in commerce

The term "declaration of bona fide intention to use the mark in commerce" means a declaration that is signed by the applicant for, or holder of, an international registration who is seeking extension of protection of a mark to the United States and that contains a statement that—

(A) the applicant or holder has a bona fide intention to use the mark in commerce;

(B) the person making the declaration believes himself or herself, or the firm, corporation, or association in whose behalf he or she makes the declaration, to be entitled to use the mark in commerce; and

(C) no other person, firm, corporation, or association, to the best of his or her knowledge and belief, has the right to use such mark in commerce either in the identical form of the mark or in such near resemblance to the mark as to be likely, when used on or in connection with the goods of such other person, firm, corporation, or association, to cause confusion, mistake, or deception.

(6) Extension of protection

The term "extension of protection" means the protection resulting from an international registration that extends to the United States at the request of the holder of the international registration, in accordance with the Madrid Protocol.

(7) Holder of an international registration

A "holder" of an international registration is the natural or juristic person in whose name the international registration is recorded on the International Register.

(8) International application

The term "international application" means an application for international registration that is filed under the Madrid Protocol.

(9) International Bureau

The term "International Bureau" means the International Bureau of the World Intellectual Property Organization.

(10) International Register

The term "International Register" means the official collection of data concerning international registrations maintained by the International Bureau that the Madrid Protocol or its implementing regulations require or permit to be recorded.

(11) International registration

The term "international registration" means the registration of a mark granted under the Madrid Protocol.

(12) International registration date

The term "international registration date" means the date assigned to the international registration by the International Bureau.

(13) Madrid Protocol

The term "Madrid Protocol" means the Protocol Relating to the Madrid Agreement Concerning the International Registration of Marks, adopted at Madrid, Spain, on June 27, 1989.

(14) Notification of refusal

The term "notification of refusal" means the notice sent by the United States Patent and Trademark Office to the International Bureau declaring that an extension of protection cannot be granted.

(15) Office of a Contracting Party

The term "Office of a Contracting Party" means—

(A) the office, or governmental entity, of a Contracting Party that is responsible for the registration of marks; or

(B) the common office, or governmental entity, of more than 1 Contracting Party that is responsible for the registration of marks and is so recognized by the International Bureau.

(16) Office of origin

The term "office of origin" means the Office of a Contracting Party with which a basic application was filed or by which a basic registration was granted.

(17) Opposition period

The term "opposition period" means the time allowed for filing an opposition in the United States Patent and Trademark Office, including any extension of time granted under section 1063 of this title.

§ 1141a. (§ 61) International applications based on United States applications or registrations

(a) In general

The owner of a basic application pending before the United States Patent and Trademark Office, or the owner of a basic registration granted by the United States Patent and Trademark Office may file an international application by submitting to the United States Patent and Trademark Office a written application in such form, together with such fees, as may be prescribed by the Director.

(b) Qualified owners

A qualified owner, under subsection (a) of this section, shall—

(1) be a national of the United States;

(2) be domiciled in the United States; or

(3) have a real and effective industrial or commercial establishment in the United States.

§ 1141b. (§ 62) Certification of the international application

(a) Certification procedure

Upon the filing of an application for international registration and payment of the prescribed fees, the Director shall examine the international application for the purpose of certifying that the information contained in the international application corresponds to the information contained in the basic application or basic registration at the time of the certification.

(b) Transmittal

Upon examination and certification of the international application, the Director shall transmit the international application to the International Bureau.

§ 1141c. (§ 63)   Restriction, abandonment, cancellation, or expiration of a basic application or basic registration

With respect to an international application transmitted to the International Bureau under section 1141b of this title, the Director shall notify the International Bureau whenever the basic application or basic registration which is the basis for the international application has been restricted, abandoned, or canceled, or has expired, with respect to some or all of the goods and services listed in the international registration –

(1) within 5 years after the international registration date; or

(2) more than 5 years after the international registration date if the restriction, abandonment, or cancellation of the basic application or basic registration resulted from an action that began before the end of that 5-year period.

§ 1141d. (§ 64)   Request for extension of protection subsequent to international registration

The holder of an international registration that is based upon a basic application filed with the United States Patent and Trademark Office or a basic registration granted by the Patent and Trademark Office may request an extension of protection of its international registration by filing such a request –

(1) directly with the International Bureau; or

(2) with the United States Patent and Trademark Office for transmittal to the International Bureau, if the request is in such form, and contains such transmittal fee, as may be prescribed by the Director.

§ 1141e. (§ 65)   Extension of protection of an international registration to the United States under the Madrid Protocol

(a) In general

Subject to the provisions of section 1141h of this title, the holder of an international registration shall be entitled to the benefits of extension of protection of that international registration to the United States to the extent necessary to give effect to any provision of the Madrid Protocol.

(b) If the United States is office of origin

Where the United States Patent and Trademark Office is the office of origin for a trademark application or registration, any international registration based on such application or registration cannot be used to obtain the benefits of the Madrid Protocol in the United States.

§ 1141f. (§ 66)   Effect of filing a request for extension of protection of an international registration to the United States

(a) Requirement for request for extension of protection

A request for extension of protection of an international registration to the United States that the International Bureau transmits to the United States Patent and Trademark Office shall be deemed to be properly filed in the United States if such request, when received by the International Bureau, has attached to it a declaration of bona fide intention to use the mark in commerce that is verified by the applicant for, or holder of, the international registration.

(b) Effect of proper filing

Unless extension of protection is refused under section 1141h of this title, the proper filing of the request for extension of protection under subsection (a) of this section shall constitute constructive use of the mark, conferring the same rights as those specified in section 1057(c) of this title, as of the earliest of the following:

(1) The international registration date, if the request for extension of protection was filed in the international application.

(2) The date of recordal of the request for extension of protection, if the request for extension of protection was made after the international registration date.

(3) The date of priority claimed pursuant to section 1141g of this title.

§ 1141g. (§ 67) Right of priority for request for extension of protection to the United States

The holder of an international registration with a request for an extension of protection to the United States shall be entitled to claim a date of priority based on a right of priority within the meaning of Article 4 of the Paris Convention for the Protection of Industrial Property if—

(1) the request for extension of protection contains a claim of priority; and

(2) the date of international registration or the date of the recordal of the request for extension of protection to the United States is not later than 6 months after the date of the first regular national filing (within the meaning of Article 4(A)(3) of the Paris Convention for the Protection of Industrial Property) or a subsequent application (within the meaning of Article 4(C)(4) of the Paris Convention for the Protection of Industrial Property).

§ 1141h. (§ 68) Examination of and opposition to request for extension of protection; notification of refusal

(a) Examination and opposition

(1) A request for extension of protection described in section 1141f(a) of this title shall be examined as an application for registration on the Principal Register under this chapter, and if on such examination it appears that the applicant is entitled to extension of protection under this subchapter, the Director shall cause the mark to be published in the Official Gazette of the United States Patent and Trademark Office.

(2) Subject to the provisions of subsection (c) of this section, a request for extension of protection under this subchapter shall be subject to opposition under section 1063 of this title.

(3) Extension of protection shall not be refused on the ground that the mark has not been used in commerce.

(4) Extension of protection shall be refused to any mark not registrable on the Principal Register.

(b) Notification of refusal

If, a request for extension of protection is refused under subsection (a) of this section, the Director shall declare in a notification of refusal (as provided in subsection (c) of this section) that the extension of protection cannot be granted, together with a statement of all grounds on which the refusal was based.

(c) Notice to International Bureau

(1) Within 18 months after the date on which the International Bureau transmits to the Patent and Trademark Office a notification of a request for extension of protection, the Director shall transmit to the International Bureau any of the following that applies to such request:

(A) A notification of refusal based on an examination of the request for extension of protection.

(B) A notification of refusal based on the filing of an opposition to the request.

(C) A notification of the possibility that an opposition to the request may be filed after the end of that 18-month period.

(2) If the Director has sent a notification of the possibility of opposition under paragraph (1)(C), the Director shall, if applicable, transmit to the International Bureau a notification of refusal on the basis of the opposition, together with a statement of all the grounds for the opposition, within 7 months after the beginning of the opposition period or within 1 month after the end of the opposition period, whichever is earlier.

(3) If a notification of refusal of a request for extension of protection is transmitted under paragraph (1) or (2), no grounds for refusal of such request other than those set forth in such notification may be transmitted to the International Bureau by the Director after the expiration of the time periods set forth in paragraph (1) or (2), as the case may be.

(4) If a notification specified in paragraph (1) or (2) is not sent to the International Bureau within the time period set forth in such paragraph, with respect to a request for extension of protection, the request for extension of protection shall not be refused and the Director shall issue a certificate of extension of protection pursuant to the request.

(d) Designation of agent for service of process

In responding to a notification of refusal with respect to a mark, the holder of the international registration of the mark may designate, by a document filed in the United States Patent and Trademark Office, the name and address of a person residing in the United States on whom notices or process in proceedings affecting the mark may be served. Such notices or process may be served upon the person designated by leaving with that person, or mailing to that person, a copy thereof at the address specified in the last designation filed. If the person designated cannot be found at the address given in the last designation, or if the holder does not designate by a document filed in the United States Patent and Trademark Office the name and address of a person residing in the United States for service of notices or process in proceedings affecting the mark, the notice or process may be served on the Director.

§ 1141i. (§ 69)   Effect of extension of protection
(a) Issuance of extension of protection

Unless a request for extension of protection is refused under section 1141h of this title, the Director shall issue a certificate of extension of protection pursuant to the request and shall cause notice of such certificate of extension of protection to be published in the Official Gazette of the United States Patent and Trademark Office.

(b) Effect of extension of protection

From the date on which a certificate of extension of protection is issued under subsection (a) of this section—

(1) such extension of protection shall have the same effect and validity as a registration on the Principal Register; and

(2) the holder of the international registration shall have the same rights and remedies as the owner of a registration on the Principal Register.

§ 1141j. (§ 70)   Dependence of extension of protection to the United States on the underlying international registration
(a) Effect of cancellation of international registration

If the International Bureau notifies the United States Patent and Trademark Office of the cancellation of an international registration with respect to some or all of the goods and services listed in the international registration, the Director shall cancel any extension of protection to the United States with respect to such goods and services as of the date on which the international registration was canceled.

(b) Effect of failure to renew international registration

If the International Bureau does not renew an international registration, the corresponding extension of protection to the United States shall cease to be valid as of the date of the expiration of the international registration.

(c) Transformation of an extension of protection into a United States application

The holder of an international registration canceled in whole or in part by the International Bureau at the request of the office of origin, under article 6(4) of the Madrid Protocol, may file an application, under section 1051 or 1126 of this title, for the registration of the same mark for any of the goods and services to which the cancellation applies that were covered by an extension of protection to the United States based on that international registration. Such an application shall be treated as if it had been filed on the international registration date or the date of recordal of the request for extension of protection with the International Bureau, whichever date applies, and, if the extension of protection enjoyed priority under section 1141g of this title, shall enjoy the same priority. Such an application shall be entitled to the benefits conferred by this subsection only if the application is filed not later than 3 months after the date on which the international registration was canceled, in whole or in part, and only if the application complies with all the requirements of this chapter which apply to any application filed pursuant to section 1051 or 1126 of this title.

§ 1141k. (§71) Duration, affidavits and fees

(a) Time periods for required affidavits

Each extension of protection for which a certificate has been issued under section 69 [15 USC §1141i] shall remain in force for the term of the international registration upon which it is based, except that the extension of protection of any mark shall be canceled by the Director unless the holder of the international registration files in the United States Patent and Trademark Office affidavits that meet the requirements of subsection (b), within the following time periods:

(1) Within the 1-year period immediately preceding the expiration of 6 years following the date of issuance of the certificate of extension of protection.

(2) Within the 1-year period immediately preceding the expiration of 10 years following the date of issuance of the certificate of extension of protection, and each successive 10-year period following the date of issuance of the certificate of extension of protection.

(3) The holder may file the affidavit required under this section within a grace period of 6 months after the end of the applicable time period established in paragraph (1) or (2), together with the fee described in subsection (b) and the additional grace period surcharge prescribed by the Director.

(b) Requirement for affidavit

The affidavit referred to in subsection (a) shall—

(1)(A) state that the mark is in use in commerce;

(B) set forth the goods and services recited in the extension of protection on or in connection with which the mark is in use in commerce;

(C) be accompanied by such number of specimens or facsimiles showing current use of the mark in commerce as may be required by the Director; and

(D) be accompanied by the fee prescribed by the Director; or

(2)(A) set forth the goods and services recited in the extension of protection on or in connection with which the mark is not in use in commerce;

(B) include a showing that any nonuse is due to special circumstances which excuse such nonuse and is not due to any intention to abandon the mark; and

(C) be accompanied by the fee prescribed by the Director.

(c) Deficient affidavit

If any submission filed within the period set forth in subsection (a) is deficient, including that the affidavit was not filed in the name of the holder of the international registration, the deficiency may be corrected after the statutory time period, within the time prescribed after notification of the deficiency. Such submission shall be accompanied by the additional deficiency surcharge prescribed by the Director.

(d) Notice of requirement

Special notice of the requirement for such affidavit shall be attached to each certificate of extension of protection.

(e) Notification of acceptance or refusal

The Director shall notify the holder of the international registration who files any affidavit required by this section of the Director's acceptance or refusal thereof and, in the case of a refusal, the reasons therefor.

(f) Designation of resident for service of process and notices

If the holder of the international registration of the mark is not domiciled in the United States, the holder may designate, by a document filed in the United States Patent and Trademark Office, the name and address of a person resident in the United States on whom may be served notices or process in proceedings affecting the mark. Such notices or process may be served upon the person so designated by leaving with that person or mailing to that person a copy thereof at the address specified in the last designation so filed. If the person so designated cannot be found at the last designated address, or if the holder does not designate by a document filed in the United States Patent and Trademark Office the name and address of a person resident in the United States on whom may be served notices or process in proceedings affecting the mark, such notices or process may be served on the Director.

§ 1141l. (§ 72) Assignment of an extension of protection

An extension of protection may be assigned, together with the goodwill associated with the mark, only to a person who is a national of, is domiciled in, or has a bona fide and effective industrial or commercial establishment either in a country that is a Contracting Party or in a country that is a member of an intergovernmental organization that is a Contracting Party.

§ 1141m. (§ 73) Incontestability

The period of continuous use prescribed under section 1065 of this title for a mark covered by an extension of protection issued under this subchapter may begin no earlier than the date on which the Director issues the certificate of the extension of protection under section 1141i of this title, except as provided in section 1141n of this title.

§ 1141n. (§ 74) Rights of extension of protection

When a United States registration and a subsequently issued certificate of extension of protection to the United States are owned by the same person, identify the same mark, and list the same goods or services, the extension of protection shall have the same rights that accrued to the registration prior to issuance of the certificate of extension of protection.

COUNTERFEITING

COUNTERFEITING

18 U.S.C. § 2318

Trafficking in counterfeit labels, illicit labels, or counterfeit documentation or packaging.

(a)(1)[1] Whoever, in any of the circumstances described in subsection (c), knowingly traffics in–

  (A) a counterfeit label or illicit label affixed to, enclosing, or accompanying, or designed to be affixed to, enclose, or accompany–

     (i) a phonorecord;

     (ii) a copy of a computer program;

     (iii) a copy of a motion picture or other audiovisual work;

     (iv) a copy of a literary work;

     (v) a copy of a pictorial, graphic, or sculptural work;

     (vi) a work of visual art; or

     (vii) documentation or packaging; or

  (B) counterfeit documentation or packaging, shall be fined under this title or imprisoned for not more than 5 years, or both.

(b) As used in this section–

  (1) the term "counterfeit label" means an identifying label or container that appears to be genuine, but is not;

  (2) the term "traffic" has the same meaning as in section 2320(e) of this title;

  (3) the terms "copy", "phonorecord", "motion picture", "computer program", and "audiovisual work", "literary work", "pictorial, graphic, or sculptural work", "sound recording", "work of visual art", and "copyright owner" have, respectively, the meanings given those terms in section 101 (relating to definitions) of title 17;

  (4) the term "illicit label" means a genuine certificate, licensing document, registration card, or similar labeling component–

  (A) that is used by the copyright owner to verify that a phonorecord, a copy of a computer program, a copy of a motion picture or other audiovisual work, a copy of a literary work, a copy of a pictorial, graphic, or sculptural work, a work of visual art, or documentation or packaging is not counterfeit or infringing of any copyright; and

  (B) that is, without the authorization of the copyright owner–

---

[1] There is no provision designated "(2)."

(i) distributed or intended for distribution not in connection with the copy, phonorecord, or work of visual art to which such labeling component was intended to be affixed by the respective copyright owner; or

(ii) in connection with a genuine certificate or licensing document, knowingly falsified in order to designate a higher number of licensed users or copies than authorized by the copyright owner, unless that certificate or document is used by the copyright owner solely for the purpose of monitoring or tracking the copyright owner's distribution channel and not for the purpose of verifying that a copy or phonorecord is noninfringing;

(5) the term "documentation or packaging" means documentation or packaging, in physical form, for a phonorecord, copy of a computer program, copy of a motion picture or other audiovisual work, copy of a literary work, copy of a pictorial, graphic, or sculptural work, or work of visual art; and

(6) the term "counterfeit documentation or packaging" means documentation or packaging that appears to be genuine, but is not.

(c) The circumstances referred to in subsection (a) of this section are–

(1) the offense is committed within the special maritime and territorial jurisdiction of the United States; or within the special aircraft jurisdiction of the United States (as defined in section 46501 of title 49);

(2) the mail or a facility of interstate or foreign commerce is used or intended to be used in the commission of the offense;

(3) the counterfeit label or illicit label is affixed to, encloses, or accompanies, or is designed to be affixed to, enclose, or accompany–

(A) a phonorecord of a copyrighted sound recording or copyrighted musical work;

(B) a copy of a copyrighted computer program;

(C) a copy of a copyrighted motion picture or other audiovisual work;

(D) a copy of a literary work;

(E) a copy of a pictorial, graphic, or sculptural work;

(F) a work of visual art; or

(G) copyrighted documentation or packaging; or

(4) the counterfeited documentation or packaging is copyrighted.

(d) **Forfeiture and destruction of property; restitution.**– Forfeiture, destruction, and restitution relating to this section shall be subject to section 2323, to the extent provided in that section, in addition to any other similar remedies provided by law.

(e) **Civil remedies.** –

(1) **In general.** –Any copyright owner who is injured, or is threatened with injury, by a violation of subsection (a) may bring a civil action in an appropriate United States district court.

(2) **Discretion of court.** –In any action brought under paragraph (1), the court–

(A) may grant 1 or more temporary or permanent injunctions on such terms as the court determines to be reasonable to prevent or restrain a violation of subsection (a);

(B) at any time while the action is pending, may order the impounding, on such terms as the court determines to be reasonable, of any article that is in the custody or control of the alleged violator and that the court has reasonable cause to believe was involved in a violation of subsection (a); and

(C) may award to the injured party–

(i) reasonable attorney fees and costs; and

(ii)(I) actual damages and any additional profits of the violator, as provided in paragraph (3); or

(II) statutory damages, as provided in paragraph (4).

(3) Actual damages and profits. –

(A) **In general.** –The injured party is entitled to recover–

(i) the actual damages suffered by the injured party as a result of a violation of subsection (a), as provided in subparagraph (B) of this paragraph; and

(ii) any profits of the violator that are attributable to a violation of subsection (a) and are not taken into account in computing the actual damages.

(B) **Calculation of damages.** –The court shall calculate actual damages by multiplying–

(i) the value of the phonorecords, copies, or works of visual art which are, or are intended to be, affixed with, enclosed in, or accompanied by any counterfeit labels, illicit labels, or counterfeit documentation or packaging, by

(ii) the number of phonorecords, copies, or works of visual art which are, or are intended to be, affixed with, enclosed in, or accompanied by any counterfeit labels, illicit labels, or counterfeit documentation or packaging.

(C) **Definition.** –For purposes of this paragraph, the "value" of a phonorecord, copy, or work of visual art is–

(i) in the case of a copyrighted sound recording or copyrighted musical work, the retail value of an authorized phonorecord of that sound recording or musical work;

(ii) in the case of a copyrighted computer program, the retail value of an authorized copy of that computer program;

(iii) in the case of a copyrighted motion picture or other audiovisual work, the retail value of an authorized copy of that motion picture or audiovisual work;

(iv) in the case of a copyrighted literary work, the retail value of an authorized copy of that literary work;

(v) in the case of a pictorial, graphic, or sculptural work, the retail value of an authorized copy of that work; and

(vi) in the case of a work of visual art, the retail value of that work.

(4) **Statutory damages.** – The injured party may elect, at any time before final judgment is rendered, to recover, instead of actual damages and profits, an award of statutory damages for each violation of subsection (a) in a sum of not less than $2,500 or more than $25,000, as the court considers appropriate.

(5) **Subsequent violation.** – The court may increase an award of damages under this subsection by 3 times the amount that would otherwise be awarded, as the court considers appropriate, if the court finds that a person has subsequently violated subsection (a) within 3 years after a final judgment was entered against that person for a violation of that subsection.

(6) **Limitation on actions.** – A civil action may not be commenced under section[7] unless it is commenced within 3 years after the date on which the claimant discovers the violation of subsection (a).

---

[7] *sic*, "this subsection"?

18 U.S.C. § 2320

§ 2320. Trafficking in counterfeit goods or services
(a) Offenses.--Whoever intentionally--

(1) traffics in goods or services and knowingly uses a counterfeit mark on or in connection with such goods or services,

(2) traffics in labels, patches, stickers, wrappers, badges, emblems, medallions, charms, boxes, containers, cans, cases, hangtags, documentation, or packaging of any type or nature, knowing that a counterfeit mark has been applied thereto, the use of which is likely to cause confusion, to cause mistake, or to deceive, or

(3) traffics in goods or services knowing that such good or service is a counterfeit military good or service the use, malfunction, or failure of which is likely to cause serious bodily injury or death, the disclosure of classified information, impairment of combat operations, or other significant harm to a combat operation, a member of the Armed Forces, or to national security,

or attempts or conspires to violate any of paragraphs (1) through (3) shall be punished as provided in subsection (b).

(b) Penalties.--

(1) **In general.**--Whoever commits an offense under subsection (a)--

(A) if an individual, shall be fined not more than $2,000,000 or imprisoned not more than 10 years, or both, and, if a person other than an individual, shall be fined not more than $5,000,000; and

(B) for a second or subsequent offense under subsection (a), if an individual, shall be fined not more than $5,000,000 or imprisoned not more than 20 years, or both, and if other than an individual, shall be fined not more than $15,000,000.

(2) **Serious bodily injury or death.**--

(A) **Serious bodily injury.**--Whoever knowingly or recklessly causes or attempts to cause serious bodily injury from conduct in violation of subsection (a), if an individual, shall be fined not more than $ 5,000,000 or imprisoned for not more than 20 years, or both, and if other than an individual, shall be fined not more than $15,000,000.

(B) **Death.**--Whoever knowingly or recklessly causes or attempts to cause death from conduct in violation of subsection (a), if an individual, shall be fined not more than

$5,000,000 or imprisoned for any term of years or for life, or both, and if other than an individual, shall be fined not more than $15,000,000.

(3) **Counterfeit military goods or services.**–Whoever commits an offense under subsection (a) involving a counterfeit military good or service–

(A) if an individual, shall be fined not more than $5,000,000, imprisoned not more than 20 years, or both, and if other than an individual, be fined not more than $15,000,000; and

(B) for a second or subsequent offense, if an individual, shall be fined not more than $15,000,000, imprisoned not more than 30 years, or both, and if other than an individual, shall be fined not more than $30,000,000.

(c) **Forfeiture and destruction of property; restitution.**–Forfeiture, destruction, and restitution relating to this section shall be subject to section 2323, to the extent provided in that section, in addition to any other similar remedies provided by law.

(d) **Defenses.**–All defenses, affirmative defenses, and limitations on remedies that would be applicable in an action under the Lanham Act shall be applicable in a prosecution under this section. In a prosecution under this section, the defendant shall have the burden of proof, by a preponderance of the evidence, of any such affirmative defense.

(e) **Presentence report.**–(1) During preparation of the presentence report pursuant to Rule 32(c) of the Federal Rules of Criminal Procedure, victims of the offense shall be permitted to submit, and the probation officer shall receive, a victim impact statement that identifies the victim of the offense and the extent and scope of the injury and loss suffered by the victim, including the estimated economic impact of the offense on that victim.

(2) Persons permitted to submit victim impact statements shall include–

(A) producers and sellers of legitimate goods or services affected by conduct involved in the offense;

(B) holders of intellectual property rights in such goods or services; and

(C) the legal representatives of such producers, sellers, and holders.

(f) **Definitions.**–For the purposes of this section–

(1) the term "counterfeit mark" means–

(A) a spurious mark–

(i) that is used in connection with trafficking in any goods, services, labels, patches, stickers, wrappers, badges, emblems, medallions, charms, boxes, containers, cans, cases, hangtags, documentation, or packaging of any type or nature;

(ii) that is identical with, or substantially indistinguishable from, a mark registered on the principal register in the United States Patent and Trademark Office and in use, whether or not the defendant knew such mark was so registered;

(iii) that is applied to or used in connection with the goods or services for which the mark is registered with the United States Patent and Trademark Office, or is applied to or consists of a label, patch, sticker, wrapper, badge, emblem, medallion, charm, box, container, can, case, hangtag, documentation, or packaging of any type or nature that is designed, marketed, or otherwise intended to be used on or in connection with the goods or services for which the mark is registered in the United States Patent and Trademark Office; and

(iv) the use of which is likely to cause confusion, to cause mistake, or to deceive; or

(B) a spurious designation that is identical with, or substantially indistinguishable from, a designation as to which the remedies of the Lanham Act are made available by reason of section 220506 of title 36;

but such term does not include any mark or designation used in connection with goods or services, or a mark or designation applied to labels, patches, stickers, wrappers, badges, emblems, medallions, charms, boxes, containers, cans, cases, hangtags, documentation, or packaging of any type or nature used in connection with such goods or services, of which the manufacturer or producer was, at the time of the manufacture or production in question, authorized to use the mark or designation for the type of goods or services so manufactured or produced, by the holder of the right to use such mark or designation;

(2) the term "financial gain" includes the receipt, or expected receipt, of anything of value;

(3) the term "Lanham Act" means the Act entitled "An Act to provide for the registration and protection of trademarks used in commerce, to carry out the provisions of certain international conventions, and for other purposes", approved July 5, 1946 (15 U.S.C. 1051 et seq.);

(4) the term "counterfeit military good or service" means a good or service that uses a counterfeit mark on or in connection with such good or service and that—

(A) is falsely identified or labeled as meeting military specifications, or

(B) is intended for use in a military or national security application; and

(5) the term "traffic" means to transport, transfer, or otherwise dispose of, to another, for purposes of commercial advantage or private financial gain, or to make, import, export, obtain control of, or possess, with intent to so transport, transfer, or otherwise dispose of.

(g) Limitation on cause of action.~Nothing in this section shall entitle the United States to bring a criminal cause of action under this section for the repackaging of genuine goods or services not intended to deceive or confuse.

(h) Report to Congress.~**(1)** Beginning with the first year after the date of enactment of this subsection, the Attorney General shall include in the report of the Attorney General to Congress on the business of the Department of Justice prepared pursuant to section 522 of title 28, an accounting, on a district by district basis, of the following with respect to all actions taken by the Department of Justice that involve trafficking in counterfeit labels for phonorecords, copies of computer programs or computer program documentation or packaging, copies of motion pictures or other audiovisual works (as defined in section 2318 of this title), criminal infringement of copyrights (as defined in section 2319 of this title), unauthorized fixation of and trafficking in sound recordings and music videos of live musical performances (as defined in section 2319A of this title), or trafficking in goods or services bearing counterfeit marks (as defined in section 2320 of this title):

(A) The number of open investigations.

(B) The number of cases referred by the United States Customs Service.

(C) The number of cases referred by other agencies or sources.

(D) The number and outcome, including settlements, sentences, recoveries, and penalties, of all prosecutions brought under sections 2318, 2319, 2319A, and 2320 of title 18.

(2)(A) The report under paragraph (1), with respect to criminal infringement of copyright, shall include the following:

(i) The number of infringement cases in these categories: audiovisual (videos and films); audio (sound recordings); literary works (books and musical compositions); computer programs; video games; and, others.

(ii) The number of online infringement cases.

(iii) The number and dollar amounts of fines assessed in specific categories of dollar amounts. These categories shall be: no fines ordered; fines under $500; fines from $500 to

$1,000; fines from $1,000 to $5,000; fines from $5,000 to $10,000; and fines over $10,000.

(iv) The total amount of restitution ordered in all copyright infringement cases.

(B) In this paragraph, the term "online infringement cases" as used in paragraph (2) means those cases where the infringer~

(i) advertised or publicized the infringing work on the Internet; or

(ii) made the infringing work available on the Internet for download, reproduction, performance, or distribution by other persons.

(C) The information required under subparagraph (A) shall be submitted in the report required in fiscal year 2005 and thereafter.

(i) Transshipment and exportation.~No goods or services, the trafficking in of which is prohibited by this section, shall be transshipped through or exported from the United States. Any such transshipment or exportation shall be deemed a violation of section 42 of an Act to provide for the registration of trademarks used in commerce, to carry out the provisions of certain international conventions, and for other purposes, approved July 5, 1946 (commonly referred to as the "Trademark Act of 1946" or the "Lanham Act").

18 U.S.C. § 2323

§ 2323. Forfeiture, destruction, and restitution

(a) Civil forfeiture.

(1) **Property subject to forfeiture.** The following property is subject to forfeiture to the United States Government:

(A) Any article, the making or trafficking of which is, prohibited under section 506 of title 17, or section 2318, 2319, 2319A, 2319B, or 2320, or chapter 90, of this title.

(B) Any property used, or intended to be used, in any manner or part to commit or facilitate the commission of an offense referred to in subparagraph (A).

(C) Any property constituting or derived from any proceeds obtained directly or indirectly as a result of the commission of an offense referred to in subparagraph (A).

(2) **Procedures.** The provisions of chapter 46 relating to civil forfeitures shall extend to any seizure or civil forfeiture under this section. For seizures made under this section, the court shall enter an appropriate protective order with respect to discovery and use of any records or information that has been seized. The protective order shall provide for appropriate procedures to ensure that confidential, private, proprietary, or privileged information contained in such records is not improperly disclosed or used. At the conclusion of the forfeiture proceedings, unless otherwise requested by an agency of the United States, the court shall order that any property forfeited under paragraph (1) be destroyed, or otherwise disposed of according to law.

(b) Criminal forfeiture.

(1) **Property subject to forfeiture.** The court, in imposing sentence on a person convicted of an offense under section 506 of title 17, or section 2318, 2319, 2319A, 2319B, or 2320, or chapter 90, of this title, shall order, in addition to any other sentence imposed, that the person forfeit to the United States Government any property subject to forfeiture under subsection (a) for that offense.

(2) **Procedures.**

(A) In general.~The forfeiture of property under paragraph (1), including any seizure and disposition of the property and any related judicial or administrative proceeding, shall be governed by the procedures set forth in section 413 of the Comprehensive Drug Abuse Prevention and Control Act of 1970 (21 U.S.C. 853), other than subsection (d) of that section.

(B) Destruction.~At the conclusion of the forfeiture proceedings, the court, unless otherwise requested by an agency of the United States shall order that any~

(i) forfeited article or component of an article bearing or consisting of a counterfeit mark be destroyed or otherwise disposed of according to law; and

(ii) infringing items or other property described in subsection (a)(1)(A) and forfeited under paragraph (1) of this subsection be destroyed or otherwise disposed of according to law.

(c) **Restitution.** When a person is convicted of an offense under section 506 of title 17 or section 2318, 2319, 2319A, 2319B, or 2320, or chapter 90, of this title, the court, pursuant to sections 3556, 3663A, and 3664 of this title, shall order the person to pay restitution to any victim of the offense as an offense against property referred to in section 3663A(c)(1)(A)(ii) of this title.

19 U.S.C. § 1526

§ 1526 Merchandise bearing American trade-mark
(a) Importation prohibited

Except as provided in subsection (d) of this section, it shall be unlawful to import into the United States any merchandise of foreign manufacture if such merchandise, or the label, sign, print, package, wrapper, or receptacle, bears a trademark owned by a citizen of, or by a corporation or association created or organized within, the United States, and registered in the Patent and Trademark Office by a person domiciled in the United States, under the provisions of sections 81 to 109 of Title 15, and if a copy of the certificate of registration of such trademark is filed with the Secretary of the Treasury, in the manner provided in section 106 of said Title 15, unless written consent of the owner of such trademark is produced at the time of making entry.

(b) Seizure and forfeiture

Any such merchandise imported into the United States in violation of the provisions of this section shall be subject to seizure and forfeiture for violation of the customs laws.

(c) Injunction and damages

Any person dealing in any such merchandise may be enjoined from dealing therein within the United States or may be required to export or destroy such merchandise or to remove or obliterate such trademark and shall be liable for the same damages and profits provided for wrongful use of a trademark, under the provisions of sections 81 to 109 of Title 15.

(d) Exemptions; publication in Federal Register; forfeitures; rules and regulations

(1) The trademark provisions of this section and section 1124 of Title 15, do not apply to the importation of articles accompanying any person arriving in the United States when such articles are for his personal use and not for sale if (A) such articles are within the limits of types and quantities determined by the Secretary pursuant to paragraph (2) of this subsection, and (B) such person has not been granted an exemption under this subsection within thirty days immediately preceding his arrival.

(2) The Secretary shall determine and publish in the Federal Register lists of the types of articles and the quantities of each which shall be entitled to the exemption provided by this subsection. In determining such quantities of particular types of trade-marked articles, the Secretary shall give such consideration as he deems necessary to the numbers of such articles usually purchased at retail for personal use.

(3) If any article which has been exempted from the restrictions on importation of the trade-mark laws under this subsection is sold within one year after the date of importation, such article, or its value (to be recovered from the importer), is subject to forfeiture. A sale pursuant to a judicial order or in liquidation of the estate of a decedent is not subject to the provisions of this paragraph.

(4) The Secretary may prescribe such rules and regulations as may be necessary to carry out the provisions of this subsection.

(e) Merchandise bearing counterfeit mark; seizure and forfeiture; disposition of seized goods

Any such merchandise bearing a counterfeit mark (within the meaning of section 1127 of Title 15) imported into the United States in violation of the provisions of section 1124 of Title 15, shall be seized and, in the absence of the written consent of the trademark owner, forfeited for violations of the customs laws. Upon seizure of such merchandise, the Secretary shall notify the owner of the trademark, and shall, after forfeiture, destroy the merchandise. Alternatively, if the merchandise is not unsafe or a hazard to health, and the Secretary has the consent of the trademark owner, the Secretary may obliterate the trademark where feasible and dispose of the goods seized—

(1) by delivery to such Federal, State, and local government agencies as in the opinion of the Secretary have a need for such merchandise,

(2) by gift to such eleemosynary institutions as in the opinion of the Secretary have a need for such merchandise, or

(3) more than 90 days after the date of forfeiture, by sale by the Customs Service at public auction under such regulations as the Secretary prescribes, except that before making any such sale the Secretary shall determine that no Federal, State, or local government agency or eleemosynary institution has established a need for such merchandise under paragraph (1) or (2).

(f) Civil penalties

(1) Any person who directs, assists financially or otherwise, or aids and abets the importation of merchandise for sale or public distribution that is seized under subsection (e) of this section shall be subject to a civil fine.

(2) For the first such seizure, the fine shall be not more than the value that the merchandise would have had if it were genuine, according to the manufacturer's suggested retail price, determined under regulations promulgated by the Secretary.

(3) For the second seizure and thereafter, the fine shall be not more than twice the value that the merchandise would have had if it were genuine, as determined under regulations promulgated by the Secretary.

(4) The imposition of a fine under this subsection shall be within the discretion of the Customs Service, and shall be in addition to any other civil or criminal penalty or other remedy authorized by law.

RULES OF PRACTICE IN TRADEMARK CASES (EXCERPTS)

TITLE 37~PATENTS, TRADEMARKS, AND COPYRIGHTS CHAPTER I~ UNITED STATES PATENT AND TRADEMARK OFFICE, DEPARTMENT OF COMMERCE PART 2~RULES OF PRACTICE IN TRADEMARK CASES (EXCERPTS)

* * *

§ 2.34 Bases for filing.

(a) The application must include one or more of the following five filing bases:

(1) *Use in commerce under section 1(a) of the Act.* The requirements for an application based on section 1(a) of the Act are:

(i) The trademark owner's verified statement that the mark is in use in commerce on or in connection with the goods or services listed in the application. If the verification is not filed with the initial application, the verified statement must allege that the mark was in use in commerce on or in connection with the goods or services listed in the application as of the application filing date;

(ii) The date of the applicant's first use of the mark anywhere on or in connection with the goods or services;

(iii) The date of the applicant's first use of the mark in commerce as a trademark or service mark; and

(iv) One specimen showing how the applicant actually uses the mark in commerce.

(v) If more than one item of goods or services is specified in the application, the dates of use required in paragraphs (ii) and (iii) of this section need be for only one of the items specified in each class, provided that the particular item to which the dates apply is designated.

(2) *Intent-to-use under section 1(b) of the Act.* In an application under section 1(b) of the Act, the applicant must verify that it has a bona fide intention to use the mark in commerce on or in connection with the goods or services listed in the application. If the verification is not filed with the initial application, the verified statement must also allege that the applicant had a bona fide intention to use the mark in commerce on or in connection with the goods or services listed in the application as of the filing date of the application.

(3) *Registration of a mark in a foreign applicant's country of origin under section 44(e) of the Act.* The requirements for an application under section 44(e) of the Act are:

(i) The applicant's verified statement that it has a bona fide intention to use the mark in commerce on or in connection with the goods or services listed in the application. If the verification is not filed with the initial application, the verified statement must also allege that the applicant had a bona fide intention to use the mark in commerce on or in connection with the goods or services listed in the application as of the filing date of the application.

(ii) A true copy, a photocopy, a certification, or a certified copy of a registration in the applicant's country of origin showing that the mark has been registered in that country, and that the registration is in full force and effect. The certification or copy of the foreign registration must show the name of the owner, the mark, and the goods or services for which the mark is registered. If the foreign registration is not in the English language, the applicant must submit a translation.

(iii) If the record indicates that the foreign registration will expire before the United States registration will issue, the applicant must submit a true copy, a photocopy, a certification, or a certified copy from the country of origin to establish that the foreign registration has been renewed and will be in force at the time the United States registration will issue. If the foreign registration is not in the English language, the applicant must submit a translation.

(4) *Claim of priority, based upon an earlier-filed foreign application, under section 44(d) of the Act.* The requirements for an application under section 44(d) of the Act are:

(i) A claim of priority, filed within six months of the filing date of the foreign application. Before publication or registration on the Supplemental Register, the applicant must either:

(A) Specify the filing date, serial number and country of the first regularly filed foreign application; or

(B) State that the application is based upon a subsequent regularly filed application in the same foreign country, and that any prior-filed application has been withdrawn, abandoned or otherwise disposed of, without having been laid open to public inspection and without having any rights outstanding, and has not served as a basis for claiming a right of priority.

(ii) Include the applicant's verified statement that it has a bona fide intention to use the mark in commerce on or in connection with the goods or services listed in the application. If the verification is not filed with the initial application, the verified statement must also allege that the applicant had a bona fide intention to use the mark in commerce on or in connection with the goods or services listed in the application as of the filing date of the application.

(iii) Before the application can be approved for publication, or for registration on the Supplemental Register, the applicant must establish a basis under section 1(a), section 1(b) or section 44(e) of the Act.

(5) *Extension of protection of an international registration under section 66(a) of the Act.* In an application under section 66(a) of the Act, the international application or subsequent designation requesting an extension of protection to the United States must contain a signed declaration that meets the requirements of §2.33.

(b)(1) In an application under section 1 or section 44 of the Act, an applicant may claim more than one basis, provided the applicant satisfies all requirements for the bases claimed. However, the applicant may not claim both sections 1(a) and 1(b) for the identical goods or services in the same application.

(2) In an application under section 1 or section 44 of the Act, if an applicant claims more than one basis, the applicant must list each basis, followed by the goods or services to which that basis applies. If some or all of the goods or services are covered by more than one basis, this must be stated.

(3) A basis under section 66(a) of the Act cannot be combined with any other basis.

(c) The word "commerce" means commerce that Congress may lawfully regulate, as specified in section 45 of the Act.

[64 FR 48919, Sept. 8, 1999, as amended at 67 FR 79522, Dec. 30, 2002; 68 FR 55763, Sept. 26, 2003 ; 73 FR 67768, Nov. 17, 2008]

* * *

§ 2.88 Filing statement of use after notice of allowance.

(a) In an application under section 1(b) of the Act, a statement of use, required under section 1(d) of the Act, must be filed within six months after issuance of a notice of allowance under section 13(b)(2) of the Act, or within an extension of time granted under §2.89. A statement of use that is filed prior to issuance of a notice of allowance is premature, will not be considered, and will be returned to the applicant.

(b) A complete statement of use must include:

(1) A statement that is signed and verified (sworn to) or supported by a declaration under § 2.20 by a person properly authorized to sign on behalf of the applicant (see § 2.193(e)(1)) that:

(i) The applicant believes it is the owner of the mark; and

(ii) The mark is in use in commerce, specifying the date of the applicant's first use of the mark and first use of the mark in commerce on or in connection with the goods or services identified in the notice of allowance, and setting forth or incorporating by reference those goods/services identified in the notice of allowance on or in connection with which the mark is in use in commerce. Where an applicant claims section 1(a) of the Act for some goods/services in a class and section 1(b) of the Act for other goods/services in the same class, the statement of use must include dates for the section 1(b) of the Act goods/services;

(2) One specimen of the mark as actually used in commerce. See §2.56 for the requirements for specimens; and

(3) The fee per class required by § 2.6. The applicant must pay a filing fee sufficient to cover at least one class within the statutory time for filing the statement of use, or the application will be abandoned. If the applicant submits a fee insufficient to cover all the classes in a multiple-class application, the applicant must specify the classes to be abandoned. If the applicant submits a fee sufficient to pay for at least one class, but insufficient to cover all the classes, and the applicant has not specified the class(es) to be abandoned, the Office will issue a notice granting the applicant additional time to submit the fee(s) for the remaining class(es), or specify the class(es) to be abandoned. If the applicant does not submit the required fee(s) or specify the class(es) to be abandoned within the set time period, the Office will apply the fees paid, beginning with the lowest numbered class(es), in ascending order. The Office will delete the goods/services in the remaining class(es) not covered by the fees submitted..

(c) The statement of use may be filed only when the applicant has made use of the mark in commerce on or in connection with all of the goods or services, as specified in the notice of allowance, for which applicant will seek registration in that application, unless the statement of use is accompanied by a request in accordance with §2.87 to divide out from the application the goods or services to which the statement of use pertains. If more than one item of goods or services is specified in the statement of use, the dates of use required in paragraph (b)(1) of this section need be for only one of the items specified in each class, provided the particular item to which the dates apply is designated.

(d) The title "Allegation of Use" should appear at the top of the first page of the document.

(e) The Office will review a timely filed statement of use to determine whether it meets the following minimum requirements:
    (1) The fee for at least a single class, required by §2.6;
    (2) One specimen of the mark as used in commerce;
    (3) A statement that is signed and verified (sworn to) or supported by a declaration under §2.20 by a person properly authorized to sign on behalf of the applicant that the mark is in use in commerce. If the verification or declaration is unsigned or signed by the wrong party, the applicant must submit a substitute verification on or before the statutory deadline for filing the statement of use.

(f) A timely filed statement of use which meets the minimum requirements specified in paragraph (e) of this section will be examined in accordance with §§2.61 through 2.69. If, as a result of the examination of the statement of use, applicant is found not entitled to registration, applicant will be notified and advised of the reasons and of any formal requirements or refusals. The statement of use may be amended in accordance with §§2.59 and 2.71 through 2.75. If the statement of use is acceptable in all respects, the applicant will be notified of its acceptance.

(g) If the statement of use does not meet the minimum requirements specified in paragraph (e) of this section, applicant will be notified of the deficiency. If the time permitted for applicant to file a statement of use has not expired, applicant may correct the deficiency. After the filing of a statement of use during a permitted time period for such filing, the applicant may not withdraw the statement to return to the previous status of awaiting submission of a statement of use, regardless of whether it is in compliance with paragraph (e) of this section.

(h) The failure to timely file a statement of use which meets the minimum requirements specified in paragraph (e) of this section shall result in the abandonment of the application.

(i)(1) The goods or services specified in a statement of use must conform to those goods or services identified in the notice of allowance. An applicant may specify the goods or services by stating "those goods or services identified in the notice of allowance" or, if appropriate, "those goods or services identified in the notice of allowance except * * *" followed by an identification of the goods or services to be deleted.

(2) If any goods or services specified in the notice of allowance are omitted from the identification of goods or services in the statement of use, the Office will delete the omitted goods/services from the application. The applicant may not thereafter reinsert these goods/services.

(3) The statement of use may be accompanied by a separate request to amend the identification of goods or services in the application, as stated in the notice of allowance, in accordance with §2.71(a).

(j) The statement of use may be accompanied by a separate request to amend the drawing in the application, in accordance with §§2.51 and 2.72.

(k) If the statement of use is not filed within a reasonable time after the date it is signed, the Office may require a substitute verification or declaration under §2.20 stating that the mark is still in use in commerce.

(l) For the requirements for a multiple class application, see §2.86.

[54 FR 37595, Sept. 11, 1989, as amended at 64 FR 48923, Sept. 8, 1999; 64 FR 51245, Sept. 22, 1999; 68 FR 55765, Sept. 26, 2003; 73 FR 67771, Nov. 17, 2008; 74 FR 54908, Oct. 26, 2009]

Trademark Manual of Examining Procedure (TMEP) – 8th Edition, October 2011 (Excerpts)

TRADEMARK MANUAL OF EXAMINING PROCEDURE (TMEP) - 8TH EDITION (EXCERPTS)

501.01(a) Assignability of Intent-to-Use Applications

In an application under §1(b) of the Trademark Act, 15 U.S.C. §1051(b), the applicant cannot assign the application before the applicant files an allegation of use (i.e., either an amendment to allege use under 15 U.S.C. §1051(c) or a statement of use under 15 U.S.C. §1051(d)), except to a successor to the applicant's business, or portion of the business to which the mark pertains, if that business is ongoing and existing. Section 10 of the Trademark Act, 15 U.S.C. §1060; 37 C.F.R. §3.16.

The primary purpose of this provision is to ensure that a mark may only be assigned along with some business or goodwill, and to prevent "trafficking" in marks.

As a general rule, the United States Patent and Trademark Office ("USPTO") does not investigate or evaluate the validity of assignments. Therefore, the examining attorney should issue an inquiry concerning the compliance of an assignment with the cited provisions of §10 only if:

(1) The application itself includes a statement indicating that the assignee is not a successor to the original applicant's business, or portion of the business to which the mark pertains, if that business is ongoing and existing; or

(2) *All* of the following conditions are present:

(a) The assignment is executed before the filing of an allegation of use;

(b) The applicant submits the assignment document for inclusion in the application record; and

(c) The assignment document fails to include the relevant language from §10 to the effect that the assignment includes the entire business of the applicant/assignor or the portion of the business to which the mark pertains.

The examining attorney should not require the submission of assignment documents to determine compliance.

If the examining attorney issues an inquiry, the applicant's statement that the assignment was in compliance with the cited provision of §10 is sufficient to resolve the issue. This statement may be entered through an examiner's amendment.

The assignment of an intent-to-use application to someone who is not the successor to the applicant's business before filing an allegation of use renders the application and any resulting registration void. Clorox Co. v. Chemical Bank, 40 USPQ2d 1098 (TTAB 1996).

* * *

1102 Initial Examination of Intent-to-Use Applications

In an intent-to-use application, the examining attorney will potentially examine the application twice: first, when it is initially filed based on a bona fide intention to use the mark in commerce under 15 U.S.C. §1051(b), and second, when the applicant files an allegation of use (i.e., either an amendment to allege use under 15 U.S.C. §1051(c) or a statement of use under 15 U.S.C. §1051(d)). See TMEP §§1104 et seq. regarding amendments to allege use and TMEP §§1109 et seq. regarding statements of use. After receipt of the application, the examining attorney will initially examine the application to determine whether the mark is eligible for registration but for the lack of evidence of use. If the mark is determined to be eligible, the mark will be approved for publication and then published for opposition. If the applicant has not submitted an amendment to allege use before approval for publication, and the application is not successfully opposed, the USPTO will issue a notice of allowance. 15 U.S.C. §1063(b); 37 C.F.R. §2.81. See TMEP §§1106 et seq. regarding notices of allowance. In such a case, the applicant must submit a statement of use. 15 U.S.C. §1051(d)(1); 37 C.F.R. §2.88.

An intent-to-use application is subject to the same requirements and examination procedures as other applications, except as specifically noted. The examining attorney must raise all possible refusals and requirements in initial examination.

* * *

1201.03(a) Use Solely by Related Company Must be Disclosed

If the mark is not being used by the applicant but is being used by one or more related companies whose use inures to the benefit of the applicant under §5 of the Act, then these facts must be disclosed in the application. 37 C.F.R. §2.38(b). *See Pease Woodwork Co., Inc. v. Ready Hung Door Co., Inc.,* 103 USPQ 240 (Comm'r Pats. 1954); *Industrial Abrasives, Inc. v. Strong,* 101 USPQ 420 (Comm'r Pats. 1954). Use that inures to the applicant's benefit is a proper and sufficient support for an application and satisfies the requirement of 37 C.F.R. §2.33(b)(1) that a §1(a) application specify that the *applicant* has adopted and is using the mark.

The party who controls the nature and quality of the goods or services on or in connection with which the mark is used should be set forth as the applicant. In an application under §1(a) of the Trademark Act, the applicant should state in the body of the application that the applicant has adopted and is using the mark *through its related company* (or equivalent explanatory wording). In a §1(b) application, the statement that the applicant is using the mark through a related company should be included in the amendment to allege use under 15 U.S.C. §1051(c) (*see* TMEP §§1104 *etseq.*) or statement of use under 15 U.S.C. §1051(d) (*see* TMEP §§1109 *etseq.*).

The applicant is not required to give the name of the related-company user, unless it is necessary to explain information in the record that clearly contradicts the applicant's verified claim of ownership of the mark.

The applicant may claim the benefit of use by a related company in an amendment to the application. *Greyhound Corp. v. Armour Life Insurance Co.,* 214 USPQ 473, 475 (TTAB 1982).

If the applicant and a related company both use the mark, and it is the applicant's own use of the mark that is relied on in the application, then the applicant does not have to include a reference to use by a related company in the application. *See* TMEP §1201.05.

1202.03 Refusal on Basis of Ornamentation

Subject matter that is merely a decorative feature does not identify and distinguish the applicant's goods and, thus, does not function as a trademark. A decorative feature may include words, designs, slogans, or other trade dress. This matter should be refused registration because it is merely ornamentation and, therefore, does not function as a trademark as required by §§1, 2 and 45 of the Trademark Act, 15 U.S.C. §§1051, 1052 and 1127.

Generally, the ornamentation refusal applies only to trademarks, not to service marks. *See* TMEP §§1301.02 *et seq.* regarding matter that does not function as a service mark.

Matter that serves primarily as a source indicator, either inherently or as a result of acquired distinctiveness, and that is only incidentally ornamental or decorative, can be registered as a trademark. *In re Paramount Pictures Corp.*, 213 USPQ 1111 (TTAB 1982).

With regard to registrability, ornamental matter may be categorized along a continuum ranging from ornamental matter that is registrable on the Principal Register, to purely ornamental matter that is incapable of trademark significance and unregistrable under any circumstances, as follows:

(1) Ornamental matter that serves as an identifier of a "secondary source" is registrable on the Principal Register. For example, ornamental matter on a T-shirt (*e.g.*, the designation "NEW YORK UNIVERSITY") can convey to the purchasing public the "secondary source" of the T-shirt (rather than the manufacturing source). Thus, even where the T-shirt is distributed by a party other than that identified by the designation, sponsorship, or authorization by the identified party is indicated. *See* TMEP §1202.03(c).

(2) Ornamental matter that is neither inherently distinctive nor a secondary source indicator may be registered on the Principal Register under §2(f), if the applicant establishes that the subject matter has acquired distinctiveness as a mark in relation to the goods. *See* TMEP §1202.03(d).

(3) Ornamental matter that is neither inherently distinctive nor an indicator of secondary source, and has not acquired distinctiveness, but is capable of attaining trademark significance, may be registered on the Supplemental Register in an application under §1 or §44 of the Trademark Act.

(4) Some matter is determined to be purely ornamental and, thus, incapable of trademark significance and unregistrable on either the Principal Register or the Supplemental Register. *See* TMEP §1202.03(a).

The examining attorney should consider the following factors to determine whether ornamental matter can be registered: (1) the commercial impression of the proposed mark; (2) the relevant practices of the trade; (3) secondary source, if applicable; and (4) evidence of distinctiveness. These factors are discussed in the following sections.

* * *

1215 Marks Composed, in Whole or in Part, of Domain Names
1215.01 Background
A domain name is part of a Uniform Resource Locator ("URL"), which is the address of a site or document on the Internet. In general, a domain name is comprised of a second-level domain, a "dot," and a top-level domain ("TLD"). The wording to the left of the "dot" is the second-level domain, and the wording to the right of the "dot" is the TLD.

Example: If the domain name is "ABC.com," the term "ABC" is a second-level domain and the term "com" is a TLD.

A domain name is usually preceded in a URL by "http://www." The "http://" refers to the protocol used to transfer information, and the "www" refers to World Wide Web, a graphical hypermedia interface for viewing and exchanging information.

Generic TLDs. The following are examples of generic TLDs that are designated for use by the public:

.com commercial, for-profit organizations
.edu 4-year, degree-granting colleges/universities
.gov U.S. federal government agencies
.int international organizations
.mil U.S. military organizations, even if located outside the U.S.
.net network infrastructure machines and organizations
.org miscellaneous, usually non-profit organizations and individuals

Each of the above TLDs is intended for use by a certain type of organization. For example, the TLD ".com" is for use by commercial, for-profit organizations. However, the administrator of the .com, .net, .org and .edu TLDs does not check the requests of parties seeking domain names to ensure that such parties are a type of organization that should be using those TLDs. On the other hand, .mil, .gov, and .int TLD applications are checked, and only the U.S. military, the U.S. government, or international organizations are allowed in the respective domain space.

Country Code TLDs. Country code TLDs are for use by each individual country. For example, the TLD ".ca" is for use by Canada, and the TLD ".jp" is for use by Japan. Each country determines who may use their code. For example, some countries require that users of their code be citizens or have some association with the country, while other countries do not.

See www.icann.org for additional information about other generic TLDs and TMEP § 1209.03(m).

1215.02 Use as a Mark
Generally, when a trademark, service mark, collective mark, or certification mark is composed, in whole or in part, of a domain name, neither the beginning of the URL ("http://www.") nor the TLD have any source-indicating significance. Instead, those designations are merely devices that every Internet site provider must use as part of its address. Advertisements for all types of products and services routinely include a URL for the website of the advertiser, and the average person familiar with the Internet recognizes the format for a domain name and understands that "http," "www," and a TLD are a part of every URL.

1215.02(a) Use Applications

A mark composed of a domain name is registrable as a trademark or service mark only if it functions as a source identifier. The mark as depicted on the specimen must be presented in a manner that will be perceived by potential purchasers to indicate source and not as merely an informational indication of the domain name address used to access a website. *See In re Roberts*, 87 USPQ2d 1474 (TTAB 2008) (irestmycase does not function as mark for legal services, where it is used only as part of an address by means of which one may reach applicant's website, or along with applicant's other contact information on letterhead); *In re Eilberg*, 49 USPQ2d 1955 (TTAB 1998).

In *Eilberg*, the Trademark Trial and Appeal Board held that a term that only serves to identify the applicant's domain name or the location on the Internet where the applicant's website appears, and does not separately identify applicant's services, does not function as a service mark. The applicant's proposed mark was WWW.EILBERG.COM, and the specimen showed that the mark was used on letterhead and business cards in the following manner:

(The specimen submitted was the business card of William H. Eilberg, Attorney at Law, 820 Homestead Road, P.O. Box 7, Jenkintown, Pennsylvania 19046, 215-855-4600, email whe@eilberg.com.)

The Board affirmed the examining attorney's refusal of registration on the ground that the matter presented for registration did not function as a mark, stating that:

[T]he asserted mark, as displayed on applicant's letterhead, does not function as a service mark identifying and distinguishing applicant's legal services and, as presented, is not capable of doing so. As shown, the asserted mark identifies applicant's Internet domain name, by use of which one can access applicant's Web site. In other words, the asserted mark WWW.EILBERG.COM merely indicates the location on the Internet where applicant's Web site appears. It does not separately identify applicant's legal services as such. *Cf. In re The Signal Companies, Inc.*, 228 USPQ 956 (TTAB 1986).

This is not to say that, if used appropriately, the asserted mark or portions thereof may not be trademarks or [service marks]. For example, if applicant's law firm name were, say, EILBERG.COM and were presented prominently on applicant's letterheads and business cards as the name under which applicant was rendering its legal services, then that mark may well be registrable.

49 USPQ2d at 1957.

The examining attorney must review the specimen in order to determine how the proposed mark is actually used. It is the perception of the ordinary customer that determines whether the asserted mark functions as a mark, not the applicant's intent, hope, or expectation that it does so. *See In re Standard Oil Co.*, 275 F.2d 945, 125 USPQ 227 (C.C.P.A. 1960).

If the proposed mark is used in a way that would be perceived as nothing more than an Internet address where the applicant can be contacted, registration must be refused. Examples of a domain name used only as an Internet address include a domain name used in close proximity to language referring to the domain name as an address, or a domain name displayed merely as part of the information on how to contact the applicant.

> *Example*: The mark is WWW.ABC.COM for online ordering services in the field of clothing. A specimen consisting of an advertisement that states "visit us on the web at www.ABC.com" does not show service mark use of the proposed mark.

> *Example*: The mark is ABC.COM for financial consulting services. A specimen consisting of a business card that refers to the service and lists a telephone number, fax number, and the domain name sought to be registered does not show service mark use of the proposed mark.

If the specimen fails to show use of the domain name as a mark and the applicant seeks registration on the Principal Register, the examining attorney must refuse registration on the ground that the matter presented for registration does not function as a mark. The statutory bases for the refusals are §§1, 2, and 45 of the Trademark Act, 15 U.S.C. §§1051, 1052, and 1127, for trademarks; and §§1, 2, 3, and 45 of the Act, 15 U.S.C. §§1051, 1052, 1053, and 1127, for service marks.

If the applicant seeks registration on the Supplemental Register, the examining attorney must refuse registration under Trademark Act §23, 15 U.S.C. §1091.

II

US – State Law (Rights of Publicity)

CALIFORNIA

CALIFORNIA
Civil Code - Division 4 (General Provisions) - Part 1 (Relief) -
Title 2 (Compensatory Relief) - Chapter 2 (Measure of Damages) -
Article 3 (Penal Damages)

§ 3344. Use of another's name, voice, signature, photograph, or likeness for advertising or selling or soliciting purposes

(a) Any person who knowingly uses another's name, voice, signature, photograph, or likeness, in any manner, on or in products, merchandise, or goods, or for purposes of advertising or selling, or soliciting purchases of, products, merchandise, goods or services, without such person's prior consent, or, in the case of a minor, the prior consent of his parent or legal guardian, shall be liable for any damages sustained by the person or persons injured as a result thereof. In addition, in any action brought under this section, the person who violated the section shall be liable to the injured party or parties in an amount equal to the greater of seven hundred fifty dollars ($750) or the actual damages suffered by him or her as a result of the unauthorized use, and any profits from the unauthorized use that are attributable to the use and are not taken into account in computing the actual damages. In establishing such profits, the injured party or parties are required to present proof only of the gross revenue attributable to such use, and the person who violated this section is required to prove his or her deductible expenses. Punitive damages may also be awarded to the injured party or parties. The prevailing party in any action under this section shall also be entitled to attorney's fees and costs.

(b) As used in this section, "photograph" means any photograph or photographic reproduction, still or moving, or any videotape or live television transmission, of any person, such that the person is readily identifiable.

(1) A person shall be deemed to be readily identifiable from a photograph when one who views the photograph with the naked eye can reasonably determine that the person depicted in the photograph is the same person who is complaining of its unauthorized use.

(2) If the photograph includes more than one person so identifiable, then the person or persons complaining of the use shall be represented as individuals rather than solely as members of a definable group represented in the photograph. A definable group includes, but is not limited to, the following examples: a crowd at any sporting event, a crowd in any street or public building, the audience at any theatrical or stage production, a glee club, or a baseball team.

(3) A person or persons shall be considered to be represented as members of a definable group if they are represented in the photograph solely as a result of being present at the time the photograph was taken and have not been singled out as individuals in any manner.

(c) Where a photograph or likeness of an employee of the person using the photograph or likeness appearing in the advertisement or other publication prepared by or in behalf of the user is only incidental, and not essential, to the purpose of the publication in which it appears, there shall arise a rebuttable presumption affecting the burden of producing evidence that the failure to obtain the consent of the employee was not a knowing use of the employee's photograph or likeness.

(d) For purposes of this section, a use of a name, voice, signature, photograph, or likeness in connection with any news, public affairs, or sports broadcast or account, or any political campaign, shall not constitute a use for which consent is required under subdivision (a).

(e) The use of a name, voice, signature, photograph, or likeness in a commercial medium shall not constitute a use for which consent is required under subdivision (a) solely because the material containing such use is commercially sponsored or contains paid advertising. Rather it shall be a question of fact whether or not the use of the person's name, voice, signature, photograph, or likeness was so directly connected with the commercial sponsorship or with the paid advertising as to constitute a use for which consent is required under subdivision (a).

(f) Nothing in this section shall apply to the owners or employees of any medium used for advertising, including, but not limited to, newspapers, magazines, radio and television networks and stations, cable television systems, billboards, and transit ads, by whom any advertisement or solicitation in violation of this section is published or disseminated, unless it is established that such owners or employees had knowledge of the unauthorized use of the person's name, voice, signature, photograph, or likeness as prohibited by this section.

(g) The remedies provided for in this section are cumulative and shall be in addition to any others provided for by law.

§ 3344.1. Deceased personality's name, voice, signature, photograph, or likeness; unauthorized use; damages and profits from use; protected uses; persons entitled to exercise rights; successors in interest or licensees; registration of claim

(a)(1) Any person who uses a deceased personality's name, voice, signature, photograph, or likeness, in any manner, on or in products, merchandise, or goods, or for purposes of advertising or selling, or soliciting purchases of, products, merchandise, goods, or services, without prior consent from the person or persons specified in subdivision (c), shall be liable for any damages sustained by the person or persons injured as a result thereof. In addition, in any action brought under this section, the person who violated the section shall be liable to the injured party or parties in an amount equal to the greater of seven hundred fifty dollars ($750) or the actual damages suffered by the injured party or parties, as a result of the unauthorized use, and any profits from the unauthorized use that are attributable to the use and are not taken into account in computing the actual damages. In establishing these profits, the injured party or parties shall be required to present proof only of the gross revenue attributable to the use and the person who violated the section is required to prove his or her deductible expenses. Punitive damages may also be awarded to the injured party or parties. The prevailing party or parties in any action under this section shall also be entitled to attorney's fees and costs.

(2) For purposes of this subdivision, a play, book, magazine, newspaper, musical composition, audiovisual work, radio or television program, single and original work of art, work of political or newsworthy value, or an advertisement or commercial

announcement for any of these works, shall not be considered a product, article of merchandise, good, or service if it is fictional or nonfictional entertainment, or a dramatic, literary, or musical work.

(3) If a work that is protected under paragraph (2) includes within it a use in connection with a product, article of merchandise, good, or service, this use shall not be exempt under this subdivision, notwithstanding the unprotected use's inclusion in a work otherwise exempt under this subdivision, if the claimant proves that this use is so directly connected with a product, article of merchandise, good, or service as to constitute an act of advertising, selling, or soliciting purchases of that product, article of merchandise, good, or service by the deceased personality without prior consent from the person or persons specified in subdivision (c).

(b) The rights recognized under this section are property rights, freely transferable or descendible, in whole or in part, by contract or by means of any trust or any other testamentary instrument, executed before or after January 1, 1985. The rights recognized under this section shall be deemed to have existed at the time of death of any deceased personality who died prior to January 1, 1985, and, except as provided in subdivision (o), shall vest in the persons entitled to these property rights under the testamentary instrument of the deceased personality effective as of the date of his or her death. In the absence of an express transfer in a testamentary instrument of the deceased personality's rights in his or her name, voice, signature, photograph, or likeness, a provision in the testamentary instrument that provides for the disposition of the residue of the deceased personality's assets shall be effective to transfer the rights recognized under this section in accordance with the terms of that provision. The rights established by this section shall also be freely transferable or descendible by contract, trust, or any other testamentary instrument by any subsequent owner of the deceased personality's rights as recognized by this section. Nothing in this section shall be construed to render invalid or unenforceable any contract entered into by a deceased personality during his or her lifetime by which the deceased personality assigned the rights, in whole or in part, to use his or her name, voice, signature, photograph, or likeness, regardless of whether the contract was entered into before or after January 1, 1985.

(c) The consent required by this section shall be exercisable by the person or persons to whom the right of consent, or portion thereof, has been transferred in accordance with subdivision (b), or if no transfer has occurred, then by the person or persons to whom the right of consent, or portion thereof, has passed in accordance with subdivision (d).

(d) Subject to subdivisions (b) and (c), after the death of any person, the rights under this section shall belong to the following person or persons and may be exercised, on behalf of and for the benefit of all of those persons, by those persons who, in the aggregate, are entitled to more than a one-half interest in the rights:

(1) The entire interest in those rights belongs to the surviving spouse of the deceased personality unless there are any surviving children or grandchildren of the deceased personality, in which case one-half of the entire interest in those rights belongs to the surviving spouse.

(2) The entire interest in those rights belongs to the surviving children of the deceased personality and to the surviving children of any dead child of the deceased

personality unless the deceased personality has a surviving spouse, in which case the ownership of a one-half interest in rights is divided among the surviving children and grandchildren.

(3) If there is no surviving spouse, and no surviving children or grandchildren, then the entire interest in those rights belongs to the surviving parent or parents of the deceased personality.

(4) The rights of the deceased personality's children and grandchildren are in all cases divided among them and exercisable in the manner provided in Section 240 of the Probate Code according to the number of the deceased personality's children represented. The share of the children of a dead child of a deceased personality can be exercised only by the action of a majority of them.

(e) If any deceased personality does not transfer his or her rights under this section by contract, or by means of a trust or testamentary instrument, and there are no surviving persons as described in subdivision (d), then the rights set forth in subdivision (a) shall terminate.

(f)(1) A successor in interest to the rights of a deceased personality under this section or a licensee thereof shall not recover damages for a use prohibited by this section that occurs before the successor in interest or licensee registers a claim of the rights under paragraph (2).

(2) Any person claiming to be a successor in interest to the rights of a deceased personality under this section or a licensee thereof may register that claim with the Secretary of State on a form prescribed by the Secretary of State and upon payment of a fee as set forth in subdivision (d) of Section 12195 of the Government Code. The form shall be verified and shall include the name and date of death of the deceased personality, the name and address of the claimant, the basis of the claim, and the rights claimed.

(3) Upon receipt and after filing of any document under this section, the Secretary of State shall post the document along with the entire registry of persons claiming to be a successor in interest to the rights of a deceased personality or a registered licensee under this section upon the World Wide Web, also known as the Internet. The Secretary of State may microfilm or reproduce by other techniques any of the filings or documents and destroy the original filing or document. The microfilm or other reproduction of any document under this section shall be admissible in any court of law. The microfilm or other reproduction of any document may be destroyed by the Secretary of State 70 years after the death of the personality named therein.

(4) Claims registered under this subdivision shall be public records.

(g) No action shall be brought under this section by reason of any use of a deceased personality's name, voice, signature, photograph, or likeness occurring after the expiration of 70 years after the death of the deceased personality.

(h) As used in this section, "deceased personality" means any natural person whose name, voice, signature, photograph, or likeness has commercial value at the time of his or her death, whether or not during the lifetime of that natural person the person used his or her name, voice, signature, photograph, or likeness on or in products, merchandise, or goods, or for purposes of advertising or selling, or solicitation of purchase of, products, merchandise, goods, or services. A "deceased personality" shall include, without limitation, any such natural person who has died within 70 years prior to January 1, 1985.

(i) As used in this section, "photograph" means any photograph or photographic reproduction, still or moving, or any video recording or live television transmission, of any person, such that the deceased personality is readily identifiable. A deceased personality shall be deemed to be readily identifiable from a photograph when one who views the photograph with the naked eye can reasonably determine who the person depicted in the photograph is.

(j) For purposes of this section, a use of a name, voice, signature, photograph, or likeness in connection with any news, public affairs, or sports broadcast or account, or any political campaign, shall not constitute a use for which consent is required under subdivision (a).

(k) The use of a name, voice, signature, photograph, or likeness in a commercial medium shall not constitute a use for which consent is required under subdivision (a) solely because the material containing the use is commercially sponsored or contains paid advertising. Rather, it shall be a question of fact whether or not the use of the deceased personality's name, voice, signature, photograph, or likeness was so directly connected with the commercial sponsorship or with the paid advertising as to constitute a use for which consent is required under subdivision (a).

(l) Nothing in this section shall apply to the owners or employees of any medium used for advertising, including, but not limited to, newspapers, magazines, radio and television networks and stations, cable television systems, billboards, and transit ads, by whom any advertisement or solicitation in violation of this section is published or disseminated, unless it is established that the owners or employees had knowledge of the unauthorized use of the deceased personality's name, voice, signature, photograph, or likeness as prohibited by this section.

(m) The remedies provided for in this section are cumulative and shall be in addition to any others provided for by law.

(n) This section shall apply to the adjudication of liability and the imposition of any damages or other remedies in cases in which the liability, damages, and other remedies arise from acts occurring directly in this state. For purposes of this section, acts giving rise to liability shall be limited to the use, on or in products, merchandise, goods, or services, or the advertising or selling, or soliciting purchases of, products, merchandise, goods, or services prohibited by this section.

(o) Notwithstanding any provision of this section to the contrary, if an action was taken prior to May 1, 2007, to exercise rights recognized under this section relating to a deceased personality who died prior to January 1, 1985, by a person described in subdivision (d), other than a person who was disinherited by the deceased personality in a testamentary instrument, and the exercise of those rights was not challenged successfully in a court action by a person described in subdivision (b), that exercise shall not be affected by subdivision (b). In such a case, the rights that would otherwise vest in one or more persons described in subdivision (b) shall vest solely in the person or persons described in subdivision (d), other than a person disinherited by the deceased personality in a testamentary instrument, for all future purposes.

(p) The rights recognized by this section are expressly made retroactive, including to those deceased personalities who died before January 1, 1985.

INDIANA

INDIANA
Title 32 (Property) - Article 36 (Publicity) Chapter 1 (Rights of Publicity)

32-36-1-1 Application of chapter

Sec. 1. (a) This chapter applies to an act or event that occurs within Indiana, regardless of a personality's domicile, residence, or citizenship.

(b) This chapter does not affect rights and privileges recognized under any other law that apply to a news reporting or an entertainment medium.

(c) This chapter does not apply to the following:

(1) The use of a personality's name, voice, signature, photograph, image, likeness, distinctive appearance, gestures, or mannerisms in any of the following:

(A) Literary works, theatrical works, musical compositions, film, radio, or television programs.

(B) Material that has political or newsworthy value.

(C) Original works of fine art.

(D) Promotional material or an advertisement for a news reporting or an entertainment medium that:

(i) uses all or part of a past edition of the medium's own broadcast or publication; and

(ii) does not convey or reasonably suggest that a personality endorses the news reporting or entertainment medium.

(E) An advertisement or commercial announcement for a use described in this subdivision.

(2) The use of a personality's name to truthfully identify the personality as:

(A) the author of a written work; or

(B) a performer of a recorded performance;

under circumstances in which the written work or recorded performance is otherwise rightfully reproduced, exhibited, or broadcast.

(3) The use of a personality's:

(A) name;

(B) voice;

(C) signature;

(D) photograph;

(E) image;

(F) likeness;

(G) distinctive appearance;

(H) gestures; or

(I) mannerisms;

in connection with the broadcast or reporting of an event or a topic of general or public interest.

32-36-1-2 "Commercial purpose" defined

Sec. 2. As used in this chapter, "commercial purpose" means the use of an aspect of a personality's right of publicity as follows:

(1) On or in connection with a product, merchandise, goods, services, or commercial activities.

(2) For advertising or soliciting purchases of products, merchandise, goods, services, or for promoting commercial activities.

(3) For the purpose of fundraising.

32-36-1-3 "Name" defined

Sec. 3. As used in this chapter, "name" means the actual or assumed name of a living or deceased natural person that is intended to identify the person.

32-36-1-4 "News reporting or an entertainment medium" defined

Sec. 4. As used in this chapter, "news reporting or an entertainment medium" means a medium that publishes, broadcasts, or disseminates advertising in the normal course of its business, including the following:

(1) Newspapers.

(2) Magazines.

(3) Radio and television networks and stations.

(4) Cable television systems.

32-36-1-5 "Person" defined

Sec. 5. As used in this chapter, "person" means a natural person, a partnership, a firm, a corporation, or an unincorporated association.

32-36-1-6 "Personality" defined

Sec. 6. As used in this chapter, "personality" means a living or deceased natural person whose:

(1) name;

(2) voice;

(3) signature;

(4) photograph;

(5) image;

(6) likeness;

(7) distinctive appearance;

(8) gesture; or

(9) mannerisms;

has commercial value, whether or not the person uses or authorizes the use of the person's rights of publicity for a commercial purpose during the person's lifetime.

32-36-1-7 "Right of publicity" defined

Sec. 7. As used in this chapter, "right of publicity" means a personality's property interest in the personality's:

(1) name;

(2) voice;

(3) signature;

(4) photograph;

(5) image;

(6) likeness;

(7) distinctive appearance;

(8) gestures; or

(9) mannerisms.

32-36-1-8 Use of personality's right of publicity

Sec. 8. (a) A person may not use an aspect of a personality's right of publicity for a commercial purpose during the personality's lifetime or for one hundred (100) years after the date of the personality's death without having obtained previous written consent from a person specified in section 17 of this chapter.

(b) A written consent solicited or negotiated by an athlete agent (as defined in IC 25-5.2-1-2) from a student athlete (as defined in IC 25-5.2-1-2) is void if the athlete agent obtained the consent as the result of an agency contract that:

(1) was void under IC 25-5.2-2-2 or under the law of the state where the agency contract was entered into;

(2) was voided by the student athlete under IC 25-5.2-2-8 or a similar law in the state where the agency contract was entered into; or

(3) was entered into without the notice required under IC 35-46-4-4 or a similar law in the state where the agency contract was entered into.

(c) A written consent for an endorsement contract (as defined in IC 35-46-4- 1.5) is void if notice is not given as required by IC 35-46-4-4 or a similar law in the state where the endorsement contract is entered into.

32-36-1-9 Submission to court jurisdiction

Sec. 9. A person who:

(1) engages in conduct within Indiana that is prohibited under section 8 of this chapter;

(2) creates or causes to be created within Indiana goods, merchandise, or other materials prohibited under section 8 of this chapter;

(3) transports or causes to be transported into Indiana goods, merchandise, or other materials created or used in violation of section 8 of this chapter; or

(4) knowingly causes advertising or promotional material created or used in violation of section 8 of this chapter to be published, distributed, exhibited, or disseminated within Indiana;

submits to the jurisdiction of Indiana courts.

32-36-1-10 Damages

Sec. 10. A person who violates section 8 of this chapter may be liable for any of the following:

(1) Damages in the amount of:

(A) one thousand dollars ($1,000); or

(B) actual damages, including profits derived from the unauthorized use;

whichever is greater.

(2) Treble or punitive damages, as the injured party may elect, if the violation under section 8 of this chapter is knowing, willful, or intentional.

32-36-1-11 Establishment of profits

Sec. 11. In establishing the amount of the profits under section 10(1)(B) of this chapter:

(1) the plaintiff is required to prove the gross revenue attributable to the unauthorized use; and

(2) the defendant is required to prove properly deductible expenses.

32-36-1-12 Attorney's fees; injunctions

Sec. 12. In addition to any damages awarded under section 10 of this chapter, the court:

(1) shall award to the prevailing party reasonable attorney's fees, costs, and expenses relating to an action under this chapter; and

(2) may order temporary or permanent injunctive relief, except as provided by section 13 of this chapter.

32-36-1-13 Unenforceable injunctions

Sec. 13. Injunctive relief is not enforceable against a news reporting or an entertainment medium that has:

(1) contracted with a person for the publication or broadcast of an advertisement; and

(2) incorporated the advertisement in tangible form into material that has been prepared for broadcast or publication.

32-36-1-14 Order for impoundment

Sec. 14. (a) This section does not apply to a news reporting or an entertainment medium.

(b) During any period that an action under this chapter is pending, a court may order the impoundment of:

(1) goods, merchandise, or other materials claimed to have been made or used in violation of section 8 of this chapter; and

(2) plates, molds, matrices, masters, tapes, negatives, or other items from which goods, merchandise, or other materials described in subdivision (1) may be manufactured or reproduced.

(c) The court may order impoundment under subsection (b) upon terms that the court considers reasonable.

32-36-1-15 Order for destruction

Sec. 15. (a) This section does not apply to a news reporting or an entertainment medium.

(b) As part of a final judgment or decree, a court may order the destruction or other reasonable disposition of items described in section 14(b) of this chapter.

32-36-1-16 Property rights

Sec. 16. The rights recognized under this chapter are property rights, freely transferable and descendible, in whole or in part, by the following:

(1) Contract.

(2) License.

(3) Gift.

(4) Trust.

(5) Testamentary document.

(6) Operation of the laws of intestate succession applicable to the state administering the estate and property of an intestate deceased personality, regardless of whether the state recognizes the property rights set forth under this chapter.

32-36-1-17 Written consent

Sec. 17. (a) The written consent required by section 8 of this chapter and the rights and remedies set forth in this chapter may be exercised and enforced by:

(1) a personality; or

(2) a person to whom the recognized rights of a personality have been transferred under section 16 of this chapter.

(b) If a transfer of a personality's recognized rights has not occurred under section 16 of this chapter, a person to whom the personality's recognized rights are transferred under section 18 of this chapter may exercise and enforce the rights under this chapter and seek the remedies provided in this chapter.

32-36-1-18 Exercise of rights and remedies post-mortem

Sec. 18. (a) Subject to sections 16 and 17 of this chapter, after the death of an intestate personality, the rights and remedies of this chapter may be exercised and enforced by a person who possesses a total of not less than one-half (1/2) interest of the personality's recognized rights.

(b) A person described in subsection (a) shall account to any other person in whom the personality's recognized rights have vested to the extent that the other person's interest may appear.

32-36-1-19 Termination of deceased person's rights

Sec. 19. If:

(1) a deceased personality's recognized rights under this chapter were not transferred by:

(A) contract;

(B) license;

(C) gift;

(D) trust; or

(E) testamentary document; and

(2) there are no surviving persons as described in section 17 of this chapter to whom the deceased personality's recognized rights pass by intestate succession;

the deceased personality's rights set forth in this chapter terminate.

32-36-1-20 Rights and remedies are supplemental
Sec. 20. The rights and remedies provided for in this chapter are supplemental to any other rights and remedies provided by law.

NEW YORK

NEW YORK
Civil Rights Law
Chapter 6 (of the Consolidated Laws)
Article 5 (Right of Privacy)

§ 50. Right of privacy

A person, firm or corporation that uses for advertising purposes, or for the purposes of trade, the name, portrait or picture of any living person without having first obtained the written consent of such person, or if a minor of his or her parent or guardian, is guilty of a misdemeanor.

* * *

§ 51. Action for injunction and for damages

Any person whose name, portrait, picture or voice is used within this state for advertising purposes or for the purposes of trade without the written consent first obtained as above provided[1] may maintain an equitable action in the supreme court of this state against the person, firm or corporation so using his name, portrait, picture or voice, to prevent and restrain the use thereof; and may also sue and recover damages for any injuries sustained by reason of such use and if the defendant shall have knowingly used such person's name, portrait, picture or voice in such manner as is forbidden or declared to be unlawful by section fifty of this article, the jury, in its discretion, may award exemplary damages. But nothing contained in this article shall be so construed as to prevent any person, firm or corporation from selling or otherwise transferring any material containing such name, portrait, picture or voice in whatever medium to any user of such name, portrait, picture or voice, or to any third party for sale or transfer directly or indirectly to such a user, for use in a manner lawful under this article; nothing contained in this article shall be so construed as to prevent any person, firm or corporation, practicing the profession of photography, from exhibiting in or about his or its establishment specimens of the work of such establishment, unless the same is continued by such person, firm or corporation after written notice objecting thereto has been given by the person portrayed; and nothing contained in this article shall be so construed as to prevent any person, firm or corporation from using the name, portrait, picture or voice of any manufacturer or dealer in connection with the goods, wares and merchandise manufactured, produced or dealt in by him which he has sold or disposed of with such name, portrait, picture or voice used in connection therewith; or from using the name, portrait, picture or voice of any author, composer or artist in connection with his literary, musical or artistic productions which he has sold or disposed of with such name, portrait, picture or voice used in connection therewith. Nothing contained in this section shall be construed to prohibit the copyright owner of a sound recording from disposing of, dealing in, licensing or selling

---

1. See § 50.

that sound recording to any party, if the right to dispose of, deal in, license or sell such sound recording has been conferred by contract or other written document by such living person or the holder of such right. Nothing contained in the foregoing sentence shall be deemed to abrogate or otherwise limit any rights or remedies otherwise conferred by federal law or state law.

TENNESSEE

TENNESSEE
Title 47 (Commercial Instruments and Transactions)
Chapter 25 (Trade practices) - Part 11 (Protection of Personal Rights)

47-25-1101 Short title.

This part shall be known and may be cited as the "Personal Rights Protection Act of 1984." [Acts 1984, ch. 945, § 1.]

47-25-1102 Definitions.

As used in this part, unless the context otherwise requires:

(1) "Definable group" means an assemblage of individuals existing or brought together with or without interrelation, orderly form, or arrangement, including, but not limited to, a crowd at any sporting event, a crowd in any street or public building, the audience at any theatrical or stage production, a glee club, or a baseball team;

(2) "Individual" means human being, living or dead;

(3) "Likeness" means the use of an image of an individual for commercial purposes;

(4) "Person" means any firm, association, partnership, corporation, joint stock company, syndicate, receiver, common law trust, conservator, statutory trust, or any other concern by whatever name known or however organized, formed, or created, and includes not-for-profit corporations, associations, educational and religious institutions, political parties, community, civic, or other organizations; and

(5) "Photograph" means any photograph or photographic reproduction, still or moving, or any videotape or live television transmission, of any individual, so that the individual is readily identifiable. [Acts 1984, ch. 945, § 2.]

47-25-1103 Property right in use of name, photograph or likeness.

(a) Every individual has a property right in the use of that person's name, photograph, or likeness in any medium in any manner.

(b) The individual rights provided for in subsection (a) constitute property rights and are freely assignable and licensable, and do not expire upon the death of the individual so protected, whether or not such rights were commercially exploited by the individual during the individual's lifetime, but shall be descendible to the executors, assigns, heirs, or devisees of the individual so protected by this part. [Acts 1984, ch. 945, § 3.]

47-25-1104 Exclusive rights, commercial exploitation after death.

(a) The rights provided for in this part shall be deemed exclusive to the individual, subject to the assignment or licensing of such rights as provided in § 47-25-1103, during such individual's lifetime and to the executors, heirs, assigns, or devisees for a period of ten (10) years after the death of the individual.

(b)(1) Commercial exploitation of the property right by any executor, assignee, heir, or devisee if the individual is deceased shall maintain the right as the exclusive property of the executor, assignee, heir, or devisee until such right is terminated as provided in this subsection (b).

(2) The exclusive right to commercial exploitation of the property rights is terminated by proof of the non-use of the name, likeness, or image of any individual for commercial purposes by an executor, assignee, heir, or devisee to such use for a period of two (2) years subsequent to the initial ten (10) year period following the individual's death. [Acts 1984, ch. 945, § 4.]

47-25-1105 Unauthorized use.

(a) Any person who knowingly uses or infringes upon the use of another individual's name, photograph, or likeness in any medium, in any manner directed to any person other than such individual, as an item of commerce for purposes of advertising products, merchandise, goods, or services, or for purposes of fund raising, solicitation of donations, purchases of products, merchandise, goods, or services, without such individual's prior consent, or, in the case of a minor, the prior consent of such minor's parent or legal guardian, or in the case of a deceased individual, the consent of the executor or administrator, heirs, or devisees of such deceased individual, shall be liable to a civil action.

(b) In addition to the civil action authorized by this section and the remedies set out in § 47-25-1106, any person who commits unauthorized use as defined in subsection (a) commits a Class A misdemeanor.

(c) It is no defense to the unauthorized use defined in subsection (a) that the photograph includes more than one (1) individual so identifiable; provided, that the individual or individuals complaining of the use shall be represented as individuals per se rather than solely as members of a definable group represented in the photograph.

(d) If an unauthorized use as defined in subsection (a) is by means of products, merchandise, goods or other tangible personal property, all such property, including all instrumentalities used in connection with the unauthorized use by the person violating this section, is declared contraband and subject to seizure by, and forfeiture to, the state in the same manner as is provided by law for the seizure and forfeiture of other contraband items. [Acts 1984, ch. 945, § 5; 1989, ch. 308, § 1; 1991, ch. 506, § 1; 2005, ch. 395, §§ 4, 5.]

47-25-1106 Injunctions; impounding or destruction of materials; damages.

(a) The chancery and circuit court having jurisdiction for any action arising pursuant to this part may grant injunctions on such terms as it may deem reasonable to prevent or restrain the unauthorized use of an individual's name, photograph, or likeness. As part of such injunction, the court may authorize the confiscation of all unauthorized items and seize all instrumentalities used in connection with the violation of the individual's rights. All instrumentalities seized pursuant to enforcing an injunction under this subsection (a) shall be liquidated and used to satisfy statutory damages, if damages are recovered by the rights holder.

(b) At any time while an action under this part is pending, the court may order the impounding, on such terms as it may deem reasonable, of all materials or any part thereof claimed to have been made or used in violation of the individual's rights, and such court may enjoin the use of all plates, molds, matrices, masters, tapes, film negatives, or other articles by means of which such materials may be reproduced.

(c) As part of a final judgment or decree, the court may order the destruction or other reasonable disposition of all materials found to have been made or used in violation of the individual's rights, and of all plates, molds, matrices, masters, tapes, film negatives, or other articles by means of which such materials may be reproduced.

(d)(1) An individual is entitled to recover the actual damages suffered as a result of the knowing use or infringement of such individual's rights and any profits that are attributable to such use or infringement which are not taken into account in computing the actual damages. Profit or lack thereof by the unauthorized use or infringement of an individual's rights shall not be a criteria of determining liability.

(2) An individual is entitled to recover three (3) times the amount to which the individual is entitled under subdivision (d)(1), plus reasonable attorney fees, if a person knowingly uses or infringes the rights of a member of the armed forces in violation of this part. As used in this subdivision (d)(2), "member of the armed forces" means a member of the United States armed forces or a member of a reserve or Tennessee national guard unit who is in, or was called into, active service or active military service of the United States, as defined in § 58-1-102.

(e) The remedies provided for in this section are cumulative and shall be in addition to any others provided for by law. [Acts 1984, ch. 945, § 6; 2005, ch. 395, § 6; Acts 2009, ch. 359, § 1.]

47-25-1107 Fair use; commercial sponsorship.

(a) It is deemed a fair use and no violation of an individual's rights shall be found, for purposes of this part, if the use of a name, photograph, or likeness is in connection with any news, public affairs, or sports broadcast or account.

(b) The use of a name, photograph, or likeness in a commercial medium does not constitute a use for purposes of advertising or solicitation solely because the material containing such use is commercially sponsored or contains paid advertising. Rather it shall be a question of fact whether or not the use of the complainant individual's name, photograph, or likeness was so directly connected with the commercial sponsorship or with the paid advertising as to constitute a use for purposes of advertising or solicitation.

(c) Nothing in this section applies to the owners or employees of any medium used for advertising, including, but not limited to, newspapers, magazines, radio and television stations, billboards, and transit ads, who have published or disseminated any advertisement or solicitation in violation of this part, unless it is established that such owners or employees had knowledge of the unauthorized use of the individual's name, photograph, or likeness as prohibited by this section. [Acts 1984, ch. 945, § 7.]

47-25-1108 Application of law.

This part applies to any individual otherwise entitled to the protection afforded under part 5 of this chapter. [Acts 1984, ch. 945, § 8.]

III

INTERNATIONAL MATERIALS

A

AGREEMENT ON TRADE-RELATED ASPECTS OF INTELLECTUAL PROPERTY RIGHTS ("TRIPS") (EXCERPTS)

AGREEMENT ON TRADE-RELATED ASPECTS OF INTELLECTUAL PROPERTY RIGHTS ("TRIPS") (EXCERPTS)

Annex IC to the Agreement Establishing the World Trade Organization, April 15, 1994, Marrakesh, Morocco

Article 1
Nature and Scope of Obligations

1.   Members shall give effect to the provisions of this Agreement. Members may, but shall not be obliged to, implement in their law more extensive protection than is required by this Agreement, provided that such protection does not contravene the provisions of this Agreement. Members shall be free to determine the appropriate method of implementing the provisions of this Agreement within their own legal system and practice.

2.   For the purposes of this Agreement, the term "intellectual property" refers to all categories of intellectual property that are the subject of Sections 1 through 7 of Part II.

3.   Members shall accord the treatment provided for in this Agreement to the nationals of other Members.[1] In respect of the relevant intellectual property right, the nationals of other Members shall be understood as those natural or legal persons that would meet the criteria for eligibility for protection provided for in the Paris Convention (1967), the Berne Convention (1971), the Rome Convention and the Treaty on Intellectual Property in Respect of Integrated Circuits, were all Members of the WTO members of those conventions.[2] Any Member availing itself of the possibilities provided in paragraph 3 of Article 5 or paragraph 2 of Article 6 of the Rome Convention shall make a notification as foreseen in those provisions to the Council for Trade-Related Aspects of Intellectual Property Rights (the "Council for TRIPS").

---

1. When "nationals" are referred to in this Agreement, they shall be deemed, in the case of a separate customs territory Member of the WTO, to mean persons, natural or legal, who are domiciled or who have a real and effective industrial or commercial establishment in that customs territory.

2. In this Agreement, "Paris Convention" refers to the Paris Convention for the Protection of Industrial Property; "Paris Convention (1967)" refers to the Stockholm Act of this Convention of 14 July 1967. "Berne Convention" refers to the Berne Convention for the Protection of Literary and Artistic Works; "Berne Convention (1971)" refers to the Paris Act of this Convention of 24 July 1971. "Rome Convention" refers to the International Convention for the Protection of Performers, Producers of Phonograms and Broadcasting Organizations, adopted at Rome on 26 October 1961. "Treaty on Intellectual Property in Respect of Integrated Circuits" (IPIC Treaty) refers to the Treaty on Intellectual Property in Respect of Integrated Circuits, adopted at Washington on 26 May 1989. "WTO Agreement" refers to the Agreement Establishing the WTO.

Article 2
Intellectual Property Conventions

1.   In respect of Parts II, III and IV of this Agreement, Members shall comply with Articles 1 through 12, and Article 19, of the Paris Convention (1967).

2.   Nothing in Parts I to IV of this Agreement shall derogate from existing obligations that Members may have to each other under the Paris Convention, the Berne Convention, the Rome Convention and the Treaty on Intellectual Property in Respect of Integrated Circuits.

Article 3
National Treatment

1.   Each Member shall accord to the nationals of other Members treatment no less favourable than that it accords to its own nationals with regard to the protection[3] of intellectual property, subject to the exceptions already provided in, respectively, the Paris Convention (1967), the Berne Convention (1971), the Rome Convention or the Treaty on Intellectual Property in Respect of Integrated Circuits. In respect of performers, producers of phonograms and broadcasting organizations, this obligation only applies in respect of the rights provided under this Agreement. Any Member availing itself of the possibilities provided in Article 6 of the Berne Convention (1971) or paragraph 1(b) of Article 16 of the Rome Convention shall make a notification as foreseen in those provisions to the Council for TRIPS.

2.   Members may avail themselves of the exceptions permitted under paragraph 1 in relation to judicial and administrative procedures, including the designation of an address for service or the appointment of an agent within the jurisdiction of a Member, only where such exceptions are necessary to secure compliance with laws and regulations which are not inconsistent with the provisions of this Agreement and where such practices are not applied in a manner which would constitute a disguised restriction on trade.

* * *

Article 15
Protectable Subject Matter

1.   Any sign, or any combination of signs, capable of distinguishing the goods or services of one undertaking from those of other undertakings, shall be capable of constituting a trademark. Such signs, in particular words including personal names, letters, numerals, figurative elements and combinations of colours as well as any combination of such signs, shall be eligible for registration as trademarks. Where signs are not inherently

---

3. For the purposes of Articles 3 and 4, "protection" shall include matters affecting the availability, acquisition, scope, maintenance and enforcement of intellectual property rights as well as those matters affecting the use of intellectual property rights specifically addressed in this Agreement.

capable of distinguishing the relevant goods or services, Members may make registrability depend on distinctiveness acquired through use. Members may require, as a condition of registration, that signs be visually perceptible.

2.   Paragraph 1 shall not be understood to prevent a Member from denying registration of a trademark on other grounds, provided that they do not derogate from the provisions of the Paris Convention (1967).

3.   Members may make registrability depend on use. However, actual use of a trademark shall not be a condition for filing an application for registration. An application shall not be refused solely on the ground that intended use has not taken place before the expiry of a period of three years from the date of application.

4.   The nature of the goods or services to which a trademark is to be applied shall in no case form an obstacle to registration of the trademark.

5.   Members shall publish each trademark either before it is registered or promptly after it is registered and shall afford a reasonable opportunity for petitions to cancel the registration. In addition, Members may afford an opportunity for the registration of a trademark to be opposed.

Article 16
Rights Conferred

1.   The owner of a registered trademark shall have the exclusive right to prevent all third parties not having the owner's consent from using in the course of trade identical or similar signs for goods or services which are identical or similar to those in respect of which the trademark is registered where such use would result in a likelihood of confusion. In case of the use of an identical sign for identical goods or services, a likelihood of confusion shall be presumed. The rights described above shall not prejudice any existing prior rights, nor shall they affect the possibility of Members making rights available on the basis of use.

2.   Article 6*bis* of the Paris Convention (1967) shall apply, *mutatis mutandis*, to services. In determining whether a trademark is well-known, Members shall take account of the knowledge of the trademark in the relevant sector of the public, including knowledge in the Member concerned which has been obtained as a result of the promotion of the trademark.

3.   Article 6*bis* of the Paris Convention (1967) shall apply, *mutatis mutandis*, to goods or services which are not similar to those in respect of which a trademark is registered, provided that use of that trademark in relation to those goods or services would indicate a connection between those goods or services and the owner of the registered trademark and provided that the interests of the owner of the registered trademark are likely to be damaged by such use.

Article 17
Exceptions

Members may provide limited exceptions to the rights conferred by a trademark, such as fair use of descriptive terms, provided that such exceptions take account of the legitimate interests of the owner of the trademark and of third parties.

Article 18
Term of Protection

Initial registration, and each renewal of registration, of a trademark shall be for a term of no less than seven years. The registration of a trademark shall be renewable indefinitely.

Article 19
Requirement of Use

1.   If use is required to maintain a registration, the registration may be cancelled only after an uninterrupted period of at least three years of non-use, unless valid reasons based on the existence of obstacles to such use are shown by the trademark owner. Circumstances arising independently of the will of the owner of the trademark which constitute an obstacle to the use of the trademark, such as import restrictions on or other government requirements for goods or services protected by the trademark, shall be recognized as valid reasons for non-use.

2.   When subject to the control of its owner, use of a trademark by another person shall be recognized as use of the trademark for the purpose of maintaining the registration.

Article 20
Other Requirements

The use of a trademark in the course of trade shall not be unjustifiably encumbered by special requirements, such as use with another trademark, use in a special form or use in a manner detrimental to its capability to distinguish the goods or services of one undertaking from those of other undertakings. This will not preclude a requirement prescribing the use of the trademark identifying the undertaking producing the goods or services along with, but without linking it to, the trademark distinguishing the specific goods or services in question of that undertaking.

Article 21
Licensing and Assignment

Members may determine conditions on the licensing and assignment of trademarks, it being understood that the compulsory licensing of trademarks shall not be permitted and that the owner of a registered trademark shall have the right to assign the trademark with or without the transfer of the business to which the trademark belongs.

Section 3: Geographical Indications

Article 22
Protection of Geographical Indications

1. Geographical indications are, for the purposes of this Agreement, indications which identify a good as originating in the territory of a Member, or a region or locality in that territory, where a given quality, reputation or other characteristic of the good is essentially attributable to its geographical origin.

2. In respect of geographical indications, Members shall provide the legal means for interested parties to prevent:

    (a)   the use of any means in the designation or presentation of a good that indicates or suggests that the good in question originates in a geographical area other than the true place of origin in a manner which misleads the public as to the geographical origin of the good;

    (b)   any use which constitutes an act of unfair competition within the meaning of Article 10*bis* of the Paris Convention (1967).

3. A Member shall, *ex officio* if its legislation so permits or at the request of an interested party, refuse or invalidate the registration of a trademark which contains or consists of a geographical indication with respect to goods not originating in the territory indicated, if use of the indication in the trademark for such goods in that Member is of such a nature as to mislead the public as to the true place of origin.

4. The protection under paragraphs 1, 2 and 3 shall be applicable against a geographical indication which, although literally true as to the territory, region or locality in which the goods originate, falsely represents to the public that the goods originate in another territory.

Article 23
Additional Protection for Geographical
Indications for Wines and Spirits

1. Each Member shall provide the legal means for interested parties to prevent use of a geographical indication identifying wines for wines not originating in the place indicated by the geographical indication in question or identifying spirits for spirits not originating in the place indicated by the geographical indication in question, even where the true origin of the goods is indicated or the geographical indication is used in translation or accompanied by expressions such as "kind", "type", "style", "imitation" or the like.[4]

2. The registration of a trademark for wines which contains or consists of a geographical indication identifying wines or for spirits which contains or consists of a geographical indication identifying spirits shall be refused or invalidated, *ex officio* if a

---

4. Notwithstanding the first sentence of Article 42, Members may, with respect to these obligations, instead provide for enforcement by administrative action.

Member's legislation so permits or at the request of an interested party, with respect to such wines or spirits not having this origin.

3.   In the case of homonymous geographical indications for wines, protection shall be accorded to each indication, subject to the provisions of paragraph 4 of Article 22. Each Member shall determine the practical conditions under which the homonymous indications in question will be differentiated from each other, taking into account the need to ensure equitable treatment of the producers concerned and that consumers are not misled.

4.   In order to facilitate the protection of geographical indications for wines, negotiations shall be undertaken in the Council for TRIPS concerning the establishment of a multilateral system of notification and registration of geographical indications for wines eligible for protection in those Members participating in the system.

Article 24
International Negotiations; Exceptions

1.   Members agree to enter into negotiations aimed at increasing the protection of individual geographical indications under Article 23. The provisions of paragraphs 4 through 8 below shall not be used by a Member to refuse to conduct negotiations or to conclude bilateral or multilateral agreements. In the context of such negotiations, Members shall be willing to consider the continued applicability of these provisions to individual geographical indications whose use was the subject of such negotiations.

2.   The Council for TRIPS shall keep under review the application of the provisions of this Section; the first such review shall take place within two years of the entry into force of the WTO Agreement. Any matter affecting the compliance with the obligations under these provisions may be drawn to the attention of the Council, which, at the request of a Member, shall consult with any Member or Members in respect of such matter in respect of which it has not been possible to find a satisfactory solution through bilateral or plurilateral consultations between the Members concerned. The Council shall take such action as may be agreed to facilitate the operation and further the objectives of this Section.

3.   In implementing this Section, a Member shall not diminish the protection of geographical indications that existed in that Member immediately prior to the date of entry into force of the WTO Agreement.

4.   Nothing in this Section shall require a Member to prevent continued and similar use of a particular geographical indication of another Member identifying wines or spirits in connection with goods or services by any of its nationals or domiciliaries who have used that geographical indication in a continuous manner with regard to the same or related goods or services in the territory of that Member either (a) for at least 10 years preceding 15 April 1994 or (b) in good faith preceding that date.

5.   Where a trademark has been applied for or registered in good faith, or where rights to a trademark have been acquired through use in good faith either:
   (a) before the date of application of these provisions in that Member as defined in Part VI; or
   (b) before the geographical indication is protected in its country of origin;

measures adopted to implement this Section shall not prejudice eligibility for or the validity of the registration of a trademark, or the right to use a trademark, on the basis that such a trademark is identical with, or similar to, a geographical indication.

6.   Nothing in this Section shall require a Member to apply its provisions in respect of a geographical indication of any other Member with respect to goods or services for which the relevant indication is identical with the term customary in common language as the common name for such goods or services in the territory of that Member. Nothing in this Section shall require a Member to apply its provisions in respect of a geographical indication of any other Member with respect to products of the vine for which the relevant indication is identical with the customary name of a grape variety existing in the territory of that Member as of the date of entry into force of the WTO Agreement.

7.   A Member may provide that any request made under this Section in connection with the use or registration of a trademark must be presented within five years after the adverse use of the protected indication has become generally known in that Member or after the date of registration of the trademark in that Member provided that the trademark has been published by that date, if such date is earlier than the date on which the adverse use became generally known in that Member, provided that the geographical indication is not used or registered in bad faith.

8.   The provisions of this Section shall in no way prejudice the right of any person to use, in the course of trade, that person's name or the name of that person's predecessor in business, except where such name is used in such a manner as to mislead the public.

9.   There shall be no obligation under this Agreement to protect geographical indications which are not or cease to be protected in their country of origin, or which have fallen into disuse in that country.

Paris Convention for the Protection of Industrial Property (Excerpts)

PARIS CONVENTION FOR THE PROTECTIONOF INDUSTRIAL PROPERTY
(EXCERPTS)

Article 2
[National Treatment for Nationals of Countries of the Union]

(1) Nationals of any country of the Union shall, as regards the protection of industrial property, enjoy in all the other countries of the Union the advantages that their respective laws now grant, or may hereafter grant, to nationals; all without prejudice to the rights specially provided for by this Convention. Consequently, they shall have the same protection as the latter, and the same legal remedy against any infringement of their rights, provided that the conditions and formalities imposed upon nationals are complied with.

(2) However, no requirement as to domicile or establishment in the country where protection is claimed may be imposed upon nationals of countries of the Union for the enjoyment of any industrial property rights.

(3) The provisions of the laws of each of the countries of the Union relating to judicial and administrative procedure and to jurisdiction, and to the designation of an address for service or the appointment of an agent, which may be required by the laws on industrial property are expressly reserved.

* * *

Article 4
[A to I: *Patents, Utility Models, Industrial Designs, Marks, Inventors' Certificates:* Right of Priority
G: *Patents:* Division of the Application]

A.

(1) Any person who has duly filed an application for a patent, or for the registration of a utility model, or of an industrial design, or of a trademark, in one of the countries of the Union, or his successor in title, shall enjoy, for the purpose of filing in the other countries, a right of priority during the periods hereinafter fixed.

(2) Any filing that is equivalent to a regular national filing under the domestic legislation of any country of the Union or under bilateral or multilateral treaties concluded between countries of the Union shall be recognized as giving rise to the right of priority.

(3) By a regular national filing is meant any filing that is adequate to establish the date on which the application was filed in the country concerned, whatever may be the subsequent fate of the application.

B.

Consequently, any subsequent filing in any of the other countries of the Union before the expiration of the periods referred to above shall not be invalidated by reason of any acts accomplished in the interval, in particular, another filing, the publication or exploitation of the invention, the putting on sale of copies of the design, or the use of the mark, and such acts cannot give rise to any third-party right or any right of personal possession. Rights acquired by third parties before the date of the first application that serves as the basis for the right of priority are reserved in accordance with the domestic legislation of each country of the Union

C.

(1) The periods of priority referred to above shall be twelve months for patents and utility models, and six months for industrial designs and trademarks.

(2) These periods shall start from the date of filing of the first application; the day of filing shall not be included in the period.

(3) If the last day of the period is an official holiday, or a day when the Office is not open for the filing of applications in the country where protection is claimed, the period shall be extended until the first following working day.

(4) A subsequent application concerning the same subject as a previous first application within the meaning of paragraph (2), above, filed in the same country of the Union. shall be considered as the first application, of which the filing date shall be the starting point of the period of priority, if, at the time of filing the subsequent application, the said previous application has been withdrawn, abandoned, or refused, without having been laid open to public inspection and without leaving any rights outstanding, and if it has not yet served as a basis for claiming a right of priority. The previous application may not thereafter serve as a basis for claiming a right of priority.

D.

(1) Any person desiring to take advantage of the priority of a previous filing shall be required to make a declaration indicating the date of such filing and the country in which it was made. Each country shall determine the latest date on which such declaration must be made.

(2) These particulars shall be mentioned in the publications issued by the competent authority, and in particular in the patents and the specifications relating thereto.

(3) The countries of the Union may require any person making a declaration of priority to produce a copy of the application (description, drawings, etc.) previously filed. The copy, certified as correct by the authority which received such application, shall not require any authentication, and may in any case be filed, without fee, at any time within three months of the filing of the subsequent application. They may require it to be accompanied by a certificate from the same authority showing the date of filing, and by a translation.

(4) No other formalities may be required for the declaration of priority at the time of filing the application. Each country of the Union shall determine the consequences of failure to comply with the formalities prescribed by this Article, but such consequences shall in no case go beyond the loss of the right of priority.

(5) Subsequently, further proof may be required. Any person who avails himself of the priority of a previous application shall be required to specify the number of that application; this number shall be published as provided for by paragraph (2), above.

E.

(1) Where an industrial design is filed in a country by virtue of a right of priority based on the filing of a utility model, the period of priority shall be the same as that fixed for industrial designs.

(2) Furthermore, it is permissible to file a utility model in a country by virtue of a right of priority based on the filing of a patent application, and vice versa.

F.

No country of the Union may refuse a priority or a patent application on the ground that the applicant claims multiple priorities, even if they originate in different countries, or on the ground that an application claiming one or more priorities contains one or more elements that were not included in the application or applications whose priority is claimed, provided that, in both cases, there is unity of invention within the meaning of the law of the country.

With respect to the elements not included in the application or applications whose priority is claimed, the filing of the subsequent application shall give rise to a right of priority tinder ordinary conditions.

G.

(1) If the examination reveals that an application for a patent contains more than one invention, the applicant may divide the application into a certain number of divisional applications and preserve as the date of each the date of the initial application and the benefit of the right of priority, if any.

(2) The applicant may also, on his own initiative, divide a patent application and preserve as the date of each divisional application the date of the initial application and the benefit of the right of priority, if any. Each country of the Union shall have the right to determine the conditions under which such division shall be authorized.

H.

Priority may not be refused on the ground that certain elements of the invention for which priority is claimed do not appear among the claims formulated in the application in the country of origin, provided that the application documents as a whole specifically disclose such elements.

I.

(1) Applications for inventors' certificates filed in a country in which applicants have the right to apply at their own option either for a patent or for an inventor's certificate shall give rise to the right of priority provided for by this Article, under the same conditions and with the same effects as applications for patents.

(2) In a country in which applicants have the right to apply at their own option either for a patent or for an inventor's certificate, an applicant for an inventor's certificate shall, in accordance with the provisions of this Article relating to patent applications, enjoy a right of priority based on an application for a patent, a utility model, or an inventor's certificate.

* * *

Article 6
[*Marks:* Conditions of Registration; Independence of Protection of Same Mark in Different Countries]

(1) The conditions for the filing and registration of trademarks shall be determined in each country of the Union by its domestic legislation.

(2) However, an application for the registration of a mark filed by a national of a country of the Union in any country of the Union may not be refused, nor may a registration be invalidated, on the ground that filing, registration, or renewal, has not been effected in the country of origin.

(3) A mark duly registered in a country of the Union shall be regarded as independent of marks registered in the other countries of the Union, including the country of origin.

Article 6*bis*
[*Marks:* Well-Known Marks]

(1) The countries of the Union undertake, ex officio if their legislation so permits, or at the request of an interested party, to refuse or to cancel the registration, and to prohibit the use, of a trademark which constitutes a reproduction, an imitation, or a translation, liable to create confusion, of a mark considered by the competent authority of the country of registration or use to be well known in that country as being already the mark of a person entitled to the benefits of this Convention and used for identical or similar goods. These provisions shall also apply when the essential part of the mark constitutes a reproduction of any such well-known mark or an imitation liable to create confusion therewith.

(2) A period of at least five years from the date of registration shall be allowed for requesting the cancellation of such a mark. The countries of the Union may provide for a period within which the prohibition of use must be requested.

(3) No time limit shall be fixed for requesting the cancellation or the prohibition of the use of marks registered or used in bad faith.

Article 6*ter*
[*Marks:* Prohibitions Concerning State Emblems, Official Hallmarks, and Emblems of Intergovernmental Organizations]

(1) (a) The countries of the Union agree to refuse or to invalidate the registration, and to prohibit by appropriate measures the use, without authorization by the competent authorities, either as trademarks or as elements of trademarks, of armorial bearings, flags, and other State emblems, of the countries of the Union, official signs and hallmarks indicating control and warranty adopted by them, and any imitation from a heraldic point of view.

(b) The provisions of subparagraph (a), above, shall apply equally to armorial bearings, flags, other emblems, abbreviations, and names, of international intergovernmental organizations of which one or more countries of the Union are members, with the exception of armorial bearings, flags, other emblems, abbreviations, and names, that are already the subject of international agreements in force, intended to ensure their protection.

(c) No country of the Union shall be required to apply the provisions of subparagraph (b), above, to the prejudice of the owners of rights acquired in good faith before the entry into force, in that country, of this Convention. The countries of the Union shall not be required to apply the said provisions when the use or registration referred to in subparagraph (a), above, is not of such a nature as to suggest to the public that a connection exists between the organization concerned and the armorial bearings, flags, emblems, abbreviations, and names, or if such use or registration is probably not of such a nature as to mislead the public as to the existence of a connection between the user and the organization.

(2) Prohibition of the use of official signs and hallmarks indicating control and warranty shall apply solely in cases where the marks in which they are incorporated are intended to be used on goods of the same or a similar kind.

(3) (a)   For the application of these provisions, the countries of the Union agree to communicate reciprocally, through the intermediary of the International Bureau, the list of State emblems, and official signs and hallmarks indicating control and warranty, which they desire, or may hereafter desire, to place wholly or within certain limits tinder the protection of this Article, and all subsequent modifications of such list. Each country of the Union shall in due course make available to the public the lists so communicated. Nevertheless such communication is not obligatory in respect of flags of States.

(b) The provisions of subparagraph (b) of paragragh (1) of this Article shall apply only to such armorial bearings, flags, other emblems, abbreviations, and names, of international intergovernmental organizations as the latter have communicated to the countries of the Union through the intermediary of the International Bureau.

(4) Any country of the Union may, within a period of twelve months from the receipt of the notification, transmit its objections, if any, through the intermediary of the International Bureau, to the country or international intergovernmental organization concerned.

(5) In the case of State flags, the measures prescribed by paragraph (1), above, shall apply solely to marks registered after November 6, 1925.

(6) In the case of State emblems other than flags, and of official signs and hallmarks of the countries of the Union, and in the case of armorial bearings, flags, other emblems. abbreviations, and names, of international intergovernmental organizations, these provisions shall apply only to marks registered more than two months after receipt of the communication provided for in paragraph (3), above.

(7) In cases of bad faith, the countries shall have the right to cancel even those marks incorporating State emblems, signs, and hallmarks, which were registered before November 6, 1925.

(8) Nationals of any country who are authorized to make use of the State emblems, signs, and hallmarks, of their country may use them even if they are similar to those of another country.

(9) The countries of the Union undertake to prohibit the unauthorized use in trade of the State armorial bearings of the other countries of the Union, when the use is of such a nature as to be misleading as to the origin of the goods.

(10) The above provisions shall not prevent the countries from exercising the right given in Article 6*quinquies*(B)(3), to refuse or to invalidate the registration of marks incorporating, without authorization, armorial bearings, flags, other State emblems, or official signs and hallmarks adopted by a country of the Union, as well as the distinctive signs of international intergovernmental organizations referred to in paragraph (1), above.

Article 6*quater*
[*Marks:* Assignment of Marks]

(1) When, in accordance with the law of a country of the Union, the assignment of a mark is valid only if it takes place at the same time as the transfer of the business or goodwill to which the mark belongs, it shall suffice for the recognition of such validity that the portion of the business or goodwill located in that country be transferred to the assignee, together with the exclusive right to manufacture in the said country, or to sell therein, the goods bearing the mark assigned.

(2) The foregoing provision does not impose upon the countries of the Union any obligation to regard as valid the assignment of any mark the use of which by the assignee would, in fact, be of such a nature as to mislead the public, particularly as regards the origin, nature, or essential qualities, of the goods to which the mark is applied.

Article 6*quinquies*
[*Marks:* Protection of Marks Registered in One Country of the Union in the Other Countries of the Union]

A.

(1) Every trademark duly registered in the country of origin shall be accepted for filing and protected as is in the other countries of the Union, subject to the reservations indicated in this Article. Such countries may, before proceeding to final registration, require the production of a certificate of registration in the country of origin, issued by the competent authority. No authentication shall be required for this certificate.

(2) Shall be considered the country of origin the country of the Union where the applicant has a real and effective industrial or commercial establishment, or, if he has no such establishment within the Union, the country of the Union where he has his domicile, or, if he has no domicile within the Union but is a national of a country of the Union, the country of which he is a national.

B.

Trademarks covered by this Article may be neither denied registration nor invalidated except in the following cases:

1. when they are of such a nature as to infringe rights acquired by third parties in the country where protection is claimed;

2. when they are devoid of any distinctive character, or consist exclusively of signs or indications which may serve, in trade, to designate the kind, quality, quantity, intended purpose, value, place of origin, of the goods, or the time of production, or have become customary in the current language or in the bona fide and established practices of the trade of the country where protection is claimed;

3. when they are contrary to morality or public order and, in particular, of such a nature as to deceive the public. It is understood that a mark may not be considered contrary to public order for the sole reason that it does not conform to a provision of the legislation on marks, except if such provision itself relates to public order.

This provision is subject, however, to the application of Article 10*bis*.

C.

(1) In determining whether a mark is eligible for protection, all the factual circumstances must be taken into consideration, particularly the length of time the mark has been in use.

(2) No trademark shall be refused in the other countries of the Union for the sole reason that it differs from the mark protected in the country of origin only in respect of elements that do not alter its distinctive character and do not affect its identity in the form in which it has been registered in the said country of origin.

D.

No person may benefit from the provisions of this Article if the mark for which he claims protection is not registered in the country of origin.

E.

However, in no case shall the renewal of the registration of the mark in the country of origin involve an obligation to renew the registration in the other countries of the Union in which the mark has been registered.

F.

The benefit of priority shall remain unaffected for applications for the registration of marks filed within the period fixed by Article 4, even if registration in the country of origin is effected after the expiration of such period.

Article 6*sexies*
[*Marks:* Service Marks]

The countries of the Union undertake to protect service marks. They shall not be required to provide for the registration of such marks.

Article 6*septies*
[*Marks:* Registration in the Name of the Agent or Representative of the Proprietor Without the Latter's Authorization]

(1) If the agent or representative of the person who is the proprietor of a mark in one of the countries of the Union applies, without such proprietor's authorization, for the registration of the mark in his own name, in one or more countries of the Union, the proprietor shall be entitled to oppose the registration applied for or demand its

cancellation or, if the law of the country so allows, the assignment in his favor of the said registration, unless such agent or representative justifies his action.

(2) The proprietor of the mark shall, subject to the provisions of paragraph (1), above, be entitled to oppose the use of his mark by his agent or representative if he has not authorized such use.

(3) Domestic legislation may provide an equitable time limit within which the proprietor of a mark must exercise the rights provided for in this Article.

Article 10*ter*
[*Marks, Trade Names, False Indications, Unfair Competition:* Remedies, Right to Sue]

(1) The countries of the Union undertake to assure to nationals of the other countries of the Union appropriate legal remedies effectively to repress all the acts referred to in Articles 9, 10, and 10*bis*.

(2) They undertake, further, to provide measures to permit federations and associations representing interested industrialists, producers, or merchants, provided that the existence of such federations and associations is not contrary to the laws of their countries, to take action in the courts or before the administrative authorities, with a view to the repression of the acts referred to in Articles 9, 10, and 10*bis*, in so far as the law of the country in which protection is claimed allows such action by federations and associations of that country.

Uniform Domain Name Dispute Resolution Policy

UNIFORM DOMAIN NAME DISPUTE RESOLUTION POLICY
(As Approved by ICANN on October 24, 1999)

1. Purpose. This Uniform Domain Name Dispute Resolution Policy (the "Policy") has been adopted by the Internet Corporation for Assigned Names and Numbers ("ICANN"), is incorporated by reference into your Registration Agreement, and sets forth the terms and conditions in connection with a dispute between you and any party other than us (the registrar) over the registration and use of an Internet domain name registered by you. Proceedings under Paragraph 4 of this Policy will be conducted according to the Rules for Uniform Domain Name Dispute Resolution Policy (the "Rules of Procedure"), which are available at www.icann.org/udrp/udrp-rules-24oct99.htm, and the selected administrative-dispute-resolution service provider's supplemental rules.

2. Your Representations. By applying to register a domain name, or by asking us to maintain or renew a domain name registration, you hereby represent and warrant to us that (a) the statements that you made in your Registration Agreement are complete and accurate; (b) to your knowledge, the registration of the domain name will not infringe upon or otherwise violate the rights of any third party; (c) you are not registering the domain name for an unlawful purpose; and (d) you will not knowingly use the domain name in violation of any applicable laws or regulations. It is your responsibility to determine whether your domain name registration infringes or violates someone else's rights.

3. Cancellations, Transfers, and Changes. We will cancel, transfer or otherwise make changes to domain name registrations under the following circumstances:

a. subject to the provisions of Paragraph 8, our receipt of written or appropriate electronic instructions from you or your authorized agent to take such action;

b. our receipt of an order from a court or arbitral tribunal, in each case of competent jurisdiction, requiring such action; and/or

c. our receipt of a decision of an Administrative Panel requiring such action in any administrative proceeding to which you were a party and which was conducted under this Policy or a later version of this Policy adopted by ICANN. (See Paragraph 4(i) and (k) below.)

We may also cancel, transfer or otherwise make changes to a domain name registration in accordance with the terms of your Registration Agreement or other legal requirements.

4. Mandatory Administrative Proceeding. This Paragraph sets forth the type of disputes for which you are required to submit to a mandatory administrative proceeding. These proceedings will be conducted before one of the administrative-dispute-resolution service providers listed at www.icann.org/udrp/approved-providers.htm (each, a "Provider").

a. Applicable Disputes. You are required to submit to a mandatory administrative proceeding in the event that a third party (a "complainant") asserts to the applicable Provider, in compliance with the Rules of Procedure, that

(i) your domain name is identical or confusingly similar to a trademark or service mark in which the complainant has rights; and

(ii) you have no rights or legitimate interests in respect of the domain name; and

(iii) your domain name has been registered and is being used in bad faith.

In the administrative proceeding, the complainant must prove that each of these three elements are present.

b. Evidence of Registration and Use in Bad Faith. For the purposes of Paragraph 4(a)(iii), the following circumstances, in particular but without limitation, if found by the Panel to be present, shall be evidence of the registration and use of a domain name in bad faith:

(i) circumstances indicating that you have registered or you have acquired the domain name primarily for the purpose of selling, renting, or otherwise transferring the domain name registration to the complainant who is the owner of the trademark or service mark or to a competitor of that complainant, for valuable consideration in excess of your documented out-of-pocket costs directly related to the domain name; or

(ii) you have registered the domain name in order to prevent the owner of the trademark or service mark from reflecting the mark in a corresponding domain name, provided that you have engaged in a pattern of such conduct; or

(iii) you have registered the domain name primarily for the purpose of disrupting the business of a competitor; or

(iv) by using the domain name, you have intentionally attempted to attract, for commercial gain, Internet users to your web site or other on-line location, by creating a likelihood of confusion with the complainant's mark as to the source, sponsorship, affiliation, or endorsement of your web site or location or of a product or service on your web site or location.

c. How to Demonstrate Your Rights to and Legitimate Interests in the Domain Name in Responding to a Complaint. When you receive a complaint, you should refer to Paragraph 5 of the Rules of Procedure in determining how your response should be prepared. Any of the following circumstances, in particular but without limitation, if found by the Panel to be proved based on its evaluation of all evidence presented, shall demonstrate your rights or legitimate interests to the domain name for purposes of Paragraph 4(a)(ii):

(i) before any notice to you of the dispute, your use of, or demonstrable preparations to use, the domain name or a name corresponding to the domain name in connection with a bona fide offering of goods or services; or

(ii) you (as an individual, business, or other organization) have been commonly known by the domain name, even if you have acquired no trademark or service mark rights; or

(iii) you are making a legitimate noncommercial or fair use of the domain name, without intent for commercial gain to misleadingly divert consumers or to tarnish the trademark or service mark at issue.

d. Selection of Provider. The complainant shall select the Provider from among those approved by ICANN by submitting the complaint to that Provider. The selected Provider will administer the proceeding, except in cases of consolidation as described in Paragraph 4(f).

e. Initiation of Proceeding and Process and Appointment of Administrative Panel. The Rules of Procedure state the process for initiating and conducting a proceeding and for appointing the panel that will decide the dispute (the "Administrative Panel").

f. Consolidation. In the event of multiple disputes between you and a complainant, either you or the complainant may petition to consolidate the disputes before a single Administrative Panel. This petition shall be made to the first Administrative Panel appointed to hear a pending dispute between the parties. This Administrative Panel may consolidate before it any or all such disputes in its sole discretion, provided that the disputes being consolidated are governed by this Policy or a later version of this Policy adopted by ICANN.

g. Fees. All fees charged by a Provider in connection with any dispute before an Administrative Panel pursuant to this Policy shall be paid by the complainant, except in cases where you elect to expand the Administrative Panel from one to three panelists as provided in Paragraph 5(b)(iv) of the Rules of Procedure, in which case all fees will be split evenly by you and the complainant.

h. Our Involvement in Administrative Proceedings. We do not, and will not, participate in the administration or conduct of any proceeding before an Administrative Panel. In addition, we will not be liable as a result of any decisions rendered by the Administrative Panel.

i. Remedies. The remedies available to a complainant pursuant to any proceeding before an Administrative Panel shall be limited to requiring the cancellation of your domain name or the transfer of your domain name registration to the complainant.

j. Notification and Publication. The Provider shall notify us of any decision made by an Administrative Panel with respect to a domain name you have registered with us. All decisions under this Policy will be published in full over the Internet, except when an Administrative Panel determines in an exceptional case to redact portions of its decision.

    k. Availability of Court Proceedings. The mandatory administrative proceeding requirements set forth in Paragraph 4 shall not prevent either you or the complainant from submitting the dispute to a court of competent jurisdiction for independent resolution before such mandatory administrative proceeding is commenced or after such proceeding is concluded. If an Administrative Panel decides that your domain name registration should be canceled or transferred, we will wait ten (10) business days (as observed in the location of our principal office) after we are informed by the applicable Provider of the Administrative Panel's decision before implementing that decision. We will then implement the decision unless we have received from you during that ten (10) business day period official documentation (such as a copy of a complaint, file-stamped by the clerk of the court) that you have commenced a lawsuit against the complainant in a jurisdiction to which the complainant has submitted under Paragraph 3(b)(xiii) of the Rules of Procedure. (In general, that jurisdiction is either the location of our principal office or of your address as shown in our Whois database. See Paragraphs 1 and 3(b)(xiii) of the Rules of Procedure for details.) If we receive such documentation within the ten (10) business day period, we will not implement the Administrative Panel's decision, and we will take no further action, until we receive (i) evidence satisfactory to us of a resolution between the parties; (ii) evidence satisfactory to us that your lawsuit has been dismissed or withdrawn; or (iii) a copy of an order from such court dismissing your lawsuit or ordering that you do not have the right to continue to use your domain name.

    5. <u>All Other Disputes and Litigation</u>. All other disputes between you and any party other than us regarding your domain name registration that are not brought pursuant to the mandatory administrative proceeding provisions of Paragraph 4 shall be resolved between you and such other party through any court, arbitration or other proceeding that may be available.

    6. <u>Our Involvement in Disputes</u>. We will not participate in any way in any dispute between you and any party other than us regarding the registration and use of your domain name. You shall not name us as a party or otherwise include us in any such proceeding. In the event that we are named as a party in any such proceeding, we reserve the right to raise any and all defenses deemed appropriate, and to take any other action necessary to defend ourselves.

    7. <u>Maintaining the Status Quo</u>. We will not cancel, transfer, activate, deactivate, or otherwise change the status of any domain name registration under this Policy except as provided in Paragraph 3 above.

8. Transfers During a Dispute.

a. Transfers of a Domain Name to a New Holder. You may not transfer your domain name registration to another holder (i) during a pending administrative proceeding brought pursuant to Paragraph 4 or for a period of fifteen (15) business days (as observed in the location of our principal place of business) after such proceeding is concluded; or (ii) during a pending court proceeding or arbitration commenced regarding your domain name unless the party to whom the domain name registration is being transferred agrees, in writing, to be bound by the decision of the court or arbitrator. We reserve the right to cancel any transfer of a domain name registration to another holder that is made in violation of this subparagraph.

b. Changing Registrars. You may not transfer your domain name registration to another registrar during a pending administrative proceeding brought pursuant to Paragraph 4 or for a period of fifteen (15) business days (as observed in the location of our principal place of business) after such proceeding is concluded. You may transfer administration of your domain name registration to another registrar during a pending court action or arbitration, provided that the domain name you have registered with us shall continue to be subject to the proceedings commenced against you in accordance with the terms of this Policy. In the event that you transfer a domain name registration to us during the pendency of a court action or arbitration, such dispute shall remain subject to the domain name dispute policy of the registrar from which the domain name registration was transferred.

9. Policy Modifications. We reserve the right to modify this Policy at any time with the permission of ICANN. We will post our revised Policy at <URL> at least thirty (30) calendar days before it becomes effective. Unless this Policy has already been invoked by the submission of a complaint to a Provider, in which event the version of the Policy in effect at the time it was invoked will apply to you until the dispute is over, all such changes will be binding upon you with respect to any domain name registration dispute, whether the dispute arose before, on or after the effective date of our change. In the event that you object to a change in this Policy, your sole remedy is to cancel your domain name registration with us, provided that you will not be entitled to a refund of any fees you paid to us. The revised Policy will apply to you until you cancel your domain name registration.

D

Protocol Relating to the Madrid Agreement Concerning the International Registration of Marks

PROTOCOL RELATING TO THE MADRID AGREEMENT CONCERNING THE INTERNATIONAL REGISTRATION OF MARKS

Adopted at Madrid on June 27, 1989

* * *

Article 2
Securing Protection Through International Registration

(1) Where an application for the registration of a mark has been filed with the Office of a Contracting Party, or where a mark has been registered in the register of the Office of a Contracting Party, the person in whose name that application (hereinafter referred to as "the basic application") or that registration (hereinafter referred to as "the basic registration") stands may, subject to the provisions of this Protocol, secure protection for his mark in the territory of the Contracting Parties, by obtaining the registration of that mark in the register of the International Bureau of the World Intellectual Property Organization (hereinafter referred to as "the international registration," "the International Register," "the International Bureau" and "the Organization," respectively), provided that,

(i)   where the basic application has been filed with the Office of a Contracting State or where the basic registration has been made by such an Office, the person in whose name that application or registration stands is a national of that Contracting State, or is domiciled, or has a real and effective industrial or commercial establishment, in the said Contracting State,

(ii) where the basic application has been filed with the Office of a Contracting Organization or where the basic registration has been made by such an Office, the person in whose name that application or registration stands is a national of a State member of that Contracting Organization, or is domiciled, or has a real and effective industrial or commercial establishment, in the territory of the said Contracting Organization.

(2) The application for international registration (hereinafter referred to as "the international application") shall be filed with the International Bureau through the intermediary of the Office with which the basic application was filed or by which the basic registration was made (hereinafter referred to as "the Office of origin"), as the case may be.

(3) Any reference in this Protocol to an "Office" or an "Office of a Contracting Party" shall be construed as a reference to the office that is in charge, on behalf of a Contracting Party, of the registration of marks, and any reference in this Protocol to "marks" shall be construed as a reference to trademarks and service marks.

(4) For the purposes of this Protocol, "territory of a Contracting Party" means, where the Contracting Party is a State, the territory of that State and, where the Contracting Party is an intergovernmental organization, the territory in which the constituting treaty of that intergovernmental organization applies.

* * *

Article 3 *bis*
Territorial Effect

The protection resulting from the international registration shall extend to any Contracting Party only at the request of the person who files the international application or who is the holder of the international registration. However, no such request can be made with respect to the Contracting Party whose Office is the Office of origin.

Article 3 *ter*
Request for "Territorial Extension"

(1) Any request for extension of the protection resulting from the international registration to any Contracting Party shall be specially mentioned in the international application.

(2) A request for territorial extension may also be made subsequently to the international registration. Any such request shall be presented on the form prescribed by the Regulations. It shall be immediately recorded by the International Bureau, which shall notify such recordal without delay to the Office or Offices concerned. Such recordal shall be published in the periodical gazette of the International Bureau. Such territorial extension shall be effective from the date on which it has been recorded in the International Register; it shall cease to be valid on the expiry of the international registration to which it relates.

Article 4
Effects of International Registration

(1) (a)   From the date of the registration or recordal effected in accordance with the provisions of Articles 3 and 3*ter*, the protection of the mark in each of the Contracting Parties concerned shall be the same as if the mark had been deposited direct with the Office of that Contracting Party. If no refusal has been notified to the International Bureau in accordance with Article 5(1) and 5(2) or if a refusal notified in accordance with the said Article has been withdrawn subsequently, the protection of the mark in the Contracting Party concerned shall, as from the said date, be the same as if the mark had been registered by the Office of that Contracting Party.

(b) The indication of classes of goods and services provided for in Article 3 shall not bind the Contracting Parties with regard to the determination of the scope of the protection of the mark.

(2) Every international registration shall enjoy the right of priority provided for by Article 4 of the Paris Convention for the Protection of Industrial Property, without it being necessary to comply with the formalities prescribed in Section 4.D of the Article.

Article 4 *bis*
Replacement of a National or Regional Registration by an International Registration

(1) Where a mark that is the subject of a national or regional registration in the Office of a Contracting Party is also the subject of an international registration and both registrations stand in the name of the same person, the international registration is deemed

to replace the national or regional registration, without prejudice to any rights acquired by virtue of the latter, provided that

(i)   the protection resulting from the international registration extends to the said Contracting Party under Article 3*ter*(1) or 3*ter*(2),

(ii) all the goods and services listed in the national or regional registration are also listed in the international registration in respect of the said Contracting Party,

(iii) such extension takes effect after the date of the national or regional registration.

(2) The Office referred to in paragraph (1) shall, upon request, be required to take note in its register of the international registration.

Article 5
Refusal and Invalidation of Effects of International Registration in Respect of Certain Contracting Parties

(1) Where the applicable legislation so authorizes, any Office of a Contracting Party which has been notified by the International Bureau of an extension to that Contracting Party, under Article 3*ter*(1) or 3*ter*(2), of the protection resulting from the international registration shall have the right to declare in a notification of refusal that protection cannot be granted in the said Contracting Party to the mark which is the subject of such extension. Any such refusal can be based only on the grounds which would apply, under the Paris Convention for the Protection of Industrial Property, in the case of a mark deposited direct with the Office which notifies the refusal. However, protection may not be refused, even partially, by reason only that the applicable legislation would permit registration only in a limited number of classes or for a limited number of goods or services.

(2) (a)   Any Office wishing to exercise such right shall notify its refusal to the International Bureau, together with a statement of all grounds, within the period prescribed by the law applicable to that Office and at the latest, subject to subparagraphs (b) and (c), before the expiry of one year from the date on which the notification of the extension referred to in paragraph (1) has been sent to that Office by the International Bureau.

(b) Notwithstanding subparagraph (a), any Contracting Party may declare that, for international registrations made under this Protocol, the time limit of one year referred to in subparagraph (a) is replaced by 18 months.

(c) Such declaration may also specify that, when a refusal of protection may result from an opposition to the granting of protection, such refusal may be notified by the Office of the said Contracting Party to the International Bureau after the expiry of the 18-month time limit. Such an Office may, with respect to any given international registration, notify a refusal of protection after the expiry of the 18-month time limit, but only if

(i)   it has, before the expiry of the 18-month time limit, informed the International Bureau of the possibility that oppositions may be filed after the expiry of the 18-month time limit, and

(ii) the notification of the refusal based on an opposition is made within a time limit of one month from the expiry of the opposition period and, in any case, not later than seven months from the date on which the opposition period begins.

(d) Any declaration under subparagraphs (b) or (c) may be made in the instruments referred to in Article 14(2), and the effective date of the declaration shall be the same as the date of entry into force of this Protocol with respect to the State or intergovernmental organization having made the declaration. Any such declaration may also be made later, in which case the declaration shall have effect three months after its receipt by the Director General of the Organization (hereinafter referred to as "the Director General"), or at any later date indicated in the declaration, in respect of any international registration whose date is the same as or is later than the effective date of the declaration.

(e) Upon the expiry of a period of ten years from the entry into force of this Protocol, the Assembly shall examine the operation of the system established by subparagraphs (a) to (d). Thereafter, the provisions of the said subparagraphs may be modified by a unanimous decision of the Assembly.[8]

(3) The International Bureau shall, without delay, transmit one of the copies of the notification of refusal to the holder of the international registration. The said holder shall have the same remedies as if the mark had been deposited by him direct with the Office which has notified its refusal. Where the International Bureau has received information under paragraph (2)(c)(i), it shall, without delay, transmit the said information to the holder of the international registration.

(4) The grounds for refusing a mark shall be communicated by the International Bureau to any interested party who may so request.

(5) Any Office which has not notified, with respect to a given international registration, any provisional or final refusal to the International Bureau in accordance with paragraphs (1) and (2) shall, with respect to that international registration, lose the benefit of the right provided for in paragraph (1).

(6) Invalidation, by the competent authorities of a Contracting Party, of the effects, in the territory of that Contracting Party, of an international registration may not be pronounced without the holder of such international registration having, in good time, been afforded the opportunity of defending his rights. Invalidation shall be notified to the International Bureau.

* * *

---

[8] Interpretive statement adopted by the Assembly of the Madrid Union: "Article 5(2)(e) of the Protocol is understood as allowing the Assembly to keep under review the operation of the system established by subparagraphs (a) to (d), it being also understood that any modification of those provisions shall require a unanimous decision of the Assembly."

Article 7
Renewal of International Registration

(1) Any international registration may be renewed for a period of ten years from the expiry of the preceding period, by the mere payment of the basic fee and, subject to Article 8(7), of the supplementary and complementary fees provided for in Article 8(2).

(2) Renewal may not bring about any change in the international registration in its latest form.

(3) Six months before the expiry of the term of protection, the International Bureau shall, by sending an unofficial notice, remind the holder of the international registration and his representative, if any, of the exact date of expiry.

(4) Subject to the payment of a surcharge fixed by the Regulations, a period of grace of six months shall be allowed for renewal of the international registration.

* * *

Article 9*quinquies*
Transformation of an International Registration
into National or Regional Applications

Where, in the event that the international registration is cancelled at the request of the Office of origin under Article 6(4), in respect of all or some of the goods and services listed in the said registration, the person who was the holder of the international registration files an application for the registration of the same mark with the Office of any of the Contracting Parties in the territory of which the international registration had effect, that application shall be treated as if it had been filed on the date of the international registration according to Article 3(4) or on the date of recordal of the territorial extension according to Article 3*ter*(2) and, if the international registration enjoyed priority, shall enjoy the same priority, provided that

(i)   such application is filed within three months from the date on which the international registration was cancelled,

(ii)   the goods and services listed in the application are in fact covered by the list of goods and services contained in the international registration in respect of the Contracting Party concerned, and

(iii) such application complies with all the requirements of the applicable law, including the requirements concerning fees.

Article 9*sexies*
Safeguard of the Madrid (Stockholm) Agreement

(1) Where, with regard to a given international application or a given international registration, the Office of origin is the Office of a State that is party to both this Protocol and the Madrid (Stockholm) Agreement, the provisions of this Protocol shall have no effect in the territory of any other State that is also party to both this Protocol and the Madrid (Stockholm) Agreement.

(2) The Assembly may, by a three-fourths majority, repeal paragraph (1), or restrict the scope of paragraph (1), after the expiry of a period of ten years from the entry into force of this Protocol, but not before the expiry of a period of five years from the date on which the

majority of the countries party to the Madrid (Stockholm) Agreement have become party to this Protocol. In the vote of the Assembly, only those States which are party to both the said Agreement and this Protocol shall have the right to participate.

Article 9*sexies [effective September 1, 2008]*
Relations Between States Party to both this Protocol
and the Madrid (Stockholm) Agreement

(1) (a) This Protocol alone shall be applicable as regards the mutual relations of States party to both this Protocol and the Madrid (Stockholm) Agreement.

(b) Notwithstanding subparagraph (a), a declaration made under Article 5(2)(b), Article 5(2)(c) or Article 8(7) of this Protocol, by a State party to both this Protocol and the Madrid (Stockholm) Agreement, shall have no effect in the relations with another State party to both this Protocol and the Madrid (Stockholm) Agreement.

(2) The Assembly shall, after the expiry of a period of three years from September 1, 2008, review the application of paragraph (1)(b) and may, at any time thereafter, either repeal it or restrict its scope, by a three-fourths majority. In the vote of the Assembly, only those States which are party to both the Madrid (Stockholm) Agreement and this Protocol shall have the right to participate.

NORTH AMERICAN FREE TRADE AGREEMENT (EXCERPTS)

NORTH AMERICAN FREE TRADE AGREEMENT (EXCERPTS)
between the Government of Canada, the Government of the United Mexican States, and the Government of the United States of America
Done at Washington on December 8 and 17, 1992,
at Ottawa on December 11 and 17, 1992 and
at Mexico City on December 14 and 17, 1992

PART SIX
INTELLECTUAL PROPERTY

Chapter Seventeen
Intellectual Property

Article 1708: Trademarks

1. For purposes of this Agreement, a trademark consists of any sign, or any combination of signs, capable of distinguishing the goods or services of one person from those of another, including personal names, designs, letters, numerals, colors, figurative elements, or the shape of goods or of their packaging. Trademarks shall include service marks and collective marks, and may include certification marks. A Party may require, as a condition for registration, that a sign be visually perceptible.

2. Each Party shall provide to the owner of a registered trademark the right to prevent all persons not having the owner's consent from using in commerce identical or similar signs for goods or services that are identical or similar to those goods or services in respect of which the owner's trademark is registered, where such use would result in a likelihood of confusion. In the case of the use of an identical sign for identical goods or services, a likelihood of confusion shall be presumed. The rights described above shall not prejudice any prior rights, nor shall they affect the possibility of a Party making rights available on the basis of use.

3. A Party may make registrability depend on use. However, actual use of a trademark shall not be a condition for filing an application for registration. No Party may refuse an application solely on the ground that intended use has not taken place before the expiry of a period of three years from the date of application for registration.

4. Each Party shall provide a system for the registration of trademarks, which shall include:
   (a)   examination of applications;
   (b)   notice to be given to an applicant of the reasons for the refusal to register a trademark;
   (c)   a reasonable opportunity for the applicant to respond to the notice;
   (d)   publication of each trademark either before or promptly after it is registered; and
   (e)   a reasonable opportunity for interested persons to petition to cancel the registration of a trademark.

A Party may provide for a reasonable opportunity for interested persons to oppose the registration of a trademark.

5.   The nature of the goods or services to which a trademark is to be applied shall in no case form an obstacle to the registration of the trademark.

6.   Article 6*bis* of the Paris Convention shall apply, with such modifications as may be necessary, to services. In determining whether a trademark is well known, account shall be taken of the knowledge of the trademark in the relevant sector of the public, including knowledge in the Party's territory obtained as a result of the promotion of the trademark. No Party may require that the reputation of the trademark extend beyond the sector of the public that normally deals with the relevant goods or services.

7.   Each Party shall provide that the initial registration of a trademark be for a term of at least 10 years and that the registration be indefinitely renewable for terms of not less than 10 years when conditions for renewal have been met.

8.   Each Party shall require the use of a trademark to maintain a registration. The registration may be canceled for the reason of non-use only after an uninterrupted period of at least two years of non-use, unless valid reasons based on the existence of obstacles to such use are shown by the trademark owner. Each Party shall recognize, as valid reasons for non-use, circumstances arising independently of the will of the trademark owner that constitute an obstacle to the use of the trademark, such as import restrictions on, or other government requirements for, goods or services identified by the trademark.

9.   Each Party shall recognize use of a trademark by a person other than the trademark owner, where such use is subject to the owner's control, as use of the trademark for purposes of maintaining the registration.

10. No Party may encumber the use of a trademark in commerce by special requirements, such as a use that reduces the trademark's function as an indication of source or a use with another trademark.

11. A Party may determine conditions on the licensing and assignment of trademarks, it being understood that the compulsory licensing of trademarks shall not be permitted and that the owner of a registered trademark shall have the right to assign its trademark with or without the transfer of the business to which the trademark belongs.

12. A Party may provide limited exceptions to the rights conferred by a trademark, such as fair use of descriptive terms, provided that such exceptions take into account the legitimate interests of the trademark owner and of other persons.

13. Each Party shall prohibit the registration as a trademark of words, at least in English, French or Spanish, that generically designate goods or services or types of goods or services to which the trademark applies.

14. Each Party shall refuse to register trademarks that consist of or comprise immoral, deceptive or scandalous matter, or matter that may disparage or falsely suggest a connection with persons, living or dead, institutions, beliefs or any Party's national symbols, or bring them into contempt or disrepute.

* * *

Article 1712: Geographical Indications

1. Each Party shall provide, in respect of geographical indications, the legal means for interested persons to prevent:

(a)   the use of any means in the designation or presentation of a good that indicates or suggests that the good in question originates in a territory, region or locality other than the true place of origin, in a manner that misleads the public as to the geographical origin of the good;

(b)   any use that constitutes an act of unfair competition within the meaning of Article 10*bis* of the Paris Convention.

2. Each Party shall, on its own initiative if its domestic law so permits or at the request of an interested person, refuse to register, or invalidate the registration of, a trademark containing or consisting of a geographical indication with respect to goods that do not originate in the indicated territory, region or locality, if use of the indication in the trademark for such goods is of such a nature as to mislead the public as to the geographical origin of the good.

3. Each Party shall also apply paragraphs 1 and 2 to a geographical indication that, although correctly indicating the territory, region or locality in which the goods originate, falsely represents to the public that the goods originate in another territory, region or locality.

4. Nothing in this Article shall be construed to require a Party to prevent continued and similar use of a particular geographical indication of another Party in connection with goods or services by any of its nationals or domiciliaries who have used that geographical indication in a continuous manner with regard to the same or related goods or services in that Party's territory, either:

(a)   for at least 10 years, or

(b)   in good faith,

before the date of signature of this Agreement.

5. Where a trademark has been applied for or registered in good faith, or where rights to a trademark have been acquired through use in good faith, either:

(a)   before the date of application of these provisions in that Party, or

(b)   before the geographical indication is protected in its Party of origin,

no Party may adopt any measure to implement this Article that prejudices eligibility for, or the validity of, the registration of a trademark, or the right to use a trademark, on the basis that such a trademark is identical with, or similar to, a geographical indication.

6. No Party shall be required to apply this Article to a geographical indication if it is identical to the customary term in common language in that Party's territory for the goods or services to which the indication applies.

7. A Party may provide that any request made under this Article in connection with the use or registration of a trademark must be presented within five years after the adverse use of the protected indication has become generally known in that Party or after the date of registration of the trademark in that Party, provided that the trademark has been published by that date, if such date is earlier than the date on which the adverse use

became generally known in that Party, provided that the geographical indication is not used or registered in bad faith.

8. No Party shall adopt any measure implementing this Article that would prejudice any person's right to use, in the course of trade, its name or the name of its predecessor in business, except where such name forms all or part of a valid trademark in existence before the geographical indication became protected and with which there is a likelihood of confusion, or such name is used in such a manner as to mislead the public.

9. Nothing in this Chapter shall be construed to require a Party to protect a geographical indication that is not protected, or has fallen into disuse, in the Party of origin.

EC TRADEMARK DIRECTIVE
(EXCERPTS)

EC TRADEMARK DIRECTIVE (EXCERPTS)
Directive 2008/95/EC of the European Parliament and the Council of 22 October 2008 to approximate the laws of the Member States relating to trade marks (codified version)

* * *

Article 1
Scope

This Directive shall apply to every trade mark in respect of goods or services which is the subject of registration or of an application in a Member State for registration as an individual trade mark, a collective mark or a guarantee or certification mark, or which is the subject of a registration or an application for registration in the Benelux Trade Mark Office or of an international registration having effect in a Member State.

Article 2
Signs of which a trade mark may consist

A trade mark may consist of any sign capable of being represented graphically, particularly words, including personal names, designs, letters, numerals, the shape of goods or of their packaging, provided that such signs are capable of distinguishing the goods or services of one undertaking from those of other undertakings.

Article 3
Grounds for refusal or invalidity

1. The following shall not be registered or if registered shall be liable to be declared invalid:
   - (a) signs which cannot constitute a trade mark;
   - (b) trade marks which are devoid of any distinctive character;
   - (c) trade marks which consist exclusively of signs or indications which may serve, in trade, to designate the kind, quality, quantity, intended purpose, value, geographical origin, or the time of production of the goods or of rendering of the service, or other characteristics of the goods;
   - (d) trade marks which consist exclusively of signs or indications which have become customary in the current language or in the *bona fide* and established practices of the trade;
   - (e) signs which consist exclusively of:
     - – the shape which results from the nature of the goods themselves, or
     - – the shape of goods which is necessary to obtain a technical result, or
     - – the shape which gives substantial value to the goods;
   - (f) trade marks which are contrary to public policy or to accepted principles of morality;
   - (g) trade marks which are of such a nature as to deceive the public, for instance as to the nature, quality or geographical origin of the goods or service;
   - (h) trade marks which have not been authorized by the competent authorities and are to be refused or invalidated pursuant to Article 6*ter* of the Paris

Convention for the Protection of Industrial Property, hereinafter referred to as the 'Paris Convention'.

2. Any Member State may provide that a trade mark shall not be registered or, if registered, shall be liable to be declared invalid where and to the extent that:

(a) the use of that trade mark may be prohibited pursuant to provisions of law other than trade mark law of the Member State concerned or of the Community;

(b) the trade mark covers a sign of high symbolic value, in particular a religious symbol;

(c) the trade mark includes badges, emblems and escutcheons other than those covered by Article 6ter of the Paris Convention and which are of Public interest, unless the consent of the appropriate authorities to its registration has been given in conformity with the legislation of the Member State;

(d) the application for registration of the trade mark was made in bad faith by the applicant.

3. A trade mark shall not be refused registration or be declared invalid in accordance with paragraph 1 (b), (c) or (d) if, before the date of application for registration and following the use which has been made of it, it has acquired a distinctive character. Any Member State may in addition provide that this provision shall also apply where the distinctive character was acquired after the date of application for registration or after the date of registration.

4. Any Member State may provide that, by derogation from the preceding paragraphs, the grounds of refusal of registration or invalidity in force in that State prior to the date on which the provisions necessary to comply with this Directive enter into force, shall apply to trade marks for which application has been made prior to that date.

Article 4
Further grounds for refusal or invalidity concerning
conflicts with earlier rights

1. A trade mark shall not be registered or, if registered, shall be liable to be declared invalid:

(a) if it is identical with an earlier trade mark, and the goods or services for which the trade mark is applied for or is registered are identical with the goods or services for which the earlier trade mark is protected;

(b) if because of its identity with, or similarity to, the earlier trade mark and the identity or similarity of the goods or services covered by the trade marks, there exists a likelihood of confusion on the part of the public, which includes the likelihood of association with the earlier trade mark.

2. 'Earlier trade marks' within the meaning of paragraph 1 means:

(a) trade marks of the following kinds with a date of application for registration which is earlier than the date of application for registration of the trade mark, taking account, where appropriate, of the priorities claimed in respect of those trade marks;

   (i)   Community trade marks;

(ii)   trade marks registered in the Member State or, in the case of Belgium, Luxembourg or the Netherlands, at the Benelux Trade Mark Office;

(iii)   trade marks registered under international arrangements which have effect in the Member State;

(b) Community trade marks which validly claim seniority, in accordance with the Regulation on the Community trade mark, from a trade mark referred to in (a) (ii) and (iii), even when the latter trade mark has been surrendered or allowed to lapse;

(c) applications for the trade marks referred to in (a) and (b), subject to their registration;

(d) trade marks which, on the date of application for registration of the trade mark, or, where appropriate, of the priority claimed in respect of the application for registration of the trade mark, are well known in a Member State, in the sense in which the words 'well known' are used in Article 6*bis* of the Paris Convention.

3. A trade mark shall furthermore not be registered or, if registered, shall be liable to be declared invalid if it is identical with, or similar to, an earlier Community trade mark within the meaning of paragraph 2 and is to be, or has been, registered for goods or services which are not similar to those for which the earlier Community trade mark is registered, where the earlier Community trade mark has a reputation in the Community and where the use of the later trade mark without due cause would take unfair advantage of, or be detrimental to, the distinctive character or the repute of the earlier Community trade mark.

4. Any Member State may furthermore provide that a trade mark shall not be registered or, if registered, shall be liable to be declared invalid where, and to the extent that:

(a) the trade mark is identical with, or similar to, an earlier national trade mark within the meaning of paragraph 2 and is to he, or has been, registered for goods or services which are not similar to those for which the earlier trade mark is registered, where the earlier trade mark has a reputation in the Member State concerned and where the use of the later trade mark without due cause would take unfair advantage of, or be detrimental to, the distinctive character or the repute of the earlier trade mark;

(b) rights to a non-registered trade mark or to another sign used in the course of trade were acquired prior to the date of application for registration of the subsequent trade mark, or the date of the priority claimed for the application for registration of the subsequent trade mark and that non-registered trade mark or other sign confers on its proprietor the right to prohibit the use of a subsequent trade mark;

(c) the use of the trade mark may be prohibited by virtue of an earlier right other than the rights referred to in paragraphs 2 and 4 (b) and in particular:

(i)   a right to a name;

(ii)   a right of personal portrayal;

      (iii)   a copyright;

      (iv)   an industrial property right;

(d) the trade mark is identical with, or similar to, an earlier collective trade mark conferring a right which expired within a period of a maximum of three years preceding application;

(e) the trade mark is identical with, or similar to, an earlier guarantee or certification mark conferring a right which expired within a period preceding application the length of which is fixed by the Member State;

(f) the trade mark is identical with, or similar to, an earlier trade mark which was registered for identical or similar goods or services and conferred on them a right which has expired for failure to renew within a period of a maximum of two years preceding application, unless the proprietor of the earlier trade mark gave his agreement for the registration of the later mark or did not use his trade mark;

(g) the trade mark is liable to be confused with a mark which was in use abroad on the filing date of the application and which is still in use there, provided that at the date of the application the applicant was acting in bad faith.

5. The Member States may permit that in appropriate circumstances registration need not be refused or the trade mark need not be declared invalid where the proprietor of the earlier trade mark or other earlier right consents to the registration of the later trade mark.

6. Any Member State may provide that, by derogation from paragraphs 1 to 5, the grounds for refusal of registration or invalidity in force in that State prior to the date on which the provisions necessary to comply with this Directive enter into force, shall apply to trade marks for which application has been made prior to that date.

Article 5
Rights conferred by a trade mark

1. The registered trade mark shall confer on the proprietor exclusive rights therein. The proprietor shall be entitled to prevent all third parties not having his consent from using in the course of trade:

(a) any sign which is identical with the trade mark in relation to goods or services which are identical with those for which the trade mark is registered;

(b) any sign where, because of its identity with, or similarity to, the trade mark and the identity or similarity of the goods or services covered by the trade mark and the sign, there exists a likelihood of confusion on the part of the public, which includes the likelihood of association between the sign and the trade mark.

2. Any Member State may also provide that the proprietor shall be entitled to prevent all third parties not having his consent from using in the course of trade any sign which is identical with, or similar to, the trade mark in relation to goods or services which are not similar to those for which the trade mark is registered, where the latter has a reputation in the Member State and where use of that sign without due cause takes unfair advantage of, or is detrimental to, the distinctive character or the repute of the trade mark.

3. The following, *inter alia*, may be prohibited under paragraphs 1 and 2:

(a) affixing the sign to the goods or to the packaging thereof;

(b) offering the goods, or putting them on the market or stocking them for these purposes under that sign, or offering or supplying services thereunder;

(c) importing or exporting the goods under the sign;

(d) using the sign on business papers and in advertising.

4. Where, under the law of the Member State, the use of a sign under the conditions referred to in 1(b) or 2 could not be prohibited before the date on which the provisions necessary to comply with this Directive entered into force in the Member State concerned, the rights conferred by the trade mark may not be relied on to prevent the continued use of the sign.

5. Paragraphs 1 to 4 shall not affect provisions in any Member State relating to the protection against the use of a sign other than for the purposes of distinguishing goods or services, where use of that sign without due cause takes unfair advantage of, or is detrimental to, the distinctive character or the repute of the trade mark.

Article 6
Limitation of the effects of a trade mark

1. The trade mark shall not entitle the proprietor to prohibit a third party from using, in the course of trade,

(a) his own name or address;

(b) indications concerning the kind, quality, quantity, intended purpose, value, geographical origin, the time of production of goods or of rendering of the service, or other characteristics of goods or services;

(c) the trade mark where it is necessary to indicate the intended purpose of a product or service, in particular as accessories or spare parts;

provided he uses them in accordance with honest practices in industrial or commercial matters.

2. The trade mark shall not entitle the proprietor to prohibit a third party from using, in the course of trade, an earlier right which only applies in a particular locality if that right is recognized by the laws of the Member State in question and within the limits of the territory in which it is recognized.

Article 7
Exhaustion of the rights conferred by a trade mark

1. The trade mark shall not entitle the proprietor to prohibit its use in relation to goods which have been put on the market in the Community under that trade mark by the proprietor or with his consent.

2. Paragraph 1 shall not apply where there exist legitimate reasons for the proprietor to oppose further commercialization of the goods, especially where the condition of the goods is changed or impaired after they have been put on the market.

Article 8
Licensing

1. A trade mark may be licensed for some or all of the goods or services for which it is registered and for the whole or part of the Member State concerned. A license may be exclusive or non-exclusive.

2. The proprietor of a trade mark may invoke the rights conferred by that trade mark against a licensee who contravenes any provision in his licensing contract with regard to its duration, the form covered by the registration in which the trade mark may be used, the scope of the goods or services for which the licence is granted, the territory in which the trade mark may be affixed, or the quality of the goods manufactured or of the services provided by the licensee.

Article 9
Limitation in consequence of acquiescence

1. Where, in a Member State, the proprietor of an earlier trade mark as referred to in Article 4(2) has acquiesced, for a period of five successive years, in the use of a later trade mark registered in that Member State while being aware of such use, he shall no longer be entitled on the basis of the earlier trade mark either to apply for a declaration that the later trade mark is invalid or to oppose the use of the later trade mark in respect of the goods or services for which the later trade mark has been used, unless registration of the later trade mark was applied for in bad faith.

2. Any Member State may provide that paragraph 1 shall apply *mutatis mutandis* to the proprietor of an earlier trade mark referred to in Article 4(4)(a) or an other earlier right referred to in Article 4(4) (b) or (c).

3. In the cases referred to in paragraphs 1 and 2, the proprietor of a later registered trade mark shall not be entitled to oppose the use of the earlier right, even though that right may no longer be invoked against the later trade mark.

Article 10
Use of trade marks

1. If, within a period of five years following the date of the completion of the registration procedure, the proprietor has not put the trade mark to genuine use in the Member State in connection with the goods or services in respect of which it is registered, or if such use has been suspended during an uninterrupted period of five years, the trade mark shall be subject to the sanctions provided for in this Directive, unless there are proper reasons for non-use.

2. The following shall also constitute use within the meaning of paragraph 1:
   (a) use of the trade mark in a form differing in elements which do not alter the distinctive character of the mark in the form in which it was registered;
   (b) affixing of the trade mark to goods or to the packaging thereof in the Member State concerned solely for export purposes.

3. Use of the trade mark with the consent of the proprietor or by any person who has authority to use a collective mark or a guarantee or certification mark shall be deemed to constitute use by the proprietor.

4. In relation to trade marks registered before the date on which the provisions necessary to comply with this Directive enter into force in the Member State concerned:

   (a) where a provision in force prior to that date attaches sanctions to non-use of a trade mark during an uninterrupted period, the relevant period of five years mentioned in paragraph 1 shall be deemed to have begun to run at the same time as any period of non-use which is already running at that date;

   (b) where there is no use provision in force prior to that date, the periods of five years mentioned in paragraph 1 shall be deemed to run from that date at the earliest.